THE CONSTITUTION TODAY

ALSO BY AKHIL REED AMAR

The Law of the Land

America's Unwritten Constitution

America's Constitution: A Biography

The Bill of Rights: Creation and Reconstruction

The Constitution and Criminal Procedure

THE
CONSTITUTION
TODAY

TIMELESS LESSONS
FOR THE ISSUES OF OUR ERA

AKHIL REED AMAR

BASIC BOOKS
New York

Published by Basic Books,
An imprint of Perseus Books, a division of PBG Publishing, LLC, a subsidiary of Hachette
Book Group, Inc.

Books published by Basic Books are available at special discounts for bulk purchases in
the United States by corporations, institutions, and other organizations. For more
information, please contact the Special Markets Department at the Perseus Books Group,
2300 Chestnut Street, Suite 200, Philadelphia, PA 19103, or call (800) 810-4145, ext.
5000, or e-mail special.markets@perseusbooks.com.

Designed by Trish Wilkinson
Set in 10.5-point Goudy Oldstyle STD

Library of Congress Cataloging-in-Publication Data

Names: Amar, Akhil Reed, author.
Title: The constitution today : timeless lessons for the issues of our era /
    Akhil Reed Amar.
Description: New York : Basic Books, 2016. | Includes bibliographical
    references and index.
Identifiers: LCCN 2016023102 (print) | LCCN 2016023606 (ebook) | ISBN
    9780465096336 (hardback) | ISBN 9780465096343 (e-book)
Subjects: LCSH: Constitutional law—United States. | BISAC: LAW /
    Constitutional. | HISTORY / United States / General. | POLITICAL SCIENCE /
    Government / General. | LAW / Essays.
Classification: LCC KF4550 .A728 2016 (print) | LCC KF4550 (ebook) |
    DDC 342.73—dc23
LC record available at https://lccn.loc.gov/2016023102

10 9 8 7 6 5 4 3

For Bob Woodward
journalist and historian, mentor and mensch

Contents

INTRODUCTION

The Constitution on Deadline

ON THE MORNING OF JUNE 28, 2012, the eyes of the world turned to the United States Supreme Court for what many thought might be the biggest constitutional ruling of the decade. Would the justices uphold or strike down the sweeping 2010 health-insurance law known as Obamacare? In particular, would the Court undermine the statute's cornerstone clause—the so-called individual mandate—requiring a wide swath of Americans to procure subsidized health-insurance policies or else pay substantial tax penalties? And if the Court did invalidate the signature domestic accomplishment of America's first black president, would this epic judicial rebuke doom Barack Obama's prospects for reelection in November? Having delivered the presidency on a silver platter to the Republican candidate in the notorious *Bush v. Gore* ruling in 2000, would a bare majority of Republican-appointed justices in effect do this again in 2012—and in the process erase the biggest consequence of the Democrats' intervening sweep in 2008?

Network cameras are not allowed in the decorous courtroom itself. Thus, as Chief Justice John Roberts began an oral summary of his ruling on behalf of a closely divided Court, television correspondents outside the courthouse were furiously speed-reading copies of the chief's simultaneously released, and quite lengthy, written opinion. On CNN, which bills itself as "the most trusted name in news," a historic headline appeared on-screen at 10:07 Eastern Time: "BREAKING NEWS: SUPREME CT. KILLS INDIVIDUAL MANDATE." Over the next couple of minutes, CNN's John King breathlessly explained to the world what this all meant: "The Court striking down that mandate is a dramatic blow to the policy and to the president,

1

politically. . . . The justices have just gutted . . . the centerpiece provision of the Obama health-care law. . . . Without a doubt, . . . the justices' throwing that out is a direct blow to the president of the United States, a direct blow to his Democratic party." As King spoke, the network posted another headline at 10:09: "INDIVIDUAL MANDATE STRUCK DOWN: Supreme Court finds measure unconstitutional."

Meanwhile, Fox News was broadcasting its own headline: "SUPREME COURT FINDS HEALTH CARE INDIVIDUAL MANDATE UNCON-STITUTIONAL." Standing on the courthouse steps at 10:08, with a copy of the Roberts opinion in her excited hands, correspondent Shannon Bream minced no words: "The mandate is gone!"

Among the millions of real-time onlookers was President Obama himself, who was watching the coverage of multiple networks in the outer Oval Office. Like so many others in that instant, he was getting his information from broadcast journalists, who were telling him that his proudest legislative achievement was kaput.

BUT IT WASN'T. The journalists had blundered, badly. In their rush to get it first, they got it wrong. They hadn't even read to the end of the Roberts opinion before they started summarizing it, erroneously, on camera. Haste in those supercharged seconds was not their only lapse. In the months leading up to that fateful day, many prominent journalists had failed to understand that Obamacare's individual mandate could be constitutionally sustained on *either* an interstate-commerce clause theory *or* a tax-clause theory. Had reporters and pundits grasped this basic legal fact about the case, they would have realized, as Roberts began narrating his opinion and they began flipping through it, that the chief justice's early pages were addressing only the former theory. No matter what those pages said, Obamacare could be upheld—as in fact it was upheld that day, as we all know now—on the latter theory.

The networks' spectacular goofs that morning remind us of two large truths about journalism. First, most professional journalists are not experts on constitutional law. Second and related, almost all journalists, by definition, act under severe time pressure. They act *on deadline*.

The very word *journalist*, from the French *jour*, captures the immediacy of the daily news and the oft-fleeting nature of the journalist's message. The unrelenting need to attend quickly to whatever the issue *du jour* might be makes it hard for the ordinary journalist to acquire genuine mastery of any single subject requiring long study—whether that subject be American constitutional law or anything else. At one time, printing presses and delivery trucks dictated journalism's tight schedules. Today, there remains the driving desire to get there first, to scoop the competition, if only by a few minutes or even seconds. This furious obsession with fastness and firstness makes a certain sense, given journalists' self-image—they are newspeople, not oldspeople—and the media's current business model. As headlines about Obamacare flashed across television screens, so did running Dow and S&P tickers. Ours is a world of continuous and instantaneous buying and selling of virtually everything, everywhere. Any news outlet that is just a hair ahead of the rest of the market on a colossal news item might help some savvy trader somewhere make a killing.

In obvious contrast to a typical newspaper essay or TV news show designed for immediate consumption, America's Constitution has a protracted shelf life. As Chief Justice John Marshall famously observed in the 1819 case of *McCulloch v. Maryland*, our Constitution aspires "to endure for ages to come."

Yet many issues of our day, like Obamacare in 2012, are also constitutional issues—issues of epochal import, issues that oblige us to simultaneously excavate a distant past and envision a faraway future as we also focus intently on the present moment and the urgent question now before us. In these situations, either ordinary journalists, despite their ingrained present-mindedness, must become constitutionalists, or professional constitutional scholars like me must become, at least momentarily, journalists of a certain sort—in a phrase, *constitutional journalists*.

THE FINAL CHAPTER of this book returns to the drama of June 28, 2012, and to my own role as a freelance constitutional journalist trying both to analyze and to influence events in the weeks and months that led up to the Court's historic ruling that day. But my career in constitutional journalism began well before Obama's presidency. Ever since I got tenure at Yale in the early 1990s, I have been a constitutional hammer in search of newsworthy nails—anything in the headlines that might give me a half-decent excuse in some news outlet to share with my fellow citizens my abiding views regarding the Constitution's letter, spirit, and contemporary significance.

My thinking was—and remains—quite simple. The Constitution cannot endure if it does not live in actual hearts and minds in the here and now. Ultimately, as a document that came from the people and that always remains amendable by the people, its specific rules and general themes must at all times be accessible to the people—not just to a professional caste of lawyers, judges, and scholars, but to ordinary citizens. Everyday people, however, have children to raise, souls to save, ball games to watch, clocks to punch. Those of us whose academic careers involve intense study of the Constitution must thus find creative ways to bring our fruits into the flow of daily American life—into newspapers, magazines, and websites aimed at a mass audience.

In my efforts to bring the Constitution to the people and the people to the Constitution, I see myself as one tiny part of a worthy tradition of popular constitutionalism stretching all the way back to the Founding. After all, in 1787–1788 the Constitution was itself a mass-produced tract reprinted in newspapers across the country; it was designed both for the ages and for immediate distribution and discussion. It was a remarkably compact text precisely because it targeted a wide popular readership: "We the People." And the most acclaimed constitutional commentary ever produced, *The Federalist*, is a series of newspaper columns initially written under tight deadlines and later arranged into a timeless book.

Now, I am no Publius, and the book you now hold in your hands surely falls short of *The Federalist*. But even as I was composing the earliest drafts of the on-deadline columns and commentaries that are revised and rearranged in this volume, I had plans to configure them one day into something more enduring—a grand colonnade of sorts. While crafting these essays at various moments over the last two decades for periodicals such as the *New York Times*, the *Daily News*, the *Wall Street Journal*, the *Washington Post*, the *Los Angeles Times*, the *New Republic*, the *Atlantic*, *Time*, the *Daily Beast*, and *Slate*, I had one eye on the minute hand and the other on the far horizon.*

This volume puts the individual puzzle pieces together for the first time. The essays are organized by subject matter so that the reader may see the larger patterns of argument that run through them. I begin each of this book's ten chapters with a freshly composed overview describing how the individual essays in that chapter originally came into being; how these pieces—le mot juste—fit together; and how my constitutional views have fared in the broader legal and public discourse in the years since these pieces

---

*The immediacy—the newness and nowness—of these periodicals is often implicit in their very names, which underscore their *time*-liness, their *daily*-ness, their *jour*-nalism. True to its title—a "slate" is something you scribble on right now, not a stone tablet you engrave for the ages—*Slate* makes a point of recording the precise minute that an item is posted.

first appeared. In countless ways, I have gently tweaked the original essays to improve this book's style, coherence, and accuracy. To preserve the integrity of the historical record, I've used this book's footnotes and endnotes to identify all important substantive changes.

Although my views have evolved on several points (all duly noted), for the most part I have been incorrigible. Yogi Berra once declared that he really didn't say everything he said. Unlike Yogi, I did say what I said, and I am now, far more systematically, saying it again.*

In so doing, I seek to offer three books in one. First, this is a book on *constitutional substance*, exploring the biggest and most bitterly contested constitutional issues of the last two decades. I aim to present a wide-angled yet detailed survey of contemporary constitutional law—that is, a survey that draws constitutional lessons from every century of our national experience and every corner of our constitutional text; that ponders the intricacies of both constitutional rights and constitutional structures; that explains the nitty-gritty of constitutional law both inside and outside the judiciary; and that folds various criminal procedure issues that are often neglected by today's mainstream constitutional law scholars back into the constitutional conversation.

Second, this is a book on *constitutional method*, illustrating by example how to do constitutional law. Constitutional law is a practice, like surgery or chess. One good way that an aspiring constitutionalist can learn and perfect the art of doing constitutional law is by carefully working through a broad cross-section of real-life case studies. Much as the chess books that I read as a youngster walked me through, with careful annotation and analysis, some of the great matches of recent memory, so this book aims to teach its readers how to do constitutional law by annotating and analyzing the real-life constitutional contests that the last twenty years have thrust to the surface of public discourse. Because the essays collected in this volume were first written on deadline and originally designed for quick mass consumption, they cut to the chase on issue after issue. The key methodological moves unfold swiftly and are easy to spot.

---

*Over the years, I've had the good fortune to work with a great set of occasional coauthors—Senator Gary Hart, journalist Timothy Noah, and Professors Vikram David Amar, Ian Ayres, Steve Calabresi, Josh Chafetz, and Neal Katyal. Roughly one-fifth of the essays collected in this book benefited from one of these collaborators.

Third, this is book on *constitutional time.* Each chapter features two temporal takes on the issues of our era: my real-time, on-deadline, in-the-heat-of-the-moment argumentation as each issue arose, and in the newly drafted overview that opens each chapter, my current assessment of how my initial arguments have come to be viewed, by me and by the wider legal and popular culture, in the coolness of time. These interlocking overviews also aim to underscore and reflect upon the temporal tension between constitutionalism and journalism, a tension created by the long-term ambitions of the former and the short-term obsessions of the latter.

I hope that you will find that this book's essays and overviews, taken together, speak clearly to many of the biggest constitutional issues of our age. I hope you will also see how each individual journalistic essay makes special sense when fitted within a more encompassing argumentative framework, as elaborated by my new overviews—how each brick works best when properly mortared alongside every other brick, as can happen only in a book such as this.

In short, I hope you will see how the pieces that follow are not a brick pile, but a building. Think once again of Publius, whose individual eighty-plus *Federalist* essays surely make special sense when read as an interlocking ensemble. I admit the analogy is imperfect. Publius's original journalistic essays were densely clustered within a nine-month span, and united by a single tightly focused rhetorical mission: to persuade readers in 1787–1788 to ratify the then-pending Constitution. The journalistic essays in this book were composed over a wider time period and are somewhat more varied in their specific argumentative aims and ambitions. But these pieces are nonetheless parts of a strongly unified constitutional project: My overarching mission is, quite simply, to help readers today understand our current Constitution. And as I explain in the chapter-opening overviews and in this book's Conclusion, the pieces within each chapter and across chapters tightly interconnect in myriad ways and on various levels.

AS WITH MY PREVIOUS BOOKS, this one has its roots in a simple-minded and old-fashioned premise: There are right and wrong answers in American constitutional law.

True, constitutional law cannot be entirely disentangled from ordinary partisan politics. Yet law differs from politics, and constitutional law when done properly cannot be reduced to partisan ideology. On several of the topics covered in this book, my constitutional views diverge from my personal and political attitudes and inclinations. For example, although guns make me nervous and I have never kept a firearm in my own house, I have long insisted that the Constitution does protect a right to keep a handgun in one's home for self-protection. (When I first started writing on this topic, mine was a distinctly minority view within the legal academy and the broader legal culture. Since then, my views on gun rights have become part of the mainstream of academic thought and have been validated by a pair of recent Supreme Court rulings.) I continue to endorse a certain constitutional theory of filibuster reform—the so-called nuclear option—even though any nuclear strike by today's Senate Republican majority would likely hurt current Senate Democrats and President Obama, whom I generally support. I also champion certain electoral-college reforms that aim to vindicate the constitutional principle of one person, one vote, despite the fact that these reforms might well disadvantage my own political party at present and for the foreseeable future.

I admit that many questions of constitutional law are close questions and that many constitutional issues may have no single right answer. But not all constitutional questions are close, and some close cases are in the end clear. In these situations, both sides have valid legal points, but when the arguments and bits of evidence are carefully sifted and tallied, one side is plainly the stronger side, legally. Even where there is not one and only one right answer to a nice question of constitutional law, there may well be a wide range of clearly wrong answers.

My previous books can be read to suggest that sound constitutional arguments usually succeed. Even if various clearly correct claims do not win at first, they ultimately sweep the field. They prevail *in time*. When the Constitution was being debated in 1787–1788, no prominent Founder ever said that a disgruntled state could unilaterally secede post-ratification. This Founding consensus is now the undeniable bedrock of our modern union, despite the fact that millions of Americans did indeed—and in deed—deny this constitutional truth in the middle of the nineteenth century. The Sedition Act of 1798 was clearly unconstitutional at the moment of its enactment; James Madison proclaimed this at the time, and eventually Madison's views prevailed in our constitutional culture. The *Dred Scott v. Sanford* decision was preposterous when rendered; Abraham Lincoln said so in real time, and *Dred Scott* is nowadays universally reviled. The Fourteenth Amendment was designed to make the Bill of Rights applicable against state and local governments; the amendment's sponsors said this loud and clear while this text was being drafted and debated, and ultimately the Supreme Court got the message. Racial apartheid was unequal and thus unconstitutional, as the first Justice Harlan insisted in his strong dissent in *Plessy v. Ferguson*; today, Harlan's view is common ground for all judges, lawyers, and citizens of good-will. The Constitution affirms a right to vote in several places, and in time judicial case law came to take that right seriously.

What might explain this striking pattern of long-run constitutional triumph? Here is one admittedly naïve and simple-minded hypothesis. On certain important issues, our Constitution really does clearly say certain things. The document's text, spirit, structure, and enactment history support an indivisible union, a robust right to criticize government officials, a broad set of fundamental rights that no state may abridge, true racial equality in the domains of civil and political rights, and so on. In the short run, ideologues and partisan politicos on and off the bench are routinely tempted to stray from the path of constitutional righteousness, and many manage to delude themselves and their political and judicial allies into thinking that their policy preferences are perfectly reflected in the Constitution itself as they choose to (mis)interpret it. For them, the Constitution is a mere mirror. But the text remains the text, and the original intent and purpose cannot be forever erased or ignored. Over the long run—precisely because Americans of all stripes have continued to pledge allegiance to the document and have continued to venerate it as the foundation of our system—slow and steady constitutional tortoises win out over fleet but fleeting constitutional hares.

Alas, there is an obvious problem with these Whiggish claims and others like them that populate my previous books on American constitutional law. Most of the constitutional issues canvassed in the preceding paragraphs and many of the issues covered in my earlier books were conclusively settled long before I came onto the scene. Perhaps I have simply written "winner's history" by first observing which side won in the end, on a particular issue, and then reverse-engineering a simplistic and triumphalist just-so story in which I depict the ultimately victorious side as legally deserving to win and legally destined to win all along. The only real constitutional method at work, a skeptic might claim, is the method of hindsight bias.

Hence this book, which seeks to illustrate and exemplify proper constitutional thinking while the issues at hand remained hotly contested, when the legal roulette balls were still in play. If in fact my constitutional arguments in the various essays in this book have aged well since their initial publication—a big if, and one that readers must judge for themselves—then this fact would be strong additional evidence for the hypothesis that there truly are constitutional right answers that can be discovered, with proper constitutional methods, long before these answers achieve universal or near-universal consensus as correct. Because proper constitutional methodology involves more than a pithy slogan or an elegant mathematical formula or a simple recipe—"start with two cups of text, add a dollop of enactment history and four tablespoons of structure, fold in the relevant precedents and evolving traditions, and then let stand for thirty minutes"—method must be illustrated and exemplified. A wide range of illustrations and examples is precisely what I provide in the chapters that follow.

One puzzle remains. If there really are more demonstrably correct constitutional answers than skeptics claim, and if there really are proper constitutional methods for finding these answers, then why do many good constitutional arguments lose the sprint and win only the marathon? My answer, in a word, is *time*. When a constitutional issue arises this afternoon, journalists who knew little or nothing about the issue this morning and who lack serious training in constitutional method can hardly be expected to analyze the issue well within a matter of hours—or even days or weeks or months.[1] After the issue is decided by a seemingly authoritative government institution—say, Congress or the president or the Supreme Court—the matter no longer commands the typical journalist's attention. He or she is on to the next story and is not particularly interested in whether a case decided fourteen months ago was in fact correctly decided.

Some might think that judges are constitutional experts, but in fact they are not. At times, they are merely opinionated lawyers with powerful political connections. At best, they are upright and hardworking generalists who must be ready in short order to rule on any legal issues that might come their way—tort law, property law, commercial law, civil-procedure law, employment law, antitrust law, and so on. Many of these legal issues involve complex regulatory codes and intricate statutes, with little or no connection to important and unsettled questions of constitutional law. Even the Supreme Court, which hears a higher percentage of constitutional law cases than do other courts, consists of generalist lawyers. Despite the justices' familiarity with Supreme Court case law, especially cases in which they themselves participated in years past, few of the justices have spent decades or even years intensely studying the Constitution itself, or the history of its enactment, amendment, and implementation across the centuries. Thus, America's legal and political system is today marred, and for much of our history has been marred, by a wide gap in truly useful constitutional knowledge and expertise.

Truth be told, only a few modern constitutional law scholars aim to bridge this gap. Most professors who teach constitutional law focus on recent Supreme Court case law, not first principles of constitutional text, history, and structure. Many gifted scholars also dream of ultimate appointment to the bench, and these dreams can seduce. Ours is a partisan world, and many a scholar picks a side, hoping that one day the phone will ring when the scholar's preferred party is in power. In the meantime, some of these politically ambitious or merely ideological scholars crank out work that is less objective than one might wish for—just objective (or seemingly objective) enough to neutralize credulous journalists and persuade or provide cover for inexpert judges and politicos who lean in the same ideological direction.

Here are two examples from this book. First, *Bush v. Gore* stinks. I said so on deadline—one week after this December 2000 ruling came down—and so did many other Democratic and Democrat-leaning constitutional scholars at that time. At first almost no leading Republican scholars echoed our cris de coeur. Some right-leaning scholars actually defended the Court; others stayed mum. But this sharp division hardly meant that neither side was clearly right. The harsh critics of *Bush v. Gore* were correct, and our criticisms have aged well. In the decade and a half since *Bush v. Gore* came down, no Supreme Court majority opinion has ever cited the case; Court insiders report that several current and retired justices now view this case with profound embarrassment; many conservative scholars now quietly admit that the case reeks; and in a recent *Time* magazine survey of constitutional scholars, *Bush v. Gore* was repeatedly condemned as one of the worst cases of the last half-century.[2]

Second, the so-called exclusionary rule is misbegotten. Rightly read, the Constitution provides next to no support for this perverse doctrine under which judges have tossed out reliable physical evidence in countless criminal cases, freeing undeniably guilty criminals and inflicting great harm on innocent victims of crime and their families. The exclusionary rule was kicked into high gear by a Democrat-leaning Supreme Court in the 1960s, and in multiple op-eds and other writings over the last two decades I have assailed the rule. Only a few Democrat-leaning scholars have joined me in this crusade, but many Republican-leaning scholars have climbed aboard this bandwagon. Here, too, the current lack of scholarly consensus does not mean that there is no right answer. On this issue, the conservative side, the Republican side, has the better constitutional argument, and this side is slowly but surely gaining ground in court. The arguments of the exclusionary rule's critics are aging well—as sound constitutional arguments generally do—and the current Supreme Court is cutting back on the exclusionary rule. For my taste these cutbacks have been too sluggish and too timid, but the general direction of doctrinal movement is now clear, and I remain hopeful that slow and steady will win this race . . . *in time.*

PART I OF THIS BOOK probes the basic structure of the modern federal government—the main institutions and offices of national power set forth in America's written Constitution. Whereas the eighteenth-century text outlines three branches, starting with the legislature, Part I has four chapters, starting with the presidency.

In the modern era, the presidency has become America's dominant political institution. Journalism itself is part of the explanation. The presidency comes with a pulpit. Unlike Congress, which is often in recess, the president is always on the job and is at every moment a perfect subject for the daily news. Far more Americans tune into televised presidential debates and vote in presidential elections than tune into congressional debates and vote in off-year congressional elections. Indeed, the very phrase "off-year" signifies the centrality of the modern presidency: Any even-year election in which the presidency is not at stake is considered "off-year" even though every single seat in the House of Representatives is on the ballot. Other factors exalting the modern presidency include the ubiquity of war and the centrality of international relations in today's world; the significance of nuclear weaponry (with the president's hand proverbially controlling the button at all times); and the reality of sharp partisan division in Congress (rendering the framers' first branch less able to act coherently and decisively than their second branch, headed as it is by a one-person chief executive).

Chapter 1's essays on the modern-day presidency pay particular attention to the recent resurgence of dynasties in our presidential politics. When I first started writing about presidential dynasties in January 2000, most Americans, if polled, might have said that the phrase "George W" referred to George Washington, and few knew that George Washington's contemporaries trusted him precisely because he was a non-dynast—precisely because he had no son of his own to succeed him.

Since I wrote that initial piece, a president's son and namesake bested senator's son and namesake for the presidency in the November 2000 election; a president's wife made a notable bid for the Oval Office in 2008; the GOP tapped the son of a previous presidential candidate as its standard-bearer in the 2012 presidential election; and the 2016 presidential contest has showcased no less than three obviously dynastic aspirants—Hillary Clinton, Jeb Bush, and Rand Paul. And let's not forget Donald Trump. True, Trump's father never sought or held the presidency; nor did his current spouse; nor did either of his ex-spouses; nor did any of his siblings. But "The Donald" (as in "The Duke" or "The Earl") did inherit vast wealth from his sire. "Dynasty" is now a word on everyone's lips.[3]

Over the years, I have aimed to give my fellow citizens a framework for thinking about similarities and differences among various kinds of dynasties—marital, parental, fraternal, and adoptive; presidential, gubernatorial, and senatorial; same-sex and opposite sex; inter- and intra-generational; plutocratic and non-plutocratic; foreign and domestic; and so on. For almost two decades I have seen dynasties everywhere, and my countrymen are now beginning to see them, too.

Chapter 2 continues my exploration of the modern-day executive branch by bringing the vice presidency into the spotlight.[4] In a non-nuclear world, it may not have mattered quite so much who was a heartbeat away from the presidency, but today's Americans live in the shadow of Hiroshima and Dallas. Two modern constitutional amendments have also combined to increase the power and visibility of vice presidents. Thanks to the Twenty-second Amendment, ratified in 1951, a president can no longer seek a third term personally, and so he must often do so indirectly via his veep. The Twenty-fifth Amendment, crafted after President John F. Kennedy's death to modernize the machinery of presidential succession, further heightened the significance of the vice presidency. Between 1804, when the Constitution was amended to downgrade the vice presidency, and 1951, when the Constitution was re-amended to upgrade the office, only 16 percent of America's vice presidents went on to win a major-party nomination to the presidency itself. Since 1952—the first election under modern rules—more than half of America's vice presidents have gone on to head their party's ticket.

The most important constitutional function of a sitting vice president is to serve as the legal linchpin of an elaborate presidential succession system. Alas, at present this legal linchpin mechanism is not entirely sturdy, and other components of our current presidential succession laws are a set of constitutional disasters waiting to happen. Or so I have argued in many journalistic venues, using a variety of news hooks to try to capture the imagination of my fellow citizens. But the worrisome cracks in our system, while real, are low-probability and low-visibility threats. Although policy wonks and senior statesmen from across the political spectrum have in recent years endorsed my general diagnosis and prescription, only Congress can fix this system and Congress seems in no hurry to do so. America's best hope is thus to get the general public—the readers of this book—far more focused on the succession problem, so that some ambitious future congressperson might find it in his or her political interest to become the reforming crusader here.

Chapter 3 covers the framers' first branch, the United States Congress, and pays particular attention to the modern Senate and its various dysfunctions—dysfunctions often rooted in or intertwined with the upper chamber's feckless disregard for the basic democratic default principle of majority rule.

In the waning hours of 2008, Professor Josh Chafetz and I publicly urged the Senate not to seat Roland Burris, who had been appointed by the crooked governor of Illinois, Rod Blagojevich, to fill Barack Obama's vacant Senate position. Josh and I lost on this one—and so did the republic, as it later became clear that Burris himself had lied about his own role in the undeniably corrupt process of his selection. Yet Senate Democrats seeking ways to overcome likely Republican filibusters seated Burris despite the stink in the air. In January 2012, journalist Timothy Noah and I also lost in our public effort to persuade President Obama and Senate Majority Leader Harry Reid to make clear that a majority of senators actually did support the recess appointments that the president had just made. Obama and Reid should have listened to this advice: When the issue reached the Supreme Court in 2014, the justices unanimously ruled against these awkwardly executed appointments.

More happily, Reid eventually did begin the process of reforming the Senate's dysfunctional filibuster rules via a simple majoritarian legal device known as "the nuclear option." In November 2013, the Senate clearly and for the first time in modern history endorsed a simple and sweeping theory of filibuster reform that was first articulated in January 2009, in a *Slate* piece that Senator Gary Hart and I coauthored. At present, Reid's reform has tamed the filibuster only in connection with certain nominations. But in future years, the Reid precedent and the ideas underlying it could well be extended, by either Republicans or Democrats, to apply to ordinary legislation—thus ending the filibuster as we now know it.

Chapter 4 trains a constitutionalist's eye on the practices and personages of the federal judiciary, suggesting some ways that the branch most often associated with the Constitution might better embody the document's deepest principles. For instance, in 2002 Federalist Society co-founder Steve Calabresi and I criticized the Supreme Court for not allowing the public to take notes at oral arguments and for not making free transcripts of these arguments quickly available to the public. Today, the Court is much better. Notes are allowed, and free transcripts issue promptly. The Court needs to go further still: Real-time National Public Radio (NPR) broadcasts of all oral arguments, please!

One other idea that Professor Calabresi and I launched back in 2002 has only begun to capture the public imagination: Why not have the justices of the Supreme Court serve somewhere within the Article III judiciary for life, but on the Court itself for only eighteen years? Or allow senior justices to remain on the Court but as back-benchers hearing cases only if the Court is short-staffed? As we explained that year in a *Washington Post* op-ed, such a reform could be accomplished by simple statute or a new informal norm, without the need for a formal constitutional amendment. Thus this reform could actually materialize in the decades to come, especially if judicial life expectancies continue to lengthen.

PART II OF THIS BOOK addresses the Constitution's role in modern America's culture wars.

Chapter 5 concentrates on constitutional criminal procedure and shows how basic constitutional provisions regarding evidence and testimony have been widely misinterpreted. In a televised 1995 trial that riveted the nation, O. J. Simpson got away with murder, thanks in part to the exclusionary rule. Happily, the Court over the last two decades has whittled down the exclusionary rule and has also moved increasingly toward my view that the touchstone of the Fourth Amendment is neither a global warrant requirement nor a global probable cause requirement, but a global reasonableness requirement. Though the justices have made no mention of my journalistic essays on this topic, they have, in five cases over the last quarter century, favorably cited my law review publications that expound these very same Fourth Amendment ideas at greater length and with more technical detail.[5] By contrast, my views on the Fifth Amendment self-incrimination clause—a clause that I believe should bar only compelled words, not any reliable physical fruit that might be found as a result of compelled words—have not been embraced by the Court.

On one of the most important issues of modern criminal procedure law—the use of DNA to solve crime—some of the edgy ideas I put forth as early as 2001 are now much closer to reality. And that, I confess, makes me nervous because my edgiest proposal—calling for the creation of a truly comprehensive and carefully guarded DNA database—holds great promise but is also fraught with peril. Of all the ideas in this book, my endorsement of a database that includes everyone's DNA may one day come to be seen by posterity as especially misguided. At present, it is too soon to tell how the promise of DNA will eventually balance out against the peril of DNA.

Chapter 6 covers several other recent battles in America's culture wars. In general, my essays and their arguments—some liberal, some conservative, some hard to classify—have stood the test of time and have been judicially vindicated. Diversity-based affirmative action in higher education, if pursued softly à la Lewis Powell in *Regents of the University of California v. Bakke*, remains constitutionally permissible. An ordinary American citizen now has a judicially recognized right to have an ordinary handgun in his or her home for self-protection, and rightly so, but all sorts of reasonable gun control measures should pass muster. Key parts of the McCain-Feingold campaign-finance bill, restricting free speech during election seasons, have been struck down, quite properly, as violative of the First Amendment. Bans on same-sex marriage are now in history's rearview mirror. So far, so good for my views on these matters, views that I made public long before the decisive judicial rulings—*Grutter v. Bollinger* (2003), *District of Columbia v. Heller* (2008), *Citizens United v. Federal Election Commission* (2010), and *Obergefell v. Hodges* (2015)—came down.

Part II ends with Chapter 7, which collects a quintet of essays that I have authored over the years to commemorate the Constitution's mid-September birthday. (For those who don't know, September 17 is officially designated Constitution Day, marking the moment in 1787 when the Philadelphia framers went public with their proposed new rules for a new world.) Of course, no scholar or journalist can objectively judge his or her own influence, but I am gratified that some of the small seeds that I tried to plant in these anniversary essays appear to be taking root. In 2005, I publicly invited my dazzling Yale Law School colleague Jack Balkin to be more "originalist"—that is, more attentive to the framers' and ratifiers' original understandings of the 1787

Constitution and its subsequent amendments. In recent years Professor Balkin has accepted my invitation, as have other prominent liberals.[6] Back in 2005, the Constitutional Accountability Center did not yet exist. Today that organization, founded by the visionary Doug Kendall and now led by his brilliant protégée Elizabeth Wydra, plays a major role in America's ongoing constitutional conversation; and the defining vision of this important and still-rising organization might be fairly summarized by my 2005 slogan, "Originalism for Liberals."

More generally, these anniversary essays, emphasizing both the democratic audacity of the Founding and the transformative meaning of later events such as the woman suffrage amendment, offer a clear counternarrative to ideologues who wrongly read the Constitution as if the crucial words were "We the Property" or "We the States" or "We the Wealthy White Men."

PART III OF THIS BOOK covers three modern presidential dramas. For each of our most recent presidents—Bill Clinton, George W. Bush, and Barack Obama—I highlight one especially suspenseful experience that future constitutional historians will likely see as particularly notable.

Chapter 8 features a series of essays that appeared in newspapers and newsmagazines before, during, and shortly after the impeachment of President Bill Clinton in 1998–1999. These essays argue that Clinton's impeachment grew out of a constitutionally flawed independent counsel statute. Building on foundations laid by Justice Antonin Scalia, I was one of the legal academy's earliest and most emphatic constitutional critics of this statute. In time, others came around. Several of the statute's most prominent scholarly supporters later conceded error; Independent Counsel Ken Starr himself eventually joined the law's critics; the statute has now lapsed; and there are no realistic prospects for its revival any time soon.

I also argued that the Clinton impeachment reflected inappropriate partisanship. No elected president should be ousted from office, or even brought to trial in the Senate, unless leaders of the president's own party, and members of the president's own electoral base, have signaled their willingness to toss their man out. House Republicans in 1998–1999 did not accept this rule of fair play, but they apparently do today, having ignored impeachment noises from party extremists in recent years—just as Democratic congressional leaders properly resisted symmetrically extreme demands for the impeachment of George W. Bush in the years between Presidents Clinton and Obama.

Chapter 9 centers on an awkward fact that colored George W. Bush's entire first term: In the roller-coaster election of 2000, his opponent, Al Gore, had undeniably won far more votes nationwide. When I first began writing about America's electoral college prior to that wild election, few Americans understood that this clumsy Founding-era electoral contraption had been designed and reinvented in the shadow of slavery; that this contraption has historically dampened and continues to dampen state incentives to expand voting rights; that federalism and attractive competition among states could continue to operate even under a system of direct national election; and that such a system could be adopted without the need for a formal constitutional amendment. Today, more Americans do understand these basic truths. As a result, there is currently a powerful political reform movement afoot—the National Popular Vote (NPV) project—to put a variant of my journalistic ideas into action. Ten states and the District of Columbia have formally enacted laws to operationalize this project. This group represents 165 electoral votes, more than 60 percent of the 270 electoral votes needed for the plan to launch a system of direct national popular election roughly tracking a journalistic blueprint that Professor Vikram David Amar and I posted online fifteen years ago and a similar blueprint published at the same time by Professor Robert W. Bennett. This new NPV system would not be tilted against the Republican Party, which so far has resisted the reform. If anything, Republicans might benefit from this plan for the foreseeable future. Whether or not the ideas in this chapter are persuasive, at least they have never been partisan.

Chapter 10 revolves around the most nail-biting constitutional conflict of Barack Obama's tenure: the intense constitutional challenge mounted against his signature health-care law. On the morning of June 28, 2012, Obamacare was upheld by the Supreme Court, and rightly so. Indeed, the essays in this chapter make clear that the case shouldn't even have been close. There were many different and constitutionally correct ways of upholding the Obamacare statute—all true roads led to constitutional validity. One particular pathway that I strongly advocated on deadline in June 2011 and again in March 2012 detoured around the interstate-commerce clause—the focus of most contemporaneous pundits and politicos—and instead traveled through Congress's taxation power and a theory of judicial modesty associated with a case called *Ashwander v. TVA*. This was the pathway that prevailed in the Supreme Court. Although the particular voting lineup that emerged on the Court, with Chief Justice John Roberts joining the Court's four Democratic appointees to uphold the health-reform law, surprised many journalistic observers, this lineup was also strongly foreshadowed by my journalistic interventions.

IN A BRIEF CONCLUSION, I offer some general thoughts about how the essays in this book might help both constitutionalists and journalists do their respective jobs better. Constitutionalists must attend—as this book tries to attend—to all three branches of government, and not just the judiciary, which is the obsessive focus of so many modern constitutional scholars. The constitutional issues of our era, like the constitutional issues of every era, have pulsed through every vital organ of the American body politic.

And like blood itself, the Constitution sustains our republic. This compact intergenerational document does not merely limit; it empowers and illuminates. For those skilled in the arts of unlocking its meaning, this document distills and preserves the wisdom of a great people over many centuries. Read right, it guides us and shapes us, giving a raucous and variegated society a common language, a handy metric, a shared set of institutions, a joint history, a collective identity, a national narrative, a genuinely unifying yet pluralist ideology.

I also offer advice for full-time professional journalists. The beginning of journalistic wisdom, I suggest, is self-knowledge. Journalists must recognize their guild's structural tendencies toward myopia and amnesia, and the particular problems that arise when constitutional issues become news. It is probably too much to expect journalists to familiarize themselves with the entire history of American constitutionalism or with every wrinkle of the written Constitution or with all the tools and techniques of proper constitutional analysis. But it is not too much to ask today's journalists to think again, with the benefit of hindsight, about the great constitutional issues that they and their colleagues have lived through and covered over the last two decades. There are doubtless many ways that today's journalists could discharge this solemn responsibility of sober self-reflection regarding the biggest constitutional issues of their era. It is utterly self-serving—but it might nonetheless be true—for me to suggest that one good thing for all good journalists to do would be to read this book.

MY GOAL AS A CONSTITUTIONAL JOURNALIST has always been to shed light on the issues of the day while simultaneously offering a more enduring set of ideas—a general road map for where constitutional law must go in the long run. Like other creatures, humans live every moment in the moment, but unlike the rest of God's creation, we humans also consciously and conscientiously plan for the distant future, not just for ourselves but for our posterity.[7]

America's Constitution embodies a particularly expansive temporal ambition. The document and the doctrines fashioned in the service of the document seek to regulate human affairs not just for today or this year, but for decades and even centuries hence. Constitutional journalists must never forget to ponder the long-run implications of their everyday work.

Having invoked the always quotable John Marshall at the outset of this Introduction, I close with another eloquent American philosopher. "If you don't know where you're going," said Yogi, "you might not get there."

PART I

MODERN BRANCHES

1

THE PRESIDENCY

A Return to Dynasty?

AT THE AGE OF NINE, I became a collector. I started amassing coins, miniature cars, marbles, baseball cards, and presidential knickknacks. As I memorized the order of the presidents and fun facts about these first men, I couldn't help noticing that there were two presidents named Adams, two named Harrison, and two named Roosevelt. (There were no presidential Bushes yet, of course.)

And then there were the Kennedys. My impressions of John F. Kennedy were almost entirely posthumous. But my emotional relationship to his two younger brothers was very different. In 1968, some of my precocious fourth-grade pals were supporters of Eugene McCarthy, but I was for Kennedy all the way—Robert, that is. In college, I fell for Kennedy yet again—another brother, Ted. Only years later, when I came to study the American Revolution and the Founding of the Constitution did I begin to see the sinister side of Camelot—a metaphor I now find downright un-American and anti-constitutional, for reasons that I unfold in one of the essays in this chapter.

As an adult, I began to see dynasties everywhere. One eye-opening experience occurred in the summer of 1992, when I read historian Gordon Wood's magisterial book, *The Radicalism of the American Revolution*. This epic tome, with its sustained focus on the monarchical, aristocratic, and clerical elements of the ancien régime that American revolutionaries hoped to sweep away, helped me see several constitutional clauses in a new light. The multiple bans on titles of nobility, the explicit guarantee of a republican form of government, the absence of property qualifications for federal public service, the promise that all federal public servants would be paid from a public treasury, the secular presidential oath clause, the repudiation of religious tests for federal officeholding, even the minimum age rules in the document—all were part of a comprehensive anti-aristocratic, anti-feudal, anti-establishmentarian vision. American government officials, especially American presidents, would be decisively different from Old World sacerdotal monarchs who inherited hallowed crowns from their fathers and passed them down, with priestly blessing, to their sons and namesakes.

Two events at the turn of the millennium—one personal and one political—heightened my sensitivity to dynastic issues. First, in 1999 I became a father and began to see the world through a father's eyes, and to experience the natural instinct to favor one's own child in ways large and small. My wife and I named our son Vikram Paul Amar after my two brothers, Vikram David Amar and Arun Paul Amar, and this surely sensitized me to various intricacies of the intergenerational name game. ("Which 'Vik' do you mean—'big Vik' or 'little Vik?'")

And then came the second momentous event—the emergence of George W. Bush onto the presidential stage. As I mention in this chapter's opening journalistic essay, "U.S. Successions Began with George (III and W)," first-name-confusion in the Bush dynasty helped W in the earliest days of the 1999–2000 presidential sweepstakes. This essay ran in the *Los Angeles Times* in January 2000 and was a harbinger of things to come: Throughout the election year, George *fils* continued to benefit from his nominal resemblance to, and descent from, George *père*.

More generally, the prism of dynasty furnished a powerful tool for refracting both sides of the 2000 election. The race between Al Gore and George W. Bush was not just a Democrat against a Republican, a wonkish progressive against a compassionate conservative, a Harvard man against a Yalie. In a nation dedicated to the proposition that all persons are born equal, the presidential election of 2000 gave voters a choice between a senator's son and a president's son—or to be more genealogically precise, between a senator's son and a president's son/senator's grandson/big-swing-state-governor's brother. (Like W, Al Gore Jr. shared both a first and last name with a legendary political officeholder—his sire was none other than Senator Albert Gore Sr.— and in W's case, we must recall that his father's father was Senator Prescott Bush of Connecticut and his kid brother Jeb was in 2000 the sitting governor of Florida.)

The Founders would not have wanted to, and emphatically did not, deny modern Americans the right to make these pro-dynasty choices. But in this chapter's essays, I suggest that the Founders would have been disappointed to see how little attention modern Americans have at times paid to the political dynasties rising up in our midst. Precisely because stories of charming princes and charmed princesses shape us all at an early age, we must as adults become aware of the immense power of these not-so-benign fairy tales, especially when backed, as they often are, by vast institutional clout and enormous intergenerational wealth.

Presidential dynasties are hardly the only ones to notice—especially if one is always on the lookout for dynastic influence. For example, Edmund G. Brown Sr. was my boyhood governor in California in the 1960s and his only son, Edmund G. Brown Jr., became California's governor in the late 1970s and early 1980s, and is once again governor, having been reelected in 2010 and 2014. At least there was minimal name-confusion here: The elder Brown was generally known as "Pat" and the younger Brown has always gone by "Jerry." Also, in his most recent two successful bids for the governorship, Jerry was surely judged more by his own track record than his father's. Note, too, that Brown's 2010 predecessor, Arnold Schwarzenegger, had never held political office prior to the governorship and was a celebrity not merely in his own right as a movie star, but also as a nephew-in-law of President John Kennedy and Senators Robert Kennedy and Ted Kennedy. And if all that isn't dynastic enough, Arnold's father-in-law, R. Sargent Shriver, was the Democratic nominee for the vice presidency in 1972.

Or to switch from one big blue coastal state to another: Recall that the current New York governor, Andrew Cuomo, is not just the son of a former governor, Mario, but was for fifteen years married to RFK's daughter Kerry.

ONE THEME OF THIS BOOK is how various constitutional ideas either play out in, or are absent from, the mass media. I see political dynasties everywhere and am eager to talk about them anytime. But when are my fellow Americans—especially the editors who stand as the gatekeepers of America's leading popular periodicals—eager to listen? Only during certain windows, alas. It is no coincidence that four of the five essays in this chapter were initially published in presidential election years—the first two in 2000, the third in 2008, and the fourth in 2012.

The fifth and final essay in this chapter, "Second Chances," is also the product of a presidential election that captured the media's attention. In the immediate aftermath of Barack Obama's reelection in 2012, the editors of the *Atlantic* contacted me to solicit an essay to be published in early January

2013 to mark his second inauguration. Although this essay does not dwell in detail on family dynasties, it does end by imagining a second President Clinton—Hillary. Its main point is also closely related to dynasty: Because even presidents are mortal, America's chiefs must look for ways to project their influence beyond their natural and political life spans. *Familial dynasties have historically been one (Old World) way to project power into the future; hand-picked succession is another (more democratic, New World) way.*

Think of handpicked succession as adopting an adult heir rather than procreating an infant namesake. Whether power descends by birth (John and John Quincy Adams; George H. W. Bush and George W. Bush) or marriage (Bill and Hillary Clinton) or de facto adult adoption (George Washington and Alexander Hamilton; Thomas Jefferson and James Madison), the important thing, I argue, is that strong presidents must find someone who will carry their flag forward when they can no longer do so themselves. The key to presidential success is . . . succession.

The concluding passages of this 2013 essay, when read alongside my 2008 musings about Hillary Clinton's dynastic dimensions, place the impending presidential election of 2016 in an interesting and unconventional light. From a conventional (and shallow) journalistic angle, Hillary Clinton looks obviously and entirely dynastic: She is simply a female version of Jack Kennedy, Bobby Kennedy, Ted Kennedy, George H. W. Bush, George W. Bush, Jeb Bush, Jerry Brown, Al Gore, Mitt Romney, and Andrew Cuomo.

But from a constitutional angle—the angle of my 2008 and 2013 pieces—we must recall that earned adult achievements are decisively different from aristocratic privileges inherited at birth or in early childhood. Unlike all the other heirs just mentioned, the baby named Hillary Rodham did not at birth inherit any position of political or economic privilege (or exalted social status, for that matter). Instead, much later in life—and after gaining admission to top schools based on her own hard-won grades and test scores and then re-proving her merit in a series of demanding professional positions—the common-born Hillary Rodham Clinton was handpicked twice (!) as a key presidential helpmate. First, from 1992 to 2001, she was Bill Clinton's two-for-the-price-of-one de facto running mate and policy adviser. Second, after a successful and high-visibility stint as a U.S. senator, she was Barack Obama's leading cabinet minister in his first term. Unlike, for example, JFK or Bush 41 or Bush 43, neither of the presidents who handpicked her was himself born into wealth or power or fame. Nor were the presidents who picked her related to her by blood or at birth. Of course as adults, Bill Clinton and she chose to partner up in many ways, with interconnections surely more complex than—but in certain respects not entirely unlike—the strong bonds that linked Washington with Hamilton and Jefferson with Madison. Both President Bill Clinton and President Barack Obama freely and democratically chose to politically team up with Hillary Clinton because both presidents perceived her as an electoral asset and a policy expert.

Seen from this angle, former New York senator Hillary Clinton's closest counterpart in American politics is not New York's highborn governor Andrew Cuomo, or New York's past highborn governors Nelson Rockefeller or Franklin Roosevelt, or New York's highborn tycoon Donald Trump, but rather New York's greatest Founding Father, the common-born Alexander Hamilton, Washington's handpicked helper. (Another not far-fetched analogy is New York's common-born Martin Van Buren, the handpicked helpmate and successor of common-born president Andrew Jackson.)

IN GENERAL, THIS CHAPTER'S ESSAYS differ in shape and feel from many of the other essays elsewhere in this book that propose specific and immediate legal results or reforms: judicial validation of Obamacare, establishment of direct presidential election, modification of the electoral calendar, abolition of the exclusionary rule, increased transparency of Supreme Court oral arguments, and so on. This chapter's essays did not presume to tell my fellow Americans exactly how to vote, or for whom to vote. With the exception of "Second Chances"—which did offer specific suggestions to the Obama administration—these pieces had no immediate policy payoff or prescription. Rather, they aimed to broadly refocus the electoral conversation— to urge Americans to consider which results on Election Night would exacerbate dynastic rule in America, and which results might tend to counteract it. This question should not always be decisive in the voting booth. But it should always, I argued, factor into the calculus of thoughtful voters.

So, too, should America's anti-establishmentarian commitment to religious pluralism and openness, as I argued in passing in an essay on the 2008 presidential candidates, and in a more sustained way in its 2012 sequel when Mitt Romney, a Mormon, made it to the finals.

America's Constitution is not merely a set of legal commands—dos and don'ts—separating what is legal/constitutional from what is illegal/unconstitutional. The Constitution is also a national narrative, a template for pondering a range of choices, all of which are legally permissible, but some of which may be constitutionally preferable—more in keeping with some of the Constitution's grand themes as distinct from its clear rules.

THREE OF THE PRESIDENTIAL-ELECTION-YEAR ESSAYS that now form the backbone of this chapter were clearly styled as musings on the unfolding campaigns of 2000, 2008, and 2012, respectively. Another one, "The Dark Side of Camelot," also offered anti-dynastic election-year commentary but had a slightly different backstory.

With interest in all things presidential running high in the autumn of 2000, the *Wall Street Journal* asked me to participate in a scholarly survey rating America's past presidents.[1] When my answers indicated that, in my view, JFK was closer to the middle of the pack than to Washington and Lincoln, the *Journal* invited me to say why, as part of a series the *Journal* was running in connection with the publication of its survey results. I suspect that the *Journal*, with its generally Republican point of view, was gleeful that a card-carrying Democratic scholar would volunteer to take the Kennedys down a notch.

But in expressing anxieties about Jack's placement of his kid brother Bobby atop the Justice Department in the 1960s, this late-November 2000 essay was also slyly hinting that *Journal* readers might sensibly wonder whether George W's team was improperly benefitting from kid brother Jeb's role atop the Florida government. Thanks to the disgraceful Katherine Harris, a close ally of the Bush dynasty, Florida's election authorities had illegally purged the voting rolls before the election and were engaging in a wide range of other legally dubious post-election actions. Whether or not the *Journal* editors saw this Floridian implication, and whether or not most *Journal* readers in November 2000 saw it, I surely saw it in late 2000—because I see dynasty everywhere.

HERE IS ONE FINAL EXAMPLE of the kinds of questions and insights that a relentless focus on dynasty makes possible: Is it purely a coincidence that Al Gore ran for president in 2000 but Dick Cheney did not in 2008? In the last sixty years, most sitting vice presidents or former veeps have not only sought the presidency when their presidents were no longer in the running but have also won their party's nomination: Richard Nixon in 1960, Lyndon Johnson in 1964, Hubert Humphrey in 1968, Richard Nixon in 1968 and

1972, Gerald Ford in 1976, Walter Mondale in 1984, George H. W. Bush in 1988 and 1992, and Al Gore in 2000. What requires explanation, then, is not that Gore ran in 2000, but that Cheney didn't in 2008. I suspect that one key factor was dynastic: Cheney in 2000 was chosen in part because he was loyal to the Bush family and would likely be too old and infirm to run in his own right in 2008—the year slotted for Jeb Bush, had this Bush grandson/son/brother chosen to run. In part because of Iraq and Hurricane Katrina, the Bush dynasty ended up not seeking a fourth term in 2008, but isn't it note-worthy that George W's choice of Cheney in 2000 nicely preserved this option?

Isn't it also noteworthy that Dan Quayle sought but did not get his party's nomination in 2000? Apparently, the president under whom he served, H. W., had another successor in mind—namely, his namesake, W. Here, too, dynastic issues would seem to be part of the story. Since the mid-1950s, the only other veeps who failed to win presidential nomination were Spiro Agnew (a disgraced felon by the time his chance rolled around in 1976), Nelson Rockefeller (dead when his first chance would have materialized in 1980), and Joe Biden (who had to contend with another Obama handpicked helper, Hillary Clinton, as I discussed in the closing passage of the 2013 "Second Chances" essay).

Summing up all the data, the big outliers are Quayle and Cheney, and the simplest explanation is the Bush dynasty.

U.S. SUCCESSIONS BEGAN WITH GEORGE (III AND W)

Los Angeles Times, Sunday, January 23, 2000

Our story of father-son succession and the U.S. presidency begins with George the patriarch and the rising George W—that is, with King George III and George Washington.[2]

As the federal Constitution was being debated in the late 1780s, every-one understood that Washington would most likely become the United States' first president. But America's George would be very different from Britain's George. As The Federalist No. 69 emphasized: "The president of the United States would be an officer elected by the people for four years; the king of Great Britain is a perpetual and hereditary prince." The U.S. Consti-tution thus decisively broke with the idea that political office should be handed down from father to son as inheritable property. In Thomas Jefferson's words, "The mass of mankind has not been born with saddles on their backs, nor a favored few booted and spurred, ready to ride them legitimately, by the grace of God."[3]

Sadly, the Constitution in practice failed to live up to this lofty idea of a republic open to talent and indifferent to blood. Plantation owners' namesakes were given spurs at birth, and slave children were saddled up. But the Constitution's language proclaimed a different, anti-dynastic ideal. Here, "We the people" would live out "a republican form of government" based on principles of equal citizenship. In two separate places, the Constitution promised that no "titles of nobility" would be allowed in America. A third clause condemning titles of nobility passed Congress as a constitutional amendment in the early nineteenth century but was never ratified.

George W's unanimous election in 1789—every member of the first electoral college supported him—reflected the Founders' strong suspicion of father-son dynasty. Put simply, Washington became father of his country in part because he was not father of his own children. He sired no heirs, and his only stepson died in 1781. Americans could breathe easier knowing that their first general and first president would not try to create a throne and crown to pass on to his namesake. In fact, the man contemporaries most feared was Alexander Hamilton, who often played the role of the son Washington never had.[4]

The history of the early presidency is striking. Thomas Jefferson had no surviving sons, at least no legitimate ones. Ditto for James Madison and James Monroe. John Adams, however, did have a son and namesake: John Quincy. Q's eventual accession to the presidency can be seen as a transition from a pre-modern world of dynastic succession to the modern world of a democracy open to talent. As historian Gordon Wood has explained, pre-revolutionary America was a world of political patriarchy: "During the half century before the Revolution, more than 70 percent of the representatives elected to the New Jersey assembly were related to previously elected legislators."

Q's accession in 1824–1825 might seem a throwback, but it can also be viewed differently. A Phi Beta Kappa graduate of Harvard and, later, a Harvard professor; an accomplished diplomat, fluent in several languages, with decades of experience in foreign affairs, including a successful eight-year stint as secretary of state—here was a man with impressive credentials and prodigious talents in his own right. And Q's entrance onto the presidential stage occurred a quarter-century after his father's exit. In 1801, when John the elder left office, Q was not old enough to run—one happy effect, and perhaps purpose, of the Constitution's rule requiring the president to be at least thirty-five was to limit regency successions of young and irresponsible namesakes.

Having considered presidential Georges and Johns from the Founding era, let's now turn to our modern presidential Georges and Johns. John F. Kennedy's electoral victory in 1960 did pose genuine concerns about dynastic succession—mainly issues of sibling rather than father-son succession. Had Robert F. Kennedy or Ted Kennedy become president soon after their elder brother, the world might well have wondered if American democracy was really so different from old-fashioned monarchy. And perhaps John F. Kennedy Jr.'s greatest service to the nation was that he did not try to claim the Camelot crown himself.

If these last points seem overwrought, consider how the rest of the world is still struggling to break free from dynastic succession. Recent years have witnessed father-son transitions in North Korea, Jordan, and Morocco; both Iraq and Syria may soon follow suit. The new vice president and heir apparent in Indonesia is the daughter of a former president; and the leader of the Congress Party in India, Sonia Gandhi, is the widow of one prime minister (Rajiv Gandhi), the daughter-in-law of another prime minister (Indira Gandhi), and the granddaughter-in-law of yet a third prime minister (Jawaharlal Nehru). In turn, Sonia's daughter, Priyanka, is beginning to build a political following. These familial successions are unfortunate throwbacks to feudalism, even in societies that have elected their leaders "democratically."

Through their names and their looks, the offspring of great leaders doubtless conjure up images of past glory in the minds of fellow citizens. But a mature democracy should insist that look-alikes and sound-alikes are truly persons of distinction in their own right before being crowned with high office. The history of great families is, alas, often a history of decline.

All this raises questions about *our* George W. One real cost of electing this namesake to the presidency would be the mixed message about democracy and dynasty it might send to the rest of the world. Granted, dynasty has some virtues: In India, Indonesia, and Pakistan, for example, it has crowned women as leaders of societies otherwise stained by rather repressive policies toward those born with two X chromosomes. Granted, also, Americans must be free to vote for the best person and should not bar someone who happens to be a president's heir. Rather than a "title of nobility," an absolute bar would resemble an unconstitutional "corruption of the blood" imposed on children of disfavored politicians.

But we should proceed carefully, lest we open a Pandora's box that the Founders tried to nail shut by electing their George W. Here are a few suggested guidelines:

First, American voters should distinguish between political dynasties and presidential ones. Gubernatorial, senatorial, and other dynasties abound, but the stakes and visibility of the presidency make it different in kind.

Second, let's focus on the time lapse between the elder's exit and the younger's entrance; dynastic dangers are greatest when these two are close together. (In addition to the Adamses, Benjamin Harrison was elected forty-eight years after his grandfather William Henry, who died after a month in office, and Franklin D. Roosevelt entered office twenty-four years after his distant cousin, Theodore Roosevelt, had left.)

Third, pay extra attention to the credentials and talents of the younger in his own right and don't assume his upbringing has properly trained him for office by osmosis. Be especially wary when the younger shares the elder's first name as well as his last name: It's disheartening when some pundits speculate that George W's early success in polls reflected confusion between père and fils.

None of this means George W should not be our next president. It does mean he deserves special scrutiny because his accession would raise special concerns about presidential primogeniture. And let's not forget about W's politically active brother, Florida governor Jeb Bush. On the other hand, at least George W does not have any sons named George III.[5]

THE DARK SIDE OF CAMELOT[6]

WALL STREET JOURNAL, MONDAY,
NOVEMBER 27, 2000, 12:01 A.M. (ET)

I grew up idolizing JFK. My first television memories come from November, 1963. In early 1964, my parents—immigrants from India—bought me a documentary record excerpting Kennedy's best speeches. I wore its grooves out. I can still recite much of his inaugural address.

But as a student of constitutional law over the last twenty years, I have come to see another, less inspiring, side of Camelot.

Begin with Kennedy and the courts. To appease southern Democrats, he stocked the lower federal bench with some notorious segregationists who proceeded to trample the Constitution. His first southern appointee, Harold

Cox, was recently described by civil rights crusader Jack Greenberg as "possibly the most racist judge ever to sit on the federal bench." Similarly, Pulitzer Prize winner Taylor Branch has noted that "the best civil rights judges in the South were Eisenhower appointees; the most egregious segregationists were Kennedy's." Publicly, Kennedy pooh-poohed the problems created by his judicial appointees, and even commended these judges at a March 1963 press conference.

JFK's two picks for the Supreme Court were better, but ultimately disappointing. Arthur Goldberg stepped down after only three years. Byron White sat for more than thirty, but somehow managed to write no truly towering opinions and leave almost no legacy. No great idea bears White's name. His most famous decision, deriding gay rights in *Bowers v. Hardwick*, was simultaneously hard-hearted and softheaded.

Now turn to JFK and civil rights more generally. His account of Andrew Johnson's impeachment in *Profiles in Courage* lionized civil rights conservatives and moderates while slighting crusaders like Charles Sumner, the true heroes of the Reconstruction story. Only two words of JFK's soaring inaugural address gestured toward the American dilemma of race, and the problem of human rights "at home" as well as abroad. Late in his administration, he addressed the nation in a famous televised speech eloquently stating the legal, moral, and geopolitical case for racial equality; but what took him so long? It may be unfair to fault Kennedy for failing to win any major civil rights legislation—his mandate was shaky and southern Democrats held key congressional posts. But it is fair to note that, on civil rights, he failed to make the most of his bully pulpit and his great gifts of expression.

At its best, Kennedy's Justice Department embodied grace and courage and decency under intense pressure. In 1968 Bobby Kennedy was my hero. But I now view Bobby's appointment as attorney general as a terrible precedent. The Justice Department should not be headed by the president's best friend and campaign manager. Although the attorney general is formally part of the executive branch who serves at the president's pleasure, the country is best served by a tradition of some informal independence in this office, where legal judgment and professional detachment temper partisan calculus and personal loyalty. Instead, Bobby's appointment begat John Mitchell's. Mitchell, indeed, was Bobby's mirror image—Nixon's campaign manager and confidant, whose later lapses during Watergate proved to us all how dangerous it can be to put the president's best buddy in charge of federal law enforcement.

Bobby's appointment also reawakened the sleeping dragon of presidential dynasty. In effect, JFK dubbed his thirty-something kid brother his political heir apparent. Americans at the Founding consciously tried to break with British dynastic rule. One key reason that George Washington became father of his country was that he was not father of any offspring. Having sired no heirs, he could be trusted not to create a throne to hand down to a young prince. Of the first five men Americans made president, only John Adams had any (legitimate) sons. Adams's heir eventually became president, of course, but long after dad had left the scene and not because the old man had named young Johnny to the cabinet. The Constitution exudes special anxiety about ascensions of young princelings: This is part of the story behind the Founders' requirement that presidents be at least thirty-five years old. Though impressionable voters might be charmed by a young kinsman of a popular president, the Constitution makes dynastic succession more difficult by insisting that only mature political figures may be chosen to fill the big chair.

The metaphor of Camelot is ultimately un-American and undemocratic, conjuring up images of crowns and dashing young princes and noble birth. Our revolutionary forbears forged an emphatically anti-monarchical Constitution that went out of its way to condemn "titles of nobility" and to promise "republican" government. Today, the world is still struggling to break free from the grip of dynasty. Perhaps we can understand dynasty's allure in places where democracy has never taken firm root: Jordan, Morocco, Pakistan, Syria, and so on. But the world's largest democracy—my parents' India—has also failed to transcend this vestige of feudalism: Prime Minister Jawaharlal Nehru's daughter Indira Gandhi and grandson Rajiv Gandhi both claimed their crowns, and now a fourth generation of Nehrus has appeared on the Indian political scene.

Indians revered JFK in the 1960s, and his dynastic ambitions taught India precisely the wrong lesson. He set a dubious precedent for the rest of the world. And for America, too.

THE CONSTITUTION AND THE CANDIDATES (2008)

SLATE, MONDAY, FEBRUARY 4, 2008, 1:25 P.M. (ET)

Our next president's first act will be to solemnly swear to uphold the Constitution. But what does that document say about who that person should be?

Of course, all the top candidates are formally eligible. The Constitution demands only that our next president must have been born a citizen, must be at least thirty-five years old, and must have resided in the United States for fourteen or more years. But if we probe these rules and ask not merely *what* the text says but *why*, interesting differences among the contenders snap into focus.

For example, why was the Constitution's age rule necessary? In the framers' world, who could ever have enjoyed enough name recognition to be elected president at the age of, say, thirty-two?

As they drafted and debated the Constitution, the Founders knew that the sitting English prime minister was William Pitt, the younger, whose father (William Pitt, the elder) had headed the ministry before the American Revolution. Young Pitt had entered Parliament at age twenty-one and had become prime minister at age twenty-four. America's Constitution aimed to prevent something similar from happening here. By age thirty-five, a favorite son of a famous father would have his own record on which he could be judged. Conversely, meritorious lowborn men would have time to rise through the ranks. George Washington was the first electoral college's unanimous choice not only because of his model military service but also because he embodied an anti-dynastic ideal. Washington became father of his country precisely because he was *not* father to any child who might seek to succeed him.

Washington himself stressed this fact when drafting his first inaugural address: "Divine Providence hath not seen fit that my blood should be transmitted or my name perpetuated by the endearing, though sometimes seducing channel of immediate offspring. I have no child for whom I could wish to make a provision—no family to build in greatness upon my Country's ruins." (Washington ultimately decided to drop this passage—the point went without saying.)

Of the first five men entrusted with the presidency, only one had any (acknowledged) sons. That was John Adams, and his namesake, John Quincy Adams, himself became America's sixth president—but only after proving his own mettle and winning the top slot long after his thirty-fifth birthday and a quarter century after his father's tenure. Q's presidential résumé included an eight-year stint as America's top diplomat under a president, James Monroe, wholly unconnected to the elder Adams. With Q and A, we can see the sensible limits of the framers' anti-dynastic ideology and the nice balance they struck. A permanent disqualification of favorite sons would have gone too far, forever preventing Americans from tapping someone whom they reasonably viewed as the nation's ablest leader.

Beyond the rule of thirty-five, the Constitution trusted the political process to resist dynastic overreach, and early presidential discourse sharply focused the public's attention on dynastic issues. In 1796, one Boston paper warned that the elder Adams, if elected, would try to install his "well born" sons as "Lords of this country," while Jefferson, with "daughters only," could be trusted. Another campaign tract reminded voters that "Adams has Sons who might aim to succeed to their father. Jefferson, like Washington, has no Son." In later eras, two presidents (John Tyler and Franklin Pierce) were governors' sons; another (Benjamin Harrison) was the grandson of a president; and yet another (FDR) was a presidential nephew-in-law and distant cousin. Each of these scions had a political track record of his own when elected, as did George W. Bush in 2000.

Consider next the Constitution's rule that the president be "a natural born citizen"—a rule that focuses not on *where* a person became a citizen, but *when*. To be eligible, one must be *born* a citizen rather than naturalized at some later date. At the Founding, a special constitutional clause provided that even those who had not been citizens at birth could nevertheless become president, if they were citizens circa 1787. Thus, Alexander Hamilton, born in the West Indies, was clearly eligible. All those already in America in 1787 could be trusted; but the framers fretted that an Old World earl or duke might someday sail across the Atlantic with a boatload of gold and bribe his way into the presidency. (Rumor had it that George III's second son, the Bishop of Osnaburgh, would soon head this way.) Thus, the "natural-born" clause's main target of concern was not immigrants generally, but wealthy European aristocrats who might wreak havoc in an America lacking strong campaign finance laws.

The Constitution's final requirement—fourteen years of U.S. residence—also focused on transoceanic travel and made clear that loyal Americans who had spent years or even decades abroad were nonetheless welcome to pursue the American presidency. (The document pointedly did not require decades of continuous and uninterrupted residence in the U.S.) After Washington, four of the nation's next five presidents could point to extended foreign residence—all as key U.S. diplomats. The framers expected that their presidents—who would take oaths to "preserve, protect, and defend" the American system—would need a deep understanding of the dangerous world outside America. Until Lincoln, every elected president save one (James K. Polk) had served as a military general and/or a top diplomat; and all but four (Washington, Madison, Polk, and Zachary Taylor) had served in the Senate, which played a special role in treaty making and ambassadorial appointments.

Also notable is what the Constitution's eligibility rules do *not* say. Almost every early state constitution imposed property requirements for candidates running for governor, yet the Constitution omitted any comparable barrier for the presidency. In dramatic contrast to most early state constitutions, which required governors to meet various religious tests, the framers omitted any such test for presidents and in another part of the Constitution went even further, banning religious tests for all federal posts.

Later amendments have further opened the door of eligibility. Nothing at the Founding required that state election laws give equal treatment to black or female voters or office seekers. The Constitution's Fifteenth and Nineteenth Amendments corrected these Founding lapses, promising blacks and women the rights to vote and to be voted for as full political equals.

Even as the Constitution says that our generation must choose for ourselves, the document and its history thus prompt us to focus on certain things—such as the dangers of dynasty, the significance of international experience, and the shining ideal of political equality for all groups. How do each of today's top four contenders appear when seen through this constitutional prism?

Mitt Romney seems the most aristocratic. If he's not richer than God, he's apparently richer than the current president and vice president put together, and that's saying something. Nor is he self-made; he began with a base of inherited wealth and inherited political celebrity. His father was not merely a corporate titan but a political heavyweight who himself ran for president. Mitt's willingness to spend tens of millions from his own coffers to advance his presidential ambitions would have worried the Founders. No one in America in 1787 had money on Mitt's scale. Only a few European aristocrats had this kind of spending power, and we have seen what the framers thought of them.

Also, Romney is the only non-senator of the bunch. He is neither a war hero (like John McCain, or JFK before him), nor a diplomat (as Hillary Clinton was, de facto, as first lady), nor someone (like Barack Obama) who has spent many years living in parts of the world that Americans know least and need to understand much better.

The best constitutional argument for Romney is one that he has never made: To make amends for America's long history of discrimination against Mormons, voters should consider engaging in electoral affirmative action for Latter-day Saints.

As an admiral's son born in the Panama Canal Zone, John McCain is fully eligible. (A citizen from birth, he would have been eligible even had he been born on undeniably foreign soil—say, Brazil.)* McCain understands foreign threats firsthand, but his "residence" abroad in a Vietnamese POW camp gives him a more combative view of the world than, say, Obama, who also spent years living abroad. (Think of the difference between the Marine Corps and the Peace Corps.) McCain instinctively understands the need to "preserve, protect, and defend" the homeland; whether he understands how to protect the Constitution is iffier. He's the only top candidate without extensive legal training, and his ballyhooed campaign finance "reform" threatened the core First Amendment freedom of criticizing incumbents at election time.[7]

---

*[Extra information for readers interested in the more recent hullabaloo about Obama's birth certificate and the questions raised about Ted Cruz's presidential eligibility: Cruz is eligible even though he was undeniably born in Canada. At the time of his birth, the relevant congressional statute conferred birth-based American citizenship on any foreign-born baby who had at least one parent who was a U.S. citizen, so long as that parent had met certain conditions of extensive prior physical presence in the United States. On the day of his birth, Cruz's mother was a U.S. citizen, even though his father was not; and his mother also met the relevant rules of extensive prior physical presence. Why then, would Obama have been any different even if he *had* been born in Kenya, as has been (preposterously but repeatedly) claimed by various critics, led by Donald Trump? Like Cruz, Obama's mother was a U.S. citizen on the day of his birth, even though, like Cruz, his father was not. And nothing in the relevant congressional statute treats a Kenyan birth as any different from a Canadian birth. The answer to this puzzle is that the congressional law on the books when Obama was born required a foreign-born child to have at least one citizen parent who had been physically present in the United States at least five years after age fourteen. Obama's mother did not clear this bar because she was only eighteen when she gave birth. So this birth had to happen in the United States to make her son a citizen at birth. Of course this birth did in actual fact happen in the United States— in the state of Hawaii—and except for the children of foreign diplomats, *anyone* born these days in the United States is a birthright citizen under the Constitution itself, whether or not the baby's parents are themselves citizens. (This birthright citizenship is the clear command of the first sentence of the Fourteenth Amendment, see pp. 240–245.) For the law on the books on Obama's birthday, see Act of June 27, 1952, 66 Stat. 235–36; Title III, ch. 1, section 301(a)(7). For more on the meaning of "natural born" see p. 42 n. 15.]

Dynasties come in different sizes and shapes, and the Clinton dynasty is both like and unlike the dynasties that worried the framers. On the one hand, Hillary Clinton's résumé is inextricably intertwined with Bill's. When she boasts far more "experience" than Obama, she doesn't really mean her seniority over him in the Senate. Rather, she means her time as a top political adviser to her husband and unofficial Minister Without Portfolio in his White House. This service makes it hard to say how much she should be made to answer for (or allowed to take credit for) what her husband did and didn't do.

On the other hand, the Clintons are largely self-made and not (yet) fabulously wealthy. (Their net worth so far is only tens rather than hundreds of millions.)[8] Their dynasty thus far is intragenerational, not intergenerational. Theirs is a relationship of choice, not blood. At the Founding, George Washington in effect adopted Alexander Hamilton as his helpmate. Hamilton was a "favorite son" of sorts—but he was chosen for, not born into, this post. Hillary is like Hamilton in some ways—a gifted lawyer, a brilliant policy analyst, a sharp partisan, and a towering lightning rod.

She is also like Eleanor Roosevelt, who, along with FDR, offered America its first two-for-one presidential package. Eleanor's dramatic redefinition of the role of first lady is best seen through a constitutional prism: Once the Constitution guaranteed women the vote, new electoral strategies became possible. A moderate male president can now appeal to moderate male voters while his crusading first lady can exploit a potential gender gap and target her own message to female liberal voters. Hillary's candidacy takes the strategy one step further as the ultimate fulfillment of the Nineteenth Amendment guaranteeing women's suffrage.

In turn, Barack Obama's candidacy marks the fulfillment of the Fifteenth Amendment guaranteeing black suffrage. Whereas Romney is the most aristocratic candidate, Obama is the least. Not because he is biracial, but because he is self-made. His parents had little wealth, prestige, and power to pass on, and both are now dead. He has chosen his own faith as an adult (Protestant Christianity, as it happens), and he remains far and away the least wealthy of the Big Four. His children are still young. In all these and other ways, the historical figure he calls most to mind is not MLK or JFK or RFK—as so many have suggested—but Abraham Lincoln.

Oh, and as some of the framers would have appreciated, he can give a pretty good speech, too.

THE CONSTITUTION AND THE CANDIDATES (2012)

DAILY BEAST, SUNDAY, AUGUST 19, 2012

When the Philadelphia framers unveiled their proposed Constitution 225 years ago—September 17 will mark the official anniversary—most Americans were white Protestants. Anti-Catholicism ran deep, no Jews held high office, most blacks were enslaved, and the Church of Jesus Christ of Latter-day Saints did not even exist. Today, while America remains predominantly white and Protestant, no white Protestant sits on the Supreme Court, which consists of four white Catholics, three white Jews, one Latina Catholic, and one black Catholic. Among the four leading men now in the presidential and vice-presidential spotlight, the only mainstream Protestant is black (Barack Obama); two of the remaining three contenders are Catholic (Joe Biden and Paul Ryan) and one is Mormon (Mitt Romney). For this extraordinary evolution, credit the Constitution.

The place where the Constitution meets religion and race remains a treacherous cultural battleground. This spring, the conservative political operative and self-styled historian David Barton hit the best-seller list with an audacious new book on Thomas Jefferson's philosophy of church, state, and race. Last week, Barton's publisher unceremoniously withdrew this publication from store shelves, as scholarly evidence mounted that the book is bunk.

Barton's fall is a cautionary tale about the perils of oversimplification. That said, here are three simple principles to remember regarding race, religion, and the Constitution.[9]

Principle One: The Constitution Is Not a Religious Document

Consider first what the Constitution's pointedly does not say. Although the Declaration of Independence, the Articles of Confederation, and several Revolution-era state constitutions had explicitly and prominently invoked God in their opening and/or closing passages, the federal Constitution conspicuously said nothing of the sort. Thus, neither the Preamble nor any other constitutional clause explicitly mentioned the "Creator" or "Nature's God" or "the Supreme Judge of the World," as had the Declaration of Independence and the New York Constitution of 1777 (which incorporated the Declaration); or "the Great Governor of the World," as had the Articles of Confederation; or the "Great Governor of the Universe," as had the Pennsylvania Constitution of 1776; or "the Great Legislator of the Universe, . . . the Supreme Being, the great Creator and Preserver of the universe," as had the Massachusetts Constitution of 1780. The South Carolina Constitution of 1778 used the word "God" nine times—a word that explicitly appeared in every Revolution-era state constitution save Virginia's. But this word appeared nowhere in the federal Constitution—a pointed omission if ever there was one.

Consider next what the Constitution does explicitly say: "No religious Test shall ever be required as a Qualification to any Office or public Trust under the United States." As of 1787, almost every state did in fact use religious tests. Nine states incorporated these tests into the very texts of their written constitutions. So the framers' emphatic rejection of religious tests for federal officeholders was not business as usual. It was big news—a truly revolutionary New World idea whose reverberations powerfully resounded last weekend, with a Mormon and a Catholic, Romney and Ryan, clasping hands as thousands of onlookers, mostly mainstream Protestants, clapped and cheered.

Consider, finally, one additional patch of constitutional text, specifically focused on the presidency. While most Founding-era state constitutions expressly included the phrase "so help me God" or some analogous reference to "God" in their obligatory oaths, the Article II presidential oath omitted all mention of God. This omission was surely pointed and purposeful, with the result that no duly selected president could be obliged to utter the word "God" or profess his belief in any supreme being.

True, the Constitution does specially privilege "Sundays" in a clause governing the ten-day window for presidential vetoes, but this provision was not expressly theological; and common days of rest can be justified on wholly secular grounds.

One textual arrow might seem to point in a different direction. Immediately preceding the thirty-nine famous signatures at the bottom of the 1787 parchment, we find the following words: "done in Convention by the Unanimous Consent of the States present the Seventeenth Day of September *in the Year of our Lord* one thousand seven hundred and Eighty seven and of the Independence of the United States of America the Twelfth. In witness whereof We have hereunto subscribed our Names" (emphasis added).

At first blush, these words might seem to contradict the central meaning of the religious-test clause and the presidential-oath clause. After all, the Constitution requires federal officials to take an oath to the Constitution itself. If that document really does proclaim that Jesus Christ is "our Lord," then isn't this oath-taking itself an improper religious test?

As it turns out—though this fact has until now not been widely understood—the "our Lord" clause is not part of the official legal Constitution. The official Constitution's text ends just before these extra words of attestation—extra words that in fact were not ratified by various state conventions in 1787–1788.[10]

Consider also the words "so help me God" in presidential inaugurations. These words are not part of the official constitutionally prescribed oath, and thus no president can be obliged to utter these words in his inauguration ceremony. But presidents may choose to add them, if they wish. Over the course of American history, many presidents have in fact chosen to add these words.[11] Similarly, the Constitution nowhere requires a president to swear his oath of office on a Bible, but a president can choose to do so—and almost all presidents, beginning with George Washington, have in fact done so. All of which leads us to our next general principle:

Principle Two: The Constitution Is Not an Anti-Religious Document

A religiously neutral Constitution should not be confused with an anti-religious or anti-Christian Constitution. Just as no unbeliever may be barred from federal service for his atheism, no true believer may be excluded for his abiding faith.

Many of those responsible for America's Constitution were folk of deep faith. Bracket, for a moment, the Founding generation. Whether or not Barton and his fellow travelers succeed in establishing that the leading framers wore religion on their sleeves, surely the generation of reformers who arose to stamp out slavery and its vestiges brought their faith dramatically into the public square. First and foremost, abolitionists believed that slavery was ungodly—and eventually they succeeded in inscribing their abiding moral principles in the Constitution itself, in a trio of Reconstruction amendments adopted after the Civil War. Long before Barton, Ralph Reed, Jerry Falwell, and others made clear the clout of America's religious right, America's religious left—the abolitionist generation—gave us the Thirteenth, Fourteenth, and Fifteenth Amendments, the crown jewels of our Constitution.

And with these amendments in view, we see our final general principle:

Principle Three: The Constitution Includes More Than the Founding

Two hundred and twenty-five years ago, slavery, race discrimination, and/or religious tests prevailed in most states. Today, all races and religions stand equal before the law, and do so not because activist federal judges have plucked liberal constitutional principles out of thin air, but because We, the People of the United States, amended our Constitution after the Civil War to hold state governments to much higher standards of religious and racial equality.

None of the four men who now stand atop the political pyramid could have scaled these heights had the rules of 1787, grand as they were for their time, remained unchanged. As America celebrates the Constitution's 225th birthday, let's give credit not just to the Founders but also to those later generations who, thank God, made amends for some of the sins of our fathers.

SECOND CHANCES

ATLANTIC, JANUARY–FEBRUARY 2013

Second terms in the White House have, in many cases, ranged from the disappointing to the disastrous. Sick of the political infighting that intensified after his reelection, George Washington could hardly wait to retire to Mount Vernon. Ulysses S. Grant's second term was plagued by political scandal and economic panic. Woodrow Wilson left office a broken man, having suffered a massive stroke during his failed crusade to persuade America to join the League of Nations. Republican Dwight D. Eisenhower was routed in his last political battle, leaving Democrats in control of the presidency, the House, the Senate, and the Supreme Court for nearly the rest of his life. More recently, Richard Nixon resigned in disgrace; Ronald Reagan was tarred by the Iran-Contra scandal; Bill Clinton was impeached; and George W. Bush watched helplessly as his opponents surged into both houses of Congress and then the White House.

Hence the legendary "second-term curse." In the early days of the republic, second-termers were by tradition discouraged from seeking another term, and nowadays, presidents are legally barred from a third term, thanks to the Twenty-second Amendment. Popular wisdom has it that second-termers are therefore lame ducks. Unable to run again, how can a term-limited president reward his allies or restrain his adversaries? If he is seen as a fading force, won't his allies hitch themselves to the next rising star? Won't his adversaries attack relentlessly?

Fortunately for Barack Obama, the situation is not that bleak. For one thing, the idea of a second-term curse fails to account for basic probability. Most presidents fail in one way or another, and many nose-dive so fast that they never get a second term. Perhaps the "curse" is actually an example of what statisticians call "regression to the mean": those presidents who beat the political odds in term one usually cannot maintain their lucky streak in term two. Nor does the curse account for several exceptional presidents whose authority increased following reelection. By looking at these two-term stars more closely, we can see how and why Obama might be more blessed than cursed.

From our nation's Founding to the present, politics has followed a tidal pattern. Once a party devises a new and successful electoral formula—a workable coalition that can consistently outnumber the opposition—that party tends to win, and keep winning, until eventually, the tide changes and the other party takes the lead. So far, U.S. history has seen four such reversals, each of which coincided with the election, and reelection, of an exceptional president. Yes, each of the four figures who presided over these great shifts—Thomas Jefferson, Abraham Lincoln, Franklin Roosevelt, and Ronald Reagan—had his share of second-term tribulations and catastrophes. (Lincoln, of course, died weeks after delivering his epic second inaugural address, and only days after Lee's surrender.) But thanks to his own exceptional skills, as well as the fragility of the opposition party, each man forged a new electoral coalition that kept winning long after he left office.

The first turning of the political tide occurred shortly after George Washington's death. In 1800, Jefferson's triumph over John Adams marked the beginning of the end of the Federalist era. In 1804, Jefferson won a second term, and in 1808 he transferred power to his political lieutenant, James Madison. Jefferson and Madison's Democratic-Republican Party (later renamed the Democratic Party) remained America's dominant presidential party until the Civil War era, when the tide turned a second time. Lincoln, a Republican, won, won again, and (in the election following his assassination) was succeeded by a political heir, Ulysses Grant. Republicans dominated the presidency until the Great Depression—and FDR's election and reelections—marked a third tidal shift. The Democrats' resulting New Deal/Great Society coalition generally held until it was ripped apart by the Vietnam War and the migration of white southern Democrats to the GOP. Enter Ronald Reagan, whose two terms marked a fourth turning of the electoral tide.

We have been living in the Reagan era ever since. But now, inexorable forces—the changing voting habits of women and young adults, the rising political power of nonwhites and immigrants—mean that the Reagan electoral formula, with its reliance on southern whites, tax-averse businessmen, evangelicals, and Catholics, no longer yields a working majority. The tide may be turning back to the Democrats. Obama's reelection is particularly historic given modern Democratic presidents' track record of failing to win the popular vote. *He is only the second Democratic president since the Civil War to win two popular majorities.* The other was FDR (who, of course, won four). Since Lincoln, in fact, only four Democrats have won even one popular-vote majority—and that tally includes Jimmy Carter, with 50.1 percent of the vote. Bill Clinton never had a popular majority.

So what lessons might Obama borrow from his successful two-term predecessors to avoid being perceived as a lame duck? First, though he cannot succeed himself in 2016, he can designate a proxy to replace him—a loyal lieutenant willing to help his friends, smite his foes, and keep his secrets long after he leaves office. Reagan fared as well as he did in part because he had designated George H. W. Bush as his wingman, and in effect won a third term when Bush became "Bush 41." By contrast, Eisenhower kept his vice president, Richard Nixon, at a distance. (When asked during the 1960 general election whether his administration had adopted any major ideas of Nixon's, Ike replied, "If you give me a week, I might think of one.") The Lewinsky scandal drove a wedge between Clinton and his wingman, Al Gore. When George W. Bush's time was up, his party tapped John McCain, a White House outsider whose relationship with the president was feisty and rivalrous.

A successor—or the lack of one—can shape not just a president's performance, but also his legacy. To put the point within our more general pattern of presidential tide-turners: Each of the four previous tide-turning presidents not only won twice but was followed in the next presidential election by a successor who had been visibly handpicked by the tide-turner himself. Madison, Grant, Harry Truman, and Bush 41 quite clearly owed their presidential elections to Jefferson, Lincoln, FDR, and Reagan, respectively.[12]

Second, Obama should take advantage of his relative youth, which gives him a distinct edge over most of his predecessors: Until recently, most second-term presidents were well past their prime, both physically and mentally. By contrast, Obama can remain a potent political force even in retirement; he should exploit this fact to enhance his current clout. (Only Grant and Clinton were younger than Obama at the start of their second terms—and think of how Clinton has remained relevant in recent years.)

If he's to beat the second-term curse, Obama will also need to go bold and big. Just as FDR's New Deal programs and Reagan's tax cuts won over whole generations of voters, Obama must find ways to entrench his own legacy—and in the process, his new base. Immigration reform, for example, could draw the kind of young, highly skilled workers who might be able to pay for Social Security benefits for retiring baby boomers. Election reform might restore the luster of American democracy—while making it easier for Democratic voters to cast ballots.

One caveat: big changes like these can't succeed unless another big change comes early in term two—Senate filibuster reform. The signature accomplishment of Obama's first term, Obamacare, crowded out other reforms because Senate Democrats had to scrape together sixty votes to avoid a filibuster, rather than the simple majority the Constitution requires for passage of a law. If Senate reformers can tame the filibuster early in Obama's second term—and it appears that Democratic leaders are indeed serious about changing the Senate's rules this January, using a party-line vote to limit the minority party's power to slow or stop legislation—then the political picture will change dramatically.

Without filibuster reform, the forty-five Republicans in the Senate can quietly block up-or-down votes, with the result being that individual senators from moderate states don't have to visibly go on record voting against popular Obama agenda items. But if the filibuster were blunted, and only fifty-one senators' votes were needed, many key bills would pass with or without the GOP, and some savvy Republicans would choose to swim with the larger electoral tide. Americans would begin to see Republicans and Democrats working together again in the Senate—and this could change dynamics in the House.

And if not, there's always 2014. When it comes to midterm elections, lameness, handled deftly, can be a source of strength. In 2008, Obama ran as a uniter; had he campaigned aggressively against House Republicans in either 2010 or 2012, he might have tarnished his image and imperiled his own reelection prospects. But this time around, there's nothing to stop him from going after those who obstruct his agenda. Beware the lame duck: he can bite hard.

By then, in any case, most eyes will be turning to the 2016 campaign trail. Which brings us back to our first and most important lesson: *Each previous tide-turning president was succeeded in the next presidential election by a handpicked ally.* Like Reagan, Obama has a possible successor in his vice president. Joe Biden could dutifully offer to replace him, thus safeguarding Obama's power throughout his second term and beyond. But Obama has at least one other outstanding option: Just as Jefferson handed presidential power to his talented secretary of state, James Madison, Obama could do the same with Hillary Clinton.

Ultimately, nothing succeeds like succession.

2

THE VICE PRESIDENCY
Nothing, but Maybe Everything

IN A 1793 LETTER to his beloved wife, Abigail, John Adams, America's first vice president, broodingly described his post as "the most insignificant office that ever the invention of man contrived or his imagination conceived." Four years earlier, in the first Senate's earliest days, Adams had offered up a less bleak and more balanced assessment: "I am nothing, but I may be everything."[1]

To most modern journalists and readers engrossed by the great events of the day, the hour, and the minute, the vice presidency is usually an irrelevance—a "nothing," an "insignifican[ce]" precisely because so few formal powers accompany the office. Notably, NPR has White House correspondents and a congressional correspondent and a legal-affairs/Supreme Court correspondent, but no single person covering the vice presidency as such.

To constitutionalists who take the long view, the matter looks very different. In a heartbeat (or its absence), he who was nothing becomes everything, and has often done so in American history. Consider Andrew Johnson, Teddy Roosevelt, Harry Truman, Lyndon Johnson, and Gerald Ford, to name just a few of history's most notable men who in a flash went from zero to 1600.

But how can the freelance constitutionalist entice the opinion page editor and the everyday reader to attend to the usually dull office of the vice presidency? The essays in this chapter try to do so in several different ways.

Unlike the pieces in Chapter 1 and in most other chapters of this book, the journalistic essays in this chapter are not configured in chronological order of original publication. Instead, these pieces are now arranged to track Adams's 1789 bon mot. The opening essays focus on the vice presidency in itself—"I am nothing"—and the ones that follow highlight aspects of the vice presidency that snap into view when succession becomes a possibility: "but I may be everything." Note that succession may occur either when a president dies or becomes disabled or steps down before his term has expired; or when a sitting or former vice president is ultimately elected president in his own right, as happened to Adams himself, and as has happened frequently in modern times. In all, five of America's most recent dozen presidents were sitting or former veeps.

THIS CHAPTER'S TWO OPENING ESSAYS adopt what might be called a Seinfeldian strategy, making a virtue out of . . . nothing. These essays, originally published when Dick Cheney sat in the second chair, explore the implications of the fact that vice presidents are often like the rest of us (and like the cast of the sitcom *Seinfeld*): they spend much of their time talking with friends and occasionally badmouthing others. Precisely because vice presidents in these episodes are doing nothing special, no special rules need apply. Thus, when Cheney was yakking with his buddies at Enron, he deserved no special immunity from oversight or investigation; conversely, when Cheney was denigrating his detractors to reporters, he merited the same First Amendment solicitude that we all deserve. At least in these two situations, there need be no special law for vice presidents. It suffices to apply the ordinary rules that apply to ordinary people.

This chapter's next pair of essays explores the drama of the vice president as a running mate—as someone entirely different from you or me, and indeed different even from other top politicians, and as such governed by a special constitutional framework. The first of this pair appeared in the *New Republic* in early February 1999, in the middle of the impeachment trial of Bill Clinton. This essay, "Take Five," sought to bring into view one intriguing situation in which a vice president might in an instant become "everything," at least temporarily: whenever a president—even a physically fit one—chooses to hand off power to his running mate. And Al Gore, as I explained in this piece, was indeed Bill Clinton's running mate, both past and future—a loyal partner whom Clinton had handpicked to run alongside him in 1992 and 1996 and who would likely be running to succeed him in 2000. How, I asked, might Clinton creatively use his constitutional option to hand off power so as to help his running mate, and also help himself, at a time when he was politically besieged?*

In December 1999, I continued my exploration of running mates in a companion *New Republic* essay, this time exploring some of the special constraints that Gore faced as a loyal veep seeking to succeed his tarnished partner. When an incumbent vice president himself runs for president—as did Gore in 1999–2000—he must be particularly careful about what he says about the incumbent president. In certain respects, he must "speak softly." And the rest of us—voters, reporters, pundits—must understand his campaign performance against the backdrop of his special constitutional role as an incumbent vice president. Precisely because he may be "everything" in the blink of an eye, the political rules for him must be different.

Most of the remaining essays in this chapter focus on the tense and tragic moments when actual presidential power must flow, either temporarily or permanently, to the vice president or someone farther down the line of succession, as a result of death or medical disability. As I explain, America faces serious vulnerabilities involving the succession rung immediately below the vice-presidency, especially because our current system fails to clearly address issues of possible vice-presidential disability and fails to maximize the odds that both the president-elect and the vice-president-elect will in fact be alive on Inauguration Day. Fortunately, there exist some simple statutory fixes that can easily be adopted today to avert the disasters that might otherwise await us. Unfortunately, Congress has yet to adopt any of these sensible fixes, perhaps because the public has failed to notice the dangerous cracks in the system.

---

* A similarly creative use of the hand-off power is imaginable when two heavyweight candidates are vying for their party's presidential nomination. If candidate A wins the nomination, how can A's party rival, B, be incentivized to work hard for A's election? In certain situations B might actually be better off if nominee A loses in November, clearing the path for B to try again in four years. But if A were to bring B onto the ticket, B's incentives might change dramatically. Suppose, however, that the second spot will not suffice to satisfy B or B's core constituents. In some scenarios running mates might do well to present themselves to the electorate as a tag team that will use the hand-off power to alternate in the Oval Office, trading back and forth as president and vice president once in office. For more details on how a tag-team candidacy and presidency could work, thanks to the Constitution's recognition of the hand-off power, see chap. 9 of my book *The Law of the Land*.

AND IN THIS FAILURE, there lie certain lessons about constitutional journalism. *Journalism* focuses on the present and on the immediate or easily foreseeable future. *Constitutionalism*, however, needs to ponder all possible future events, even low-probability events—at least if these low-probability events might result in constitutional catastrophe.

When the presidential succession system is on the precipice of cataclysmic failure or actually fails disastrously, journalists will doubtless become interested. As I know from past experience with other constitutional crises, my phone at such a moment would start ringing off the hook. But at that point it is too late. Long before the system fails, how can a freelance constitutionalist journalist get editorial gatekeepers and the public to focus on the problem?

When originally published, the various essays collected here tried to use various hooks—the first anniversaries of the crazy election of 2000 and of the 9/11/2001 attack; the 2003 season debut of a popular TV show, *The West Wing*; the 2010 election of David Cameron in Britain; the political implosion of Newt Gingrich in the early presidential sweepstakes of 2011–2012— to engage the popular imagination, and to retell some basic truths about past presidential successions and presidential transitions that every American should know and that almost no American does know.*

---

*An important note on terminology. A presidential "transition" typically occurs when, as a result of the Constitution's quadrennial presidential clock, one president leaves office and a new president enters on January 20. A subset of these transitions, often referred to as "successions," occurs when the outgoing president on January 20 has in effect handpicked or blessed the incoming "successor" president—as would occur if Hillary Clinton "succeeds" Barack Obama on January 20, 2017. This was the kind of "succession" alluded to in the closing sentence of the previous chapter: "Ultimately, nothing succeeds like succession." A different kind of "succession" occurs *intraquadrennially*—at some moment in the middle of a presidential term—when, as a result of death or physical or mental disability or political choice, presidential power devolves permanently or temporarily to the vice president or to some other officer lower down in the chain of command, which is also referred to as "the line of succession."

A general theme of this chapter is that these two kinds of succession—January 20 and non-January 20, quadrennial and intraquadrennial—are interrelated in interesting and intricate ways that have not been well understood. Thus, in "Take Five," written in the middle of Bill Clinton's 1999 impeachment trial, I explored whether Clinton could have used the intraquadrennial power to hand off authority to his veep, Al Gore, in ways that would have also affected Gore's prospects for election in his own right to the presidency the following year. By temporarily succeeding Clinton intraquadrennially in 1999, Gore might have been more likely to succeed Clinton in the standard electoral way in 2000–2001. In the companion "Speak Softly"

In the case of the *West Wing* episode, there is an interesting backstory. Over the years, I had occasionally consulted with the writers of this show, who were aware of my worries about the holes in our current succession safety net. When these writers chose to dramatize some of these defects in a season-ending cliffhanger, public interest was piqued. As the new television season began in September 2003, with millions poised to watch how the fictional crisis would end, the *Washington Post* agreed to run my op-ed on the real-world issues of presidential succession, and two Senate committees decided to hold a joint hearing on the matter and to solicit my testimony. Thank you, President Bartlet!

Even with Hollywood's help, however, I have not succeeded in getting my succession-reform plan off the drawing board and onto the congressional floor for enactment and then onto the president's desk for signature. Several of the reform ideas presented in this chapter have won the general support of a bipartisan Continuity of Government Commission, which issued a major report on presidential succession in 2009, explicitly citing and endorsing my general approach.[2] This commission was sponsored by both the conservative American Enterprise Institute and the center-left Brookings Institution; and its members included former House speakers Tom Foley (a liberal Democrat) and Newt Gingrich (a conservative Republican), along with an impressive array of scholars across the disciplinary spectrum, including law professors, historians, and political scientists.* But this commission's strong support for

---

piece in 2000, I explored the converse situation: How, even as he was running to succeed Clinton in the standard electoral way in 2000, Gore had to be ever attentive to the possibility that he might be called upon to succeed Clinton intraquadrennially in case of mishap—presidential death or disability. In "How to Thwart Electoral Terrorism," I explored how death or disability of a presidential or vice presidential candidate at the end of a standard election campaign could result in a gap in the intraquadrennial line of succession, were a January 20 Inauguration Day to dawn without both a living president-elect and a living vice-president-elect ready to take their respective oaths of office. And in "Insta-Gov," I showed how presidential transitions after standard elections could be speeded up through creative use of the Twenty-fifth Amendment—an amendment centrally focused on the vice presidency and the mechanisms of intraquadrennial succession.

* The willingness of two former House speakers to concur in a report advocating removal of House speakers from the line of succession, per my proposal, is particularly notable and laudable. For discussion of Independent Counsel Ken Starr's eventual willingness—similarly notable and laudable—to join ranks with those of us who had long insisted that the congressional law creating and structuring the very office of independent counsel was ill-conceived and unconstitutional, see pp. 279–280.

my ideas marks only the first step on a long road. My aim has always been, and still remains, not merely a bipartisan commission report, but a bipartisan congressional statute.

Virtually all experts agree that our current succession statute needs to be revised. Even if the statistical likelihood of double-death or double-disability is much lower than I fear, it is still north of zero. The time to make the needed statutory repairs is now—precisely when the worst imaginable succession scenarios are still only imaginary.

CHENEY, ENRON, AND THE CONSTITUTION

TIME.COM, SATURDAY, FEBRUARY 2, 2002

Waving the banner of executive privilege,[3] Vice President Dick Cheney refuses to disclose details of meetings he held last year with Enron officials. If Congress ultimately decides to press the issue, Cheney would be wise to yield.

The phrases "executive privilege" and "separation of powers" do not appear in the Constitution. Nevertheless, the Constitution clearly creates three distinct departments, and some sort of executive privilege may properly be deduced from this general tripartite structure.

But what sort? In the 1974 Nixon Tapes case, the Supreme Court recognized that presidential conversations with executive staff are presumptively privileged, but then proclaimed that, unless national security were involved, this executive privilege must yield whenever courts had need for specific, material, and relevant evidence. This is a rather puny privilege. *Anyone* can resist a subpoena that is overbroad or irrelevant. When husbands speak with wives, clients with attorneys, patients with doctors, or penitents with priests, these conversations are all entitled to far more protection than the Nixon Tapes Court gave to presidents speaking with staffers.

Cheney rightly worries that the Nixon Tapes case and later lower court opinions have eroded executive privilege. In a system of separated powers, each branch must have some internal space—a separate house—to deliberate free from the intermeddling of other branches. Senators must be free to talk candidly with colleagues and staff in cloakrooms; judges need similar freedom to converse with each other in judicial conferences and with clerks in closed chambers; jurors deliberate in secret; and for similar reasons presidents need room for confidential conversations with staff.

Imagine that the president is considering appointing some rising political star to high office. Aides brief the president on potential objections to the appointment, reporting facts and rumors about the star, her family, and her inner circle. To do his job right, the president needs this candid advice and information, but is unlikely to get it if the conversation can easily be subpoenaed in a lawsuit designed to embarrass the administration or the potential nominee. For this reason, Chief Justice John Marshall explicitly refused to force Attorney General Levi Lincoln to disclose confidential conversations with President Jefferson in the famous 1803 case, *Marbury v. Madison*. (The Nixon Tapes Court somehow overlooked this part of *Marbury*.) The principle that cabinet officers report directly to the president, rather than to Congress or the courts, draws additional support from a little-noticed part of the Constitution known as the opinions clause.

But Cheney's case raises special complications. He is neither the president nor a cabinet or subcabinet official wholly within the executive branch. Constitutionally, he is also an officer of the legislature—indeed, the Senate's presiding officer. Enron officials at these meetings were themselves not governmental officers of any sort. Nor was the topic here some purely executive issue like an appointment or a prosecution or pardon; rather it was what legislation to propose to Congress. When Senate Minority Leader Trent Lott meets with lobbyists about their legislative wish lists, these meetings are not privileged, even if Lott is acting in political partnership with the president and will later report to him. Constitutionally, how are Cheney's conversations with Enron decisively different?

It's a stretch to think the Enron officials themselves can claim "executive privilege." If the company itself can be directly subpoenaed, why can't Cheney be likewise subpoenaed to provide the same information? When a client talks to her lawyers with others in the room, she generally is deemed to have waived attorney-client privilege; so, too, when penitents speak to priests outside the confessional seal. By similar logic, executive privilege is waived, or at least weakened, when executive officials meet with outsiders.

Also, executive privilege is weakest when Congress itself seeks to pierce it. Private plaintiffs and unelected special prosecutors lack a democratic mandate to obstruct a president chosen by the American people; but Congress is elected to oversee the executive, and where necessary to enact reform laws. If Congress itself were to subpoena Cheney, he should not lightly disregard the people's representatives. (In 1974, the House Judiciary Committee voted to impeach Richard Nixon for defying certain congressional subpoenas.) The matter, however, is rather different if Congress continues to hide behind the politically unaccountable General Accounting Office rather than confront Cheney directly.

If the Bush administration seeks to limit the damage already done to executive privilege, it should find a stronger case in which to assert it—a case involving purely executive officers making an executive decision where there is no reason to think the government is trying to cover up any misconduct. Both the Nixon and Clinton administrations pushed executive privilege on bad facts, and lost. Surely the Bush administration can find a better place to make a last stand for privilege than Fort Enron.

STEALING FIRST

SLATE, TUESDAY, JULY 18, 2006, 4:07 P.M. (ET)

In an administration not known for its love of the Bill of Rights, Vice President Dick Cheney may soon find himself in a new role: defender of the First Amendment.

Along with several other current or former administration officials, Cheney is being sued by Valerie and Joseph Wilson, who claim that, in response to an anti-administration op-ed Joseph Wilson published in July 2003 in the New York Times, the defendants violated the Wilsons' constitutional rights by organizing a vicious whispering campaign against them. One result of this campaign was a newspaper column, authored by journalist Robert Novak, that outed Valerie Wilson (née Valerie Plame) as a CIA operative.

Now, Cheney's first instinct may be to assert, brusquely, that he is legally immune from damage suits challenging his actions as vice president. In 1982, the Supreme Court held, in Nixon v. Fitzgerald, that Richard Nixon could not be sued for damages by Ernest Fitzgerald, a government employee whom Nixon fired after Fitzgerald had blown the whistle on the administration. According to the Court, even if Nixon had acted unconstitutionally, he was absolutely immune from a civil damage suit, given that he was acting within the "outer perimeter" of his presidential powers, which include the power to fire executive-branch subordinates. Cheney may well feel that the same basic rule should apply to vice presidents, and that he, too, should be absolutely immune from civil liability, even if he violated the Constitution. (On this imperious view, constitutional accountability is for the little people.)

But does Richard Cheney really want to go down in history next to Richard Nixon? Wouldn't it make more sense for him to position himself in the law books alongside John Peter Zenger?

Zenger—a publisher sued for libel in the 1730s—famously defended freedom of expression, and Cheney should do likewise. In other words, Cheney should use this as a teaching moment, to explain how a proper understanding of First Amendment principles actually supports him and not the Wilsons, who have claimed that Cheney violated their free-expression rights. The result would be an elegant First Amendment jujitsu, using all the Wilsons' free-press momentum against them, to defeat their lawsuits.

Here is the key fact that Cheney should stress: Unlike Nixon, who fired a government whistle-blower, Cheney did not fire the Wilsons. He merely *spoke out* against them. True, he did so furtively, in what many might view as an underhanded whispering campaign. But the First Amendment protects a wide variety of speech and expression, encompassing the right to print, orate, and yes, to whisper—even to whisper anonymously and with petty or partisan motivation.

And to whom were Cheney and his fellow defendants whispering? To the press! This is the other key fact for the New Dick Cheney, the Zorro-Zenger Defender of the First Amendment. The Wilsons claim that they were being punished for speaking out against Cheney and the administration. But if the Wilsons have a right to criticize Cheney in the press, Cheney can claim that he has an equal right to criticize the Wilsons when talking to the press, whether on the record or off.

Of course, not all words are absolutely protected by the First Amendment. For example, the words "you're fired" may be properly viewed as constitutionally unprotected conduct rather than pure speech. So, too, the words "kill him" when the Godfather is ordering his hit man into action.

The Wilsons' suit in effect claims that the outing of Valerie Wilson is like a hit ordered by a mobster. But is it? While there are criminal laws on the books that prohibit the improper outing of CIA agents, it does not appear that these laws were violated. Indeed, the special prosecutor in charge of investigating the leak, Patrick Fitzgerald, has not brought any criminal charges under the anti-outing laws, even as he has filed other—perjury-related—charges growing out of the Wilson affair.

Of course, the Wilsons need not prove that the leak was criminal to win their civil suit. For example, although firing a government whistle-blower to punish his speech might not be criminal, it might nevertheless be unconstitutional. But it is at precisely this point in the legal argument that Cheney should reiterate that he and his fellow whisperers were speaking to *responsible journalists*, and that the whisperers' purpose was to give the journalists background for understanding the possible bias of Joseph Wilson and certain groups within the CIA.

The Wilsons do not allege that Cheney said "kill Valerie"—and in general, courts should not lightly assume that criticism of a government agency (such as the CIA) is the same as an open call to assassination or some other express advocacy of illegal violence. If courts did indulge this assumption, Cheney should add, a great many government critics would be unduly vulnerable to prosecution or civil liability. Given that even ordinary citizens have robust rights of free expression, so should vice presidents, Cheney should argue. For he, too, was in effect criticizing a certain public official (Joseph Wilson, a longtime public servant) and a certain government agency (the CIA).

In short, rather than hiding behind the claim that he, like the president, is somehow above the law, Cheney should assert that he—like any ordinary citizen!—has a legally protected right to speak to the press.

Coming from Cheney, any effort to claim this First Amendment high ground might initially be greeted with skepticism. But, in truth, several aspects of the Wilsons' legal complaint—filed last Thursday in federal district court—should trouble thoughtful civil libertarians:

Casual use of the "T" word. The complaint opens—quite oddly for a legal document—by quoting the first President Bush railing against "insidious . . . traitors" who compromise undercover operatives. But treason is defined very narrowly in the Constitution, and for good reason. Not all disclosures—even of sensitive information—are treasonous or even unpatriotic. A great deal depends on intent and context, and to use the "T" word loosely is to engage in McCarthyism. Loose talk of treason is especially dangerous in a legal document seeking to invoke the coercive power of the judiciary. Indeed, if the complaint's loose language were taken seriously, it would pose a serious threat to responsible journalists who are in the business of making hard decisions about what information should properly be brought to the public's attention. If the outing of Valerie Wilson was really treason, then journalist Robert Novak would be in dire legal peril. Yet special prosecutor Fitzgerald has cleared Novak of criminal wrongdoing.

Promiscuous use of tort law to chill public expression. The Wilsons also complain that defendants committed the tort of "publication" of "private facts." This is a tort that has a proper place in American law—as when, for example, a newspaper gratuitously publishes an account of an otherwise non-newsworthy person's closeted sexual identity or publishes graphic and unconsented-to telephoto pictures of such a person in his bathroom. But courts and commentators have stressed that this tort needs to be very strictly limited to protect First Amendment rights of speakers to publish politically important facts and thereby vindicate the public's right to know. The truthfulness of the published information is not generally a defense to this tort. Thus, this tort, if construed as broadly as the Wilson complaint urges, could become as dangerous as libel law was in the pre-Zenger era, when truth was no defense. If the Wilsons were to win on this ground, we could well end up with an oppressive tort-law version of an Official State Secrets Act, not merely cloaking a private domain for private citizens but also shielding the press (and the public) from potentially relevant political information about public servants. And if Cheney and his gang are liable, why not Novak and his newspaper? The newspaper, after all, is where the "widespread publication" that the Wilsons complain of actually occurred.

Seeking damages without strong proof of financial harm. Another flaw of old-fashioned libel law was that a plaintiff could receive a massive damage award even though there was no proof that a libelous expression caused him any real financial harm. But in 1964 the Supreme Court put an end to this racket in the famous First Amendment case of *New York Times v. Sullivan*. The Wilson complaint seeks unspecified damages. Unmentioned in the complaint is a major (and apparently quite lucrative) book deal just signed by Valerie Wilson.

The threat of broad civil discovery at the expense of journalistic privilege. Perhaps the Wilsons' real goal here is not to win the lawsuit but simply to get civil discovery against the defendants, thereby enlisting the coercive power of the courts to oblige the defendants and other witnesses to tell all—to divulge who said what to which journalist when. In a criminal case, journalists' claims of privilege may sometimes properly take a backseat to the broader public interest in catching the bad guys or clearing an innocent defendant who has been wrongly accused. But to allow every private plaintiff with a private grudge to compel journalists to divulge their sources is a very different matter. Here, too, the Wilsons' complaint may raise a serious threat to the very press freedom that it purports to champion.

There is much to criticize in Cheney's and his allies' conduct during this whole sorry mess. But it is doubtful that tort law à la Wilson is the solution. Much as it might gall him to do so, Cheney's best response to the Wilsons' complaint would be to wrap himself in the First Amendment and fight. And while he is at it, perhaps he might read the amendment—heck, the whole Bill of Rights!—and think of the rest of us.

TAKE FIVE

NEW REPUBLIC, MONDAY, FEBRUARY 8, 1999

According to his detractors, Bill Clinton's grip on power is so fierce that it would take the Jaws of Life to pry him from office. But suppose Clinton were to confound his critics and actually do something noble: Step down from office, temporarily, until the end of his impeachment trial. What would be the constitutional and political implications of this unprecedented reaction to an unprecedented impeachment of a duly elected president? (Recall that the 1868 impeachment defendant Andrew Johnson had become president not via all men's ballots but because of one man's bullet.)

The constitutional mechanism enabling Clinton to step aside, temporarily, is elaborated in the Twenty-fifth Amendment, adopted in the wake of President Kennedy's assassination. Under section 3 of this amendment, "Whenever the President transmits . . . his written declaration that he is unable to discharge the powers and duties of his office, and until he transmits . . . a written declaration to the contrary, such powers and duties shall be discharged by the Vice President as Acting President." Note that the inability here need not be physical. Clinton could simply say that, during the pendency of his trial, he deems it politically and morally better for the country that the high powers of the presidency be wielded by someone who is not under any cloud, and that he will retake the office only once the cloud has lifted, upon his due acquittal by the Senate. Legally, Clinton would be free at any time to take back the reins of power—but his pledge not to do so until the end of the trial would, as a practical matter, make it hard for him to renege.

Clinton could have stepped down a while ago, of course. But, before January 20 of this year, any such move by Clinton would not have been very sporting to his loyal vice president, Al Gore. January 20 marks the exact midpoint of Clinton's second term, which began at noon on January 20, 1997, in keeping with the constitutional calendar mandated by the Twentieth Amendment. Under the Twenty-second Amendment, adopted after FDR's unprecedented tenure in office, "No person shall be elected to the office of the President more than twice, and no person who has held the office of President, or acted as President, for more than two years of a term to which some other person was elected President shall be elected to the office of the President more than once." If Clinton had stepped aside before January 20, and if he were eventually to be convicted in the Senate, President Gore would have been limited to a maximum possible tenure of six years in office—eligible to run in 2000, but not in 2004. But, if Clinton steps down any time from now on, Gore would be allowed to serve out the remainder of Clinton's term and would still be able to run for two terms in his own right.

Far from an act of disloyalty—turning Gore into a premature lame duck—any temporary transfer of power from Clinton to Gore henceforth would be an act of great fidelity and fealty to his number two, a dramatic endorsement by Clinton of Gore as a worthy occupant of the Oval Office.

And what's in it for Clinton? Just possibly the recovery of his honor and a shot at redemption. Stepping aside temporarily would be a penance he imposed on himself rather than a penalty forced upon him by others. Too often, his concessions thus far have come just one step ahead of the law. He admitted the truth about his relationship with Monica Lewinsky only after the DNA results proved that his past statements were lies; he proposed censure only to fend off impeachment; he mouthed words of contrition without really exhaling. The time to make concessions and show contrition is when you are winning—and in that sense now is the most opportune moment since the scandal broke, because it seems clear that, if he stands pat, he will win in the Senate. (Indeed, the ideal time to be a little self-sacrificing would be now, in the wake of his post–State of the Union bounce.)

Yes, by stepping aside temporarily, he imperils his presidency—he utterly unsettles matters and risks losing all. But it is precisely this willingness to take the risk of losing what he loves—power—that may help redeem him in the eyes of his countrymen and history. If he declines to step down, odds are that he will "win" in the Senate and stay in office—but he may well win by losing: A majority of the Senate might in fact vote to oust him, but he will remain in office and formally be acquitted so long as the vote against him falls short of two-thirds. Will he be able to lead after this, or will he just mark time? Won't any "victory" in the Senate taste sour unless he can somehow bring a measure of nobility back to himself and his office?

By contrast, if he wins in the Senate after stepping down—sacrificing himself and making it easier to vote against him—any acquittal would seem a more genuine vindication, a more dramatic rebirth. Given that some Republican senators may currently be tempted to vote against him knowing that their votes won't suffice to convict and remove him, Clinton could even say that, unless an absolute Senate majority votes to acquit, he will not return; if he wins this high-stakes gamble, he wins with genuine credibility and a true vote of confidence. True, any offer to step down permanently if a majority votes against him risks sliding our separated-powers system toward British-style parliamentarianism, but, with impeachment under way, that specter is already upon us. With a bold move, Clinton might actually enhance the presidency by seizing moral high ground and redefining himself rather than letting others define him.

Now consider Al Gore. The biggest structural problem of the vice presidency is that its occupant lacks a personal mandate from the people. In many states, voters cast separate ballots for governor and lieutenant governor (not to mention other statewide offices like attorney general), but in no state do citizens vote separately for the national vice presidency. A vice president is merely the bottom half of a presidential ticket, and most voters pay no attention to this office, focusing instead only on the top of the ticket. (Pop quiz: Name Ross Perot's 1992 and 1996 running mates.) In short, Americans vote for president, and the vice president simply piggybacks into office. The Constitution does not require this perverse way of picking vice presidents and most of the time it is harmless. However, when something happens to the president, and the vice president must take over temporarily or permanently, our electoral system creates a legitimacy gap because we end up with a chief executive no one squarely voted for. The problem is compounded by the parties' practice of ticket balancing, creating succession situations in which Americans vote for the avatar of one wing of a party as president and end up with a representative of the other wing. (Think about Abraham Lincoln and Andrew Johnson, or James Garfield and Chester Arthur.)

If Clinton were to stand pat now and ultimately be convicted, the transition to Gore would be awkward—all the more so because no one really expects it to happen, even at this late date. But, if Clinton were to temporarily step down now and then be convicted, the transition to Gore would be smoother, since Gore would already be in place, installed with a personal and unforced vote of confidence from Clinton himself when it counted. Conversely, if Clinton were ultimately acquitted, Gore would have had a chance to prove his presidential mettle—as the de jure acting president of the United States—in the most dramatic way imaginable.

Finally, consider the Senate. In keeping with the command of Article I, section 3, each senator has taken an oath to do "impartial justice." One meaning of such an oath is that each senator should be "impartisan"—utterly inattentive to the demands of political party. A Republican senator should imagine herself to be a Democrat, and a Democratic senator should imagine himself to be a Republican. But this is hard to do, psychologically, and pundits are predicting that the eventual vote in the Senate may well break down cleanly along party lines.

If so, this might be greatly disheartening to the nation. But having Al Gore physically occupying the Oval Office during the remainder of the trial might wonderfully concentrate the minds of the senators and confound perceptions of partisanship. If Republicans vote to convict and Democrats vote to acquit, it will be more clear to Americans that this is not necessarily pure partisanship at play. Pro-conviction Republicans, after all, would be voting in the most emphatic way to keep Al Gore in the White House—and immeasurably strengthen him for a bid in 2000. Conversely, pro-acquittal Democrats would be seen as weakening their presidential prospects for 2000 in order to affirm their sincerely held view that Clinton was duly elected and has suffered enough.

In short, by stepping down temporarily, Bill Clinton could step up morally and politically, in a way that would benefit the vice presidency, the Senate, the country, and even himself. Don't hold your breath—but keep in mind that the Twenty-fifth Amendment offers creative opportunities for the comeback kid to find a place to come back from.

SPEAK SOFTLY

New Republic, Monday, December 6, 1999

Suddenly Al Gore can't put enough distance between himself and President Clinton. What began a few months ago as a gentle and carefully worded condemnation of Clinton's promiscuity has swelled into a general rebuke of the president's political persona, culminating in a New Yorker interview that appeared last week. "Bill Clinton sees a car going down the street and says,

'What are the political implications of that car?'" Gore told the magazine. "I see a car going down the street and I think, How can we replace the internal combustion engine on that car?"

As if that weren't enough, the *New York Times* followed with a front-page headline, for a story about a U.N.-dues deal between Clinton and anti-abortion Republicans, that proclaimed, "Gore Splits with the White House." The *Times* quoted a senior Gore official who said the vice president had "strong reservations" about the deal and "opposed what the White House ended up doing." The adviser almost certainly spoke with the campaign's blessing: Distance from the president is precisely the image Gore's handlers want to project. Separation, they seem to believe, is the only antidote to "Clinton fatigue," and most of the pundits seem to agree.

But the handlers and the pundits need to take the Constitution into account. Politically, shouting out his independence—or even picking a fight with Clinton—might be the best thing Gore could do. But constitutionally it's risky business. A sitting vice president running for president is different from all other contenders. Unlike the others, he could become president at any moment, and so he must not say things that could compromise his delicate role as next in line. History makes clear what's at stake.

Start with the Founding. The vice presidency emerged late in the Philadelphia Convention, largely as a device to grease the presidential selection process. Having Congress select the president every time would make the executive branch too dependent on the legislative branch. But southerners wouldn't stand for direct popular election of the president because slave states would get no credit for their human chattel. Thus, the framers settled on a complex electoral-college scheme—based on the notorious three-fifths compromise—that effectively guaranteed Virginia the most electoral clout even though the state disenfranchised a large fraction of its population. Not surprisingly, Virginians dominated the early presidency, holding the office for thirty-two of the first thirty-six years of its existence.

But this system for tallying electoral votes state by state created problems. If each state voted for its favorite son, no winner would emerge, which would throw presidential elections into Congress and weaken the presidency. That's where the vice presidency came in: According to the final Philadelphia plan, each state would cast two votes for president, one of which had to go to an out-of-state candidate. To discourage states from simply wasting the second vote, the Constitution provided that the person who came in second in the presidential race would automatically become vice president.

This system did not last long. It was destabilizing to automatically place the president's biggest and perhaps fiercest political rival in the position of number two, a heartbeat away from the top. This awkwardness became readily apparent once George Washington, who had no real challengers, left the presidency after two terms. John Adams won the office in 1796, with Thomas Jefferson coming in second and thereby securing the vice presidency. By 1798, the two men were bitter foes, and the election of 1800 featured the disquieting spectacle of the sitting vice president sharply and publicly challenging the sitting president. Energized by this open feud, political parties began to emerge, polarizing the electorate. Had the partisan frenzy led to an attack on Adams or to his assassination—both imaginable scenarios, given the goings-on in France at the time—the Founders' system would have been partly to blame.

In response to the 1800 election, the Twelfth Amendment was adopted. Henceforth, members of the electoral college would vote separately for president and vice president. Thus each national political party would be free to run a two-man ticket clearly designating one candidate for the top slot and a running mate for the number-two position. The amendment's immediate impetus was the confusion arising from the 1800 race: Jefferson and his running mate, Aaron Burr, had technically both been candidates for the presidency, and the formal inability to designate Burr as merely a vice-presidential candidate had caused a great deal of mischief. The effect of the change, however, was to redefine the relationship between America's top two officers—quelling the animosity once built into the system. What ultimately emerged under the Twelfth Amendment's umbrella was a closer partnership between presidents and vice presidents.

Yet, even with this change, the relationship between chief executives and their running mates remained delicate, especially because of the parties' common practice of balancing tickets with men from opposite wings. Indeed, it was only because of the discretion of vice presidents that the new system worked. For example, shortly before his death, Abraham Lincoln proclaimed his openness to black suffrage; his vice president, Andrew Johnson, disagreed but kept mum. Had he publicly blasted Lincoln, Johnson's succession to the presidency upon Lincoln's assassination would have been that much harder for an already divided nation to accept. (According to reliable historical accounts, when Lincoln first publicly floated the idea of giving blacks the vote, John Wilkes Booth was present in the audience, was horrified by Lincoln's proposal, and muttered then and there that he would do Lincoln in. Three days later, Booth tried to visit Johnson only hours before the assassination, leading some conspiracy theorists to speculate that the two men were in cahoots.)

The next presidential assassination illustrated the problem even more vividly. In 1880, the Republicans balanced a "Half-breed"[4] and a "Stalwart": the top slot went to James Garfield, who seemed open to a professional civil service, and the second spot went to Chester Arthur, who preferred a spoils system. Four months after the inauguration, a disgruntled spoilsman shot Garfield and, upon his arrest, informed the police, "I am a Stalwart and Arthur will be president." In his pocket, police found a letter, addressed to Arthur, making various recommendations for cabinet reshuffling. Arthur, in fact, knew nothing of this madman and had done little to undercut his president. Had he been sharply and publicly critical, however, Arthur's succession could have led to a serious constitutional crisis.

Presidents can be felled by impeachers as well as by assassins. And so Gore's effusive praise of Clinton on the day of his House impeachment, while politically wounding to the vice president, was constitutionally noble. Imagine if, on that day, Gore (or his staff) had joined the Clinton bashers, even subtly, and then the Senate had gone on to remove the president from office. Presidents who take over after assassinations or impeachments already suffer a legitimacy gap because they were not elected on their own. Any hint that Gore had participated in a palace coup—et tu, Al?—would have made his own presidency that much weaker. In fact, at a time of great uncertainty and division, the president would have been a constitutional cripple.

Once again, a quick look at American history clarifies matters. When Congress impeached Johnson in 1868, the vice presidency stood vacant, having been opened up by Johnson's accession. (Prior to the passage of the Twenty-fifth Amendment, which was adopted after John F. Kennedy's assassination, there was no constitutional procedure for filling a vice-presidential vacancy.) The man who thus stood next in the line of succession was the Senate president pro tem, Ben Wade. Wade had helped lead the charge against Johnson and was widely rumored to have already picked his cabinet before voting to convict. Wade's obvious self-dealing offended the public's sensibilities, and, years later, this lingering disgust led to a new statute redefining the rules of presidential succession.

So the first reason for a sitting vice president to hold his tongue is clear enough: He has a unique obligation to do nothing that might destabilize the country or compromise a transition of power. If American history has taught us anything, it is that presidential mishaps can happen at any time and without warning. At any moment, the country may need the vice president to smoothly step in.

The second reason for restraint is that the vice president has no independent electoral mandate. Despite the Twelfth Amendment, current election laws do not allow ordinary Americans to vote separately for presidents and vice presidents. Instead, citizens cast a single ballot for a joint ticket. Thus, a vice president serves not because Americans voted for him personally but solely because he was handpicked by his running mate, for whom the people did vote. When a vice president criticizes the president, therefore, he risks pulling the legitimacy rug out from under himself.

What is called for, then, is a delicate constitutional etiquette balancing the roles of vice president and presidential aspirant. Gore must be Clinton's partner today and his own man tomorrow. In this delicate balance, he may carefully distance himself from Clinton—for instance, geographically. (By moving his campaign headquarters to Nashville, he signals that, although he covets the Oval Office, he is content to wait until 2001 to move in; until then, it's Clinton's show. Historically, many vice presidents have spent most of their time far from Washington, DC. Indeed, Walter Mondale was the first vice president to have a permanent office in the West Wing, and Spiro Agnew's staff didn't even have White House passes.) Gore is also free not to push for certain administration policies; nothing in our Constitution or our traditions requires him to work for the president. But that doesn't mean he may openly and sharply criticize Clinton.

Al Gore has the right to be the best presidential candidate possible and the duty to offer us his personal vision. But, until he is elected president in his own right, he must also remain a loyal vice president who could, if necessary, insure the peaceful and legitimate transition of power at the very moment our government is weakest: when a president goes down.

THWARTING ELECTORAL TERRORISM[5]

WASHINGTON POST, SUNDAY, NOVEMBER 11, 2001

A year ago this month, a freakishly close presidential election focused Americans' attention on the glitches of election codes and voting machines, and spurred talk of election reform. Now, different images haunt our imagination and anti-terrorism legislation is the order of the day. It is not much of a stretch to imagine that future terrorists might target the very foundations of our democracy—the elections themselves.

Election reform, meet anti-terrorism legislation.

Over the past year, more than 1,500 election bills have been introduced in legislatures across America proposing fixes for what has gone wrong in the past—everything from modernizing tabulation technology to repealing the electoral college and making Election Day a national holiday. And then the terrorists struck.

Our new awareness of the possibility of terrorism brings into focus problems that have shadowed our voting system for decades. Natural disasters can compromise elections, as can a candidate's election-eve death or incapacitation, whether from natural causes or assassination. If tragedy were to strike in late October or early November, would voters be able to weigh their remaining electoral options? The fallout could be far more destabilizing than the few weeks of uncertainty we lived through last year.

Think back for a moment to the reason September 11 was a specially marked date on New Yorkers' calendars: It was a local election day, with contests that included the city's mayoral primary. As the horrific events unfolded, Governor George Pataki understood that an orderly and democratically satisfactory election that day was impossible. State law allowed him to postpone the balloting. But current federal law does not permit a similar delay of congressional and presidential elections. The law mandates an election on the first Tuesday after November 1, come hell or high water, terror or trauma.

So suppose that a major presidential or vice-presidential candidate dies or is incapacitated shortly before Election Day. A patchwork of state laws governs ballot access and counting, and most states allow national parties to substitute new candidates. But in some situations, parties would lack time to deliberate and state officials would lack time to print revised ballots. Without some postponement, voters might not even know whom they were really voting for. If presidential candidate Smith died, would a vote for Smith be counted as a vote for his or her vice-presidential running mate Jones, or for some player to be named later by a conclave of party bigwigs?

An issue of this kind arose last year in Missouri. There, U.S. Senate candidate Mel Carnahan died in mid-October, but voters nevertheless elected him in November in the expectation that his wife, Jean Carnahan, would be installed in his stead. She was. But had he died closer to the election or had the loser—then senator John Ashcroft—been less gracious and more litigious, Missouri might have been almost as tumultuous as Florida last December.

The 1963 assassination of President John F. Kennedy spurred reformers to enact the Twenty-fifth Amendment, which streamlined issues of vice-presidential succession. But the assassination five years later of the late president's brother—presidential candidate Robert F. Kennedy—failed to prompt comparable reform to address the death or disability of presidential candidates. Indeed, had RFK been shot hours before the general election rather than hours after the California primary, the vulnerability of the current system would have been obvious to all—and would likely have prompted serious discussion of election-postponement legislation.

Election reform to protect against such dramatic assaults will require hard choices. The tight timetable we now have was created by the Twentieth Amendment in 1933 to shrink the lame-duck period between a president's election and inauguration. The idea was that an incumbent president should yield as quickly as possible—on January 20, to be precise—to a new president with a fresh electoral mandate. But shortening that period any further would not only leave less time for counting, recounting, and resolving any complaints that arise, it would also make it harder for the eventual winner to assemble his new administration before inauguration. (Last year's shortened transition period surely complicated life for George W. Bush.)

One option would be for federal law to move the federal Election Day to October, with provision for postponement in rare circumstances. This, of course, would widen the very gap between election and inauguration that the Twentieth Amendment sought to shrink. A better response would thus be to keep Election Day as is, but allow brief postponement in rare circumstances, with streamlined voting technology, statutes, and court procedures to ensure enough time for proper counts and recounts.

A sound reform law might also allow for the postponement of the electoral college meeting. State laws often purport to bind electors to vote for the candidate who won the state's popular vote; but what if this candidate has died or become disabled between Election Day and the day of the meeting?

This actually happened in 1872, when Democrat Horace Greeley died shortly after losing to incumbent Ulysses S. Grant. Some loyal electors voted as pledged—for the dead man—and Congress later disregarded their votes. Little turned on Congress's ruling, given that Greeley had clearly lost in November. Had he won, however, surely the fairest result would have been to credit his electoral votes to his running mate. Otherwise, the party that won the presidency on Election Day could conceivably lose it before the inauguration. But Congress in 1873 simply tossed Greeley's votes aside, and that precedent remains a source of potential mischief today. Like ordinary voters, electors should understand in advance whether and how their votes will be counted, and should be able to cast these votes in an atmosphere of calm deliberation. And that may mean allowing for the postponement of the electoral college meeting in a crisis.

The question remains of how—and by whom—a postponement should be triggered. Handing this power to the chief justice risks sucking the Supreme Court into partisan politics, the danger of which is well illustrated by last year's controversy surrounding *Bush v. Gore*. The current Federal Election Commission may likewise lack the necessary credibility and impartiality. One possibility would be to let each major party (defined as the top two vote-getters in the previous election) trigger a postponement upon request. Parties would hesitate to delay elections for frivolous or partisan reasons because the voters could immediately punish any postponements seen as gamesmanship.

A final issue is whether, in an emergency, to postpone all federal elections or simply the presidential one. Once again, a law could be drafted to specify the decision maker and vest that person with considerable discretion. Because federal law controls only federal elections, each state would decide whether to postpone elections for state officers so as to coordinate with the delayed federal election, or whether instead to hold two elections in short order for state and federal officers, respectively.

However all these wrinkles are ironed out, the experiences of this past year have made it clear that election reform proposals cannot afford to focus exclusively on fixing the problems of the past. Our democratic processes need to be protected from much less predictable threats.

CONSTITUTIONAL ACCIDENTS
WAITING TO HAPPEN . . . AGAIN

FINDLAW, FRIDAY, SEPTEMBER 6, 2002 (WITH VIKRAM DAVID AMAR)

September presents haunting reminders that bad things sometimes happen to good people and a great nation. One hundred and one years ago today, William McKinley was shot by a politically motivated assassin. McKinley died several days later, on September 14, 1901. In mid-September, 1881, President James Garfield also died from gunshot wounds inflicted by a politically motivated assassin. And then of course there is the date that will live in infamy, September 11, 2001.

America cannot always prevent tragedy, but America often can, with relative ease, minimize the constitutional damage resulting from political assassins and other acts of political violence. Yet the country's current legal framework for presidential succession is notably flawed—a series of constitutional accidents waiting to happen, and in some cases waiting to happen again. There are simple nonpartisan solutions that lawmakers should adopt now to address these potential problems, before tragedy strikes again.

The Twenty-fifth Amendment, adopted after JFK's assassination, provides a detailed framework for determining whether the president is so severely disabled as to justify allowing someone else to act as president for the duration of the disability. But the amendment says nothing about possible vice-presidential disability, and federal statutes are likewise silent on the topic.

Suppose, for example, that the vice president is in a coma, whether from natural causes or because of some attempted assassination. Current law offers no framework for determining that the vice president is disabled and therefore unfit for the job until he recovers; and in the absence of such a framework he formally retains all the powers and duties of his office. Nor does current law allow someone other than the vice president or president to initiate determinations of presidential disability.

These legal gaps yield several scenarios of needless vulnerability. First, there is the problem of vice-presidential disability combined with presidential death. If the vice president is not fit to take the helm, but there is no proper legal mechanism for making this determination, then what happens if the president dies—whether because of some assassination or political terrorism, or from natural causes? The comatose vice president would now become the comatose president.

Even worse, in this scenario there is no statutory or constitutional framework in place to determine his unfitness *as president* once he ascends to that office! Unless a president voluntarily steps aside (which is unlikely if he is comatose), the only constitutional or statutory mechanism now in place to establish that a president is disabled is one triggered by the vice president. But in the scenario described here, there is no longer any vice president in office.

Similar problems arise under a scenario in which both the vice president and the president are disabled. Imagine that the vice president is comatose, and the president does not die but himself becomes severely disabled—whether from some terrorist incident or from natural causes. Here, too, the problem is that current law requires that (unless the president himself voluntarily steps aside) the vice president initiate the machinery for determining presidential disability. If the vice president is himself incapacitated, the machinery simply freezes up, and there is no clearly established legal framework for determining presidential disability.

Consider also a related scenario involving a disabled acting president, in which a president becomes disabled first, and a fit vice president steps up to assume the role of acting president. If that acting president later becomes arguably or even clearly incapacitated, who could trigger the process of making the disability determination?

Now consider two vice-presidential vacancy scenarios: Either the vice president has died and has not yet been replaced, or the president has died and the former vice president has become president but has not yet installed a new vice president. In these scenarios, there is once again no vice president in place to trigger the disability-determination process in the event the president suffers some serious physical or mental setback.

Although the Twenty-fifth Amendment does not itself address these scenarios, neither does it preclude a congressional statute that would solve these problems. Indeed, other language in the Constitution—in Article II—invites Congress "by law" to provide for cases of presidential and vice-presidential death and disability. In the event both the president and the vice president have died or become disabled, Article II gives Congress power to decide by law "what Officer" should act as president. At least two questions arise: Who should be that officer? And, in the event of double death in the executive branch, how long should that officer serve?

The presidential succession statute currently in place, enacted in 1947, answers these two questions but gives a plainly unconstitutional answer to the first question—the "who" question—and arguably errs on the second, "how long," question.[6] According to the act, in the event of a double death, the speaker of the House becomes president. The line of succession continues with the president pro tempore of the Senate, and then members of the cabinet, beginning with the secretary of state. The act also specifies that the successor president serves out the remainder of the deceased president's term.

But as James Madison argued in 1792, congressional legislators are not "officers" of the United States, as the Article II statutory succession clause uses the word. (Here is the relevant language, with emphasis added: "Congress may by law provide for the case of removal, death, resignation or inability, both of the President and Vice President, declaring what *officer* shall then act as President.") In the Constitution, "officers" generally means executive and judicial officials, not legislators. (Otherwise the Article I rule that "no Person holding any Office under the United States, shall be a Member of either House during his Continuance in Office" would be incoherent.)

The Article II statutory succession clause envisioned that a cabinet secretary handpicked by the president himself would substitute in the sad event of double death or double disability. This rule of cabinet succession (which was in place for sixty years before Congress changed the law in 1947) helps maximize the policy continuity between the president that Americans voted for on Election Day, and the statutory successor who ends up taking his place.

In sum, Article II empowers Congress to choose which cabinet position is next in line after the vice president, but it does not empower Congress to choose one of its own members instead. If the American people voted for a Republican presidential ticket, they should not end up with a Democratic statutory successor president; and vice versa. (We first criticized the 1947 law publicly in 1995 when the Democrats controlled the presidency and Republican Newt Gingrich stood next in line as speaker of the House. But we feel the same way about the issue today, when the White House is controlled by the Republicans and when Democrat Richard Gephardt would be speaker of the House if the Democrats win a few more seats in the upcoming off-year election.)

As to the question of the successor's term in office, because no cabinet secretary enjoys a personal mandate from a national electorate—nor, of course, do congressional leaders picked within individual states and districts— perhaps the cabinet successor who takes over in the event of double death should serve only as long as is necessary to arrange a special off-year presidential election, to choose someone to finish out the term. That way, the nation spends as little time as possible with a president lacking a personal national electoral mandate.[7]

Finally, if personal mandates from the American people are important, isn't there something odd about America's current system of choosing vice presidents? Voters often pay little attention to the bottom of the ticket. At times, America has elected vice presidents who, according to exit polls, could never have won the vice presidency (to say nothing of the presidency) head to head against their leading opponent.

If people vote for a presidential ticket despite the vice-presidential candidate, then what would that vice president's mandate be were he to become president, after a terrorist incident or otherwise? Why should the American people be led by a president who never did, and perhaps never could, win the support of the nation? (Remember Dan Quayle?)

One way to strengthen the vice president's personal mandate would be to allow voters to vote separately for president and vice president, just as many states allow separate votes for governors and lieutenant governors. Nothing in the Constitution prevents states from giving voters this option—but it does raise several complexities.[8]

All of our suggestions today raise important issues of principle and detail. Some readers will doubtless find our proposed solutions imperfect, or worse. Perhaps some readers may have better solutions. But the time for citizens and policy makers to start discussing these issues is now, before tragedy strikes again and does needless damage to American democracy.

AFTER THE VEEP, REDRAW THE LINE

WASHINGTON POST, SUNDAY, SEPTEMBER 14, 2003

Life and art (or at least television) converge this month as both the U.S. Senate and NBC's *The West Wing* focus on America's bizarre presidential-succession rules.

On Wednesday, September 24, fans of the fictional president Josiah "Jed" Bartlet will learn whether he regains his office after having temporarily abandoned it. At the end of last season, terrorists kidnapped Bartlet's daughter, exposing him and the country to possible political extortion. With his vice president having recently resigned, Bartlet, a staunch Democrat, found himself obliged for the good of the nation to hand over power to the Republican speaker of the House, played by John Goodman.

Now flash back to the real world. On Tuesday, the Senate will hold hearings to consider whether our law should indeed put the speaker in the West Wing if both the president and vice president resigned, died, or became disabled. Of course, such a double disaster is a low-probability event—but then, so was the electoral train wreck of 2000. Wise lawmakers must plan for highly destabilizing contingencies—earthquakes, blackouts, voting-machine foul-ups, terror attacks, assassinations—before they happen. This week's

hearings are part of a broader process of post-9/11 reassessment now under-
way, aimed at maximizing continuity of government in the event of crisis.

The proper starting point for planning is the Constitution, which says
that if both the president and the vice president are unavailable, presidential
power should flow to some other federal "Officer" named by law. The framers
clearly had in mind a cabinet officer—presumably, one who had been picked
by the president himself before tragedy struck. In fact, no less an authority
than James Madison insisted that the constitutionally mandated separation
of executive and legislative powers made congressional leaders ineligible. Yet
the current succession statute, enacted in 1947, puts the House speaker and
then the Senate president pro tempore—historically the majority party's
most senior senator, who presides over the Senate in the vice president's
absence—ahead of cabinet officers, in plain disregard of Madison's careful
constitutional analysis.

In truth, 1947 was not the first time Congress chose to ignore Madison. In
the early years of George Washington's presidency, Madison's argument for
cabinet succession stumbled into a political minefield. Which cabinet position should head the list? Secretary of State Thomas Jefferson thought his
office deserved top billing, but Treasury Secretary Alexander Hamilton had
other ideas. Eventually, in 1792, Congress detoured around the minefield by
placing the Senate president pro tem at the top of the line of succession, followed by the House speaker. Though the 1947 law flips this order, it suffers
from the same constitutional flaws that Madison identified two centuries ago.

Constitutionality aside, the 1947 law also defies common sense. Suppose
that a president is not dead but briefly disabled, and the vice president is also
unavailable, for whatever reason. Because separation-of-powers principles
prohibit a sitting legislator from serving even temporarily in the executive
branch, the statute says that a House speaker must quit Congress before moving into the Oval Office, as happened on West Wing. But if the disabled president then recovers and reclaims power, the former speaker will have no job
to return to. That hardly seems a fitting reward for faithful public service in a
crisis. A more sensible law would let a cabinet officer step up for the duration
of the disability and then step down whenever the president recovered.

In another wrinkle, the 1947 law allows the speaker to play an ugly wait-
and-see game. If he thinks a disability will not last long—and, again, if the
vice president is out of the picture—he can allow a cabinet officer to act as
president. If the disability then worsens, the speaker can, with a snap of his

fingers, bump the cabinet secretary out of the Oval Office and put himself in. Even if this constitutionally dubious option were never exercised, its mere existence encourages political gamesmanship, weakens the presidency itself, and increases instability at a moment when tranquillity should be the nation's top priority.

Current law may even encourage a more disruptive sort of gamesmanship. Whenever legislative leaders help impeach and remove the president or vice president, they themselves move up one notch in the succession order as long as the vice presidency remains vacant. Might this conflict of interest compromise their roles as impeachment judges and jurors?

In fact, when President Andrew Johnson was impeached in 1868, Senate leader Ben Wade stood at the top of the succession list, thanks to the 1792 law. (There was no vice president in 1868; Johnson himself had been elected to this post in 1864 but left it vacant when he became president upon Lincoln's assassination in 1865.) Even as Wade sat in supposedly impartial judgment over Johnson, he had already begun making plans to move into the White House. Though Johnson ultimately was acquitted, the Wade affair prompted reformers in 1886 to remove all legislative leaders from the line of succession. But in 1947, the lessons of 1868 were forgotten, and legislators returned to the top of the succession list.

Other conflicts of interest arise under the current law when a president seeks to fill a vacant number-two spot by nominating a new vice president to be confirmed by Congress. Such vacancies should be filled quickly, but the statute gives congressional leaders perverse incentives to delay confirmation. In 1974, it took a Democratic Congress four months to confirm Republican President Gerald Ford's nominee, Nelson A. Rockefeller. Had something happened to Ford in the meantime, Democratic Speaker Carl Albert would have assumed power.

Which highlights perhaps the biggest problem: If Americans elect a president of one party, why should we get stuck with a president of the opposite party—perhaps (as in the fictional West Wing) a sworn foe of the person we chose? Cabinet succession would avoid this oddity.

Supporters of the 1947 law say that presidential powers should go to an elected leader, not an appointed underling. But congressmen are elected locally, not nationally. Legislators often lack the national vision that characterizes the president and his cabinet team. Historically, only one House speaker, James K. Polk, has ever been elected president, compared with six secretaries of state.

Some have suggested that, if existing cabinet slots are deemed unsuitable to head the succession list, Congress could create a new cabinet post of "second" or "assistant" vice president, to be nominated by the president and confirmed by the Senate in a high-visibility process. This officer's sole responsibilities would be to receive regular briefings preparing him or her to serve at a moment's notice and to lie low until needed: in the line of succession but out of the line of fire. The democratic mandate of this assistant vice president might be further enhanced if presidential candidates announced their prospective nominees for the job well before the November election. In casting ballots for their preferred presidential candidate, American voters would also be endorsing that candidate's announced succession team.

If the proposed assistant vice president's job description seems rather quirky—doing almost nothing while remaining ready to do everything—this is of course also true of the vice presidency itself. And because, despite every precaution, mishap might befall the assistant vice president, a new statute would, like the current one, need to put existing cabinet officers on the next rungs of the succession ladder.

However the details are resolved, America needs to address the anomalies in the current law, and to do it quickly. At present, any shift from congressional to cabinet succession would be a partisan wash—from one set of Republicans to another. But if a divided government returns after the 2004 elections, reform will be much harder to achieve. Although any statutory fix will come too late to help President Bartlet next week, now is the perfect time to enact reforms that might assist President Bush and his successors in the real West Wing.

INSTA-GOV

SLATE, FRIDAY, MAY 14, 2010, 4:40 P.M. (ET)

As the world speeds up, can American constitutional democracy keep pace? This month floods hit, terrorists plotted, oil gushed, markets nosedived (then rebounded), and ash spewed. In response, our government moved at warp speed to operate floodgates, nab suspects, redeploy ships, calm investors, and tweak airline rules. But what if a month like this coincided with a period in which the wrong people are in power—that is, in the lame-duck moment when our country is being run by leaders who have just been evicted by the voters but have yet to vacate the premises?

On this score, Britain and America offer a study in contrast. In Britain, voters vote and losers leave almost instantly, as we have just witnessed. Gordon Brown is dead, electorally speaking; long live David Cameron! But in America, George W. Bush continued to hold office for months after his policies were decisively repudiated by the voters in early November 2008. Even as the economy continued to crater, the people's choice, Barack Obama, had no right to take charge.

American history serves up other particularly awkward transitions. On November 8, 1932, Herbert Hoover lost the presidency to Franklin Delano Roosevelt by a whopping margin of 472 to 59 electoral votes (57 percent to 40 percent in the popular vote count), yet remained in power until March 4, 1933, as the nation drifted further downward and government did . . . nothing. Between Abraham Lincoln's election in November 1860 and his inauguration in March 1861, the nation plunged into its deepest crisis ever because the electorally repudiated incumbent, James Buchanan, refused to nip secession in the bud. For most of the nation's first century and a half, voters waited even longer for a new Congress—thirteen months after Election Day for the House (yes, from a November election until December of the following year) and also for the Senate, elected via state legislatures.

Now we wait ten weeks for the whole federal government to turn over, thanks to the Twentieth Amendment, ratified shortly after FDR thumped Hoover. But could America sync up with the twenty-first century's pace and transfer power with the speed of Britain and other parliamentary democracies? It is widely thought not: Because various dates are fixed in our written Constitution, Americans have generally assumed that we could never approximate British briskness without a major constitutional overhaul. But in fact, Americans could speed things up dramatically without any need to amend our good old Constitution. All we need to do is creatively revise our political customs and tweak our election statutes.

Begin with the executive branch. Imagine that in November 2012, Mitt Romney and Chris Christie decisively best Barack Obama and Joe Biden on Election Day.* In fact, Romney could become president in a matter of minutes after the concession speeches, regardless of the official timetables in the Constitution. First, Vice President Biden could graciously step down,

---

* [Readers should recall that these words were written more than two years before the Republican Party chose its actual 2012 ticket, Romney and Paul Ryan, who ultimately lost to incumbents Obama and Biden.]

Gordon Brown style. Next, President Obama could nominate Romney to be vice president, under the Twenty-fifth Amendment, the one that enabled Richard Nixon to nominate Gerald Ford in 1973 after Spiro Agnew resigned. Congress could immediately confirm Romney by simply voting yes for him, just as Congress eventually voted yes for Ford in 1973. And then Obama could gracefully step aside for President Mitt Romney.

Romney, in turn, could immediately use the Twenty-fifth Amendment to install Christie as the new vice president, just as Ford, after becoming president in 1974, named Nelson Rockefeller. President Romney could also name his slate of cabinet officers, and the Senate could confirm these secretaries in a few days, in keeping with America's honeymoon tradition of deference to an incoming president's cabinet choices. (The first time in American history that a newly elected president was denied his choice for a cabinet position was in 1989, when the Senate refused to confirm John Tower to serve as George H. W. Bush's secretary of defense.) In thinking about a quick change-over of the executive branch, we should also remember that most senators are old hands at the confirmation game, and that the Senate's staggered election calendar ordinarily ensures that at any given moment at least two-thirds of the body are seasoned veterans.

Of course, if Obama and Biden were willing to do all this in November 2012, they should announce their intentions long in advance, so that their Republican opponents and the voters are not caught by surprise. And they could even cite precedent. Nearly a century ago, President Woodrow Wilson devised a similar plan to approximate British-style transitions. When running for reelection in 1916, Wilson decided that he would resign shortly after the election in the event that he was defeated by Republican Charles Evans Hughes. The plan was for Wilson to name Hughes secretary of state, an office that at the time was first in the line of succession after the vice president. Thus, if both Wilson and his vice president, Thomas Marshall, resigned after Hughes's confirmation, Hughes could take over as acting president long before his formal inauguration in March.

As things actually turned out, Wilson won reelection and nothing came of his early resignation idea, which was probably just as well, since he did not properly announce his intentions. But if Obama and Biden were to revive Wilson's idea, future incumbents might feel morally bound to follow their precedent, much as presidents after George Washington typically felt obliged to follow his lead of resigning after a maximum of two terms long before the Twenty-second Amendment required them to do so.

Now turn to House and Senate elections. Here, too, creative resignations could dramatically shorten the current lame-duck period. If every incumbent representative and every senator facing the end of his or her six-year term were to formally resign the day before the November election, that election could in effect do double duty. First, the election could determine, as it does now, who will serve in the new Congress that will begin service on January 3. But it could also operate as a special vacancy-filling election, with the winner entitled to fill out the remainder of the term for the resigning Congress member. Of course, any incumbent who runs for reelection and wins immediately fills the seat she just officially vacated by resignation. But any incumbent who loses would leave early. If we were worried about the very short continuity-in-government gap between resignations and certifications of replacements, then each resignation could be drafted so as to operate conditionally—"effective when my successor's election shall have been certified." (Several recent Supreme Court justices—most recently, Sandra Day O'Connor—have drafted just this sort of conditional resignation, formally effective only upon the seating of a successor.)[9]

Custom, rather than law, would drive this new system. Formally, losing presidents and vice presidents would be choosing to resign, and incumbent lawmakers would likewise be opting to step down earlier than required by law. But the same is true in Britain—it is longstanding custom that obliged Gordon Brown to step down as soon as it became clear that his political opponents had managed to form a majority coalition. (A legalized alternative would be to move American elections to late December, but this approach leaves little margin for error in the event of an Election Day or electoral college mishap.)

If Americans truly want to streamline our transfers of power, the Constitution does not stand in the way. The question is thus not whether we can easily emulate the Brits. It's whether we want to.

WHY SPEAKERS OF THE HOUSE
SHOULD NEVER BE PRESIDENT

NEW REPUBLIC, THURSDAY, JANUARY 12, 2012

Are there lessons to be learned from the implosion of Newt Gingrich's presidential campaign over the past month? Several come easily to mind, from the virtues of campaign organization to the importance of message discipline.

But there's another that deserves attention: namely, that serving as speaker of the House is a highly dubious qualification in preparation for assuming the presidency. The recent stumblings of current House Speaker John Boehner—including his failed bid last month to negotiate with President Obama over payroll tax cuts—are further testimony to this point.

The fact is, most speakers have limited skill sets. They are amateurs on the world stage and hyper-partisans to boot. In other words, most speakers are un-presidential—an unfitness that becomes dramatically apparent when a speaker goes head to head against a president or seeks the presidency itself. Some politically astute observers see this mismatch as a source of amusement. But it's much more than that: Given that current law places the speaker atop the line of presidential succession, it's a disaster of epic proportions waiting to happen.

Some background. The Constitution does not specify who should step up if both the president and vice president are dead or disabled. The document instead empowers Congress to legislate which "officer" should fill the breach. By "officer," the framers meant a cabinet officer; strictly speaking, congressional leaders were not "officers" within the meaning of the Constitution's succession clause. But in 1792, Congress could not decide which cabinet secretary deserved top billing, Thomas Jefferson or Alexander Hamilton. Over the constitutional objections of James Madison, Congress finessed the feud by (surprise, surprise) favoring itself: Congressional chieftains, not cabinet secretaries, topped the 1792 succession list. Congress later replaced this law with a proper regime of cabinet succession in 1886, but reversed course in 1947, placing the speaker atop the succession order.

The unconstitutionality of the 1947 law is reason enough to scrap it. But what gives the issue particular urgency is the recent polarization of the parties and the extreme partisanship this polarization has instilled in the House of Representatives and the speakers who lead it. When Democrat Harry Truman gave hell to congressional Republicans in the late 1940s, many of Congress's most conservative members were southern Democrats and some of the body's most progressive members were northern Republicans. No more. Today's congressional Democrats are all to the left of today's congressional Republicans.

Presidents, too, must now more clearly pick a side than was true in the late 1940s. Nowadays, there is no one like Ike, who ran as a Republican but could have won as a Democrat.

In today's polarized landscape, the 1947 succession law becomes hugely destabilizing. What legitimacy would the conservative Republican Boehner have, were tragedy to befall the center-left Democrats, Barack Obama and Joe Biden, who won the 2008 presidential election? Would Secretary of State Hillary Clinton quietly accept this massive power shift—effectively undoing the election—or would she instead insist that, legally, she was next in line, given the unconstitutionality of the 1947 law? Whom would the military salute? Would opposing mobs clash in the streets? Would the Supreme Court get sucked into the vortex—another *Bush v. Gore* fiasco?

These nightmare scenarios become even worse if we imagine—as history and realism demand that we imagine—successions triggered by suspicious acts of violence. In 1865, Andrew Johnson's task of national reconciliation was complicated by the fact that Lincoln's killer had tried to visit Johnson only hours before the assassination. In 1963, Lyndon Johnson likewise faced wild conspiracy theories stressing that President Kennedy was killed in Johnson's home state of Texas. In 1881, the madman who shot James Garfield had penned a letter advising the soon-to-be president, Chester Arthur. In all three cases, presidential power peacefully shifted to the dead president's own running mate. But when power instead shifts to the opposite party in the person of an intensely controversial partisan, conspiracy theories may be much more virulent, disaffection far more extreme.

And make no mistake, speakers are by the very structure of their posts intensely partisan figures. Speakers become speakers by winning repeatedly in reliably safe districts that are either far more conservative or far more liberal than the nation. Presidents must win votes of the middle of America; speakers must win the votes of the middle of the party. The skills required of each could hardly be more different.

And while intense partisanship is built into the speaker's job, foreign policy expertise is not. Refreshingly—but dangerously, given current succession law—Boehner has no pretentions to global vision. To him, Cairo means Illinois, not Egypt. While Gingrich is full of global pretensions, as a speaker he had little exposure to matters such as treaty negotiation or ratification. Gingrich's intemperate comments about Palestinians and Muslims reflect this inexperience. Diplomacy-savvy Republicans like Condoleezza Rice, James Baker, and Richard Lugar do not talk this way.

Of course, we should not single out Boehner and Gingrich. Many of the same things could be said of most modern speakers.

And therein lies hope. Precisely because speakers of both parties have typically been unfit for the presidency, both parties should favor reform.

Every one of the last eight presidents except Jimmy Carter has faced an opposition-party speaker. By now, both sides should agree that whenever a party wins the presidential vote, that party should hold the presidency for four years, because that is what Americans voted for and because even good opposition-party speakers would be bad successor presidents.

Given the current fluidity of the American mood, the 2012 election could give us a Democratic president and a Republican speaker, or a Republican president and a Democratic speaker. Now is thus the perfect time for both parties to embrace real reform by putting cabinet officers—the president's handpicked helpmates, who understand the world and share the president's worldview—back atop the line of succession.

3

THE CONGRESS
How to Fix a Broken Branch

THE ELECTION OF BARACK OBAMA in November 2008 was a remarkable event, and not just because of his race or his name. Only once before in the previous century and a half had a non-incumbent Democrat decisively swept into the White House, and the only man who had accomplished this feat, FDR, had done so way back in 1932.[1] But within weeks of Obama's storybook moment in American and world history—indeed, even before Obama entered office—his career hit a constitutional low point when his vacant Senate seat was filled via a process utterly unworthy of a great republic. As he left the Senate to prepare for his inauguration, an undeniably corrupt governor used an intrinsically corrupt process to select a presumptively corrupt replacement senator. The undeniably corrupt Illinois governor—Rod Blagojevich, nicknamed "Blago"—eventually went to prison, but Blago's presumptively corrupt Senate pick, former state attorney general Roland Burris, was allowed to sit and vote and serve out the entirety of his rump term as a senator in good standing.

As the story of Blago and Burris was unfolding shortly before and after New Year's Day 2009, most journalists did not understand the constitutional rules and principles applicable to Senate vacancies. And why should anyone expect the journalists to have done better? Members of the press are not constitutional experts; the constitutional questions here were technical and intricate; and the facts were unusual, to say the least.

Even among scholars, few correctly understood the matter. Most constitutional experts focus on courts, but the Senate vacancy issue involved Congress. Although the Constitution itself does have something to say about the matter of filling Senate vacancies, most academics who study constitutional law do not focus on the naked constitutional text in exquisite detail, nor are they experts on the Founding history that generated the text. Rather, constitutional scholars typically study the precedents and practices that are currently in place, precedents and practices that have glossed and sometimes virtually superseded the text itself. But on the matter of Blago and Burris, the relevant precedents were the precedents of the Senate itself, a tiny corner of constitutional law familiar only to a few academic specialists, most of them political scientists rather than law professors.

To be sure, there was one notable Supreme Court case on the power of each congressional house to refuse to seat a putative member—a case involving Adam Clayton Powell, a controversial 1960s congressman who was accused of corruption. But the Court's 1969 landmark opinion in *Powell v. McCormack* runs more than sixty pages, with nearly a hundred footnotes. Few constitutional law professors have ever read the case in its entirety, and at any given moment fewer still have read it recently. In most constitutional law casebooks, the gist of *Powell* is presented in a paragraph or two.

But as luck would have it, I teach *Powell* from start to finish every year. I showcase this ruling in my syllabus because the case is a particularly good modern exemplar of textual and structural constitutional analysis. And I teach the case in its entirety to impress upon students that they must read comprehensively and with care. Footnotes matter, and in *Powell*, key footnotes limit and refine the Court's holding.

So when Burris sought to be seated, I was ready to weigh in quickly because I had already done most of my homework. Most, but not all: I was far from expert on past Senate practice and precedent. Thank goodness for my former students—and for one star student in particular, Josh Chafetz, a Rhodes scholar and constitutional law professor at Cornell University. Not only had Josh just published a book on the history of parliamentary practice and procedure in both England and America, but he was (and still is) also an accomplished freelance journalist, with placements in many of America's top periodicals. So as soon as I heard the news that Blago had purported to name Burris to the Senate, I called Josh to get his take. We saw eye to eye and within a few hours we were ready to publish our analysis, in the hope that the public and the Senate would pay attention.

Our piece, "How the Senate Can Stop Blagojevich," was posted on *Slate* in the waning hours of 2008, and it now appears as this chapter's opening essay. In it, Josh and I made several key moves. First, as our title signaled, we targeted Blago, not Burris. Blago was undeniably corrupt. Audiotapes of this crooked man trying to auction off Obama's vacant seat had already been made public. (The audiotapes were part of a federal investigation that would later culminate in a multiyear prison sentence.) Second, and related, any process involving Blago was per se corrupt, intrinsically corrupt—corrupt precisely because Blago was corrupt and had already been captured on tape being corrupt in connection with the very Senate seat at issue. Third, Josh and I argued that the Senate did not need to conclusively prove that Burris himself was corrupt. As we saw it, the Senate needed only to say that *no one* whom Blago might pick, ever, would be acceptable. The factual questions about Burris himself could be sidestepped with a blanket legal presumption.

At the time our *Slate* piece came out, Burris was swearing up and down and sideways that he had made no deal whatsoever with Blago. But it later came out that he had indeed promised Blago certain things in exchange for his seat. Surprise, surprise.

When eventually caught red-handed, Burris's disgraceful defense was that his promises to Blago were insincere when made. But surely it makes no difference whatsoever whether Burris was merely a liar or was also a briber. By his own later confession, he had gotten his job on at least doubly false pretenses—having admittedly lied to Blago and having later lied to the Senate when he had denied having promised anything to Blago. On any view of the matter, his conduct stank, and he was not fit to sit in America's highest legislative council. But by the time all these facts came out, the damage was done and he had already been seated—contrary to the strong pleas that Josh and I had made when the chips were down.

At the heart of our *Slate* essay was an emphatic claim about constitutional law: Both the Constitution itself and the *Powell v. McCormack* decision, when read with care, clearly authorized the Senate to flatly refuse to seat Burris, just as that chamber could properly refuse to seat any would-be senator chosen in a rigged election. The Constitution makes the Senate itself the "judge" of fair elections and fair appointments to the Senate, and *Powell* had basically conceded this point while making clear that Congress lacked carte blanche to exclude members who were in fact fairly elected and constitutionally eligible.

WITH THE BENEFIT OF HINDSIGHT, I continue to think that Josh and I got this one exactly right. But in early 2009, Burris had two cards up his

sleeve that enabled him to prevail in the Senate itself, which chose to seat
him less than two weeks after Josh and I had weighed in.

First, Burris played the race card. Here was a black man seeking to fill a
seat vacated by a duly elected black man, Barack Obama. With Obama's departure, no African Americans were left in the Senate. Since Reconstruction, only three blacks had *ever* served in the Senate.[2] The optics of an
all-white club excluding a black man without conclusive evidence against
the man himself were terrible.

These optics were made all the worse by the famous facts of the one
Supreme Court case most on point, *Powell v. McCormack*. Adam Clayton
Powell, too, was a black man who had run into trouble gaining admission to
a white-dominated house of Congress. At the time of his exclusion from the
House, Powell was a political celebrity—the most senior African American
in Congress, representing perhaps the most iconic black district in America,
Harlem. Powell had been wrongfully excluded from the House in a process
that seemed racially biased to many observers. In a concurring opinion in
Powell v. McCormack, Justice William O. Douglas declared that Powell's exclusion had "racist overtones." (Note Douglas's word choice: not merely "racial" but "racist.") To the press and other nonexperts in early 2009, the
Burris episode seemed like *Powell* all over again.

But it wasn't, and this should be clear to anyone who has actually read
the case in its entirety. Adam Clayton Powell was duly elected, again and
again. His Harlem constituents loved him. Although Powell was alleged to
have engaged in some shady financial dealings, there was absolutely nothing
improper or corrupt in his election itself—in the process by which he came
to the Hill and demanded his seat. By contrast, everything about the process
that had brought Burris to the Hill smelled wrong. Plus, no one had ever
voted for Burris for this seat, unless we count Blago himself—but why should
we count anything Blago did here as kosher?

In early 2009, there was one sure way to defeat Burris's race card. If the
Senate is the world's most exclusive "club," there was, so to speak, an Ace of
Clubs to overcome Burris's Jack of Clubs. And the man who held that trump
card, that Ace of Clubs, was none other than Barack Obama. Obama
himself—as president-elect; as the man who had won the very Senate seat at
issue fair and square (in equity, it was his seat and not Blago's); as the head of
the Democratic Party; and as the moral leader of all America and especially
of black America—could have publicly and forcefully spoken out against
Burris and thereby given the Senate cover to do the right thing. But Obama

failed to intervene, and this failure must count as one of the low points in his storied career.

WHICH BRINGS US TO THE SECOND CARD up Burris's sleeve, the second reason that he was seated and Josh and I were ignored: the filibuster.

As New Year's Day 2009 dawned, the Democrats were mapping out an ambitious legislative agenda, including what would eventually become Obamacare. After years in the political wilderness, Democrats would once again control all three parts of the lawmaking process: the House, the Senate, and the presidency. But filibuster rules then in place meant that important bills would effectively need sixty votes in the Senate in order to become law. Without filling Obama's vacant seat, pronto, the Democrats would at best have fifty-nine. So Blago and Burris had Senate Dems over a barrel: Unless the Senate seated Burris, Senate Republicans could block almost anything, including, crucially, statutes and appointments. The Democratic Senate majority leader, Harry Reid, was not inclined to scrap the filibuster in early 2009. So he and his fellow Democrats closed their eyes, stoppered their ears, and held their noses, welcoming Burris into the club and onto their team.

NOW FLASH FORWARD exactly three years—to early January 2012. Reid still lacked sixty votes. Indeed, he was down to fifty-something, thanks largely to the intervening midterm election. Given this math, Republicans in the previous months had succeeded in thwarting various Obama nominations, which could not go through unless sixty senators were willing to end debate and proceed to a final vote. A frustrated President Obama responded by trying to exploit a loophole of his own. When the Senate took a series of short holiday breaks early in 2012, the president unilaterally appointed various nominees to temporary slots, claiming that these temporary appointments could be justified by special constitutional rules that apply during any "recess" of the Senate. Given the shortness of each of the Senate breaks in question, this Obama move seemed like an extremely aggressive escalation of the conflict between the branches.

But like Wagner's music, Obama's move was not as bad as it sounded. Or so I argued in an essay on the New Republic's website, coauthored with journalist Timothy Noah. As Noah and I explained, what at first looked like an executive-legislative gunfight was really nothing of the sort. It was just a standard tug-of-war between the two parties. A majority of the Democrat-led Senate most likely supported what Obama was doing; fifty-one senators (or fifty senators plus Vice President Joe Biden) surely backed every Obama recess nominee but had been prevented from casting a decisive yes vote because of Republican filibusters and other dilatory tactics.

The solution, Noah and I suggested, was simple. President Obama himself should publicly call upon his former colleagues in the Senate Democratic caucus to sign a letter or some other instrument endorsing his actions. So long as the envisioned statement had at least fifty signatures, it would be clear to the American public—and also to later courts, which might be called to rule on the matter—that the president had been acting *with* a Senate majority, not against it.

But as in the Blago-Burris affair, the president failed to act decisively and publicly when it counted, and Majority Leader Reid failed to do the right and smart thing on his own. (This time around, he did not need an engraved invitation from the president; there was no race card to complicate matters.) Eventually, in June 2014, the Supreme Court unanimously invalidated the president's January 2012 recess appointments. This judicial spanking of the president was both foreseeable and avoidable. As events were unfolding, Noah and I had shown how Reid and Obama could have bulletproofed or at least buttressed these recess appointments, and in the process could have highlighted that the real problem was not a dictatorial president but a dysfunctional Senate.

And speaking of dysfunction. . . . Although most of the essays in this chapter place the Senate under the constitutional microscope, the modern House of Representatives has also been an interesting and sometimes ugly place. Some of the most embarrassing constitutional moments occurred when the House in the late 1990s voted to impeach Bill Clinton in partisan fashion—the subject of a series of essays later in this book. In the current chapter, I have included only one essay on House dysfunction, focusing on a 2012 episode in which House Republicans proved themselves every bit as disappointing as Senate Democrats had been in the 2008–2009 Burris matter.

Here, too, the controversy centered on congressional power and procedure—in this case, the source, scope, and limits of the House's power to subpoena witnesses and to "hold" various witnesses in "contempt" for misconduct in congressional hearings. Here, too, some of the constitutional answers to the questions of the hour lay not in the past decisions of the Supreme Court, but in the basic structure of the Constitution itself and in the history of prior Congresses stretching all the way back to the Founders.

Here, too, the situation combined complex racial optics and crass partisanship, as another prominent black man—America's first African American attorney general, Eric Holder—found himself pitted against another awkwardly monochromatic set of white congressional leaders, this time epitomized by a hard-driving House Republican, Darrell Issa. This time, however, the black man at the center of the storm was, unlike Burris, a man of recognized rectitude.

Alas, in neither episode did Congress shine. Burris got far better congressional treatment than he deserved; Holder, far worse.

WHEN THE BURRIS episode arose in early 2009, Majority Leader Reid was hostile to major filibuster reform. But by November 2013, Reid was willing to embrace what had come to be called, in the course of many years of debate over the uses and misuses of the filibuster, the "nuclear option"—a procedural tactic empowering a simple Senate majority to curtail or even eliminate dilatory minority tactics. Specifically, in late 2013 Reid was willing to push through a dramatic version of this option—eliminating the filibuster rule for an important subset of Senate actions, doing so by a simple majority vote, and muscling this through on an ordinary day in the middle of the legislative term rather than on the first day of a new legislative session.

What had happened to change Reid's mind and the minds of fifty-plus other Senate Democrats? I'd like to think that one contributing factor was my journalistic intervention via pop essays in 2011 and 2013, essays that now appear in the middle of this chapter. These two pieces offered an entirely new set of constitutional arguments for how and why the Senate should "go nuclear."

The first piece, "How to End the Filibuster Forever," was originally published in *Slate* on January 6, 2011, just after a freshly elected House had convened on January 3 to kick off the 112th Congress. During the preceding month, talk was in the air that the Senate might use the January 3 opening day to modify that chamber's rules of debate. Many journalists and scholars had suggested that the Senate could indeed change its rules on opening day, and could do so by simple majority vote, but could do so *only* on opening day—only, that is, at the start of a new Congress. My *Slate* piece was designed to show that these pundits were precisely wrong. Contrary to conventional wisdom, the Senate could change the rules on any day, not just Day One, and thus, I suggested, reformers should keep up the pressure throughout the 112th Congress.

This was a new move in the debate over the filibuster, and it had dramatic implications. Recall the Burris fiasco of 2009. One reason that Reid was disinclined to attempt filibuster reform in January 2009 was that on opening day of the 111th Congress, he did not completely control the Senate. Pursuant to the Constitution's Twentieth Amendment, the lame-duck Republican vice president, Dick Cheney, was in the chair as the new Congress convened on January 3; and Cheney had a right to remain in the chair until January 20, at which point the newly inaugurated Democrat, Joe Biden, could take over. And the conventional wisdom in 2009 was that major filibuster reform could occur only on Day One, January 3, via a parliamentary maneuver that was widely believed to require the cooperation of the Senate chair—the vice president. But this was, as I later insisted, exactly the wrong way to think about how filibuster reform can lawfully occur.

The Senate is a body that reveres tradition. In 2009, Reid may also have believed that the filibuster was a basic Founding principle and practice, deeply rooted in the oldest traditions of the Senate, even if not in the Constitution's formal text. This is what many others believed in 2009, both in and out of the Senate. But this is a canard, as the 2011 *Slate* piece showed, and as I later elaborated elsewhere.[3] The framers believed in Senate majority rule as a basic premise of their system.

Two simple questions for anyone who doubts this. One: Can you name any important bill that was filibustered to death prior to the Civil War? Two: If simple majorities did not rule in the antebellum Senate, then why was the Compromise of 1850, giving free states the slimmest of majorities over slave states in the Senate, such a big deal?

Although nothing nuclearish happened in the 112th Congress, the *Slate* essay began to circulate among various senators and staffers, and some minds began to change. Having a highly respected alumnus of the Senate, Gary Hart, as my *Slate* coauthor had measurably enhanced the credibility of this piece, and the mere mention of his name opened more than a few doors in Senate office buildings as I occasionally made the rounds in DC and pitched my ideas to any and all who would listen.

When the 113th Congress convened and once again did nothing on opening day—January 3, 2013—I once again ran a mid-January essay explaining the underlying logic of the nuclear option. This time, I published in *Roll Call*—a periodical targeted directly at senators and staffers. My basic message was the same: Reform could happen any day, so reformers should keep pushing throughout the session.

In truth, I doubted that anything would happen anytime soon. But boy, was I wrong. On November 21, 2013, Reid went nuclear, and did so using my theory: Backed by almost every Senate Democrat, he changed the filibuster rules by simple majority (52–48), and on an ordinary day as opposed to an opening day. Although his reform applied only to certain appointments, the precedent has now been established in actual Senate practice as opposed to mere academic theory. On any future day, the Senate can extend Reid's reform to any other aspect of Senate business, including ordinary legislation. We now live in a nuclear world, and there is no going back.

As I made clear in the final essay in this chapter, which I posted online within hours of hearing the stunning news about Reid's turnabout, the rules that apply when Democrats are in control must surely apply equally whenever Republicans are in charge. I helped the governing Senate Democrats go nuclear in 2013, and I will now gladly help the governing Senate Republicans stay nuclear. Indeed, I hope the Republicans will eventually go further than Reid by applying his 2013 precedent to all appointments and also to legislation.

Which brings me back to a major theme of this book: Although all the essays collected in this volume were written on deadline, with one eye on the minute hand and the latest unfolding events, the analysis was designed to endure over the long haul. Senate majority rule is a basic constitutional principle. It applied at the Founding; it applies today; and (unless the Constitution is amended) it will apply a century hence. The rules for Democrats in 2013 must be the same for Republicans in 2016 and for whichever party is in power hereafter. That is what keeps us all honest. The genius of our constitutional project is precisely that it obliges principled constitutionalists to process the issues du jour by thinking far back and far ahead.*

---

*Although the issue of majority rule is most obviously implicated in the three essays in this chapter directly addressing filibuster reform, it is worth reemphasizing that both the Burris fiasco and the recess appointment flap occurred in obvious response to the modern Senate's feckless departures from majority rule. Today's upper chamber is far too indulgent of routine filibustering and other routine forms of minority obstructionism. Burris was wrongly seated in order to get to sixty Senate votes, when fifty-one Senate votes were all that should have been necessary for ordinary Senate business. Likewise, Obama used aggressive recess appointments tactics in response to dysfunctional Senate rules allowing Senate minorities to thwart Senate majority rule across the board in the appointments context.

The most notable House dysfunction highlighted in this chapter is precisely the opposite tendency of the lower chamber to be hyper-majoritarian and

HOW THE SENATE CAN STOP BLAGOJEVICH

SLATE, WEDNESDAY, DECEMBER 31, 2008, 6:23 P.M. (ET)
(WITH JOSH CHAFETZ)

Does the Constitution allow the Senate to refuse to seat Roland Burris, Illinois Governor Rod Blagojevich's surprise appointee? In a word, yes. Here's why.

Following English parliamentary tradition and early colonial and state practice, the framers made the Senate its own gatekeeper and guardian. Each house of Congress is "the Judge of the Elections, Returns, and Qualifications of its own members," according to Article I, section 5, of the Constitution. At the Founding, senators were elected by state legislatures. If the Senate believed that legislators in a given state had been bribed into voting for a particular candidate, the Senate could refuse to seat him.

Because of the word "returns" in section 5, what is true of elected senators is equally true of appointed senators. According to the *Oxford English Dictionary*, a "return" in the time of the framers involved a report of an appointment made by a sheriff or other official. If the Senate may refuse to seat a person picked in a corrupt election, it likewise may refuse to seat a person picked in a corrupt appointment process. (Alternatively, we might think of an appointment as an "election" by one voter.)

A simple majority of the Senate would suffice to exclude Burris. Majority rule is the general default principle established by the Constitution, except where text, structure, or tradition indicates otherwise. When the Senate tries to expel a misbehaving member who has already been seated, the rule is two-thirds, as it is when the Senate sits as an impeachment court. But the framers clearly understood that simple majority rule would apply when the Senate was judging the accuracy and fairness of elections or appointments.

---

hyper-partisan—even when the written Constitution expressly provides for a super-majoritarian rule (which protects the minority party), as that document in fact does provide in the impeachment context. No Senate can convict an impeachment defendant without a two-thirds vote; and a constitutionally sensitive House of Representatives should internalize this basic fact in pondering possible politicized impeachments that lack bipartisan and supermajoritarian support. This is one of the key points of this chapter's essay on Darrell Issa and Eric Holder, and this key point is further elaborated in the chapter 8 essays on the ill-advised, hyper-partisan, insufficiently supermajoritarian impeachment crusade against President Bill Clinton in the late 1990s.

The power to judge elections and returns has been used on countless occasions in American history, at both the state and federal level, to exclude
candidates whose elections and appointments were suspect.

Specifically, the Senate has been called upon to judge the return of an
appointed senator at least twice. In 1893 the Montana legislature adjourned
without electing a senator. After the adjournment, Governor John E. Rich-
ards appointed Lee Mantle to fill the vacant seat, using as his justification
that the (pre-Seventeenth Amendment) Constitution provided that, "if Vacancies happen by Resignation, or otherwise, during the Recess of the Legislature of any State, the Executive thereof may make temporary Appointments
until the next Meeting of the Legislature, which shall then fill such Vacancies." By a narrow three-vote margin, the Senate determined that a vacancy
that the legislature had known about and failed to fill was not the sort of
vacancy that the governor was empowered to fill. Mantle was, accordingly,
denied the seat.

In 1913, just after the Seventeenth Amendment had been ratified, Senator Joseph Johnston of Alabama died. The Alabama legislature was in recess,
and the governor appointed Frank Glass to fill the vacancy. The last provision of the Seventeenth Amendment reads, "This amendment shall not be
so construed as to affect the election or term of any Senator chosen before it
becomes valid as part of the Constitution." If the amendment was operative
with regard to the Alabama seat, then the appointment of Glass was unconstitutional, as the seat would have to be filled by special election; if, however, the amendment was not yet operative, then Glass was entitled to the
seat. The Senate determined that Glass was not entitled to the seat, because,
while the amendment did not affect the length of any senator's term, the
vacancy provision became operative immediately upon ratification. Glass
was not seated, and the seat was filled by special election.

True, in the 1969 case of *Powell v. McCormack*, the Supreme Court properly held that the Constitution imposes limits on the power of the Senate
and the House to exclude members. Some legal commentators say this decision trumps the Senate's power to exclude Burris. But the letter and spirit of
Powell actually cut against Burris. The case involved an elected congressman,
Adam Clayton Powell, whom the voters had clearly chosen in a fair election
and whom the House nevertheless excluded—wrongly, the Court held. The
key fact is that there was no doubt whatsoever that Powell was the people's
choice, and in issuing its ruling, the Warren Court repeatedly stressed this.
The justices insisted that their ruling was aimed at protecting the people's

right to vote. None of that spirit applies here. And that's why the case doesn't stand in the Senate's way now.

Powell also said that each house could "judge" the qualifications laid out in the Constitution (such as age) but could not make up new qualifications. Thus, if the Senate were to plausibly decide in good faith that a candidate failed to meet the Constitution's age requirement, *Powell* nowhere suggests that this senatorial determination should be set aside by ordinary federal courts. For similar reasons, federal courts should not interfere when the Senate plausibly and in good faith decides an election or return to be improper or corrupt. The critical point here is that the Constitution itself sets up the Senate as the highest court of Senate elections. When the Senate speaks as this court, its adjudications are legal judgments that no other court may properly reopen. If the Senate convicts a federal judge in an impeachment court, no other federal court may properly interfere. So, too, for Senate elections and returns.

What are the counterarguments in favor of seating Burris? Both he and Blagojevich say that the Senate should not hold the governor's sins against his would-be senator. To be sure, there is no evidence Burris bribed the governor to get this seat. But imagine if Burris had won election only because other candidates were wrongly and corruptly kept off the ballot. Surely the Senate could properly deem this an invalid election. Similarly, it now seems apparent that there were candidates that Blagojevich refused to consider for improper reasons—because one refused to "pay to play" early on, or because another is at the center of the impending criminal case against the governor. With the appointments process so inherently and irremediably tainted, the Senate may properly decide that nothing good can come from a Blagojevich appointment.

(And let's not feel too sorry for Burris, who, it must be said, has shown dubious judgment in accepting the nomination, given the circumstances. Weeks ago, Senate leaders announced that no Blagojevich appointee would be allowed to sit. What is Burris thinking? Many other arguably better candidates doubtless refused to have any dealings with Blagojevich once his crimes came to light; Burris got his shot at the Senate at their expense.)

Nor does it matter, from the Senate's point of view, that Blagojevich hasn't yet been convicted. In this context, the Senate itself is a judge, in the words of the Constitution, and can decide facts for itself. It need not follow the rules of criminal courts. That means it need not find Blagojevich guilty beyond reasonable doubt, as a court would need to find if his liberty were in jeopardy. It is enough for the Senate to reject Blagojevich's appointee if a majority of senators are firmly convinced that Blagojevich is corrupt and that any nomination he might make is inherently tainted by such corruption.

Houses of Congress have, in the past, found that certain elections were so systemically tainted that the returned member should not be seated. For example, in 1854, it was alleged that the election for a (nonvoting) territorial delegate from Kansas was disrupted "by an armed invading force" from Missouri—the beginning of the "Bleeding Kansas" episode in American history. A congressional committee determined that, under the conditions then existing in Kansas, "a fair election could not be held," and the returned delegate was not seated. More sweepingly, in the mid-1860s the Reconstruction House and Senate famously refused to seat various putative southern senators and representatives who had been elected under conditions that the Reconstruction House and Senate deemed utterly unfair and undemocratic.[4]

To make sure its ruling sticks, the Senate should follow its own procedures with due deliberation. Burris's case can be referred to a committee for careful review. He need not be seated while this committee does its work, and it will be very hard for Burris to persuade any federal judge to interfere in the meantime, especially if Senate Democrats and Republicans unite. With any luck, Blagojevich will be out of office soon enough and a new appointments process (or a special election) can begin that would supersede the attempted Burris appointment.

Finally, the Senate can bulletproof its vote to exclude Burris by adopting an anticipatory "sense of the Senate" resolution declaring that if Burris were ever to take the matter to a federal court and prevail, the Senate would immediately expel him. Expulsion would ultimately require a two-thirds vote. If two-thirds of the Senate is ready to vote against Burris now, an anticipatory resolution would discourage him from going to court in the first place. It would also discourage any activist judges who might be tempted by his case. Whether to seat Burris is the Senate's call: It easily has the brute power—and the constitutional right—to stop Blagojevich.

HOW TO END THE FILIBUSTER FOREVER[5]

SLATE, THURSDAY, JANUARY 6, 2011, 2:11 P.M. (ET) (WITH GARY HART)

Is the United States Senate like Cinderella—does it have the power to transform itself in only one limited moment, at the opening of the new Congress?

That is one of the two big questions in the filibuster-reform debate that is now taking center stage in the Senate. The other is whether the Senate can change the filibuster rule by a simple majority vote, regardless of what the rule itself seems to say. The short answers to these questions are that there are no magic moments in the Senate and no need to muster sixty votes to repeal the filibuster rule. The upper house has the clear constitutional authority to end the filibuster by simple majority vote on any day it chooses.

Let's address the timing question first. Magical things happen to Cinderella on a special day before the clock strikes twelve. According to the editorial board of the *New York Times* and other commentators, the time window every other year in January when the old Congress ends and a new one begins is similarly special. The idea is that only at this magical moment may a simple majority of the Senate lawfully modify the filibuster rules that in recent years have effectively required sixty votes for any important action in the upper house.

The *Times* and others are right about the power of the simple majority—more about why in a minute—but wrong about the Cinderella power of the Senate's opening day. A simple majority of determined senators may lawfully change the filibuster rules, even if the existing Senate rules say otherwise, *at any time*.

The confusion arises from missing the basic difference between the House and the Senate. Constitutionally, the House is indeed an entirely new body at the beginning of every odd year. The old House legally dies and a wholly new House springs to life. A thirty-year veteran who has been speaker for the last decade is no more already a member of the new House than is an incoming freshman.

Thus, Day One of a new House is indeed a special moment. Who organizes the House on Day One? Who sits in the chair and who guards the doors? Who decides who decides? All of this and more is up for grabs, and the new House must quickly adopt various procedural and parliamentary rules in its opening moments—which is why John Boehner can needle the Democrats by tweaking a lot of rules that applied in the previous House but do not automatically carry over into the new one.

But ever since the Founding, the Senate has been very different from the House on almost everything related to Day One. Indeed, the Constitution carefully structured the Senate precisely to ensure that the upper house, unlike the lower house, would never turn over all at once. Thus two-thirds of the Senate's members remain in their seats after an election, and at any single moment the vast majority of senators are typically duly seated holdovers.

Unlike the House, the Senate need not begin its session by approving procedural rules. The internal Senate rule allowing filibusters—Senate Rule 22—is not approved biennially at the outset of each new congressional term. Rather, this old rule, initially adopted by the Senate in the 1910s and significantly revised in the 1970s, simply carries over from one Congress to the next by inertia, since the Senate is a continuing body. Similarly, on Day One in the Senate, no leadership elections need occur. The old Senate's leaders simply continue in place, and the Senate can oust the old leaders at any time—by a simple majority vote. The same goes for old rules, including the filibuster rule. It's that simple.

But why can the Senate change the sixty-vote rule with only fifty-one votes? On its face, Rule 22 says otherwise. It provides that any motion to change it cannot be voted on unless a supermajority of senators agrees to end debate. Thus, the rule seems to block a simple Senate majority from first amending Rule 22 itself and then proceeding to pass a given bill. That's some catch, that catch-22.

But the catch-22 in fact makes Rule 22 unconstitutional, which means a simple majority of the Senate may at any time choose to ignore it. This big idea is what's now making the rounds in Washington, DC.

The principle that each chamber of Congress acts by majority rule unless the Constitution otherwise specifies was a self-evident truth for the Founders. As John Locke had explained in his canonical *Second Treatise of Government*, majority rule was the natural default principle of all assemblies: "In assemblies impowered to act by positive laws, where no number is set by that positive law which impowers them, the act of the majority passes for the act of the whole and, of course, determines, as having by the law of nature and reason the power of the whole." Building on Locke, Thomas Jefferson's mid-1780s booklet, *Notes on the State of Virginia*, declared that rule by simple majority "is the natural law of every assembly of men, whose numbers are not fixed by any other law." In written remarks read aloud to the Philadelphia Convention in 1787, Benjamin Franklin described majority rule as "the Common Practice of Assemblies in all Countries and Ages." None of his fellow delegates said otherwise. When state ratification conventions decided whether to adopt the Constitution in 1787–1788, nothing in the text specified that they should act by simple majority rule, but this is what every convention did, and in a manner that suggested that this was self-evident.

The Founders wove the majoritarian default rule into the fabric of the Constitution. Whenever the document authorized a federal institution to make a certain decision using some principle *other* than simple majority rule, the exception was specified in the document itself. Several of the Constitution's provisions prescribing supermajorities make little sense unless we assume that majority rule was the self-evident default rule.

Thus, Article I presupposed that each house would pass bills by majority vote—except when trying to override presidential vetoes, which would require a *special* supermajority. If the Senate may entrench (that is, enact and insulate from simple majoritarian repeal) a rule that sixty votes are required to pass a given bill, it could likewise entrench a rule that seventy votes are required. But such a rule would plainly violate the letter and logic of Article I, section 7, which provides that a two-thirds majority always suffices in the Senate, even when the president vetoes a particular bill. Surely it follows that something less than a two-thirds vote suffices in the absence of a veto. And that something is simple majority rule.

The supermajorities for constitutional amendments likewise were designed to be *more demanding* than the simple majorities for ordinary statutes, and the Senate supermajority for treaty ratification was meant to erect a *higher* bar than Senate agreement to ordinary legislation (a higher bar meant to offset the absence of the House in the formal treaty-making process). Similarly, the *exceptional* supermajority rule that applied when a chamber sought to expel properly elected and eligible members is distinct from the simple majority required to exclude improperly elected or constitutionally ineligible candidates.

In an effort to parry this basic argument, some scholars have asked why, if majority rule truly went without saying, the framers felt the need to specify, as they did in Article I, that a majority of each house would constitute a quorum. The obvious answer is that state constitutions and British practice varied widely on the quorum question, and thus there was no obvious default rule from universal usage.

For example, Pennsylvania set the quorum bar at two-thirds, whereas the English rule since the 1640s had provided that any forty members could constitute a quorum of the House of Commons. But neither Parliament nor any state in 1787 generally required more than simple house majority votes for the passage of bills or the adoption of internal house procedures, even though in many of these states no explicit clause explicitly specified this voting rule. In America in 1787, majority rule in these contexts thus truly did go without saying.

It has also been noted that the Constitution's electoral college clauses speak of the need for a majority vote. In this context, involving *candidate* elections, majority rule did not go without saying as the obvious and only default rule. Plurality rule furnished a salient alternative (and indeed the rule that even today remains the dominant one for candidate contests in America). But this point about candidate elections did not apply to the enactment of house rules or the exclusion of members under Article I, section 5, or the enactment of laws under Article I, section 7—all of which involved binary decisions against the status quo, and all of which are properly governed by majority rule.

From the Founding to the present, the majority-rule principle has always governed the House of Representatives and the Supreme Court. Five votes trump four on today's high court, and in the House, 218 beats 217. (Court tradition allows a minority of four justices to define the preliminary Court agenda, but this "rule of four" exists in the shadow of majority rule on the Court. At any time, a Court majority could change the "rule of four" and even without amending the rule, a simple Court majority may dismiss at any time any case that four members have placed on the Court's docket.)

There is nothing in the Constitution that suggests the Senate is any different. And throughout the Founding era, the Senate practiced and preached majority rule. Senate history prior to the 1830s offers no big examples of organized and obstructionist filibustering—and absolutely nothing like a pattern of systematic, self-perpetuating, entrenched frustration of Senate-majority rule. As Jefferson wrote as vice president and the Senate's presiding officer, "No one is to speak impertinently or beside the question, superfluously or tediously. . . . The voice of the majority decides."

Even as Senate minorities began to develop stalling tactics by the mid-nineteenth century, they typically did so with the indulgence of the Senate majority. Long-winded speechifying occasionally delayed the Senate's business without preventing majorities from ending debate at some point and taking a vote. The Senate was smaller and had less business to transact in those days, and it often indulged individual senators as a matter of courtesy. In turn, the indulged senators did not routinely try to press their privileges so as to prevent Senate majorities from governing. According to one expert treatise, before the 1880s "almost every obstructed measure was eventually passed despite filibustering opposition."

Only in the late twentieth and early twenty-first centuries has the filibuster metastasized into a rule requiring a sixty-vote supermajority for every important piece of Senate business. Over the years, the Senate has flirted with getting rid of Rule 22, the root of the trouble, but never pulled it off. Perhaps the most noteworthy attempt occurred in 1975, when a majority of the Senate upheld a constitutional ruling of the vice president—sitting in the presiding chair—that a simple majority could end debate on filibuster reform and scrap the old rule. Shortly thereafter, however, the Senate voted to reconsider its earlier action. In 2005, Republican senators frustrated by the success of the Democratic minority in blocking votes on various judicial nominations loudly threatened to revise the old filibuster rule by a simple majority vote—the so-called nuclear option. But this never came to a conclusive floor vote. Instead, Democrats moderated their obstructionism and Republicans stowed their nukes.

So where does all this leave us today? Here is one clean way of pulling together the basic argument: It is obvious that the Senate must use some specific voting rule for setting its own rules for proceeding—a rule for how to vote on how to vote. If majority rule is not that implicit rule, what is? Especially since that is the rule the Senate used at the start, in 1789. Just as the first House and the first Senate each used majority rule to decide its procedures, every subsequent House and Senate may and must do the same, for nothing in the Constitution made the Congress of 1789 king over later Congresses. Our founding document makes all Congresses equal in this respect.

In fact, neither house has ever formally prescribed a supermajority rule for formal amendment of its rules. Not even Senate Rule 22 has the audacity to openly assert that it cannot be repealed by simple majority vote. Rather, the filibuster rule says that *debate* on its own repeal cannot be ended this way. If Rule 22 simply means that it should not be repealed without a fair opportunity to debate the repeal, then it is fully valid. But insofar as Rule 22 allows repeal opponents to stall interminably so as to prevent a majoritarian vote from ever being held, then Rule 22 unconstitutionally entrenches supermajority rule. It's a question for each senator to decide for him- or herself—and then to act on, by simple majority rule, just as the framers intended.

HOW TO RESOLVE THE
RECESS APPOINTMENT CRISIS

NEW REPUBLIC, JANUARY 6, 2012, 12:00 A.M. (ET)
(WITH TIMOTHY NOAH)

Earlier this week, President Obama made several recess appointments, in effect making an independent judgment that the Senate is in recess. Senate Republicans howled in indignation that the Senate is *not* in recess; they'd pressured the Democratic majority to keep the Senate technically in session in order to prevent the president from appointing Richard Cordray (or anyone) director of the Consumer Financial Protection Bureau. (Cordray was one of the people Obama appointed yesterday.)

In the past, the question of what's a Senate recess and what isn't has been worked out through agreements between the executive branch and the Senate. If the constitutional problem with Obama's appointments is that they depart from this tradition, why not get the Senate—which, after all, has a Democratic majority—to sign on?

Senate Majority Leader Harry Reid has said he supports Cordray's appointment to the CFPB, which implicitly means that Reid thinks the president is acting within his constitutional powers. Given the Senate's elaborate system of parliamentary checks on the power of the majority—most significantly, the much-abused filibuster—it's unlikely Reid could pass a resolution formally stating the Senate's agreement that it is in recess. But perhaps the Senate doesn't need to act in any official capacity. Perhaps a letter would suffice, signed by fifty-one senators stating that the president is entitled to make a recess appointment when the Senate actively denies him that constitutional power through procedural gimmicks—gimmicks defined however they like, or not defined at all, if they prefer.

It might be argued that Senate Minority Leader Mitch McConnell would immediately launch a judicial challenge to such a handshake deal between the Senate majority and the president. But in *Byrd v. Raines* the Supreme Court ruled in 1997 that no member of the Senate minority has standing in federal court in such matters; in situations like this, the Senate must bring suit as a whole or not at all. It's true that, say, a nonbank bank regulated by the CFPB might bring suit, alleging that some action against it is not legal because the CFPB does not have a lawfully appointed director. But would such a nonbank have any genuine right of its own to complain about—apart from the (possible) violation of the rights of the Senate? If not, it's not entirely clear that any entity other than the Senate as a whole would or should be allowed to go to court.

A private letter of the sort we are proposing would have several advantages and implications. First, it would serve to limit the precedent of presidential adventurism in the Cordray affair, by making clear that the president in this case was not really defying or circumventing the Senate, but actually facilitating the preferences of the Senate majority itself. Second, it would be an opportunity for senators to accept responsibility by actually doing something rather than ducking responsibility by doing nothing at all—which the Senate of late has turned into an art form.

Third, it would be a measured move in the direction of filibuster reform—not across the board, not even in all cases involving appointments, but just in situations involving recess appointments. When Republicans controlled the Senate they loudly threatened to use "the nuclear option"—to destroy certain filibusters by a parliamentary maneuver that required only a simple majority vote of the Senate as a whole. Here, Senate Democrats would be doing the same thing, but on a smaller scale (involving only recess appointments). Such a move might be less likely, marginally, to enrage the other side. Call it a tactical nuke.

So get to it, Senator Reid. Fifty-one signatures is all you need.

THREATENING HOLDER WITH CONTEMPT IS JUST CHEAP TALK[6]

DAILY BEAST, FRIDAY, JUNE 22, 2012

The duel between Darrell Issa and Eric Holder is the latest chapter in a checks-and-balances story that traces back to an epic 1796 showdown between James Madison and George Washington. Courts should stay clear of this duel. Its proper umpires are not life-tenured judges, but ordinary citizens.

Congressman Issa, backed by fellow Republicans in a key House Oversight Committee (and only by Republicans—more on that later), is demanding that Attorney General Holder produce Justice Department documents that Issa believes will evidence executive-branch bungling and/or dishonesty. In particular, Issa wants documents that explain why Holder and his aides originally offered erroneous testimony to Congress and then later decided to retract that testimony.

Holder is resisting Issa, claiming that he needs to protect internal executive-branch deliberations. Much as justices need to confer confidentially among themselves and with their clerks before issuing their official court opinions, executive-branch officials need some confidential space to candidly formulate executive-branch policy. If these conversations can easily be subpoenaed and publicized by a separate branch, candor within the executive branch will suffer. Officials will end up whispering to each other secretly rather than using e-mails and memos, and the ultimate policy may end up being less carefully considered.

This isn't just Holder's view; the president himself has officially invoked "executive privilege" to resist the latest round of subpoenas.

So who is right? The explicit words of the Constitution itself don't provide clear answers. The terse text nowhere explicitly provides for "executive privilege"—and also nowhere explicitly provides for congressional "oversight" as such. The text does not even say that Congress has power to subpoena witnesses or punish no-shows.

But the Constitution's overall structure and two centuries of traditional practice do provide strong guidance. Beginning with the First Congress, each house has asserted broad inherent power—that is, unenumerated power, implicit power, the kind of power that "strict constructionists" and Tea Party types claim the federal government lacks entirely—to oversee the functioning of the executive branch, backed by the implicit power to issue subpoenas and to hold noncompliant witnesses in contempt. On the other side of the ledger, when James Madison and other House leaders demanded that the Washington administration hand over various diplomacy-related documents for inspection in 1796, Washington refused, and the House backed down, establishing an early precedent in favor of executive privilege in certain situations.

Washington prevailed in 1796 because he ultimately had public opinion on his side. And in the Issa-Holder duel, public opinion should and will ultimately decide the matter.

One important element of this duel, however, is not currently well understood by the public: What, exactly, does it mean to "hold" someone "in contempt"? For example, many of Holder's supporters doubtless hold Issa in contempt, in a manner of speaking. But if Issa is ultimately backed by Speaker John Boehner and a majority of the House, then the House is legally empowered to hold a defiant witness in contempt in a far more literal way: the House may *hold* a witness in its *hold*—in a prison cell in the Capitol itself. The House can keep the witness there, using its own enforcer—its "sergeant at arms"—until the House session ends. In fact, each house of Congress exercised this power early on in our nation's history.

But if Issa and Boehner tried to hold Holder, the optics would be ugly, and Mr. Chairman and Mr. Speaker would risk alienating fair-minded voters. Also, no House has ever tried to hold the president himself—commander in chief of the U.S. Army—or a cabinet officer. And any House attempt to hold Holder would be particularly awkward, as it would effectively undo an appointment made by the president and the Senate—an appointment process in which the Constitution pointedly excludes the House itself.

Issa and Boehner are not, however—at least not yet—threatening to lay hands on Holder. Instead they want to issue a "contempt citation" against Holder that will supposedly oblige Justice Department prosecutors to begin a process of judicial punishment of Holder.

But this is all just cheap talk. The attorney general and all lower-level U.S. attorneys in the Justice Department are executive-branch officials who ultimately answer not to Issa or Boehner or the House sergeant at arms—but to the chief executive, Barack Obama, who has already made clear that he sides with Holder. So the attorney general and all other prosecutors in the Justice Department are entitled to disregard the House "contempt citation." The paper has no more authority than a competing piece of paper written by Holder saying "I have contempt for Issa and Boehner."

Ultimately, courts should stay out of this knife fight altogether. This is a legislative-executive tussle—a classic "political question" beyond the proper province of the judiciary. For the Constitution gives Congress itself the means necessary to deal with a dishonest and/or corrupt cabinet officer. It's called impeachment.

But if Boehner and Issa do pursue this constitutionally proper path, then their failure to attract any support from their Democratic colleagues may ultimately doom their efforts. Even a House impeachment means nothing— just more cheap talk—unless the Senate actually convicts. And this conviction requires a two-thirds vote, a vote that cannot happen unless Senate Democrats turn on Holder. So if Boehner and Issa are serious, they must either convince some Democratic colleagues to join their crusade or persuade the great middle of the country, comprising millions of fair-minded voters, that there are real witches here that need to be hunted.

FILIBUSTER REFORM MADE SIMPLE[7]

ROLL CALL, TUESDAY, JANUARY 22, 2013

A simple question: Is the Senate a continuing body? It turns out the answer is not so simple. Getting the right answer matters for sensible filibuster reform in the weeks ahead.

Many who want an overhaul of the filibuster have assumed that changes can occur at the outset of a new Congress because a special constitutional window opens when the "old" Senate ends and a "new"—discontinuous—Senate begins. Filibuster supporters have cried foul. In their view, the Senate is a smoothly continuous body—it does not begin anew biennially—and thus no magic Senate window exists at the outset of a new Congress. Each side is partly right and partly wrong.

For some purposes, the Senate is surely a continuing body. Whereas the incoming House of Representatives had to affirmatively vote for John A. Boehner as its speaker, no similar drama unfolded in the Senate: Senators Harry Reid and Patrick J. Leahy continued in place as majority leader and president pro tempore purely by inertia, with no fuss or fanfare.

For other purposes, however, the Senate is not a continuing body. All the bills that passed the Senate before January 3 went poof as the clock chimed midnight. Most obviously, the $60 billion Superstorm Sandy relief package approved by the Senate in late December turned to dust at the witching hour. Thus a new relief bill had to be affirmatively re-passed by the new Senate, alongside the new House.

So the correct answer to our simple yes-or-no question is yes *and* no. Law often works this way. For example, are corporations persons? Yes and no. Surely yes, for some purposes: Government cannot deprive a corporation of its property without due process. But for other purposes, corporations are properly not treated as persons. The axiom of one person, one vote applies only to flesh and blood.

The House is obviously not a continuing body. Every two years its entire membership comes before the voters, who are free to choose a completely new slate. Legally, no House member holds over from one House to the next. Because each House begins anew biennially, all House legislative bills legally expire when that House expires and a new House arises to replace it. In the spirit of bicameral symmetry and coordination, the same rules about legislative bills sensibly apply to the Senate: All Senate bills die when one

Congress ends and a new one begins. Such has been the practice since the Founding.

But on matters other than bicameral lawmaking, the Constitution generally allows each chamber to govern itself, and neither need mirror the other. The House must choose its leaders and its own internal rules of procedure at the outset of each new Congress because all its members have been freshly elected by the voters. By contrast, only a third of the Senate's membership comes before the voters in any given election, so this chamber can simply allow its internal procedures and its internal leadership to continue by inertia.

Which brings us to filibuster reform. The old Senate's rules permitting filibusters carry forward by inertia. Of course, they can be changed when a new Congress begins, but they can also be changed on any other day—just as the Senate leadership can be changed at any time.

But there is at least one basic constitutional principle that cannot be changed: majority rule. The Constitution makes no sense without this rule as the implicit backdrop. Constitutional amendments require supermajorities precisely because ordinary statutes do not; overruling a president's veto requires a two-thirds vote of each house precisely because passing an ordinary law requires something less, namely, a simple majority.

Notably, the Senate's existing filibuster rules do not themselves purport to require a supermajority vote to change them. But they do purport to require a supermajority vote to end debate on the question of a filibuster overhaul.

To counter this catch-22, the Senate must insist that its own rules of debate stay within their constitutional bounds and do not unconstitutionally morph into entrenched supermajority voting rules. Thus, the Senate on any future day may decide that filibuster overhaul opponents are actually preventing filibuster changes from ever coming to a vote and have thereby transformed a proper rule of debate into an unconstitutional supermajority rule of decision. In response, a simple majority of the Senate can rule any filibuster out of order, as a violation of constitutional first principles.

Those who want a filibuster overhaul should not concede (as many appear wont to) that whatever rule changes or reinterpretations they are able to accomplish this January are the only changes that may be made during the 113th Congress. And filibuster supporters, for their part, need to reacquaint themselves with the basic small-r republican principle of majority rule. Unless the Constitution itself explicitly specifies otherwise, as it does for veto overrides, impeachment trials, and so on, the Senate always—every day—

operates by ultimate majority rule. Every Senate rule and procedure must be amendable by a determined Senate majority, if that determined majority deems the old rule unsuitable. It's just that simple.

THE NUCLEAR-OPTION GENIE
IS OUT OF THE BOTTLE

SLATE, THURSDAY, NOVEMBER 21, 2013, 5:38 P.M. (ET)

Today's vote to restore majority rule in the Senate is politically earth-shaking. The principle that a simple majority of truly determined Senators may properly modify filibuster rules on any day—and not just on one magic day at the beginning of a new congressional term—has now been firmly established in actual Senate practice, and there is no going back. The nuclear-option genie is now out of the bottle.

The filibuster-reform vote applies only to certain nominations—Supreme Court slots are not covered—but tomorrow (or any day thereafter) the Senate is free to sweep in the Supreme Court confirmation votes, or ordinary legislative votes, or anything else. When the Republicans next control the Senate—and of course one day, they will—they, too, will be free to insist on simple majority rule. What goes around comes around.

The current Democratic majority would thus be wise to allow minority Republicans very broad (but not endless) freedom of speech, as a matter of courtesy and comity; everyone should get to speak, and then all should get to vote. If the Democrats govern the Senate with a kinder, gentler version of majority rule than do the House Republicans, today will rightly be seen by future Americans as one of the great days in the history of the republic.

Oh, and by the way, you heard it here—first!—in *Slate*: the constitutional theory undergirding today's vote initially appeared way back in January 2011, in a piece that I co-wrote with former senator Gary Hart.

4

THE JUDICIARY

Who Judges the Judges?

SUPREME COURT JUSTICES have high-paying, high-status, life-tenured jobs. Most journalists get paid less and have far less secure employment situations. Members of Congress and even presidents resemble journalists insofar as they, too, lack lifetime job security. Congresspersons are never far from an election whose result could send them packing, and no president can stay in office for more than a decade. Like journalists, elected politicians thus cannot afford to ignore the short term. They, too, are on deadline.

The Supreme Court's justices have considerable discretion in defining their agenda. They pick the cases that they will hear, guided by their understanding that their basic mission is to correct certain kinds of mistakes that have been made by other parts of government, and especially by lower courts. But what happens when the justices themselves goof? Who judges the top judges?

Not the journalists. Or, to put my point more modestly, not just the journalists. As this book has repeatedly sought to emphasize, in the complex encounter between journalism and constitutionalism, professional journalists generally lack the time, the temperament, and the training to do all that needs to be done to keep the constitutional system honest. Even professional journalists who do have legal training are typically not general constitutional scholars.

If not the fourth estate, then how about the three branches? Of course, inter- and intra-branch checks and balances are crucial parts of our constitutional system—ambition checking ambition, and all that. But it is awkward for lower federal court judges to take it upon themselves to keep their bosses in check. The formal lines of appeal run from bottom to top, not the other way around. More generally, federal inferior court judges are self-interested actors within the larger governmental system, as are state judges, other state officials, and other federal officials. None of these actors has a credible claim to complete independence and disinterestedness.

The organized bar surely has a role to play in judging the justices, but lawyers also practice before the Court, and those who want to win may aim to please. Winning lawyers generally command higher fees and higher status. These realities blunt the willingness of top lawyers to always speak truth to power—here, judicial power. Besides, the ultimate touchstone for judging the judges (and all other government actors) is the Constitution itself—and how much do most top lawyers really know about the Constitution and all its parts?

Enter the constitutional law professor.

Although my academic position was not intentionally designed for the purpose of judging the judges and keeping them honest, my job does have the right features. I, too, have life tenure, which enables me to take a long view of both the Constitution and the Court (as well as other organs of government). I have had years of training in constitutional law, and I know how the judiciary works. (My most notable law job before becoming a professor was serving as a judicial law clerk—to a judge who is now a justice, as it turns out.) Like the justices, I have been afforded considerable leeway to define my own agenda. Thanks to manageable teaching loads and a generous compensation package—not to mention winter, spring, and summer breaks—I am able to do deep-drilling, time-consuming research, which is difficult for most journalists, given the parlous economic condition of the modern fourth estate. I am not a governmental actor seeking to increase the power and privileges of my own coercive branch. Thus, I can credibly adopt a neutral and disinterested stance vis-à-vis competing branches, acting as an umpire of sorts. Because I do not practice law before the justices themselves—because I do not litigate—I do not need to flatter the members of the Court in order to put food on my table or win points in a status hierarchy. Instead, I can perform a useful social function by both praising and criticizing the justices as I see fit, as a sincere and relatively disinterested, albeit fallible, professional observer—a true friend of the Court. And I can do all this in a public way—sometimes in newspapers and magazines and books aimed at the general public, and other times in more specialized works of legal

scholarship designed mainly for lawyers, judges, and other expert governmental officials.

This at least is how I have come to answer the question of what my professional mission in life is and should be, what niche I should aim to fill
within the contemporary American constitutional ecosystem. The essays
collected in this chapter reflect my efforts to be the Court's true friend—
neither a sycophant nor a scold but a genuine *amicus*.

THE FIRST TWO ESSAYS in this chapter were aimed directly at the Court
itself on a topic of internal judicial administration: In October 2002, I published a pair of pieces arguing that the justices were erring on issues involving courtroom protocols, and that the Court should fix the mess it had
created for itself. Happily, the Court in recent years has done much of what I
advocated, though it still is not quite where it should be.

The first piece of this pair ran in the *New York Times* and was designed to
coincide with the beginning of the Court's term on the first Monday in October. (Recall that a chronic challenge for a freelancer such as myself is to try
to find some timely news hook on which to hang a broader argument that
extends far beyond the news event putatively prompting the piece.) One
could not ask for a more prominent venue than the *Times*, but this venue
typically comes at a cost: space. Just as Manhattan real estate is among
the most coveted on the planet, so, too, is the tightly bounded territory of
the *Times* op-ed page. I aimed to use this small spot to plant a tall flag and
stake out a position that I could thereafter elaborate elsewhere, as I tried to
do later that month in a follow-up essay on a less-crowded website.

As these two pieces chronicle, there was a time, not so long ago, when
members of the general public in the Supreme Court's gallery could not even
take notes while listening to the give-and-take between justices and oral advocates; and when citizens across the land lacked access to free and timely
verbatim transcripts of oral argument. The Court has in recent years righted
these wrongs, but it has not yet moved all the way to my most expansive proposal: live NPR audio broadcasting of all oral arguments.

With the benefit of hindsight, it's easy to see why the Court abandoned its
earlier practices. First, these practices were utterly outlandish—inconsistent
with the Court's own preaching about free expression and public discourse
in a democracy; violative of a presumption of governmental openness that
should generally apply to American officialdom; and contrary to the practices

of every comparable court in the land. The *Times* op-ed took pains to bring to light this last point, based on research that I had done over the previous spring and summer surveying every state supreme court and federal circuit court.

Second, the reform advocated in these two pieces involved matters of internal judicial administration that could be modified by the Court itself, easily and quietly, without any need for an act of Congress. So, unlike some other reforms envisioned by other pieces in this book, this one was an especially quick fix.

Third, there was nothing remotely ideological in this particular call for reform—a point I tried to dramatize by inviting one of my oldest and dearest friends, Steve Calabresi, to be my *Times* coauthor. Steve is a conservative who clerked for Antonin Scalia and before that, for Robert Bork. In the 1980s he cofounded the Federalist Society and today he ranks as one of America's most acclaimed constitutional scholars and perhaps the preeminent conservative constitutionalist of his and my generation. (I say "perhaps" to avoid offending other leading conservative constitutionalists.) By contrast, on most things I consider myself a liberal, and I am a former law clerk of Justice Stephen Breyer, who is also generally reckoned a liberal. But on the basic issue of the need for more openness at the Supreme Court, Steve Calabresi and I were singing from the same hymnal, as were conservatives and liberals more generally.

And so were journalists across the spectrum. Professional journalists have long championed the cause of governmental openness; they had been doing so well before Steve Calabresi and I came onto the scene and they have continued to bang the drum after Steve and I sought to join this parade. In many contexts, the willingness of the institutional press to champion the broader rights of the public has been rather noble. For example, by giving Steve and me a venue to make our case and by advocating more Court openness in its own editorials, the *Times* was in a certain sense hurting itself.

Recall the rules in 2002: Only those in the courtroom itself could hear and know in real time what was being said at oral argument. The *Times* and a few other national outlets could afford to be in Court every day; but if the rest of us wanted to find out what was said, we usually had to buy the *Times* or one of the other papers. If PBS or C-SPAN or some other news outlet wanted someone to offer timely commentary on the oral argument, these organizations typically had to turn to a *Times* journalist or some other journalistic member of the Court's regular press corps (or, perhaps, to a DC-based constitutional law professor).*

But today, the Court allows radio broadcasting of certain especially significant cases, and in virtually all cases, verbatim transcripts are freely available within hours or days of oral argument. All of which is great for professorial constitutionalists who live in, say, New Haven, Connecticut, and cannot easily pop into the Supreme Court building to hear a given oral argument. We can now compete on a more level field with the *Times* (and with our academic colleagues headquartered in DC), and for that, we have the *Times* to thank.

And this, in turn, undercuts—but does not entirely destroy, I hope—my earlier claims about my own relatively disinterested niche within the broader constitutional ecosystem. I confess: I have personally and predictably benefited from the reform I advocated in 2002. (For example, only because of NPR's real-time broadcasting of the oral argument in the 2012 Obamacare case was I able to comment upon it quickly.)[1] No one this side of eternity is perfectly disinterested—a point that readers should keep in mind throughout this book.

AS IN CHAPTER 2 (and also Chapters 5 and 6), the essays in this chapter do not unfold in strict chronological order of initial publication; they have been rearranged to enable readers to follow distinct thematic threads more easily. Whereas this chapter's opening pair of essays address judicial protocols and courtroom procedures, the other pieces in this chapter focus more directly on judges themselves. When should we trust judges and when should we mistrust them? How are these men and women selected? How might these selection procedures be improved? And how have the most academically inclined members of the modern Supreme Court conceived of the judicial role when writing about it off the bench?

This section on the judges themselves begins with the harshest judgment that I have ever pronounced on the Court, berating its embarrassing

---

*In the modern media world, the only time to have a radio or TV show or op-ed about oral argument is the week of the argument itself. To wait two or three weeks— even though the basic constitutional issues of course remain unchanged in this short span—is unthinkable to modern present-minded media gatekeepers. "We are a news operation!" each editor or producer tells herself.

performance in *Bush v. Gore*. Although issues of presidential selection were obviously central to this controversy, the Court's cockeyed ruling also turned America's constitutional system of judicial selection on its head. The Constitution takes pains to put democratically chosen and politically accountable actors in charge of judicial selection. Constitutionally, presidents (and senators) pick justices, not vice versa. When justices pick presidents, as they did in *Bush v. Gore*, they thereby in effect help pick their own successors and judicial underlings—a power that the Founders purposefully withheld from the Court. And when in December 2000 the Court acted by such a painfully partisan final vote—with five conservative Republican justices picking a conservative Republican president who could then in turn pick conservative Republican replacements for the conservative Republican justices themselves, as well as a host of conservative Republican lower-court judges—the Constitution's basic structures of both presidential and judicial selection were warped almost beyond recognition. The Court should never have insinuated itself into this matter. The Constitution clearly makes Congress and not the Court the constitutional judge of electoral-college disputes (as clearly confirmed by the adjudicatory role that Congress and not the Court played in the sharply contested presidential elections of 1800–1801 and 1876–1877, and also in 1872–1873, when an interesting issue of electoral-vote validity arose in a less contentious context).[2]

Thus, the *Bush v. Gore* Court was wrong to hear the case, wrong to act in such a partisan fashion, and also wrong in almost everything that it said on the merits, as I attempted to explain in the *Los Angeles Times* shortly after the decision was announced, and as I have elaborated in much more detail in more recent scholarly work.[3] America's judges, I repeat, are not themselves above judgment. It is the right and duty of true friends of the Court to judge the judges in real time and for posterity to judge friends and judges alike in the coolness of time, as readers of this book can now do.

Supreme Court justices, of course, are not the only important judicial actors in the American judicial system. In 2002, I turned my attention to the state judiciaries in a piece entitled "Judicial Elections and the First Amendment." Coauthored with Professor Vikram David Amar, this essay maps out a route by which states may involve ordinary citizens in the process of state judicial selection without suffering some of the worst consequences of this selection mode. Although no state since 2002 has followed this road map, in many states today there exists deep dissatisfaction with the emergence of no-holds-barred and openly partisan judicial elections. Perhaps the ideas put forth in this essay are thus worth a second look.

The next piece in this section, "Term Limits for the High Court?" was coauthored with Steve Calabresi and ran in the *Washington Post* in the summer of 2002, a couple of months before our *Times* essay on unfree speech in the Court. In this *Post* piece, Steve and I launched a genuinely new idea into the broader constitutional conversation. We suggested several ways by which, *without a constitutional amendment*, Supreme Court justices could be made to serve limited terms (we proposed eighteen years) on the high court. The italicized words in the preceding sentence are the key. Amendments are nearly impossible to pull off, but Steve and I showed how improvisation could occur within the existing constitutional system. In this regard, this 2002 essay is broadly similar to other pieces in this book explaining, for example, how Americans could achieve direct election of the president without an amendment and could avoid congressional and presidential lame ducks without an amendment.[4]

When Steve and I published this piece, we were not aware of anyone else in the world of journalism or constitutional law who had ever put forth comparable ideas in print.[5] Today, there is a great deal of talk about these proposals, at least among constitutional scholars. In the summer of 2006, Steve followed up our *Post* essay with an extensive scholarly article, coauthored with Professor Jim Lindgren, fleshing out the basic reasons for and details of our reform idea. In 2009, Paul Carrington, a distinguished constitutional law scholar at Duke University, coordinated a petition signed by over thirty law professors across the country endorsing the basic outlines of the Amar-Calabresi proposal.[6]

It is still too soon to tell whether anything will come of this movement, but the momentum thus far does highlight one obvious advantage of journalistic interventions such as the essay Steve and I published in the *Post*: They enable scholars to get ideas out quickly to a wide swath of both policy makers and fellow scholars.

Which brings me to a piece coauthored with my brilliant Yale Law colleague Ian Ayres and first published in 2009 in the *Los Angeles Times*. Although there is a loose connection between the big idea of this piece—vice justices—and some of my own work on vice presidents and statutory successors to vice presidents in other pieces in this book,[7] the essay was more Ian's brainchild than mine.

Arguably, the reform idea this essay presents is too academic, too unprecedented. No state has a system of vice justices, and in America most of the successful new ideas for federal reform build in some way on state prototypes.

Indeed, the other reform ideas in this chapter are imaginable precisely because they highlight ways in which federal officials can learn from the states or vice versa. If state supreme courts all across America let citizens take notes and allow radio broadcasts, why shouldn't the U.S. Supreme Court? Given that no-holds-barred elections are not the way federal judges are picked, shouldn't at least some states rethink their drift toward this means of picking state jurists? In light of the fact that almost no state supreme court justice has life tenure, might we try to rethink life tenure for U.S. Supreme Court justices?

The clever idea of vice justices is not comparably grounded in state practice or prior federal practice. Thus, I don't see America moving anytime soon toward this idea. I nevertheless include the essay in this book precisely because it thinks outside the box. (Ayres is, famously, the coauthor of an entire book on outside-the-box thinking: *Why Not?: How to Use Everyday Ingenuity to Solve Problems Big and Small*.) For anyone who is truly into foundational questions of constitutional law—and if you have made it this far into the book, that means you—this piece is three minutes of rollicking good fun.

In 2009, Ian and I openly speculated about possible judicial exit strategies for Justice Antonin Scalia at a time when none of us could be sure what the future would hold for this highly visible and highly opinionated jurist. In early 2016, Justice Scalia died unexpectedly, and President Obama nominated a distinguished federal judge, Merrick Garland, to fill the Court vacancy. In response, I penned a pair of pieces for *Slate*, trying to place the Garland nomination within a broader constitutional framework. These essays sketch out an emerging modern model of Supreme Court replenishment, a model that intertwines elements of legal meritocracy and bare-knuckle politics. Judges judge individual Americans day by day and case by case; but Americans collectively, albeit indirectly, judge judges—and judge the politicians who pick judges—on Election Day. As this book goes to press, the Garland nomination is still pending; and the future of the Court itself is obviously on the ballot, de facto, in the upcoming presidential and senatorial elections.

This chapter's final pair of essays review two recent books by the modern Court's most self-consciously academic jurists: Antonin Scalia—now deceased, but very vibrant indeed when this review first appeared—and Stephen Breyer. Although I have always felt myself free to shower commendation or condemnation on either jurist—and have in the course of my career showered both on both—these reviews generally praised Breyer and panned Scalia. At one point in the Breyer review, I even called Scalia "a jerk."

For a typical practicing lawyer who regularly appears before the Court, it would be awkward, to say the least, to be quite this candid in a review. What might clients think? For better or worse, I have never had to worry about such matters. As I see it, my only client is truth itself. An academic fool can rush in where others fear to tread.

UNFREE SPEECH[8]

NEW YORK TIMES, SATURDAY, OCTOBER 5, 2002
(WITH STEVEN G. CALABRESI)

If recent history is any guide, the Supreme Court's new term, which begins Monday, promises to be another good one for freedom of expression— except, that is, within the courtroom itself. The justices support a broad view of free speech in their rulings, but they practice something very different in their own Court.

In the last eight terms, the Court has invoked free-speech principles to invalidate actions of other branches of government in no fewer than twenty-five cases. Yet the Court bars television cameras and radio microphones from its own public oral arguments. Transcripts of the dialogue between lawyers and the justices are not posted on the Court's website until weeks later. Spectators in the gallery may not even take notes about what is being said in open court.

These Court policies do not literally abridge free speech. But they inhibit the kind of robust and timely public discourse that, according to the Court's own doctrine, lies at the very core of the First Amendment. Oral arguments take place in open court. The lawyers may take notes, as may those with official press credentials. Members of the public deserve the same right.

These restrictive rules are at odds with the practices of other courts. Every federal appeals court and state supreme court allows note taking by the public. The Court's approach also contrasts with the openness practiced by other branches of government. Americans can watch Congress live on C-SPAN and read verbatim transcripts of congressional debate on Congress's website, updated daily. Presidential press conferences are also customarily carried live on C-SPAN.

The Supreme Court, like other courts, has not allowed TV cameras in the Court. Opponents of televised proceedings typically argue that lawyers are likely to play to the camera; that commercial news programs might broadcast short clips of trials out of context; and that witnesses would lose privacy as their faces become more publicly recognizable.

But these are arguments against televising ordinary civil and criminal trials. Appellate cases before the Supreme Court are different. There are no witnesses, and lawyers before the Court face strict limits on their time and arguments. Granted, it can be misleading to broadcast excerpts out of con-text; justices sometimes ask provocative questions or make arguments merely to sharpen debate. But this is precisely why Americans should be allowed to see the entire transcript and watch the argument uncut and free of commer-cials. Citizens could then judge for themselves what a questioner may have meant. Even if the Court continues to bar television cameras, the justices have no excuse for preventing public radio stations from broadcasting oral arguments live.

The First Amendment protects free expression so that the people can monitor and debate what is done by government on their behalf. The jus-tices are public servants. Americans deserve the right to see and hear how they conduct the public's business.

MORE ON UNFREE SPEECH[9]

FindLaw, Friday, October 18, 2002

The Supreme Court prohibits network television cameras and radio micro-phones from its public oral arguments. Transcripts of the back-and-forth be-tween attorneys and the justices are not posted on the Court's website until weeks have passed and the public's interest has waned. Members of the public may not even take notes in the gallery about what is being said in open court.

Meanwhile, in its opinions, the Court trumpets the importance of free speech and press access.

On the topic of free expression, why doesn't the Supreme Court practice what it preaches? That was the question Steve Calabresi and I recently posed in an op-ed in the *New York Times* marking the opening of the Supreme Court's term earlier this month. Here, I will expand on the Court's reluctance to welcome the First Amendment into its own courtroom.

The First Amendment is the darling of the current Court. Though sharply divided on many other issues, justices across the spectrum agree that free expression rights should be construed broadly.

But the Court's love affair with the First Amendment is a relatively modern development. Less than a decade after the adoption of the Bill of Rights, circuit-riding justices enthusiastically enforced a 1798 sedition law that made it a federal offense to criticize the president. Early in the twentieth century, the Court upheld punishment of a newspaper publisher for editorializing against state judges. During World War I, the justices sent Eugene Debs, a notable presidential candidate, to prison for peacefully criticizing the government. Indeed, before 1925, the Court had never—not once!— used free-expression principles to invalidate government censorship, even as it routinely construed property rights broadly to invalidate economic regulation.

Today's justices have repudiated this repressive legacy, but the residue of the early Court's indifference to free expression remains visible in the Court building itself, as the aforementioned rules and practices indicate.

Perhaps these Court rules and practices do not literally abridge freedom of speech or of the press, but if not, they sure come close. After all, the apparent purpose of these rules is precisely to limit free expression and free thought.

Consider the rule against note taking. A person in the courtroom can clean his wallet or twiddle his thumbs or tug his earlobe, or engage in countless other mindless activities, but is prohibited from engaging in the cognitive and expressive activity of writing down what he hears the justices saying, along with his own comments or questions or criticisms.

Consider also the rule against the media's cameras. The Court's rules do not bar security cameras in the courtroom and such cameras may well be in the room for all we know. What the justices are banning is thus not cameras per se, but *network television* cameras, cameras that might broadcast information about the Court to the American public.

The "harms" that these rules seek to prevent are harms that pivot on the acts of thought and expression themselves. And these are the very sorts of "harms" that government typically may not seek to prevent under the Supreme Court's standard First Amendment case law.

To put the point another way: no Supreme Court rule bars carrying a pencil into the courtroom, or wearing a chopstick in one's hairdo. The ban is not based on security concerns, but is rather directly aimed at expressive activity per se: using one's pencil to take notes.

More generally, one of the core purposes of the First Amendment is to protect a robust and timely public discourse about government officials and government decision making—including, of course, judicial officials and judicial decision making. But that discourse is precisely what is dampened by the Court's own rules about its own building.

This is especially so because the day of oral argument is one of the two days—the other being the day a final Supreme Court decision is announced— that the American public and the American media are most likely to focus on a given legal issue. If discourse that day is dampened, the public has lost a unique and irreplaceable occasion for democratic discussion and deliberation.

When it comes to other government arenas—post offices, airports, school grounds, and so on—the Court has typically insisted that such forums allow as much speech as is functionally compatible with the basic purpose of the arena. Yet in its own building, the Court represses expressive activity without any strong showing of incompatibility or disruption. There is a word for this and it is spelled H-Y-P-O-C-R-I-S-Y.

The Court's transcript policies are also unfree in another sense. In the days after oral argument, the transcripts are anything but free. The Court gives a temporary monopoly to a private company, which in turn charges high fees for transcripts. The Court would never (nowadays, at least) give a private company a monopoly over its written opinions. Why should its oral arguments be treated any differently?

There is nothing secret or confidential about oral argument. Unlike judicial conferences where justices deliberate privately among themselves, oral arguments take place in open court. They are public events conducted by public servants with public money. The public deserves full access.

To recast the point in the language of federalism: Americans outside the beltway deserve electronic access comparable to the ability of those who live in Washington, DC, Virginia, and Maryland to attend arguments in person. If television cameras are not acceptable, at a minimum the arguments should be carried live on public radio—as happened in December 2000 for *Bush v. Gore*—and transcripts should be freely available immediately. (Television is more intrusive upon certain privacy interests. Not all current justices are easily recognizable at the grocery store, and several like it this way. As with

TiVo for television, radio broadcasts can also be accessed asynchronously via streaming audio on the Internet and other technologies.)

Without these rules of equal access, only those with official press passes or those who live near the Court could write a timely op-ed about the oral argument that reliably quoted what the justices actually said in open Court. Why shouldn't a law professor in New Haven have the same access as a journalist in Washington?

The Supreme Court of Canada allows note taking. The Canadian Supreme Court also allows its oral arguments to be televised on CPAC, the Canadian counterpart of C-SPAN. Similarly, many appellate courts and state supreme courts allow electronic broadcasting in some form.

If the nine justices don't clean up their act and open up the Court, is there anything anyone can do?

For starters, Congress should legislate rules of open access as part of the regular appropriations bills for the Court building, or as part of Congress's general power to structure the Court and its procedures.

Also, senators in all future confirmation hearings should publicly ask each Supreme Court nominee to state his or her view of the access issue, and should hesitate to confirm any new justice who refuses to pledge to open up the Court. (Such a pledge would of course be quite different than a pledge to rule a certain way on a future case before the Court, which would be patently improper. The permissible pledge would concern Court administration, not Court doctrine.)

If all else fails, perhaps members of the press and the public should consider suing Court officials for carrying out Court policies that run afoul of general First Amendment doctrine and basic First Amendment principles.

When other branches of government are involved, the modern Court has read the First Amendment very broadly—indeed, perhaps too broadly. Founders like James Madison aimed to shield political expression (especially anti-government speech), religious expression, and literature. In contrast, modern cases have protected commercial advertising (of liquor, cigarettes, and casinos), nude dancing, and the Playboy channel.

In reading the First Amendment so broadly, the justices risk losing sight of the amendment's core concern: protecting a system of free expression whereby the people can monitor and criticize our public servants.

Those public servants include the justices themselves, and the spirit of the First Amendment argues for the broadest rights of democratic access to the Court consistent with safety and decorum. Measured by that standard—the standard the Court preaches elsewhere—the Court's own practices fall embarrassingly short.

SHOULD WE TRUST JUDGES?[10]

LOS ANGELES TIMES, SUNDAY, DECEMBER 17, 2000

What will I tell my students at Yale Law School in the aftermath of *Bush v. Gore?* Alas, it will be my painful duty to tell these earnest youngsters, "Put not your faith in judges."

A few words of background. I am a true believer in the rule of law. I have devoted my professional life to the United States Constitution—four books, a hundred articles. I have tried to get beyond partisan ideology, and pride myself on my mentorship of, and friendship with, both liberals and conservatives. I consider myself a friend of the Court and of many of its current justices—at times a critic, but always in the spirit of friendship.

The Court, in its long history, has made many mistakes. I do not hide these from my students. We read large chunks of *Dred Scott*, and *Plessy v. Ferguson*. We discuss the Court's Gilded Age transformation of amendments drafted to promote freedom and equality into doctrines protecting the rich and powerful while ignoring the rights of others. We openly discuss the obvious failures of legal analysis in *Roe v. Wade* and its progeny; and consider whether some of the results of these pro-abortion cases might nevertheless be sustainable under alternative legal theories slighted by the Court. We critique the Court's perverse criminal procedure doctrines, which often help guilty defendants at the expense of innocent defendants and innocent victims.

And now, to the list of dubious precedents that I must teach to my students, I will add *Bush v. Gore*. I will teach it as I teach most other cases—by carefully parsing its language and logic. Students will be graded on their work; and so I need to show them what counts as good legal analysis and what cannot count. In effect, I grade opinions as a way of explaining how I will ultimately grade exams and student papers.

Judged by ordinary standards of legal analysis, *Bush v. Gore* gets low marks. The core idea is that because the statewide recount of Florida's presidential ballots was proceeding under somewhat uneven standards, it violated constitutional principles of equal protection. In some counties, dimpled chads might be counted; in other counties, not. And so on.

At first, this argument sounds plausible. But let's test it by traditional legal tools. As a matter of logic: If the Florida recount was constitutionally flawed, why wasn't the initial Florida count equally if not more flawed? It, too, featured uneven standards from county to county. Different counties used different ballots (including the infamous butterfly ballot); and even counties using the same ballot used different interpretive standards. This happened not just in Florida, but in many—perhaps most—states. Are all these elections unconstitutional?

Now think about history and tradition. The idea that the Constitution requires absolute perfection and uniformity of standards in counting ballots is novel, to put it mildly. Americans have always been asked to put their X marks in boxes, and human umpires have had to judge if the X is close enough to the box to count. On Election Day, different umpires in different precincts have always called slightly different strike zones. (It would be impossible to demand that all ballots be viewed by the same pair of eyeballs.) Assuming that all these judgments are made within a small zone of "close calls," and are made in good faith with no systematic skew, it seems hard to call this practice unconstitutional. If it is unconstitutional, then every election America has ever had is unconstitutional.

Now think about precedent. No Supreme Court case ever decided comes remotely close, on its facts, to supporting the *Bush* majority. There is indeed grand voting-equality language in Supreme Court case law—but on their facts these are cases about citizens simply being denied all right to vote (typically on race or class lines); or being assigned formally unequal voting power, with some (typically white) districts being overrepresented at the expense of other (typically black) districts. And as a precedent for future cases, the *Bush* Court tries to limit itself to its unique facts—judicially presided recounts—but fails to support its limits with any neutral principle. The justices might as well have said, "We promise to follow this case in all future cases captioned *Bush v. Gore*."

As a matter of constitutional text, history, and structure: The equal protection clause was, first and foremost designed to remedy the inequalities heaped upon blacks in America. The Fifteenth Amendment extended this idea by prohibiting race discrimination in the vote. Yet southern governments mocked these rules for most of the twentieth century—and with the Court's blessing. For decades, most American blacks were simply not allowed to vote. When Congress finally acted to even things up in the 1960s, inequality still persisted as a practical matter. In Florida, for example, black

precincts typically have much glitchier voting machines that generate systematic undercounts many times the rate of wealthier (white) precincts with
sleek voting technology. Undermaintenance of voting machines, chad
buildup, and long voting lines in poor precincts—these are the real ballot
inequalities today. If we are truly serious about real equality, as envisioned by
the architects of Reconstruction, then we need not and should not ignore
the voting machine skew. Rather we should do our best to correct for it, albeit imperfectly, via manual recounts. Even if such recounts are not required
by equality, surely they are not prohibited by equality. In fixating on the
small glitches of the recount rather than the large and systemic glitches of
the machines, the justices turned a blind eye to the real inequality staring
them in the face, piously attributing the problem to "voter error" and inviting "legislative bodies" to fix the mess for future elections.

As a matter of consistency, the justices score slightly higher on my scale.
Indeed, the Court, by the same 5–4 bottom-line vote in *Bush*, has similarly
inverted constitutional equality in a series of cases involving redistricting.
In these cases, governments have drawn district lines so as to increase the
likelihood that our legislatures themselves will be racially integrated. These
lines are not formally race based—anyone can move into any house and
vote there. No government agency enforces a color code (as under Jim
Crow), and each citizen is free to vote however she likes—to consider race
or not, to vote for a member of her race or some other race. Yet the Court
has called these efforts to integrate legislatures "apartheid" and has held that
they violate principles of equal protection. Why? Because the district lines
look odd to some justices. And the recount in Florida likewise looked odd:
Dimpled ballots look weird. But this is not the rule of law—it is the rule of
subjective sensibility. Weirdness is in the eye of the beholder; and the Constitution tells judges to be on the lookout for something else, something remotely like the subjugation of blacks that led to the adoption of the equal
protection clause.

Finally, consider issues of constitutional statecraft. The Florida courts,
the Florida legislature, and Congress are all electorally accountable. The
U.S. Supreme Court is not, yet it snatched the case away from these alternative decision makers.[11] The biggest electoral check on the Court is the ability of presidents to appoint new justices, yet the five justices Al Gore has
specifically criticized handed the presidency over to his opponent by preventing a recount that might have proved that he was indeed the choice of
Florida's voters, as well as the nation's. The Court majority reached this

result by a single vote.* (Two other justices were willing to correct some of the imperfections of the recount, but only if the improved recount could then proceed.) And by refusing to hear these equality issues in its first review of the Florida mess several weeks ago, the Court denied itself the benefit of amicus briefs of scholars and experts who might have helped clarify matters by anticipating and exposing the Court's eventual illogic.

Ironies abound. Justices who claim to respect states savage state judges. Jurists who condemn new rules make up rules of breathtaking novelty in application. A Court that purports to frown on ad hoc, after-the-fact decision making gives us a case limited to its facts. A Court that claims it is defending the prerogatives of the Florida legislature in fact unravels that legislature's statutory scheme vesting power in state judges and permitting geographic variations. (The real problems in Florida identified by the justices were problems in the election laws themselves, not the Florida courts.) The man who wants to unite us, George W. Bush, has divided the Supreme Court in a way that may permanently affect the Court's stature for those of us who love the law. The case that bears the name of a professed strict constructionist is as activist a decision as I know.

America's ultimate Supreme Court is not composed of nine men and women in a marble temple in Washington, DC. Our highest Court, in the long run, is the Court of public opinion, the Court of history, the Court in which those who judge in our name are ultimately judged by us—We, the People of the United States. And in that ultimate Court, *Bush v. Gore* will not, I predict, fare well. When my students ask about the case, I will tell them that we should and must accept it. But we need not, and should not, respect it.

JUDICIAL ELECTIONS AND THE FIRST AMENDMENT

FindLaw, Friday, August 9, 2002 (with Vikram David Amar)

Yogi Berra once said, "When you come to a fork in the road, take it!"

All nine justices in the Supreme Court's June ruling on state judicial elections seemed to follow Yogi's advice. In *Republican Party of Minnesota v.*

---

* [Recall that the lineup was not merely 5–4, but an ideologically polarized and partisan 5–4. No liberal—not a single justice either appointed by a Democratic president or who would later resign so as to enable a Democratic president to name his replacement—joined the five in shutting down the recount.]

White, five justices—the usual five: William Rehnquist, Sandra Day O'Connor, Anthony Kennedy, Antonin Scalia, and Clarence Thomas—veered one way, using the First Amendment to strike down a Minnesota law that prohibited candidates for judicial office from speaking out on issues of the day. Four justices—the usual dissenters: John Paul Stevens, David Souter, Ruth Bader Ginsburg, and Stephen Breyer—swerved in the other direction, voting to uphold the scheme as a legitimate effort to promote the reality and appearance of judicial impartiality.

But was the road before the Court really forked? Was there a less visible but promising middle path that all nine justices, rushing to reach their respective end points, missed?

These questions are important not just for analyzing *White* itself, but also for thinking about how *White* should affect the dozens of other states that, like Minnesota, hold and regulate judicial elections. There was indeed a middle course available in *White* that should have been found and explored by the justices. And this middle course, which should provide guidance to other states, suggests that relatively small fixes to the Minnesota law should have changed the result.

The Minnesota law at issue in *White* prohibited a candidate for judicial office, whether an incumbent judge or a non-judge challenger, from "announc[ing] his or her views on disputed legal or political issues." The prohibition went beyond candidate "promises" and forbade, for example, a candidate from criticizing a past court decision and indicating a willingness to consider a different result in similar cases down the road.

Strong sanctions accompanied Minnesota's prohibition. Judicial candidates who as sitting judges violate the Minnesota ban are subject to discipline, including removal, censure, civil penalties, and suspension without pay. Lawyers who run for judicial office and violate the rule are subject to, among other things, disbarment, suspension, and probation from the practice of law.

Minnesota defended its law by arguing that it needed to regulate candidate speech in order to ensure that the public believes that judges are sufficiently open-minded about important matters that might come before them. According to the Court, however, whatever gain in public confidence the Minnesota law achieved was inadequate to overcome the free speech interests of the candidates, because of the "imperative that [candidates] be allowed to freely express themselves on matters of current public importance." Justice Kennedy, whose concurrence took a similar route, added that these

First Amendment rights enjoyed by an individual are not surrendered simply because he has thrown his hat into the election ring.

The dissenting justices' approach was quite different. For them, this case was not so much about the First Amendment as it was about states' rights—in particular, the freedom of states to structure their judicial selection procedures to promote judiciousness.

Judicial elections, said the dissent, authored by Justice Ginsburg, are not like other "political" elections, because "there is a critical difference between the work of the judge and the work of other public officials." Judges must be, and must be perceived to be, impartial and free from politics in a way that legislative and executive officials are not. Because of this, states must "not be put in an all or nothing choice of abandoning judicial elections or having elections in which anything goes."

The majority and dissenters end up in very different places. If one follows the majority, states are going to have a hard time discouraging judicial candidates from speaking their mind, however irresponsibly. Yet if one follows the dissent, states have a pretty free hand to deter people who want to criticize existing judicial rulings and doctrines, no matter the First Amendment costs this might entail. Neither of these destinations seems very attractive.

But there is another place to go, a place where both free speech and judicial impartiality can be protected, a place where the First and Tenth Amendments can peacefully coexist, a place that acknowledges both the centrality of anti-incumbent speech in an election and the right of a state to fill its judiciary with judicious people.

This middle path is based on two key thoughts. First, speakers should not be punished for core political and anti-incumbent speech. Second, there is no First Amendment right to be a judge, and it is not unconstitutional punishment to be kept off the bench for injudicious speech.

In a nutshell, the First Amendment protects one's right to speak about the bench, but not to sit on it; and the Tenth Amendment gives states broad power to structure state officeholding—especially judicial officeholding—but it does not give states free rein to censor and punish free-spirited critics and candidates.

Begin with our second point: It is simply not a punishment that violates the First Amendment for a state to deny a person high public office because of the views he has expressed. That happens all the time in the executive branch, under the (perfectly constitutional) system of patronage used to reward party loyalists with plum government posts. There is, in short, a First

Amendment right to be a Democrat, but not a First Amendment right to be a Democrat in a Republican president's cabinet.

Consider also the selection of judges at the federal level, where the president and the Senate certainly, and permissibly, may refuse to make someone a judge because of what that person has said, even though such refusals are undeniably content-based and indeed viewpoint-based, and thus, in other contexts, might run afoul of basic First Amendment principles.

A president is perfectly within his rights to withdraw a judicial nomination if the nominee says injudicious things. There is a right to say foolish things, but not a right to both say them and be nominated or confirmed despite them.

If it is not a violation of the First Amendment (and it is surely not) for the Senate to pass an internal Senate rule saying they "will not confirm to the federal bench anyone who has expressed racist views in public," neither is it a violation of the First Amendment for the Senate to announce that it will not confirm any person who speaks out "injudiciously" about the current Supreme Court or any other issues of the day during the confirmation process.

We are not saying the Senate can refuse to consider someone for a judgeship on any ground at all. The fact that a nominee is black, for example, cannot be a disqualifying characteristic because of constitutional principles rooted in the Fourteenth and Fifteenth Amendments, among other places. But the content and timing of the nominee's expressed views surely can be taken into account without violating the First Amendment.

A counterargument to our position might run as follows: In Minnesota, judges are selected not by the governor and state Senate, but by the *people* in an *election*. Once Minnesota has turned over the process of picking judges from government institutions to the people themselves, the counterargument goes, surely the state must allow the people to have access to all relevant information about the candidates.

Perhaps—although pinning down the precise source and scope of this constitutional intuition is no easy matter. One possible argument might take this form: When a state decides to hold a true "election" to determine a contest, the voters in that election should not be constrained in doing their job, lest people be confused or deceived about what powers they are being given or denied.

But suppose Minnesota tweaked its process ever so slightly, so as to avoid any possible deception or voter confusion. Suppose, for example, that the state made crystal clear that the vote of the people was not the final word, but rather only, formally speaking, a strong opinion poll (a "beauty contest," in election lingo) that a governmental agency—perhaps a special committee of the state Senate—should take into account in making the final decision about whom to appoint to the bench.

Consistent with the Constitution, any state could cut the people out of the loop altogether, and give judicial selection powers entirely to a governor and state senators, who would be free to take into account the views and statements of judicial applicants. (Indeed, there is strong Supreme Court case law suggesting such state choices are central to the Tenth Amendment and American federalism.) Given that this is so, why can't a state decide to involve the people, but with less finality?

So long as the final decision is made on grounds (judiciousness) plainly relevant to the nature of the office (the judiciary), how is the Constitution violated by this popular "beauty contest" system?

Popular-vote beauty contests may be unusual nowadays, but are certainly not unheard of in America. Before the Seventeenth Amendment, which provides for direct popular election of U.S. senators, several states held beauty-contest popular elections that were then used by the state legislatures in their decisions about whom to elect to the Senate.

Similarly, in presidential elections, states in the early republic were free to use popular-vote beauty contests to give the state legislatures information that legislators could then use to decide whom to send to the electoral college.

And even today, a state could, without violating the First Amendment, prospectively legislate that it will award its electoral college votes to the winner of the popular vote in that state only if that "winner" has, say, participated in state-sponsored debates, or has refrained from endorsing racial segregation.

This is so even though the First Amendment would forbid truly *punishing* someone for boycotting a debate or spewing racist rhetoric at an open political rally. In short, there is no ultra-strong First Amendment right to be a president. Or a judge. The right to speak does not encompass the right to hold either of these jobs no matter what one says.

But isn't there a presumptive right to ply one's lawful private legal practice free from penalty for one's anti-incumbent political expressions? And doesn't the Minnesota regime go too far when it threatens *disbarment* (and not just ineligibility for the bench) for any non-incumbent judicial candidate who speaks out too politically during the campaign?

Yes it does, and *this* was the aspect of the Minnesota law that should have been stressed by the majority and was altogether missed by the dissent. When Minnesota not only denies high government jobs to intemperate speakers but also threatens to take away their private livelihoods without clear evidence that they are unfit to hold those occupations, then the state's actions become punitive in a way that the First Amendment prohibits.

Allowing Minnesota to disbar lawyer critics of incumbent judges and existing judicial rulings would severely dampen core political discourse, whether we call the bench-filling process an "election," a "selection," or a "beauty contest." Punishing private citizens for speaking out against existing laws and judges is precisely what the First Amendment at its core is designed to prevent.

All of this suggests that if Minnesota were to change its election to a beauty contest, and limit the consequences of intemperate speech to judicial ineligibility, its laws should survive First Amendment attack. That much narrower result in *White* should have been the one the Court reached—and should, indeed, have commanded unanimity, as it satisfies the concerns of all nine justices. This result also would provide a map for other states, as they revisit their own judicial selection procedures to decide which way they want to go.

TERM LIMITS FOR THE HIGH COURT?

WASHINGTON POST, FRIDAY, AUGUST 9, 2002
(WITH STEVEN G. CALABRESI)

Supreme Court justices traditionally announce their retirements in summer, but this summer no one is budging. Nor has anyone budged since the most junior justice, Stephen Breyer, joined the Court eight years ago this week. Never before have any nine justices served together for so long a stretch.

America's political clock and internal court rules explain why senior justices might prefer to stay put—for now. But such explanations also call into question the wisdom of judicial life tenure as currently practiced. Whenever the next Court vacancy occurs, Congress should try to nudge the justices toward a better model of judicial independence based on fixed judicial terms.

Currently each justice is tempted to time his or her departure with one eye on the political calendar and one finger in the political wind. For example, Justice John Paul Stevens, age eighty-two, holds many liberal legal views that would probably not be shared by any replacement nominated by President Bush. Why should Stevens retire now rather than wait?

The Court's other two most senior members, Chief Justice William Rehnquist, seventy-seven, and Justice Sandra Day O'Connor, seventy-two, generally hold conservative legal views compatible with those of likely Bush appointees. But the Senate is now controlled by Democrats, who might contest a conservative appointee. Why not wait until after this November's elections, when the Republicans may regain control?

If justices actually make such partisan calculations, the independence of the judicial mind from raw politics is lessened. Even if they resist the temptation to think like pols, the public perception of their doing so is hard to escape, especially in the shadow of *Bush v. Gore*.*

Above and beyond specific issues of political timing, the Court's seniority system gives more experienced justices increased power to speak for the Court and thus encourages justices to stay past their prime. Perverse incentives also exist at the other end of the age spectrum: Life tenure encourages presidents to nominate young candidates with minimal paper trails and maximal potential to shape the future.

Only one of the fifty states copies the federal government's particular brand of unelected life tenure for its highest court, and no major democracy abroad does so. Most state and foreign constitutions prescribe a fixed number of years in office or a mandatory retirement age, or both.

Although the federal Constitution itself vests justices with life tenure, there are a variety of measures, short of amending the Constitution, by which

---

*[Granted, a justice who times his or her retirement politically is not committing the same magnitude of judicial sin as did the justices who anointed George W. Bush president in *Bush v. Gore*. Unlike individual, noncoordinated, and staggered decisions to step down, the five members of the *Bush* majority acted in simultaneous and collective coordination; the *Bush* justices acted with all the formal trappings of a court of law in the context of deciding a legal case (whereas a retiring justice acts, formally, as a mere human being stepping down without any pretense of sitting in judgment in a lawsuit or saying what the law is); unlike a quiet retirement, the *Bush* majority issued loud and embarrassingly bad legal expositions on the meaning of the Constitution and relevant case law; unlike a retiree who by stepping down affects only the fate of his own seat, the *Bush* majority influenced the selection of scores if not hundreds of lower-court judges destined to be appointed by the incoming president; and unlike a retiree who is legally and morally entitled to decide for herself how to spend her golden years, the *Bush* majority usurped decisional authority rightly belonging to others, namely, Congress's authority to definitively arbitrate electoral-college disputes.]

Congress and the president could move future justices toward a tradition of fixed terms—say, eighteen years. For example, some commentators have proposed a clever statutory solution under which judges would technically sit on the Supreme Court "by designation" for a fixed number of years, after which they would have the option to serve the remainder of their life tenure on some lower federal court.

Alternatively, the Senate could insist that all future Court nominees publicly agree to term limits, or risk nonconfirmation. Though such agreements would be legally unenforceable, justices would feel honor bound to keep their word. Unlike a promise to rule a certain way on a particular issue, a promise to resign on a fixed date comports with judicial integrity. Congress could also restructure judicial salaries, pensions, office space, and other perks to give future justices incentives to honor their promises.

Current justices should not be affected; the system should be purely prospective, applicable to all future nominees of both parties and all ideologies. Ideally, politicians should announce their preference for this fixed-date retirement system even before the next vacancy arises, so that all concerned understand that it's nothing personal.

Beginning with George Washington, early presidents established a tradition of leaving after two terms even though the Constitution permitted them to run again. Similarly, future justices could, with a little nudging, establish a tradition of leaving after a fixed term or at a set age. Once this tradition took root, the Constitution might eventually be formally amended to codify it. Or perhaps the justices themselves might collectively codify retirement guidelines in Court rules modifying the seniority system or creating an ethical norm of retirement at certain milestones, just as the House in 1994 adopted internal term limits for certain committee chairs.

A justice seeking to outfox the new system might be tempted to resign before the end of his or her term whenever early resignation might offer advantage to a preferred successor. Such manipulation should be deterred by a general sense of fair play. In an analogous situation, a president might be tempted to resign a few months before the end of his final term, thus placing his handpicked vice president in power before the November election. Yet all past presidents facing this situation—most recently, Eisenhower, Johnson, Reagan, and Clinton—have spurned this sort of manipulation. If even elected presidents pursue nonpolitical exit strategies, America should demand no less from unelected justices.

WHY NOT NOMINATE VICE JUSTICES
FOR THE SUPREME COURT?

LOS ANGELES TIMES, THURSDAY, MAY 7, 2009 (WITH IAN AYRES)

As if President Obama did not have enough on his plate, he will soon need to nominate a Supreme Court justice to replace David H. Souter, who intends to retire. While Obama is at it—and to make things easier next time around—perhaps he should consider nominating a second justice now, to fill whatever vacancy might arise after Souter's departure.

Souter's formal letter to Obama indicates that he will step down at the end of this term—presumably late June. But nothing prevents the president from nominating now and the Senate from confirming next month, while Souter is still a sitting justice. This would hardly be unusual. In a letter sent to President George W. Bush in July 2005, Justice Sandra Day O'Connor wrote that her resignation would become "effective on the nomination and confirmation of my successor"—an event that did not occur until the middle of the following term. Chief Justice Warren Burger and Justices Thurgood Marshall and Harry Blackmun also continued to sit during the process of nominating and confirming their successors.

But if the president may nominate a justice before a formal vacancy occurs, why can't he do so before an informal announcement of a planned retirement? Why shouldn't the president feel free in the next few weeks to nominate two people to the Court—an heir and a spare, one to fill Souter's seat and one to fill the next vacancy when it arises?

Consider first the efficiency advantages. Sitting justices would be free to leave whenever they wanted, without fear that the Court would be crippled until they were replaced. Likewise, an unexpected death would not leave the Court short-staffed, because a preapproved replacement justice would be ready to step in, much as vice presidents and lieutenant governors stand ready to fill executive branch positions that suddenly open up.

There was a time when Senate confirmations were quick. The Senate confirmed George Washington's first six nominees to the Court in two days. As late as 1975, Justice John Paul Stevens was confirmed less than three weeks after his nomination. But those days are gone. Since Robert Bork's failed nomination in 1987, the Senate has typically taken months to confirm even uncontroversial Court nominees. Most recently, seven months elapsed between O'Connor's conditional resignation letter and the filling of her seat by Samuel A. Alito Jr.

Consider next the political and policy advantages. A president might entice a justice to retire by naming a replacement the justice has special reason to respect. For example, Justice Antonin Scalia is seventy-three years old, but no one expects that he will voluntarily resign any time soon and thereby give a liberal president carte blanche to appoint a replacement. But if Obama and the Senate moved first and named a true moderate of extraordinary distinction, Scalia would face a very different calculus. The president could move the Court in his desired direction, but Scalia could have some confidence that it would not move too far.*

As this example illustrates, the president could choose to nominate either a general-purpose vice justice, who would fill whatever vacancy might arise, or a seat-specific vice justice, who would be eligible only to fill, say, the seat currently held by Scalia when that seat becomes vacant.

If two nominees this season are OK, why not nine or nineteen? What is to stop an administration from stealing from future administrations by trying to fill seats that will open up only in the distant future? The Constitution's formal rules offer rock-solid protections for future presidents. Even a nominee who has been confirmed by the Senate cannot take office until a vacancy actually exists; and the sitting president at the time that vacancy arises has the lawful authority to decline to commission even someone already nominated by his predecessor and confirmed by the Senate. Thus, even if Obama were to try to name nine vice justices, the next president would decide for himself or herself whether to honor the Obama slate or start afresh.

Indeed, even Obama would not be legally bound to commission someone whom he himself had nominated years earlier; but as a practical matter it would be very hard, politically, for him to renege, especially if a sitting justice had chosen to step down as a result. (Similarly, a president is free to veto a bill he has pledged to sign, but one who does so pays a heavy price for the double cross.)

---

* [When these words were written in 2009, no one, including Justice Scalia and President Obama, could know with certainty whether this conservative Republican justice would outlast this liberal Democratic president. As we now know, Scalia in fact was obliged (by death) to leave office in early 2016 and thereby create a vacancy on Obama's watch.]

The idea of anticipatory vice justices may strike many observers as a big change of the rules, even if justified by the recent slowing of the Senate confirmation process. Perhaps the vice-justice system should not go into effect until after the next presidential election. During that election, candidates can speak to the voters about their competing visions for the Court, and any candidate who endorsed the vice-justice system would have a genuine mandate to try it. For now at least, perhaps Obama needs to add only one new item to his plate, even though the Constitution gives him the option to do even more.

JUDGING JUDGE GARLAND (PART I)[12]

SLATE, THURSDAY, MARCH 17, 2016, 1:49 P.M. (ET)

It's been a great week for Hillary Clinton, Merrick Garland, and Barack Obama. Each is the very embodiment of merit, competence, and hard work. Interestingly enough, all have roots in the Land of Lincoln, but their success also sheds light on how some of Lincoln's legacy is now under stress.

Clinton ran the table in Tuesday's primaries, and then Garland got the nod from Obama on Wednesday. Some left-leaning commentators expressed disappointment that the president did not use the nomination to achieve more demographic diversity on the Court, but their objections give too much weight to crude identity politics.

Consider Clinton and Obama. Yes, Hillary is a woman, but so is Carly Fiorina and so is Sarah Palin and neither of the latter has what it takes to lead America and the world in these parlous times. Neither does Ben Carson, though his skin color resembles Obama's.

Clinton is winning and deserves to win not simply because she is a woman, thrilling as that is to behold in a would-be president. She is winning and she deserves to win because she is the most competent, the most experienced, the most knowledgeable, and the hardest-working candidate in modern presidential history.

The presidency is a nearly impossible job. Most presidents in history are failed presidents. There is no great training for the office. But Clinton brings more to the race than anyone else, as a former presidential candidate, former first spouse, former big-state senator, and former secretary of state. (She has also lived in three of America's four main regions—the Midwest, the South, and the Northeast—and has spent time on six continents.) She is a policy wonk par excellence, and she has learned a great deal about a vast number of distinct domains that a president must master. Plus, she is intentionally presenting herself as an heir of Obama, who also embodies brains and hard work.

Garland is like Clinton in many ways—but without the high negatives. He is as smart as they come, and no one works harder. Being a justice, like being president, is much more difficult than it looks—at least if one aspires to soar rather than coast. Very few justices have in fact soared, because few have been both brilliant and workaholics. (The late Antonin Scalia, for example, was whip-smart but far less knowledgeable about American constitutional history than he needed to be in order to rank as a truly towering, or even genuinely credible, originalist; he spent his spare time talking too much and reading too little.) Like a president, a Supreme Court justice must master a vast range of old and new issues over the course of many years, and genuine mastery requires a rare combination of talents and temperament. Garland is as good a bet as I know in the talent and temperament departments. He has been a top judge on a high-powered court for many years. On the Supreme Court, he also might be a force multiplier if he can occasionally win over one or more of the Court's Republican appointees. Despite the expressed concerns of the National Organization for Women—which was hoping that Obama would name a third woman in a row to the Court—it's exciting to contemplate how a Justice Garland might teach us all how men can be credible feminists.

In announcing Garland's nomination in the Rose Garden on Wednesday, Obama pointedly invoked the phrase "Land of Lincoln." He, Clinton, and Garland are all Lincoln's children in obvious ways. None is highborn, nor was Lincoln. All exemplify smarts and sweat. A woman, a black man, and a Jewish man—what better trio to remind us of Lincoln's principle that all persons are created equal?

This is the profound American ideal under assault from Donald Trump and even many anti-Trump elements in the putative party of Lincoln. Trump himself is a highborn American aristocrat who stokes resentment against or spurs ridicule of those whom he treats as being born below him—those who are born nonwhite, or born outside America, or born to non-American parents, or born Muslim, or born disabled, or born with shortness genes. Trump's leading rival for the Republican presidential nomination, Ted Cruz, proudly promises a return to a legal regime degrading those Americans who happen to be born gay, denying them their equal entitlement to the pursuit of marital happiness.

So hooray for Lincoln and for his metaphoric children—Barack, Hillary, and Merrick. But here is the difference between him and them and the dark side of the rise of modern meritocracy: Lincoln did not go to a fancy college or law school. In fact, he had less than a year's formal education from cradle to grave. He rose late in life. By contrast, Obama, Clinton, and Garland are all Ivy Leaguers. So was Scalia, and so are all the current justices. Garland himself is a double Harvard grad. To be sure, he was a scholarship kid—not unlike Obama, Clarence Thomas, and Sonia Sotomayor at various stages in their illustrious academic careers. But the gateway to the modern Supreme Court seems to narrow early in life; apparently, late bloomers and non-Ivies need not apply.

This narrowing is happening not just at the Court but also in the presidency. Each of our four most recent presidents attended Harvard, Yale, or both, as did the runners-up in five of the seven most recent elections (Michael Dukakis, George H. W. Bush, Al Gore, John Kerry, and Mitt Romney). The last time Americans voted for a president without a Harvard or Yale graduate on the ballot was 1984. If we include vice-presidential candidates in our tally, we have to go all the way back to 1968 to find a year when none of the top four candidates went to one of these two schools.

Obama, Garland, and Clinton thus embody a brave new world in which we are all formally born equal, but inequality begins to set in quite early in life, based on early grades, early test scores, and early extracurriculars. New World elites are not quite the same as the Old World elites, but the emerging schoolocracy makes me nervous, even as I myself have been a huge beneficiary. Admissions officers goof, and not all roses bloom early.

JUDGING JUDGE GARLAND (PART II)[13]

SLATE, FRIDAY, MARCH 18, 2016, 8:48 P.M. (ET)

The next justice will have an impact based on his or her votes, voice, and vision. As for votes: For the near future, regardless of whether the next justice is a crusader or moderate, the Court's swing voter will shift from Justice Anthony Kennedy to Justice Stephen Breyer and no further. Although many in today's Democratic Party love crusaders, a moderate may actually be more likely from time to time to convince persuadable Republican appointees to rule with the liberal bloc.

That's where voice comes in. Remember, John Roberts is still chief justice and remember that he was the key to upholding Obamacare. Remember, also, that Kennedy was the key to same-sex marriage. Now ask yourself whether Garland or some generic crusading liberal ideologue would be more likely to persuade Roberts or Kennedy on an intimate Court in which the justices do not merely vote but make legal arguments both orally and in print. (It's worth noting that Roberts and Garland, after similar stints at Harvard, both clerked for the same circuit judge, Henry J. Friendly, who emphatically believed that proper judging was quite different from pure partisanship or ideological politics. True, the Supreme Court is by its nature more political than a typical lower court—but even when it comes to the Supremes, I'm with Friendly, Garland, and Roberts in believing in a law-politics distinction.)

As for the final component—vision—if transformative vision is what one seeks, one is not likely to find it on the lower-court bench. Judging ordinary legal issues day in and day out leaves little time to think deeply about the system as a whole. The mice in the maze cannot easily levitate themselves to see the entire grid from above. So if you want such transformative vision, à la Justice Hugo Black, you might be better off fishing in the waters of the academy or the Senate for the likes of a Larry Lessig, or a Randy Kennedy, or an Elizabeth Warren. (Perhaps President Hillary Clinton could one day appoint Justice Barack Obama!)

For those of us who are on Team Garland, the key question is: What is his best path forward to get confirmed? My proposed compromise is to take the Republican senators at their word and construe their position with maximal charity. What is at stake, Republicans correctly remind us, is the swing seat on the Court. True, the Democrats won the presidency in 2012, but Republicans won the Senate in 2014. In the view of Senate Republicans, it's now a tie—and the tiebreaker should go to the political party that wins this November. On this view, the Court's future should be informed by the people themselves in the upcoming election. Obama's legacy is on the ballot, de facto; the Court is on the ballot, de facto; and presidential candidates and swing senators are on the ballot, de jure. Let the people decide!

To which I say: OK, but if we want the people to decide, and decide intelligently—if popular elections of presidents and senators and the Constitution's openly political process of filling Court vacancies are features of the system and not bugs—then let's enable the people to decide intelligently. Let's do our best to structure the 2016 election so that the people can better understand the Court at its current crossroads. Let's devise a system so that the people can assess the current Court, Merrick Garland, and the various claims of his supporters and his detractors. In short: *Let's have hearings! Sometime soon—before the election!* And let's encourage the American electorate to listen in and decide for themselves who are the grown-ups in the room.

The Senate as a whole need not take a final vote on Garland's nomination until after the election, and by then the people will have spoken with their eyes and ears open. If Donald Trump or some other Republican presidential candidate wins, then Garland goes down. But if Hillary Clinton wins—and wins in part based on her strong support of Garland—then the Senate could confirm Garland, pronto, in early November. He could then quickly join the Court and ensure that its next term will operate relatively smoothly, with a full complement of nine justices. Even if Clinton loses, if the Democrats somehow manage to retake the Senate, they would be free to confirm Garland when the new Senate convenes in early January after reforming the filibuster with one simple vote—the nuclear option.

In fact, a Democrat-controlled Senate would even be free to confirm two more hypothetical Obama nominees in the window between the start of the congressional session on January 3 and the presidential inauguration on January 20 were, say, Ruth Bader Ginsburg and Breyer to offer to step down as a rebuke to obstructionist Republicans. Of course this will not happen and should not happen. But this admittedly fanciful resignation scenario is a reminder to us all of the desirability of keeping the political hardball game of Court replenishment within the lines of fair play.

ANTONIN SCALIA AND THE ABSURDITY DOCTRINE[14]

DEMOCRACY JOURNAL, WINTER 2013

A simple question for Antonin Scalia and Bryan A. Garner: Who presides at a vice president's impeachment trial? The Constitution's text seems straightforward: According to Article I, section 3, "The Vice President of the United States shall be President of the Senate," and "The Senate shall have the sole power to try all Impeachments." So if we follow the text's literal meaning, the vice president gets to preside over his own impeachment.

Is this plain-meaning argument decisive? Of course not, as I explain in the opening pages of my 2012 book, *America's Unwritten Constitution: The Precedents and Principles We Live By*. But in their own new book, *Reading Law: The Interpretation of Legal Texts*, Scalia and Garner appear to embrace an approach that would indeed allow vice-presidential self-dealing of this grotesque sort. The key issue here is how judges and other interpreters should respond when the literal text seems to direct an absurd result—allowing, for example, a person to preside over his own case, or enabling a man to inherit the estate of the rich aunt whom he murdered in cold blood precisely in order to profit from his wrongdoing.

Were the authors of *Reading Law* merely obscure legal scribblers, the book's overreliance on apparent textual plain meaning, and its undervaluation of various venerable exceptions to literalism such as "the absurdity doctrine" (as it is widely called), might not be cause for alarm. But of course, Antonin Scalia enjoys special authority as an intellectually ambitious and stylish jurist—a former professor at several leading law schools, and currently the senior associate justice on the Supreme Court. In this book, targeted especially at lawyers, law students, and lower-court judges but also attempting to draw in a wider circle of civic-minded citizens, Scalia and his erudite co-author (also a law professor and the current editor in chief of the prestigious *Black's Law Dictionary*) aim to offer a treatise-like account of the rules and principles of statutory and constitutional interpretation. The result is a sprawling patchwork comprising dozens upon dozens of self-contained subsections, each exploring a different canon of legal interpretation.

I am not an expert on all or even most of these canons, and several of them are far more notable in ordinary statutory interpretation than in constitutional exegesis—my own area of expertise. Indeed, one overall weakness of *Reading Law* is that it does not clearly and in one place explain all the ways in which constitutional interpretation might sensibly differ from ordinary statutory interpretation. A strongly literalistic approach might make sense when dealing with prolix and often technical statutes drafted by and for legal insiders and easily amended by sitting legislatures. But does a similar willingness to emphasize letter at the expense of spirit make sense when dealing with the written Constitution—a uniquely terse and hard-to-amend document designed to be broadly accessible to lay folk and to serve as a unifying cultural symbol setting forth first principles? Also, unlike most statutes, the written Constitution is a temporally extended text, uniting amendments spanning centuries. All of its amendments have simply been tacked on to the end of earlier versions of the document without comprehensively rewriting earlier language. Doesn't the very nature of such a document involve unique interpretive questions about how broadly to reread earlier patches of constitutional text to harmonize with the purpose and spirit and logic of later amendments?

Scalia and Garner do not spend enough time pondering constitutional questions such as this; but they do purport to offer a reliable synthesis of the basic rules of legal interpretation—especially the rules of ordinary statutory construction. Alas, on one particular rule of interpretation—the "absurdity doctrine," a canonical principle that I did study at length long before reading *Reading Law*—I must sadly report that Scalia and Garner have badly misstated the matter.

To expound and analyze the "absurdity doctrine," both Scalia-Garner and I rely in part on the same old book—William Blackstone's *Commentaries on the Laws of England*, first published in the 1760s, and one of the two most cited law books (along with Montesquieu's *The Spirit of the Laws*) in America during the late eighteenth century. (Blackstone himself, interestingly enough, can be seen as a precursor to Scalia—a judge who wrote an ambitious legal treatise aimed at both legal insiders and a broader public.) But Scalia and Garner's reading of Blackstone—and of the absurdity doctrine more generally as that hoary doctrine has been understood by a long line of jurists across the centuries—is flatly erroneous, and this error in turn raises questions of whether similar errors of research and reporting infect their treatise as a whole.[15]

According to Scalia and Garner, if the literal meaning of a legal enactment, such as a statute or a Constitution, would lead to a weird result, judges may disregard the literal meaning and deviate from the text under the absurdity doctrine—but only when two conditions are met. First, "[t]he absurdity must consist of a disposition that no reasonable person could intend." A merely odd or suboptimal outcome does not suffice to trigger the absurdity doctrine and warrant a judicial disregard of the enactment's plain meaning. Second, "[t]he absurdity must be reparable by changing or supplying a particular word or phrase whose inclusion or omission was obviously a technical or ministerial error. . . . The doctrine does not include substantive errors arising from a drafter's failure to appreciate the effect of certain provisions."

In other words, if the drafters obviously meant to say "up" but instead said "down" or surely meant to say that attorney's fees should be paid to the "winning" party but instead said the "losing" party, judges can correct this simple slip of the pen. Because it was obvious what the legislators in fact plainly envisioned and intended, a judge who disregards a scrivener's error is in fact fulfilling the lawmakers' true intent. Typos happen, and good readers overcome them.

Fair enough. But the absurdity doctrine, as expounded by Blackstone and many other authoritative jurists, goes far beyond the correction of scriveners' errors. Blackstone made clear that in certain unusual situations that the legislature did not squarely consider when it crafted general language, judges could deviate from the literal meaning of legislative enactments in order to avoid absurdity:

> Where some collateral matter arises out of the general words, and happens to be unreasonable; there the judges are in decency to conclude that this consequence *was not foreseen by the parliament*, and therefore they are at liberty to expound the statute by equity, and [as to this collateral matter] disregard it. . . . [T]he rule is, where words bear . . . a very absurd signification, if literally understood, we must a little deviate from the received sense of them. . . . [S]ince in laws *all cases cannot be foreseen or expressed*, it is necessary, that when the general decrees of the law come to be applied to particular cases, there should be somewhere a power vested of excepting those circumstances, which (*had they been foreseen*) the legislator himself *would have* excepted. [Emphasis added.]

In their discussion of the absurdity doctrine, Scalia and Garner quote only a short snippet from Blackstone. But as is obvious when we examine the entirety of Blackstone's discussion, the absurdity doctrine goes beyond fixing scriveners' errors—what Scalia and Garner refer to as "obviously a technical or ministerial error." Indeed, Blackstone himself offered up two vivid illustrations of the absurdity doctrine in action, and each involved something far more substantive and interesting than a mere scrivener's error.

First, Blackstone explained that a law punishing anyone who "drew blood in the streets" should obviously not apply to a doctor performing an emergency surgery upon a stricken pedestrian—a situation that the enacting legislature simply did not envision and that therefore required judges to do more than merely correct a "technical or ministerial error" of draftsmanship.

Blackstone's second example is even more eye-opening, and is in fact stunningly apt in helping us to think about our own Constitution's language concerning vice-presidential impeachments: "[I]f an act of parliament gives a man power to try all causes [cases], that arise within his manor of Dale; *yet, if a cause should arise in which he himself is party, the act is construed not to extend to that; because it is unreasonable that any man should determine his own quarrel.*" [Emphasis added.]

The idea that no man should be a judge in his own case is tightly intertwined with the very idea of the rule of law, and surely this background precept should inform a proper reading of the constitutional clauses governing impeachment trials. Or at least that's what Blackstone would say, as would the vast majority of the Founding Fathers, who considered Blackstone to be the gold standard on many legal issues.

But Scalia and Garner say something very different. In their effort to constrain improperly activist judicial policy making, Scalia and Garner have gone too far in the other direction, mangling the absurdity doctrine as laid down by Blackstone and many others. The authors apparently fear that once it is openly admitted that judges can address weird situations that the legislature did not anticipate, all judicial restraint would be lost, and judges would be able simply to displace proper legislative judgments at the drop of a hat. But of course, nothing of the sort follows from Blackstone's doctrine, properly understood and properly applied. The constraints highlighted by Scalia and Garner's first condition—that judges should act only in cases of true absurdity, not mere suboptimal policy, and should act only to avoid a result that "no reasonable person" could favor—suffice to keep the absurdity doctrine from becoming judicial carte blanche.

Elsewhere in their book, Scalia and Garner discuss a situation in which a murderer stands to inherit from his victim—say, a rich aunt—because no statute explicitly bars this result, and because the murderer falls within the general next-of-kin language in the inheritance statutes on the books at the time of the murder. Prior to the mid-twentieth century, some judges barred murderers from profiting from their own crimes in this way; others permitted the inheritance. Scalia and Garner side with the permissive judges who reached the "textually correct"—their words—outcome.

But this result is absurd—morally obtuse. Surely this is not what any legislature ever intended. Indeed, Scalia and Garner themselves admit that "[a]s a general matter of right and wrong, all of us"—*all of us!*— "recoil from the thought that a murderer could advance his heirship." And the authors take solace in noting that today, "all states have statutes that explicitly deal with this problem." But surely it was evident, even before all state legislatures explicitly addressed this unusual issue, that lawmakers would have wanted to bar murderers from profiting from their crimes in this way—that, as a matter of first (if unwritten) principles, murderers should be judicially estopped from inheriting from their victims.

Granted, when construing statutes, perhaps judges should in genuinely close cases err on the side of literalism, and rely on legislatures to revise ill-considered language. But the statutory revisions necessary to anticipate every wrinkle and every exception may tend to make statute books longer and more technical. By contrast, the Constitution must necessarily be a more compact document if it is to remain accessible to ordinary people. (This was one of Chief Justice John Marshall's main insights in the landmark 1819 case of *McCulloch v. Maryland*.) Thus, might it make sense for judges to strike a different balance between textual literalism on the one hand and commonsense holistic interpretation on the other when confronting constitutional language as distinct from the words of, say, the tax code? For lay readers who are more passionate about constitutional law than statutory interpretation, it would have been nice if the authors of *Reading Law* had devoted more focused and sustained attention to questions of this sort.

It is tempting at this point in the analysis to move from the lapses in Justice Scalia's latest book to the lapses in his general jurisprudence on the Court. But this detour would not be fully fair to coauthor Garner, nor would it be fair to Scalia himself, whose book deserves to be judged on its own merits regardless of what one thinks of his overall body of work as a jurist, either in general or in the specific domains of statutory and constitutional interpretation. (For what it is worth, in my classroom, I point to several prominent Scalia opinions as exemplary, and to others as execrable.) William Blackstone himself, it is worth noting, did not make much of a mark on the bench, but did write a toweringly influential treatise. By contrast, Scalia's body of work as a justice may well prove far more influential than his academic writings. He is no Blackstone—and nowhere is this more evident than in the part of his new book that purports to channel Blackstone and the absurdity doctrine that Blackstone famously expounded.

By misstating the venerable doctrine of absurdity, Scalia and Garner champion results that are, quite literally and precisely, absurd. Scalia and Garner's mangling of this doctrine raises questions about the general reliability of *Reading Law* as a work of sound scholarship. The book is undeniably ambitious. But is it perhaps too ambitious—too sure of itself, too quick to overlook important counterarguments and complicating evidence? Given the authors' fondness for hoary Latin maxims, the two words that seem most appropriate, in light of the foregoing analysis, are *caveat emptor*.

LAW AND DIPLOMACY

Los Angeles Review of Books, Tuesday, November 24, 2015

These are good times for Stephen Breyer. For most of his twenty-one years as a Supreme Court associate justice, he has been on the losing end of many of the biggest cases. But beginning with the Court's 5–4 decision upholding Obamacare in 2012, Breyer has won more than he has lost in the cases that matter most. In the last two years, he has generated his two greatest judicial opinions. Rarely in history has a justice made his most notable contributions this late in his time on the bench. After years of merely reacting to and counterpunching against an intellectual agenda defined largely by the Court's conservatives, led by Antonin Scalia and Clarence Thomas, Breyer has begun to shape an ambitious affirmative reform agenda of his own. And now, he has penned perhaps his best book, *The Court and the World*.

It is really four books in one. Each minibook is good, and one of the four—on justices as diplomats of sorts—is particularly provocative.

But before we get to the four minibooks, some general background and disclosure. I first met Stephen Breyer on the page, learning administrative law in 1982 from an outstanding casebook he had coedited several years before as a Harvard Law School professor. The book wowed me and the following year I applied to be his law clerk. By that point, he had been named to a federal appellate court in Boston, while continuing to teach part-time at Harvard—the man has always had tremendous energy. When he offered me the job, I accepted immediately and enthusiastically. (There was only one other judge at the top of my wish list—a smart young appellate judge on the opposite coast named Anthony Kennedy.) Working for Breyer in 1984–1985 was a wonderful experience. The judge was a remarkably generous boss, fun to talk to, filled with ideas, and amazingly quick on his feet. Discussing law with him was like playing lightning chess with a grandmaster. He helped me land my dream job in the legal academy and has remained a friend ever since. I admire him tremendously and have sent many of my best students to clerk for him. We former clerks enjoy swapping stories about him, and although we sometimes poke fun at his quirks and foibles, our tales are always told with affection. No one who knows Stephen Breyer well has ever spoken ill of him. He is a mensch.

But that has never stopped me from critiquing his opinions—sometimes harshly—both to his face and in print. One of the things I most admire about him is that he welcomes constructive criticism.

In that spirit, I must confess that until recently I am not sure that I could name a toweringly great Breyer opinion, an opinion for the ages. One reason is that he was often on the losing side, with few chances to speak for the Court in marquee cases. Long ago, when I complimented him on one particularly fine dissent that he had authored, he said nothing, but flashed a sad smile and held up four fingers. The game was to count to five, and in that case he had fallen one vote and one finger short.

But now things are looking up. Two terms ago, he penned his masterpiece in a case involving both administrative law, his first love, and constitutional law, the Court's main focus. The case, *National Labor Relations Board v. Noel Canning*, implicated first principles of both substance and method. Never before had the Court issued a major ruling on the constitutional clause at issue—a clause concerning the president's power to make certain appointments unilaterally when the Senate is in recess. The case also pitted narrow literalism, championed by Justice Scalia (himself an administrative law maven and former law professor) against Breyer's preferred interpretive method emphasizing broader constitutional purpose and common sense, and reflecting deep respect for how the political branches of government have in fact operated and glossed the constitutional text over the centuries. Breyer's victory in *Noel Canning* was all the sweeter because Scalia had raised the stakes, doubling down with a fierce rebuttal. But this time—at last!—Breyer could raise a full five-fingered fist in triumph, backed as he was by his fellow liberals (Justices Ruth Bader Ginsburg, Sonia Sotomayor, and Elena Kagan) and also, critically, by swing justice Anthony Kennedy.

If *Noel Canning* was Breyer's greatest triumph, another huge success quickly followed, in last term's follow-up Obamacare case, *King v. Burwell*. The case involved nice issues of statutory construction and administrative law—Breyer's wheelhouse. (In addition to being an administrative law expert, he is a former congressional staff attorney.) And the Court's opinion—this time 6–3—was classic Breyer, closely attentive to the overall structure of the statute, deeply respectful of Congress's main purpose, and impressively policy-wonkish in its grasp of this complicated enactment. And here's the kicker: Not only did this classic Breyeresque opinion win the votes of Chief Justice John Roberts and swing justice Anthony Kennedy, but Roberts himself wrote the opinion! Breyer has now gotten inside Roberts's head—the true measure of genuine intellectual influence—and in effect he got the chief to write the very opinion he himself would have written. Once again, Justice Scalia was relegated to a minority position, gnashing his teeth and rending his tunic in obvious frustration at being outmaneuvered.

Which brings us to Breyer's latest book, which is also aimed, albeit subtly, at Scalia. In 1997, Breyer and Scalia famously clashed, in a federalism case called *Printz v. United States*, about whether and how foreign constitutional law might be useful in interpreting the U.S. Constitution. Breyer was on the losing end of that case, and in his new book, he generally purports to detour around this delicate subject. Instead he focuses on the role of foreign and international law (1) in deciding national-security issues (which often involve persons and events beyond U.S. shores); (2) in pondering whether various ambiguous American statutes are best read to regulate conduct outside the U.S.; and (3) in construing federal treaties, which by their very nature implicate foreign governments—our treaty partners. In all three contexts—in each of these three minibooks—Breyer skillfully shows that American courts must think carefully about foreign and international legal materials.

The indispensable role of foreign and international law in the context of extraterritorial statutes and treaties is almost self-evident; Breyer's main contribution here is to show in rich detail how non-American legal elements have interacted with American law in a wide range of actual Supreme Court cases, many of them cases in which he himself participated. The role of foreign and international law in domestic national-security cases is less self-evident, and here, Breyer makes a particularly nice move by highlighting the fact that the rights revolution in American case law, under the Warren Court, roughly coincided with the 1948 Universal Declaration of Human Rights, the 1959 birth of the Human Rights Court in Strasbourg, and the emergence of strong constitutional courts in many advanced democracies outside the United States.

Left largely unstated is Breyer's apparent premise that as American judges become more familiar with non-American legal sources in these three areas, these very same American jurists will naturally begin to think globally and to ponder foreign legal materials even in plain-vanilla cases of American constitutional law that do not directly involve foreign events or foreign persons—that is, in cases such as *Printz*.

Consider, for example, the death penalty. If state X wants to impose capital punishment on a certain kind of state resident—say, a youthful offender or a low-IQ offender or an offender who did not himself pull the trigger—American courts do consider how many of state X's sister states would allow capital punishment in similar situations. But should American courts also consider the punishment practices of other civilized countries in deciding whether the death penalty in the American case at hand would be impermissibly cruel and unusual? In recent cases, the Court has indeed at times considered foreign-law practices, much to the delight of Justice Breyer and the disgust of Justice Scalia. Last term, Breyer wrote a separate opinion in a case called *Glossip v. Gross*, raising the stakes dramatically by suggesting that perhaps all death penalties in America should be deemed unconstitutional. One fact favoring Breyer's new drift toward abolitionism is that many of the world's leading democracies have entirely abolished capital punishment within their own societies.

Breyer also uses his new book to subtly challenge Scalia on general interpretive method. The U.S. Constitution does not itself contain a detailed set of instructions about whether it should be read literalistically à la Scalia or with greater attention to spirit and purpose à la Breyer. Nor do most congressional statutes specify just how much judges should emphasize context and general legislative purpose, or whether legislative history (Scalia's bête noir) should count for much. But in treaty law—the subject of Breyer's third minibook—there does exist a treaty that explicitly prescribes general rules for treaty interpretation. And this treaty on treaties—the Vienna Convention on the Law of Treaties—emphatically sides with Breyer against Scalia. It explicitly highlights the importance of a given treaty's overall "context in light of its object and purpose." It finds relevant "subsequent practice" above and beyond original intent. (This was a big theme of Breyer's in the non-treaty case of *Noel Canning*.) It expressly authorizes judges to consult key pieces of legislative history. To repeat, this treaty only governs treaty interpretation. But once American judges become increasingly comfortable with this sort of interpretive process in treaty cases, Breyer apparently believes (though he does not quite say, explicitly) that similar interpretive habits will carry over into plain-vanilla cases of statutory and constitutional interpretation.

Perhaps the most interesting section of *The Court and the World* is its fourth and final minibook, "The Judge as Diplomat." If American judges increasingly engage foreign law and foreign judges, these judges in turn, Breyer argues, will likely pay more attention to American law, and thus America's soft power and influence will increase. On this view, diplomacy is not limited to presidents, ambassadors, and senators. Federal judges can also play their part in burnishing America's influence abroad.

It is an interesting argument, and also classic Breyer. He is a conversationalist par excellence and an extremely collegial jurist. He worked hard to befriend Sandra Day O'Connor in his early years on the Court, and now, perhaps, he is at last beginning to forge a bond with Chief Justice Roberts. Thus, with Breyer's fourth minibook he is once again bringing his ideas about domestic adjudication to bear on international and foreign-law matters. (Here, too, Justice Scalia is the anti-Breyer. Although Scalia can be utterly charming when he wants to be, at times he can be and has been—there is no nice way of saying this—a jerk. He alienated O'Connor at the same time Breyer wooed her. He has attacked Kennedy with special ferocity in a wide range of cases.)

But if Breyer is brilliant in pondering the possible significance of French law and Swiss law and English law and the law of many other modern democracies, he is less good at mastering the full constitutional history of America itself. They say the past is a foreign country. But this is a country that Breyer has not visited enough. He knows far less about the Founding and the Reconstruction than he should—and this is all the more unfortunate because there is a great deal of historical American material that in fact supports many of his best ideas. Good as it is, Breyer's latest book stumbles in its account of both the Civil War and the Revolution. On the Civil War, he is, characteristically, too kind to another judge—in this case, Chief Justice Roger Taney; and as for the Revolutionary War, he conflates the 1783 Treaty of Paris with the very different 1814 Treaty of Ghent—a small slip in itself, but one that reflects his larger lack of mastery of American constitutional history.

True, the past cannot be cajoled and befriended and charmed in the same way that Breyer can work his personal magic on his fellow justices or on foreign judges. Studying the past is less fun, perhaps, than seeing the sights in London and Paris. But to reach the next level of greatness, Stephen Breyer needs to visit the Founding and the Reconstruction.

PART II

CULTURE WARS

5

CRIMINAL PROCEDURE

From O. J. to DNA

WHY DOES THIS BOOK CONTAIN SO MUCH MATERIAL—fifteen essays in all—on crime and punishment? In part because of the ubiquity of the topic. Even as crime has receded somewhat in the last generation, America is still America, with extraordinarily high rates of criminal violence and incarceration. Crime happens—everywhere, all the time.

When it happens—the instant it happens—journalists cover it. The formula of many a local TV news show has long been: "If it bleeds, it leads." Crimes are news, and so are all the administrative and judicial elements that define the modern American criminal justice system—the all-points bulletins and suspect descriptions, the grand jury sessions, the arrests and perp walks, the arraignments and bail hearings, the suppression motions, the pervasive plea deals and the occasional trials with drama from voir dire to verdict, the sentencing phases, the inevitable appeals and eventual habeas filings, the rare retrials, the pardon petitions and emotional appeals for last-minute clemency, the grisly death watches and public executions.

Ordinary Americans understand a big chunk of the criminal justice system and even some of its fine points. Thanks to fictional TV shows and blockbuster movies, virtually all Americans have been Mirandized countless times and have heard opening and closing arguments in multiple murder trials. High-profile criminal trials also function as real-life detective shows and morality plays. Who done it and who deserved it? These are questions that capture the imagination of ordinary Americans, topics on which everyone feels entitled to have (and often does have) a strong opinion. In contrast to the subtleties of our presidential succession law, the rules regarding Senate vacancies, the details of recess appointments, and the intricacies of Senate cloture rules, bedrock questions of criminal justice fascinate not only the denizens of Washington, DC, but also the good people of Walnut Creek, CA. Crime plays in Peoria.

As a result, whenever I have had a point to make about a constitutional issue related to crime and punishment, I have not had to wait very long for an opportunity to make my case in a timely, relevant way in a major newspaper or newsmagazine.

MY EARLIEST WORK IN CONSTITUTIONAL LAW, in the late 1980s, did not involve any sustained engagement with the Fourth, Fifth, and Sixth Amendments, which regulate searches, seizures, self-incrimination, jury trials, counsel rights, and other aspects of criminal procedure law. In the early 1990s, I began to study these amendments in more detail, in connection with my developing ambition to understand what each part of the Constitution's text originally meant, and how all these parts should now be read to fit together in the modern world.

By the summer of 1994, I had completed an initial round of criminal-procedure research and had placed long, heavily footnoted articles in the *Harvard Law Review* and the *Michigan Law Review* elaborating the importance of truth-seeking in the criminal justice system. Our Constitution was designed, I believed then and still believe now, to sort the innocent from the guilty; and various constitutional doctrines that suppress reliable physical evidence—exclusionary rules that modern courts have fashioned in the name of the Fourth and Fifth Amendments—were and are precisely wrong.

As I was in the midst of excavating the historical and conceptual foundations of constitutional criminal procedure, Nicole Brown Simpson and Ron Goldman were brutally murdered in Brentwood, California, on June 12, 1994. Nicole's head was nearly severed by a knife—the act of an obviously powerful and presumably enraged killer. We all know now—and many of us suspected early on, even before the trial had started—that the famous football player and TV star O. J. Simpson (Nicole's ex-husband) was the murderer. Even before the blood on Simpson's driveway had been tested, his lawyers were trying to suppress the evidence. Why would they do this if he were innocent? If innocent, wouldn't he want the blood tested so that it might lead to the real killer?*

My first two solo ventures in journalism as a law professor occurred in connection with the criminal and civil suits brought against O. J. Simpson. As I saw it then and still see it, the civil suit against O. J. got to the truth— he did it—in part because some of the appalling exclusionary rules that judges have invented and imposed upon the criminal justice system are, fortunately, inapplicable in civil litigation.

The O. J. Simpson affair obliged Americans to ponder the complex and politically charged relationship between race and the modern criminal justice system. The racial dynamics of Simpson's criminal trial—and the racial aspects of an earlier southern California trial of white police officers who had brutalized a black motorist named Rodney King—formed the backdrop against which I composed the third essay in this chapter, which highlighted another notable case where white police officers had arrayed themselves against a black private citizen. This time around—unlike the Simpson case—the wrongdoers were the officers, who had unjustifiably shot and killed an innocent and unarmed black man. Many years later, this basic fact pattern remains hauntingly familiar.

I used this 2000 essay about the death of Amadou Diallo at the hands of the police to stress the role that local juries played at the Founding, and should still play today, in holding criminals accountable. The Constitution says that criminal trials should generally be held in the venue where the crime occurred and judged by a jury of the vicinage where the blood was spilled. This rule had not been followed in the Simpson case. Even though the blood had spilled in a largely white and suburban community—Brentwood—the

---

* Even without explicit evidentiary suppression, the exclusionary rule hung over the case. In order to avoid exclusion at a pretrial suppression hearing, detectives had denied that O. J. had been a formal suspect in the case when they went to his house shortly after discovering the dead bodies. Had Simpson been a formal suspect at that moment, a warrant might have been necessary, and the cops had not procured a warrant. So in order to be allowed to introduce absolutely reliable physical evidence at the impending trial, the cops at this pretrial hearing played linguistic word games: At the time of the search, they said, O. J. was not a "suspect" but merely, in effect, a *potential suspect*. Police doublespeak such as this, even though in the service of introducing genuinely strong and honest evidence, may well have caused some jurors to disbelieve everything these same cops later said at trial about other key issues in the case.

trial was held in a different part of Los Angeles with a larger black population, in an apparent attempt to avoid a repeat of the horrible optics of the Rodney King case. (In that earlier case, the trial of the brutal white police officers was wrongly moved away from the urban crime scene to the officer-friendly suburban venue of Simi Valley.) Thus, in three notable and racially charged criminal cases—the Rodney King cop case, the O. J. Simpson criminal trial, and the prosecution of the officers who killed Amadou Diallo—three improper venue transfers occurred. Each trial ended in a miscarriage of justice. Three wrongs made three wrongs.

THE NEXT CLUSTER of essays in this chapter provides further background on the original meaning of the Fourth and Fifth Amendments. My constitutional rejection of judicially fabricated rules that wrongly exclude reliable physical evidence forms a strong thematic thread connecting these individual pieces. On this issue, I have consistently been and still remain to the right of every member of the modern Supreme Court. But over time, the Court has crept closer to my Fourth Amendment views, both on the exclusionary rule itself (see, in particular, my essay "The Battle of Hudson Heights"), and on the antecedent question of the proper meaning of Fourth Amendment rights. As I see it, the amendment does not invariably require warrants or probable cause. Rather, it requires reasonableness.

Although this gradual judicial drift in my direction on both Fourth Amendment rights and Fourth Amendment remedies has caused considerable heartburn in some liberal circles, it shouldn't. As to rights, a proper reasonableness framework can often be more protective of racial and gender equality, bodily liberty, privacy, free expression, private property, and other bedrock constitutional principles than a regime based solely on warrants and probable cause. Even if probable cause exists in a given situation, certain governmental intrusions may still be unreasonable, and only a general reasonableness analysis can truly keep government on a proper leash. On this point, see in particular my 2001 *Los Angeles Times* essay, "An Unreasonable View of the Fourth Amendment," which chronicles and critiques a case in which a Texas cop did have probable cause but nevertheless acted in a beastly fashion.

As this piece also makes clear, remedies beyond exclusion are vital to protecting constitutional freedom. Where the cops expect to find no evidence and in fact find no evidence, the exclusionary rule is useless—there is nothing to exclude!—and we must rely on other mechanisms, such as damage actions, to prevent police brutality, police harassment, police intimidation, and many other forms of unreasonable police behavior.[1]

The essays in this chapter also offer a fresh way of thinking about the Fifth Amendment's self-incrimination clause, a way that differs dramatically from current doctrine. In my view, compelled testimony from criminal defendants should be inadmissible because such compelled words might be unreliable; but physical fruits—blood, bloody gloves, murder weapons, fingerprints, loot, and so on—should virtually always be admissible, even if the government finds these fruits as a result of compelled testimony. The judiciary has not yet come close to embracing my proposed reconceptualization of the self-incrimination clause. But if the Fourth Amendment exclusionary rule continues to erode, my Fifth Amendment ideas may well come to seem more attractive decades hence, because these Fifth Amendment ideas and my Fourth Amendment critique of the exclusionary rule stem from the same conceptual root structure. I still haven't given up here.

One virtue of my proposed reconceptualization is that it would enable broader legislative inquests into possible wrongdoing of both public officials and private actors. Under current doctrine, valuable legislative fact-finding hearings can end up compromising equally valuable criminal investigations; if the legislature forces a witness to say what he/she knows, prosecutors may have to fold their tents. In this chapter, this analytic point is made in connection with a 2001 legislative hearing into wrongdoing by Enron officials. But this is hardly the only example in recent years. The same problem has arisen in connection with more recent congressional investigations of IRS misconduct and of the alleged mishandling of Hillary Clinton's State Department e-mails, and with state legislative investigations into the New Jersey "Bridgegate" scandal. Current Fifth Amendment doctrine is not only messing up the judicial system; it is also obstructing proper legislative oversight of all sorts of possible high-level misconduct.

THE PENULTIMATE SECTION OF THIS CHAPTER brings together a trio of 2002 essays on various surveillance and preventive detention issues growing out of the post-9/11 war on terrorism. I confess that there is much less in this book on the war on terrorism than the intrinsic importance of this vast topic warrants. The simple reason for the skimpiness of my treatment is that many of the issues involved—for example, the Patriot Act and its infinite intricacies, the legal status of Guantánamo, and the proper scope of habeas corpus for various subcategories of detainees—lie near or beyond the boundary of my expertise. These issues are not purely questions of ordinary criminal procedure; rather, these topics also implicate broad and deep questions of national security law and international law. It is thus not coincidental that this section ends on a sincere note of self-doubt: "Part of issue-spotting is identifying what you don't know and need to learn."

In retrospect, there may be rather too little self-doubt in the various pieces of this book—an occupational hazard of being a constitutional law professor, perhaps?

THE CONCLUDING ESSAYS in this chapter present my evolving thinking about one of the most promising and most terrifying developments in modern science: our increasing ability to reliably reconstruct past events by using DNA evidence. One future utopia would be a world in which DNA not only frees the innocent and finds the guilty but also prevents various crimes from ever occurring because these crimes will be so easy to solve that would-be criminals will forbear. But in a future dystopia, scheming government officials could use DNA databases to probe and expose all sorts of private matters in order to harass or intimidate political opponents. For example, DNA can prove that the actual biological father of A is not B (as both A and B thought) but C. In my earliest piece on DNA, a 2001 essay in the *American Lawyer* entitled "A Safe Intrusion," I was too glib, treating DNA as just an improved version of fingerprinting. But fingerprints cannot prove or disprove paternity, and paternity issues are intimately connected with sexual privacy in ways that I did not adequately appreciate in 2001. Thus, in a later piece published in the *New York Times* in 2002, "A Search for Justice in Our Genes," I tried to address the matter with more precision. In both pieces, I called for the creation and super-strict regulation of a truly comprehensive DNA database that would effectively include the DNA of all Americans. In issuing this call I was years ahead of courts and most commentators.[2]

In 2013, the Supreme Court took a big step in my direction by the slimmest of margins in a landmark case, *Maryland v. King*, which allowed DNA to be taken from mere arrestees, as opposed to actual convicts. (The case is discussed in this chapter's closing essay, which Neal Katyal and I cowrote for the *New York Times* shortly after the *King* decision came down.) America is still years, perhaps decades, away from the world that I envisioned in 2001 and 2002, a world in which virtually everyone's DNA is part of a comprehensive, secure database. But we appear to be moving in that direction.

As a matter of equality and fairness, why should mere arrestees, and only arrestees, be forced into providing DNA samples? Some arrestees are innocent persons who are never subsequently convicted of any wrongdoing. If arrestees are disproportionately nonwhite, the database will be racially skewed in ways that put blood relatives of arrestees (also disproportionately nonwhite) at greater risk of government detection in situations involving partial DNA matches. (Recall that unlike fingerprints, DNA generates information implicating biological relations. Although Maryland's database system has special rules limiting familial searches, other jurisdictions are less punctilious.) *Maryland v. King* may thus be merely a way station on the road to a more comprehensive DNA-collection system at some later date—a system that, though more intrusive in certain obvious respects, would also be more racially equal than the status quo. (By analogy, airports today oblige everyone to go through metal detectors, not just those who look faintly Middle Eastern.)

Although I was among the first in the American legal academy to advocate for this end result, I confess that, years later, I am extremely nervous about this prospect. Of all the issues discussed in this book, DNA databases may be the topic on which I am now the most uneasy about how my ideas will eventually be judged by posterity.

HOW COURTS LET LEGAL GAMES HIDE THE TRUTH

WASHINGTON POST, SUNDAY, APRIL 16, 1995

A criminal trial is not a football game, even if it stars O. J. Simpson. But viewers of the Simpson case proceedings could be forgiven for confusing the two. Who can doubt, as they watch Johnnie Cochran do battle with Marcia Clark, that a sporting-match mentality has come to dominate American criminal procedure? And, entertaining as the match may be, who can escape the queasy feeling that something important is being overlooked?

That neglected something is, of course, the truth. Truth, once thought to be the main concern of the judicial process, is now too often lost in the gladiatorial excesses of our current system. But perhaps some good will come from the very extravagance of the Simpson trial, following hard, as it does, on the heels of other extravaganzas such as the Menendez brothers murder trials and the William Kennedy Smith rape trial. Perhaps it will fuel reform projects now afoot—projects designed to move our system away from a Sporting Model and back to a Truth Model of criminal justice.

Why, you may ask, can't we have both? A darn good fight and truth and justice, too?

Begin with the basics. We watch sports for fun. A good football game is played well—with quick moves, hard hits, big plays, surprising turns, a close score. But in the grand scheme of things (sorry, Vince Lombardi) it hardly matters who wins and who loses.

A criminal trial is different. From the point of view of the larger society (if not from that of the producers of Court TV), it is less important that a trial is played well—with clever lawyering, high drama, and nail-biting suspense—and more important that it ends well, with truth and justice prevailing. When a trial reaches the wrong result, the system suffers. When an innocent man is erroneously found guilty and punished—losing his good name, his liberty, perhaps even his life—a terrible tragedy has occurred. And when a guilty man is erroneously found innocent and walks free, with a grin on his face, the victim suffers anew and we are all a little less safe.

To put the point another way: A sporting event *makes* winners and losers—the rules of the game itself determine who was the better team on this day. Of course, sometimes a team that deserved to win ends up losing, but it's no big deal. Wait till next year!

Trials, by contrast, do not *make* the defendant guilty or innocent (though they do at times determine whether defendants' actions were justified). Instead, they seek to *find* a preexisting truth: Either O. J. did it or he didn't. And if he did it, he is—in a way that matters as much as anything on this earth ever does—guilty, regardless of what a jury decides. This is why, strictly speaking, a person is not "innocent until proved guilty but rather "*presumed* innocent until proved guilty."

A trial, then, should be about truth, but too often it is about playing well and winning. Lawyers on both sides want to win. Like sports stars, the more they win, the more fame they get, the more money they make. The media covers a big trial the way it covers the playoffs—with elaborate pre-game hype; up-close-and-personal profiles of colorful characters; evening news highlight footage; and unending post-game analysis by pundits who diagram plays, expound on tactics, and so on.

Worst of all, some of the rules of the courtroom itself have gradually been diverted from their truth-seeking mission. Consider, first, the so-called exclusionary rule.

Even before his jury was impaneled, O. J.'s lawyers fought fiercely to prevent the jury from learning about the blood found in his car, on his driveway, in his house. Why? Because the blood was somehow unreliable evidence that would divert the jury from the truth of whodunit? Hardly. Modern science makes blood one of the most reliable of all forms of evidence—far more reliable than notoriously inaccurate recollections of eyewitnesses. Guilty defendants may dread the power of new blood-testing technology, but innocent defendants should applaud it: The blood test, after all, can clear an innocent suspect. Indeed, some innocent men who were once on death row walk free today because new tests performed years after their trials have proved that it was actually someone else's blood.

Simpson's lawyers' plea for exclusion, then, may have had far more to do with gamesmanship than with truth. The police, they claimed, conducted searches without jumping through the right procedural hoops, and so the reliable evidence must be excluded. Government broke the rules, so it must be penalized. Fifteen years for unsportsmanlike conduct—and the truth be damned.

Gamesmanship aside, the arguments for exclusion are strikingly weak. The constitutional provision that bars unreasonable searches and seizures—the Fourth Amendment—says nothing about exclusion. English common law, the source of the amendment, has never excluded unreasonably obtained but otherwise reliable evidence. Inclusion was the clear rule in every American court, state or federal, for more than a hundred years after independence, and still is in civil courts.

Some have argued that a court would lack integrity if it allowed in "tainted" evidence. But this "integrity" argument leads to results that often undermine rather than affirm judicial integrity. Ultimately, the integrity of trials is tightly linked to their truth-seeking mission: Banning truthful evidence also threatens judicial integrity. Seeing this, many judges instead refuse to exclude evidence by cheating, dishonestly claiming that an unreasonable search really was okay, so that the evidence can come in. Here is the exclusionary rule in action: Truth is banned in some cases, and judges in other cases lie, all in the name of maintaining the "integrity" of our courts.

Sometimes it is claimed that we must exclude evidence to prevent government from profiting from its own wrong. But what about the murderer who profits from his wrong when reliable evidence is excluded and he walks free? If the government improperly searches and finds a ton of cocaine, must it give the drugs back to the dealers? If not—if it is allowed to keep the drugs, and sell them for legitimate medicinal purposes, as is now the law—why can't it also use the drugs to put criminals behind bars?

The only real argument for exclusion is deterrence: Government must be discouraged from violating citizens' rights. But exclusion is neither necessary nor sufficient for this goal; in fact, it's a dumb deterrence scheme. If the government knows you're innocent but wants to hassle you (say, because of your race, or politics), the exclusionary rule is no deterrent. The government isn't trying to convict you, and (predictably) finds nothing, so there's nothing to exclude. The exclusionary rule benefits only the guilty; and the guiltier you are—the more the cops find—the more there is to exclude and the more you benefit. (Many criminal defense attorneys don't see this as a problem because they are less concerned with innocence than with winning.)

To protect the innocent victims of government searches and seizures, we need devices other than the exclusionary rule: administrative disciplinary mechanisms against abusive cops, damage actions and punitive damages for outrageous government behavior, attorneys' fees for law-abiding citizens who prove the government violated their rights, and so on. Rodney King's successful tort suit against the Los Angeles Police Department shows how powerful a robust civil damage system could be, even for indigent victims, if given a fair chance. This is exactly the thrust of pending crime legislation, sponsored by Senators Orrin Hatch and Bob Dole, now being considered on Capitol Hill: civil deterrence rather than criminal exclusion.[3]

Interestingly, the reforms would conform precisely to the model of the Fourth Amendment framers: The most famous case in the Anglo-American world of the late eighteenth century—the O. J. case of its day—was an English case involving civil damages rather than criminal exclusion. Government had searched unreasonably, and so the citizen target sued and won huge damages. Americans cheered the result and lionized the plaintiff, John Wilkes, and the judge, Lord Camden. (Just look at any map, and the fame of the case is clear: Wilkes-Barre, Pennsylvania; Wilkes County, Georgia; Wilkes County, North Carolina; Camden, New Jersey; Camden, South Carolina; Camden, Maine; and many other places were named to honor these men. By contrast, there are no cities named in honor of the criminals freed by the exclusionary rule.)

Closely related to the Fourth Amendment's exclusionary rule is the question of exclusion under the Fifth Amendment, which says that government may not compel someone to be a witness against himself in a criminal case. And so when Oliver North was forced to testify in Congress, his compelled testimony could not later be read against him in his criminal trial: Otherwise, he would have been made an involuntary witness against himself in his own case.

But suppose North had admitted that he embezzled fifty grand in gold from the government, and that the gold was buried in his backyard. And suppose the government then dug up the gold and tried to introduce it and it alone—with North's fingerprints on it, but without his statement—in a criminal case. Under a Sporting Model, even reliable physical fruits of testimony should be excluded. In a game, you have to score on your own; you can't make your opponent do your work. But if the idea is to find the truth rather than to stage a good game, reliable fruit should come in. It can help convict the guilty, but it can also clear the innocent.

Compelled testimony—witnessing—is rightly banned because compelled words may be unreliable. An innocent man may be tricked into misleading concessions by a crafty lawyer trying to trap him—a prosecutor seeking to win rather than find the truth. But physical fruits—gold bars with fingerprints—are different. They are reliable. They are not "witnessing" and should come in.

Thirty years ago, the Warren Court began to move in this direction when it allowed prosecutors to force defendants to give blood samples. Blood, said the court, was not witnessing, so the government could compel it. This is why O. J. can be compelled to give his blood, but not his story. Similarly, if the cops fail to read a suspect his rights, a prosecutor can't use the words, but she can use the fruits—reliable physical evidence that the cops uncovered as a result of the words.

But if all this is so, supporters of the Truth Model ask, why shouldn't the gold bars be admissible in our North hypothetical? Why shouldn't the government be allowed to require a defendant to turn over (or tell the government where it can find) reliable physical evidence, as is done routinely in civil litigation?

Consider, finally, issues of legal ethics. In a Sporting Model, one team doesn't have to hand over its playbook to the other side. But in a courtroom, strategic efforts to surprise one's opponent are frowned upon. If you plan to put on a witness, the other side should be told well in advance. Lawyers who want to win are tempted to flout those rules, as has been made vividly clear by tactics on both sides in the O. J. case.

Cross-examination raises a related issue. Sports teams try to fake each other out. A fake handoff freezes the linebacker to set up a play-action pass.

But what are the ethical limits on lawyers' deception in the courtroom? Lawyers are not allowed today to suborn perjury—to put on the stand a witness whom they know will lie—but currently they are allowed to vigorously cross-examine a witness whom they know is telling the truth in an effort to trick the jury into thinking that the witness is lying. Is this just? In a rape case, should a defense attorney who knows his client did it be free to use all his arts to convince the jury that the victim is making it up? Here, too, an emphasis on truth over winning calls for possible reform of courtroom rules.

These reforms will at times make it harder for defense attorneys to win if their clients are guilty, but reform can also help innocent defendants who are now hurt by a sporting theory of justice. Consider an inmate on death row convicted in a perfectly fair trial. Both sides played by the rules, and he lost. But now, new reliable physical evidence—though improperly obtained, let's say—makes clear that he is in fact innocent. Should we exclude this evidence on the grounds that it was obtained improperly? Should we send this man to the gallows because his trial was a fair fight?

Or should we, instead, choose truth and justice over sportsmanship? And if we do choose truth, as various civil libertarians are rightly pressing upon the Supreme Court in high-profile new-evidence cases, shouldn't we also choose truth when it proves guilt rather than innocence? After all, the sword of truth in the hand of Lady Justice cuts both ways.

A SECOND CHANCE AT JUSTICE

New York Times, Thursday, February 6, 1997

If at first you don't succeed, try, try again.

Now that O. J. Simpson has been tried again—this time in a civil court—we are faced with two verdicts that appear to conflict, and some serious questions about our justice system. One lesson we can draw from the Simpson legal drama is that the civil process is better than the criminal at unlocking the truth.

A criminal defendant, for example, can refuse to answer pretrial questions: What was he doing? When? With whom? At the trial, he can wait until the state has played its cards, then trump up a convenient story. But in a civil case, a defendant must answer questions during pretrial depositions. He will then be more inclined to tell the truth during the trial, because his story is already on record. If he changes his story, he is likely to be reminded of his earlier statements under oath.

In the Simpson civil case, depositions locked in Simpson's story that he never owned a pair of Bruno Magli shoes; in the criminal case, he was not obliged to tell pretrial investigators a thing—and Simpson's truthfulness on this subject never became an issue.

Why not put a criminal defendant through a courtroom deposition before trial, with his lawyer present and a judge presiding? Since 1892, the Supreme Court has said that such a process would violate the Fifth Amendment's protection against self-incrimination, but that interpretation misreads the Constitution.

Strictly speaking, the clause prevents government from compelling a defendant to be a "witness" at trial in a criminal case. But if his pretrial deposition is never introduced before a jury, the defendant will not be a "witness" against himself. And if, as a result of the deposition, physical evidence is discovered, that evidence should be admissible in court.

Prosecutors should also be able to subpoena incriminating physical evidence from criminal defendants, just as civil defendants can be forced to hand over evidence that hurts their case.

Though these proposals may shock defense attorneys, they shouldn't. Congress explicitly endorsed such a system in the 1860s, around the time it applied to the states the Constitution's clause protecting against self-incrimination. And most criminal courts operated this way before 1892.

The Court may be drifting back in that direction. In a landmark case in 1966, a defendant was compelled to provide a blood sample. Giving blood, the Court said, wasn't the same as being a witness at trial, and besides, blood is highly reliable as evidence.

More recently, the Court has said that when police obtain a confession without reading a suspect his rights, the confession must be excluded, but any reliable physical evidence found as a result is admissible. If evidence gathered by police conduct can be used in criminal court, why not evidence generated by depositions?

Reliable evidence should always be welcome. But the so-called exclusionary rule, which only applies in criminal cases, breeds cynicism among police, judges, and ultimately jurors. For instance, to get evidence admitted that may otherwise be tossed out of court, detectives may initially deny that someone is a suspect.

The police in the Simpson case did just that. In the criminal trial, they implausibly denied that Simpson was a suspect just after the crime. As long as he was not, any evidence they seized at his home that otherwise might have been suppressed, such as blood, could be admitted in court.

Simpson's lawyer, Johnnie Cochran, exploited the fuzziness of the police story, suggesting grander conspiracies, and jurors voted to acquit.

Whether or not justice was done in either O. J. Simpson trial, criminal courts, like civil courts, should try harder to seek the truth.

A TALE OF TWO CITIES

FINDLAW, MONDAY, MAY 1, 2000

Shots ring out in a fast-moving altercation, and a black man lies dead on a city street. The white officers claim self-defense, saying they sincerely (if erroneously) thought they were in danger. A jury acquits. As the country is now aware, these are the basic facts of the Amadou Diallo case. But they also describe the Boston Massacre of 1770.

Of course history never repeats itself exactly. Five men died in Boston, and only one, Crispus Attucks, was black. The Boston victims were looking for trouble—pelting the officers with sticks and snowballs—whereas Diallo was simply reaching for his wallet. Not all Boston defendants won complete acquittals, but most did. Nevertheless, the comparison between the two trials is instructive.

Despite their similar factual scenarios and results, there was a sharp difference between the Diallo and Massacre trials. The Diallo trial was shifted from the Bronx to Albany, in a move that was designed to avoid unfair prejudice to the defendants, and that may have been responsible for the officers' controversial acquittals. The Massacre trial, in contrast, took place in the city where the tragedy occurred. And rightly so.

Remembering the Massacre trial, and its similarities to the Diallo case, can remind us of what the Founders well knew: a criminal trial is about not only the rights of defendants, but also the rights of communities. And a verdict rendered by jurors from the very community that has suffered the loss enjoys a legitimacy, and public acceptance, that no foreign verdict can muster. If we forget the Founding history that taught these lessons, including the Massacre trial itself, we do so at our peril.

The Massacre trial's Boston venue was no coincidence. Any attempt to move the trial to some "cooler" (and presumably more defendant-friendly) locale would have been viewed by our liberty-loving forefathers as an outrage. As in the Diallo case, passions ran high and virulent anti-defendant pre-trial publicity existed. Sam Adams and the Sons of Liberty could probably teach Al Sharpton and company a thing or two about how to whip up resentment against quick-triggered officers. Yet for the colonists, unlike the court that transferred venue in Diallo, such passions and publicity provided reasons for—not arguments against—impaneling a local jury.

The common law—the body of law, taken from England, that colonists demanded as their sacred birthright—promised a jury of the "vicinage": one composed of citizens of the locality where the blood had spilled. The vicinage rule derived from the local community's right to self-government, a right to judge for itself, via the jury, what had happened and how to respond. That a community might feel passionate about the fates of its own members would have seemed, to the colonists, patriotic, not inappropriate.

This concern for the community was hardly unusual in early America. Then, community rights frequently trumped defendants' desires. Thus, defendants were often barred from waiving jury trials even if they might have preferred to entrust their fate to fact-finding judges. And regardless of the wishes of the defendant, the public itself had a right to attend all criminal proceedings, in part to make sure that the judge—a permanent and paid government official—did not cut the defendant any special breaks. (This risk of favoritism was especially acute when the defendant, too, was a fellow government officer who might expect special treatment from his judicial brethren.)

A modern commentator might protest that the respect for community rights underlying the vicinage rule comes only at a cost to the rights of criminal defendants. But the Massacre trial itself provides a powerful counterargument: like the Diallo defendants, most of the Massacre defendants won complete acquittals, suggesting that they received a fair trial even in a community where passions against them ran high.

The colonial commitment to local trials ran deep. Indeed, it played a part in inspiring the American Revolution. After the Massacre trial, in 1774, Parliament declared that future British officers accused of murdering Americans would be tried in England, far from the madding crowd. Incensed Americans quickly dubbed the statute an "Intolerable Act," one of several outrageous laws that triggered the American Revolution. Indeed, the Declaration of

Independence—authored with the assistance of the Boston Massacre defense attorney, John Adams—thundered against the act as a "Mock Trial" regime. In the wake of the Revolution, the federal Constitution preserved community rights by promising that every federal crime would be tried in the state where the crime occurred; and the Bill of Rights further pledged that federal trials would always be "public."

How did we come to forget these Founding lessons? Part of the answer may be found some fourscore years after the American Revolution, when our Constitution was reconstructed in the shadow of the Civil War. The Revolution had pitted liberty-loving localists against an oppressive imperial center; and the local jury embodied all that patriots held dear. But after the Civil War, the central government emerged as the friend of liberty, and local juries, especially in the South, were not always to be trusted to protect liberty, especially the liberty of African Americans.

Nevertheless, it would be passing strange to invoke the spirit of Reconstruction to support the venue transfer in Diallo, a venue transfer that made it far less likely that blacks would compose a majority or near-majority of jurors. The Fourteenth Amendment adopted after the Civil War surely reflected heightened concern with the rights of individuals, but the individuals at the center of this concern looked more like Amadou Diallo than the armed state officials who shot him.

Nowadays, we have become too accustomed to venue transfers in high-profile cases, state and federal. Thus Los Angeles cops accused of brutalizing Rodney King were prosecuted in officer-friendly Simi Valley rather than the community where the beating occurred; and Timothy McVeigh was tried outside of Oklahoma, contrary to the Constitution's letter and spirit. The result is verdicts that may lack community legitimacy, failing to provide the scarred community the satisfaction of a local trial, and ultimately failing to provide defendants the repose of a legitimate verdict.

When the Simi Valley acquittals predictably raised public suspicion that the venue-shifting judiciary had improperly favored fellow government officers, the federal government was obliged to restore public confidence with a second prosecution. Though technically not double jeopardy (the first trial occurred in state court, the second in federal court), double prosecution nevertheless raised serious fairness concerns in the case of the Rodney King defendants. Federal officials are reportedly considering possible civil rights charges in Diallo, too—running the risk of triggering the same fairness concerns if they ultimately go forward. How much better for all concerned if the first trial is done right—done, that is, where the blood was spilled.

High-profile cases require special safeguards in order to ensure fairness to all concerned. But as the Boston Massacre trial teaches, venue transfers are generally not the answer. The basic idea of jury trial in cases like the Boston Massacre, the Rodney King beating, and the Diallo killing is that the people directly affected by government officers should be the ones who judge them. Community members are best positioned to decide how passive or aggressive they want their cops to be because they are the ones who must live with—and who may die from—the consequences of their choice. Our Founders understood this basic idea; why don't we?

THE FIRST PRINCIPLES
OF THE FOURTH AMENDMENT[4]

AMERICAN LAWYER, NOVEMBER 2001

As security experts propose new forms of searches, seizures, and surveillance to combat terrorism, civil libertarians will rhetorically rally round the Constitution. But that document does not quite say what most libertarians—or most judges, for that matter—think it does. Indeed, the document is far wiser than the standard libertarian line and the conventional judicial interpretation.

The key constitutional text is the Fourth Amendment: "The right of the people to be secure in their persons, houses, papers, and effects, against unreasonable searches and seizures, shall not be violated, and no Warrants shall issue, but upon probable cause, supported by Oath or affirmation, and particularly describing the place to be searched, and the persons or things to be seized."

Note what the amendment does not say. It does not say that every search or seizure must have a warrant. Nor does it require that each intrusion must be backed by probable cause, or even individualized suspicion. Nor does it command that whenever an unconstitutional intrusion occurs, judges must exclude the evidence obtained, and its fruits, from any criminal prosecution.

Founding history confirms this straightforward reading of the text. Arrests—highly intrusive seizures—did not require warrants at the Founding. (Nor do they today. Most arrests in fact occur without warrants.) The very Congress that proposed the Fourth Amendment authorized searches of certain ships without probable cause or even individualized suspicion. Before 1776, and for more than a century thereafter, no English or American judge ever excluded reliable evidence simply because it had been found in an improper search.

Common sense also supports the amendment's plain meaning. Metal detectors at airports and courthouses are now commonplace even though these search regimes lack warrants and probable cause. Metal detectors are indiscriminate—everyone, suspicious-looking or not, must pass through—but indiscriminateness alone does not make them unconstitutional. In fact, the general lack of discrimination may make metal detectors constitutionally more attractive on egalitarian grounds.

Common sense also balks at the extreme libertarian argument that evidence found in an illegal search must always be suppressed because government must never profit from its own wrong. Government does not, and should not, return stolen goods to a thief, even if it finds them in an illegal search. Rather, government restores stolen goods to their rightful owner, just as it would restore a kidnapped child to her parents. We do not insist that if cops find the child in an unconstitutional search, they must give her back to her kidnapper, close their eyes, count to twenty, and then start looking again. For similar reasons, government should constitutionally be allowed to use leads found in illegal searches to track down violent partners in crime, and to use all reliable evidence to put perpetrators behind bars, thereby protecting future victims.

If the Constitution does not require warrants, probable cause, individualized suspicion, or the exclusionary rule, what does it require? Simply this: Every search and seizure must be reasonable. This is less vague than it might sound, for the Constitution gives us considerable guidance about what is reasonable, why, and who should decide.

The Fourth Amendment affirms Americans' right to be secure. The right runs against government, but threats to security posed by thieves and thugs affect the constitutional calculus. For example, well-placed metal detectors may make us a little less secure against government, but can also make us a lot more secure against terrorists. Greater private threats may justify greater governmental intrusions. Americans may disagree about whether a given governmental intrusion makes them, on balance, more secure overall. But that is the key issue to debate, as opposed to the presence or absence of warrants and probable cause. And in thinking about security, we should openly focus on the intrusiveness and proportionality of the government's response.

For example, in contrast to full-blown arrests or strip-searches, metal detectors at airports are relatively modest intrusions, proportionate to the real threat of airline hijacking. A dragnet search of a neighborhood to find a stolen watch would ordinarily be disproportionate, even though a similar search to find a missing child might not be.

The amendment affirms a right of the people. At the Founding, juries embodying the people played leading roles in deciding which intrusions were unconstitutional. (Warrants—addressed in the second half of the amendment—were generally disfavored because they issued from judges in secret proceedings that cut juries out of the loop. Thus, warrants required certain special safeguards—probable cause, oaths, particular description— not required generally for all searches and seizures.)

If the government searches a broad cross-section of citizens, allegedly to enhance their security, those citizens are well positioned to assess the reasonableness of the search, and judges should not completely ignore popular sentiment. But when only a few individuals or members of disfavored minority groups are specially targeted, the people en masse may be poor judges, happy to impose intrusions on others that they would not willingly bear themselves. Ironically, sometimes a broader search, intruding on a much greater portion of society, is constitutionally preferable. The people can judge best when they are both the subjects of a search and its alleged beneficiaries.

The Bush administration has recently proposed to expand the powers of judges to issue wiretap warrants. But because judges issuing such warrants typically act in secret, the public and the people are in effect cut out of the loop here. Given the Fourth Amendment primacy of popular input, additional safeguards should be considered. For example, the law could require that, in addition to getting a court order, the Justice Department must periodically report the names of those to be subjected to wiretapping to a Senate committee with special security clearance. Exceptions could be made only if personally approved by the president and attorney general. This reporting requirement would tighten the link between governmental intrusion and popular judgment; unlike federal judges, senators and presidents are elected by the people.

The amendment mentions persons, houses, and papers, above and beyond all other effects. When government searches or seizes human bodies (persons), it must take special care to minimize unnecessary intrusions upon liberty and dignity. Houses deserve more protection than other buildings because they are unique seats of intimacy and family. Rifling through citizens' papers can threaten free expression, and so here, too, government must tread cautiously. Once we understand these special Founding values of bodily dignity, privacy, and free expression, we can guard against high-tech intrusions that threaten these values in nonliteral but real ways. For example, overly broad wiretaps and electronic eavesdropping can jeopardize expressive freedom even if papers are not literally involved.

Equality is another vital Fourth Amendment value. The very word *people* implies democratic equality among citizens, in contrast to the elaborate class distinctions of the Old World from which America revolted. The rule that warrants can be supported by either oath or affirmation embodies religious tolerance and pluralism; some religions reject oath-taking, and the amendment aims to accommodate these minority groups. Most important, the Fourteenth Amendment, adopted after the Civil War, glossed the Fourth Amendment's command of reasonableness. Antislavery crusaders inserted into the Constitution the word "equal," which the slaveholding Founders had omitted in the context of individual rights. The Fourth Amendment and all other Founding-era provisions should nowadays be read through the prism of Reconstruction, with its emphatic commitment to a republic of equal citizens. Airport searches targeted only at those citizens who look faintly Arabic are thus troubling; one way to symbolically affirm the equality of these Americans, while accommodating the need to be on the lookout for persons matching the description of specific suspects, might be to offer token compensation to passengers subject to special airport intrusions—say, free headsets or upgrades. This is how we currently show respect for those passengers bumped off airline flights, who endure special inconveniences to benefit their fellow passengers. In effect, we should try to spread the costs of fighting terrorism to the people more generally, rather than to the unlucky minority group members who are specially intruded upon.

Finally, the Fourth Amendment tells us that its provisions shall not be violated. Thus, we must deter unreasonable governmental intrusions and punish them when they occur. But the exclusionary rule is not the right way to do this. It punishes crime victims, who must watch grinning criminals walk free. It makes ordinary people less secure by unleashing thugs and thieves. It also provides no real remedy for innocent citizens targeted by government: there is no evidence to exclude in these cases. Thus, the Founders sensibly relied on systems of civil remedy rather than criminal exclusion to give the Fourth Amendment teeth. Such systems could be made to work again today, if judges and libertarians were willing to think creatively.

Reasonableness, security, popular sentiment, bodily dignity, privacy, free expression, equality, deterrence—these are the true Fourth Amendment values that should organize democratic debate about search and seizure policy in the difficult days ahead. The Constitution does not give us all the answers, but, when read carefully, it helps us ask the right questions.

AN UNREASONABLE VIEW
OF THE FOURTH AMENDMENT

Los Angeles Times, Sunday, April 29, 2001

Picture this: Returning home from soccer practice with her two young children, a mother slowly drives her pickup down a quiet street. A cop notices the car's occupants are not wearing seat belts, and pulls the vehicle over. Yelling at the mother as he approaches, he scares the kids. He tells her that she is going directly to jail, and refuses to allow her first to take the crying youngsters to a neighbor's house. As the incident unfolds, friends arrive and shepherd away the youngsters. The policeman proceeds to search the truck (finding nothing), handcuff the mother, put her in his car (without seat belts!) and haul her to the station, where she is booked and placed in a jail cell for an hour. She posts bond and is released, only to find that her pickup has been towed away. Eventually, she pleads guilty to the seat-belt infraction, and pays the maximum fine of $50.

This is what Gail Atwater said happened to her in Lago Vista, Texas, in 1997. She sued the cop and the city for damages, claiming violations of her Fourth Amendment right to be free from unreasonable searches and seizures. Last week, the Supreme Court, by a 5–4 vote, ordered that her lawsuit be dismissed because her allegations did not add up to a constitutional violation.

Justice David Souter's opinion for the majority is learned and lawyerly. It provides a magisterial exposition of early English and American cases and commentary concerning warrantless arrests for petty offenses. It surveys a broad range of modern legal scholarship, including some of my own. But it misses the point: the cop's alleged behavior was obviously unreasonable and thus unconstitutional.

Why jail a resident who was no flight risk, given that the underlying infraction itself could not be punished with jail time? Why the handcuffs? The yelling? The truck search? Each of these aspects compounded the intrusiveness of the overall encounter; none was justified on the facts of the case. At oral argument, Justice Anthony Kennedy said that "it is not a constitutional violation for a police officer to be a jerk." Perhaps not, but it is a constitutional violation for a police officer to be unreasonable in seizing a person. This much should be clear from the opening words of the Fourth Amendment: "The right of the people to be secure in their persons, houses, papers, and effects, against unreasonable searches and seizures, shall not be violated."

But what makes a search or seizure unreasonable? Many lawyers and judges have focused on the amendment's remaining words, which discuss "warrants" and "probable cause." On one reading of the amendment, any search or seizure lacking a warrant or probable cause is unreasonable and thus unconstitutional (except perhaps in an emergency). But the amendment does not quite say this, and history emphatically contradicts it. For example, officers for two centuries have generally been allowed to arrest a suspected felon without warrant, even if a warrant could easily have been obtained. The majority in the *Atwater v. Lago Vista* case held that a similar rule should hold true for petty offenses: an officer does not need a warrant to make an arrest for a violation he has witnessed firsthand.

The Court's majority was on solid ground in insisting that a warrantless arrest is not automatically unreasonable. But Atwater didn't need to prove this to prevail. All she needed to show was that, all things considered, *her* arrest was unreasonable, that the cop acted in a disproportionate and unjustified way. Granted, the cop was justified in stopping—arresting, if you will—Atwater's vehicle and temporarily detaining her to verify identity and issue a citation. But the other elements of the seizure—the handcuffing, the search, the jailhouse, and so on—seem obviously excessive given that the underlying seat-belt offense is treated so lightly by Texas law.

Indeed, on the stipulated facts, the Court seemed to concede that Atwater was seized unreasonably. To quote from the majority opinion: "In her case, the physical incidents of arrest were merely gratuitous humiliations imposed by a police officer who was at best exercising extremely poor judgment." The problem, said the Court, was that it would be hard to frame a general rule broad enough to protect Atwater, yet specific enough to give all future cops clear guidance. But two obvious candidates spring to mind: Full-blown arrests and jailhouse detentions could be deemed presumptively unreasonable where the infraction itself is punishable only by a petty fine or, more broadly, where arrests and detention are very far from standard police practice for a given offense. Under either version, an officer would be allowed to point to some special circumstance (such as some unusual danger) to justify his heavy-handedness.

More generally, the Constitution does not require the Court to frame a general rule for every conceivable fact pattern. The genius of the framers' Fourth Amendment is that juries of ordinary Americans can sometimes decide which intrusions are so unreasonable as to require abusive officers to pay damages. The landmark English search-and-seizure cases that inspired the framers were themselves civil-damage suits where juries helped determine whether government officials had acted reasonably. The amendment's very text suggests the importance of popular input on the question of reasonableness by describing the right against unreasonable intrusion as a right of "the people." Elsewhere in the Constitution, the words "the people" conjure up themes of popular sovereignty and public opinion. An early draft of the Seventh Amendment, which safeguards jury trials in damage suits like Atwater's, described the jury as "one of the best securities of the rights of the people." The striking linguistic harmony between this draft and the Fourth Amendment—both speak of the "right of the people" and use the language of "security"—confirms the founding link between civil juries and Fourth Amendment reasonableness.

Granted, many issues might be unfit for jury determination, requiring judges to frame bright-line rules that cops may never do this and must always do that. But surely there is a middle category of cases where the search issue is more fact-specific and fine-grained: Did this officer act reasonably in this situation, all things considered? The facts of *Atwater* seem tailor-made for a jury decision, yet the Court arrogated the issue to itself.

It might be feared that juries will be too hard on the cops or, alternatively, too insensitive to plaintiffs. But jurors standing between the aggrieved citizen and the accused officer are often poised to strike a sensible balance between liberty and order. If they unreasonably handcuff the cops, their community will suffer; and if they allow the cops to handcuff citizens unreasonably, they are likewise putting themselves at risk. Damage suits like Atwater's can educate jurors about actual police conduct and encourage police officers to internalize the norms of the citizens they are called to serve. Juries can foster a kind of community-based policing, providing interactive feedback between the citizenry and officialdom. As the officer was slapping the cuffs on Atwater, society should want him to be asking himself, "Could I justify my behavior here to the civilian community?"

Juries can make mistakes, but so can judges. One of the Rehnquist Court's trademark mistakes has been to inflate its own role at the expense of other, more democratic institutions empowered by the Constitution. Article II gives key roles in deciding presidential elections to Congress and state officials, but the Court snatched power to itself in *Bush v. Gore* last December. The Reconstruction amendments explicitly empower "Congress" to enforce them, yet the Rehnquist Court has struck down a slew of congressional civil-rights laws in recent years—every one of these invalidations an unjustified assault on a coequal branch. In its latest decision, the Court similarly gave insufficient thought to the possibility that someone other than itself—in this case, a jury of ordinary Americans—might be trusted to do the right thing.

THE BATTLE OF HUDSON HEIGHTS

SLATE, MONDAY, JUNE 19, 2006, 3:01 P.M. (ET)

Another front in the culture wars heated up last week. The proper scope of the exclusionary rule and the central purposes of the Fourth Amendment were debated anew as the Supreme Court announced its sharply contested decision in the case of *Hudson v. Michigan*.

The immediate battleground—the precise fact pattern at issue in *Hudson*—is but a speck on the vast map of American constitutional law. Yet given the precise location of this battleground and the particular tactics of the justices in struggling over it, *Hudson* may be seen one day as a decisive crossroads. Essentially, the judicial battle of Hudson Heights involved a fierce contest for high conceptual ground, and the victors have now secured a strong base for further action that could broadly reshape the lines of the exclusionary rule.

First the facts. The cops in *Hudson* had a search warrant authorizing them to enter a house and look for drugs and guns. They found both. But the way they entered the house was constitutionally improper. Instead of waiting a reasonable period (say, twenty seconds) after announcing their presence at the front door—as generally required under long-standing Anglo-American tradition and modern Fourth Amendment doctrine—the police simply announced themselves, opened the (unlocked) door, and began searching. They found lots of cocaine, later introduced as evidence to convict the homeowner of drug possession.

Led by Justice Stephen Breyer, four dissenters found this a textbook case for exclusion: The police violated the Fourth Amendment, so the drugs must be suppressed and the guilty man must go free. Next case.

Not so fast, said five justices on the other side, led by Justice Antonin Scalia. Although the Fourth Amendment was violated, this violation made absolutely no difference so far as the drugs were concerned. Had the cops properly waited an extra twenty seconds they still would have found the cocaine.

To this, Breyer responded with an ultrastrict version of "coulda, woulda, shoulda." It is not enough, he said, that the government could have found the drugs in a lawful search. Generally, the government must *in fact* find the drugs in a *perfectly* valid search *wholly independent* of the tainted search.

But as the Scalia opinion emphasized, the *Hudson* cops did in fact have a valid search warrant that authorized the successful drug search—even if the warrant didn't authorize the overhasty entrance. Nothing in law or logic requires that judges must always lump together the improper entrance and the otherwise proper search, rather than treating these as two independent events. For example, if the warrant had authorized only a search of the house, and the cops instead searched both the house and a nearby barn, why should drugs found in the house be excluded just because the barn search was invalid? Why shouldn't only items found in the barn be suppressed in court?

The majority also stressed that the Supreme Court's previous case law, which Breyer claimed was the source of his ultrastrict test, is actually a mixed bag of rules and exceptions. One exception to the exclusionary rule is called "inevitable discovery," and as its very label makes clear, the test is whether a piece of evidence "*would have*" inevitably come to light in a lawful search. Nor have previous Court opinions consistently read this test in the superstrict way Breyer was now urging.

But Breyer was right to observe that, if aggressively applied, the "inevitable discovery" doctrine could outflank the exclusionary rule in a wide range of cases. With *Hudson* on the books, state and federal prosecutors should now try to find the next perfect test case, which would look something like this: The cops have very good reasons (what lawyers call "probable cause") to conduct a given search and thus the police could easily get a warrant from a judge. But they decline to get the warrant because they reasonably—though it turns out erroneously—believe that the facts fall into one of the umpteen categories for which the court has said that warrants are not required. Armed with probable cause and good faith, but no warrant, the cops search and find a smoking gun or a bloody knife—proof positive of a violent crime.

Similar cases have come before the Court previously, and the justices have at times mindlessly suppressed the evidence. But none of the Court's past cases has squarely addressed the strong argument of inevitable discovery, combined with police good faith. With *Hudson* now on the books clarifying the scope and logic of inevitable discovery, the government can argue in our test case as follows: "The cops *could have* easily gotten a warrant and surely *would have* done so, had they only better understood often-complex Court doctrine. Because the cops acted in good faith and because the evidence would have been found if the cops had strictly complied with the Fourth Amendment—a warrant would inevitably have been issued, had it been sought—the case should be treated just like *Hudson*."

It's not guaranteed that a Court majority would buy this argument. Justice Kennedy, while joining almost all of Scalia's *Hudson* opinion, wrote separately to insist that "the continued operation of the exclusionary rule, *as settled and defined by our precedents*, is not in doubt." Kennedy also took pains to note that in *Hudson* the drugs were discovered "because of a search pursuant to a lawful warrant"—which would not quite be true in the test case.

Yet Kennedy also embraced virtually all of Scalia's opinion, which vigorously cataloged various vices of the exclusionary rule and called for a tighter fit between right and remedy. One big problem with the exclusionary rule, Scalia argued, is that the rule often fits poorly with important Fourth Amendment values. If cops brutalize or humiliate citizens or destroy personal effects within a home—thereby violating core Fourth Amendment principles—there is no real link between these unreasonable intrusions on persons and property and the finding of evidence for use in a criminal case. Indeed, in many situations the cops may find no evidence at all, and they might not even be looking for evidence. If the exclusionary rule were the only remedial game in town, it would be open season on the innocent.

Of course, as Scalia and Kennedy made clear (joined by Justice Thomas and by the Court's two newest members, Chief Justice Roberts and Justice Alito), the exclusionary rule is not the only—and in many cases, not the best—way to vindicate Fourth Amendment values. In fact—though Scalia did not stress this point—no Founding Father ever called for a Fourth Amendment exclusionary rule, and no court in America ever followed such a rule in the entire century after the Declaration of Independence. Instead, the framers believed that punitive-damage suits brought by aggrieved Americans against overbearing government searchers and seizers would properly protect Fourth Amendment values.

What Scalia did stress is that—in sharp contrast to the situation faced by the early Warren Court, which was the first to use the federal Constitution to apply the exclusionary rule to ordinary state crimes—today a wide range of civil rights laws and regimes offers a superior model for enforcing the Fourth Amendment via damage suits by innocent citizens and other devices rather than suppression motions by the guilty.

Hudson's facts illustrate the point nicely. Why does the Fourth Amendment generally require the cops to knock and wait for a few seconds? Not to give a crook a twenty-second window to destroy evidence, but rather to give an innocent citizen a twenty-second chance to, say, put on a bathrobe. And this right would best be vindicated in a punitive-damage suit brought by, for example, an innocent women in her negligee who was surprised by overbearing cops, rather than by a drug dealer caught red-handed and seeking a get-out-of-jail-free card.

The Founders' Fourth Amendment, in short, was designed to protect the innocent; yet the later, judge-made exclusionary rule perversely springs the guilty. Although the *New York Times* has said that Scalia seemed to trivialize the Fourth Amendment knock-and-announce rule when he emphasized the bathrobe/negligee issue,[5] Scalia was in fact describing part of the amendment's core—a right of privacy and personal dignity. It was largely this core value that led Scalia, writing for the court in 2001, to invalidate freewheeling use of high-tech thermal detection devices aimed at personal residences, since such James Bond–like ray guns would improperly allow the government to learn "at what hour each night the lady of the house takes her daily sauna and bath—a detail that many would consider 'intimate.'"

This is hardly some personal obsession of Scalia's. The Fourth Amendment's framers had a remarkably similar view of the amendment's core rights and core remedies. According to one 1787 pamphlet, if a constable searching "for stolen goods, pulled down the clothes of a bed in which there was a woman and searched under her shift . . . a trial by [civil] jury would be our safest resource, [and] heavy damages would at once punish the [offending constable] and deter others from committing the same."

Although none of the justices in *Hudson* quoted this remarkably apt passage from the Founding Fathers, it strongly supports the *Hudson* Court's shift toward Fourth Amendment remedies that protect the innocent rather than reward the guilty. In the latest round of the culture wars, score one for Scalia.

PAPER CHASE

NEW REPUBLIC, MONDAY, DECEMBER 15, 1997

Dear Diary: It's time to compose the final exam for my criminal procedure class. Better avoid O. J.—I've already ridden that nag hard enough this semester.

Maybe a question from the Unabomber case instead? Federal agents have seized Ted Kaczynski's diaries in a raid on his mountain shack. Now prosecutors have made public these most intimate of Kaczynski's writings and plan to introduce them in court as evidence, not merely of the alleged Unabomber's guilt, but also of his cold-blooded criminal intent. And that, the government hopes, will convince the jury to mete out the death penalty. Kaczynski's diaries create a troubling picture of a man bent on committing murder and frustrated when he failed.

But that only raises the constitutional stakes. Isn't there something unsettling about the state's breaking into a man's house, pawing through his most private writings, and then using them to brand him an enemy of the state and put him to death?

The Unabomber judge has given the government the green light. But there are serious arguments on the other side—arguments rooted in at least three of the ten amendments in the Bill of Rights.

A good student analysis should probably start with opening words of the Fourth Amendment: "The right of the people to be secure in their persons, houses, papers, and effects, against unreasonable searches and seizures, shall not be violated." Here we see an obvious accent on the notion of privacy— on a citizen's body (his private "person"), on his private abode (his "house" as opposed to other buildings), and on his private "papers" above and beyond all other stuff (his "effects").

And the historical context in which the Fourth Amendment was drafted also suggests that privacy weighed heavily in the Founders' deliberations. They were undoubtedly thinking about the two most famous search-and-seizure cases in the Anglo-American world, *Wilkes v. Wood* and *Entick v. Carrington*. When George III's henchmen broke into John Wilkes's and John

Entick's houses in Britain during the 1760s and rummaged through their private papers, Wilkes and Entick brought suit and won huge jury damage awards for the outrages upon their privacy, in landmark cases presided over by Lord Camden. The colonists loved the rebuke to the king's ministry, and so Wilkes and Camden became genuine American folk heroes.

Camden's language was sweeping, proclaiming that "private papers" are a person's "dearest property" and that even in cases of "atrocious" crime "our law has provided no papersearch."

No doubt some Founders read these words as absolute in their meaning. On the other hand, the Fourth Amendment text does not rule out all "paper-search," but says only that searches must be "reasonable." Camden's "atrocious" was a rhetorical excess—the searches that rightly outraged him were aimed at anti-incumbent pamphleteers, not serial killers. England lacked a First Amendment protecting political scribblers, so libertarian judges like Camden stretched procedural search law to fill the breach. But Americans needn't be so tender toward criminal suspects since we have made it clear that mere political opposition may never be criminalized in the first place.

So the Fourth Amendment means what it says: paper searches are not per se unconstitutional, but they raise special concerns and must always be "reasonable." When the government tries to rifle through newspaper files or bursts into the headquarters of opposition parties, we must beware.

Extra credit if students mention that the Supreme Court missed the boat in the 1978 *Zurcher v. Stanford Daily* case, in which the justices upheld a search of newspaper files where there was reason to believe the *Daily* had incriminating photos of student rioters. If that were enough to go prowling through press files, Richard Nixon could have sent his plumbers to rummage through the drawers of the *Washington Post* whenever the *Post* ran a story about some illegality in the District of Columbia. What was lacking in the *Stanford Daily* case was good reason to think—and a proper judicial finding—that the newspaper was itself part of the illegality it was reporting. Congress said as much when it effectively overruled *Stanford Daily* with the Privacy Protection Act of 1980.

So where does this leave us? It's outlandish to say that Kaczynski, though a political writer of sorts, has a strong First Amendment claim to resist all searches of his papers. His lawyers could claim that he is in fact a noteworthy author: he's published in the *New York Times* and the *Washington Post*! But I doubt even Alan Dershowitz would have the chutzpah to make that argument. And, unlike in the *Stanford Daily* case, the government established probable cause to believe that Kaczynski was himself guilty of serious criminal wrongdoing, and it did so before searching.

There is, of course, the general issue of reasonableness—not to mention the argument that searching for and reading a man's diary is wildly intrusive. But this only means that the government must have a very good reason to search a person's papers—for example, a high probability that he has committed a string of murders and that his papers will contain important evidence. Telephone conversations can be pretty intimate, too, but no one thinks that the state may never wiretap suspected mobsters.

Are there any other Fourth Amendment issues that students should spot? Maybe that, even if the Founders deemed a search unconstitutional, they never would have dreamed that the evidence found should therefore be excluded. No court in early America ever excluded unconstitutionally seized evidence, and England has never had an exclusionary rule. Of course, this doesn't mean that Founding-era Americans winked at Fourth Amendment violations. Rather, the Founders believed in punishing violations through civil damage suits, along the lines of *Wilkes* and *Entick*, rather than excluding evidence and, quite possibly, unleashing the guilty.

Exclusion of illegally obtained evidence is an invention of the twentieth-century Supreme Court; modern-day exclusionists say that the rule is required lest government profit from its own wrong. But that's a misshapen claim of principle. If the government finds an illegal bomb in an unconstitutional search, must it give the bomb back lest it wrongly profit? Must it restore kidnap victims to kidnappers, illegal drugs to dealers, and stolen goods to thieves? As the Court now admits, introducing reliable evidence in a criminal case is ordinarily not in itself wrong, nor does it compound the wrong of an earlier unconstitutional search.

Certainly, Kaczynski's is not an ordinary case, and it raises a nice nuance. (A good test for separating the honors students from the rest!) Perhaps reading a man's diary in open court is itself an additional, and highly intrusive, invasion of his privacy. It's one thing to search for and read a man's diary in private, and another to broadcast his most intimate thoughts. Note that this argues for a certain kind of exclusion of evidence—not as a remedy for an earlier wrong, but to prevent a new privacy violation from taking place in the courtroom itself. The argument might hold even if the government lawfully acquired the diary—in a legal search, or pursuant to a lawful subpoena, or if a cop simply found it on the sidewalk.

Then again, if it was reasonable to break open doors and rifle through personal papers to find incriminating passages in a diary, it will usually be reasonable to read them in open court. It's true that, in a few places, the law is more absolute: to preserve certain types of interpersonal privacy, some things are absolutely privileged from view in open court, like conversations between doctors and patients, priests and penitents, husbands and wives. If Kaczynski had vented to a shrink, or a priest, or a wife, his interpersonal venting would be privileged; why not when he vents intrapersonally to his diary?

But there's a good answer to that: Maybe those communications are privileged because society has an interest in channeling possibly antisocial men into churches and marriages and other interpersonal relationships that may tame and socialize these men. Wives and pastors and therapists who listen to the ventings of the violent may well moderate their most antisocial tendencies. Diaries, on the other hand, may encourage inward obsession. (I'm not sure anyone else will buy this argument, but surely you, Dear Diary, will understand!) And it's hard to imagine a more literally antisocial lifestyle than a hermit's—Norman Bates with his mommy dearest and Theodore Kaczynski with his dearest diary.

I know, I know—I've left out the obvious: What about the Fifth Amendment privilege against compelled self-incrimination? In *Entick*, Camden made a cryptic allusion to self-incrimination, and in 1886, the Supreme Court in the *Boyd v. United States* case built on *Entick* to say that a person's private papers could never be read against him in a criminal case, lest he in effect be compelled to be a witness against himself. But *Boyd* is no longer good law; the Supreme Court has twice proclaimed that the case has not withstood "the test of time." If a man writes something down of his own free will, he was not "compelled" to be a witness against himself, even if that writing is later introduced against him, says the modern Court—although it has never squarely so held in the context of diaries, and has technically left the diary question open.

So good students should ask themselves whether we should cheer *Boyd's* demise and applaud the modern Court's narrower view of compelled witnessing. To answer, students will need to discuss why defendants have the right to take the Fifth in the first place.

And they should know what I have argued in class: The best theory of the Fifth focuses on reliability and innocence-protection. Many innocent defendants, if forced to take the stand, might be made to look guilty by a wily prosecutor skilled in courtroom forensics and artificial courtroom rules of evidence and procedure. On this theory, diaries look rather different from compelled in-court interrogation. Maybe what a person tells his diary is more like what he might say to a neighbor in a candid moment than what he might say when being cross-examined by a crafty prosecutor.

Well, I guess I've found my exam question. And I suppose it's not too hard to see how I myself would answer this question: Kaczynski loses his constitutional case. Civil libertarians are right to be nervous about Bill of Rights violations, but Kaczynski's lawyers can't prove the government acted unreasonably. But I better be careful in next week's review session not to blurt out too much about Kaczynski! This whole discussion, Dear Diary, is strictly between you and me.

"YOU HAVE THE RIGHT TO . . . "

LOS ANGELES TIMES, SUNDAY, DECEMBER 12, 1999

I have a confession to make: I've been Mirandized more times than I can remember. I've never actually been arrested or hauled down to a police station. But like virtually everyone else in America, I've been treated to the *Miranda* warning countless times on television. Its words are now burned into my brain as indelibly as the lyrics of "Hey, Jude" or "The Star-Spangled Banner."

Last week, the Supreme Court agreed to hear a case, *Dickerson v. United States*, that could result in the formal overruling of *Miranda*. Civil libertarians quickly began sounding alarm bells, while some of *Miranda*'s fiercest critics started popping champagne corks. More than three decades after it was decided, *Miranda* still gets people excited.

But all the noise last week misses the point. For better or worse, *Miranda* has been woven into the fabric of daily life: into the standard operating procedures of police departments around the country; into the expectations of most judges and prosecutors (to say nothing of defense lawyers); and, most important, into the cultural literacy and mind-set of virtually every American, rich or poor, black or white. Overruling *Miranda* cannot take us back to the world that preexisted *Miranda*, even if we wanted to go there. We have all been Mirandized too many times, if only on television.

Before the Supreme Court decided *Miranda v. Arizona* in 1966, well-settled law held that a police-station confession was admissible against a criminal defendant only if he had given the statement "voluntarily." No single factor marked the line between inadmissible coerced statements and admissible voluntary ones. Instead, judges considered each case on its own and pondered all the details: the length of the interrogation; the background, age and intelligence of the suspect; the harshness of the conditions of police-station confinement (was the suspect offered coffee and sandwiches?); and so on.

Miranda dramatically changed this legal landscape. By a 5–4 vote, the Warren Court held that unless cops allowed defense lawyers into police-station interrogations, and unless cops further warned suspects of their rights to keep silent and have lawyers present, then the confessions would be categorically inadmissible.

But *Miranda* contained a key ambiguity: Was the new warning required by the Constitution, or was it merely one clean way to guard against coerced confessions? If the latter, then perhaps Congress could repeal *Miranda* in favor of some other regime designed to guard against coerced confessions. In 1968, Congress passed a law that purported to abolish *Miranda*. But instead of providing for an elaborate alternative regime to prevent police-station abuse, Congress purported merely to reinstate the pre-*Miranda* system of case-by-case determinations of voluntariness.

The 1968 statute was a slap in the Court's face—demolishing the justices' activist edifice without erecting any substitute—and for many years most prosecutors hesitated to invoke the statute in court. But in *Dickerson*, a recent bank-robbery case arising out of a federal prosecution in Virginia, the Fourth Circuit Court of Appeals looked at the dormant 1968 statute and ruled that Congress had indeed lawfully repealed *Miranda*. Last Monday, the Supreme Court agreed to review that decision later this term.

Ironically, one of the best arguments for repealing *Miranda* is that the case has exceeded the wildest expectations of its supporters. Even if the 1968 Congress failed to offer any alternative to *Miranda*'s mousetrap, our society over the last three decades has serendipitously devised a better way of protecting police-station suspects than *Miranda* envisioned. It's called television.

Consider two possible enforcement regimes and ask yourself which gives Americans better notice of their police-station rights and thus guards against coerced confessions. In the first regime, if you are ever arrested and taken downtown, the cops Mirandize you. But at that precise moment, you are typically disoriented, and the warning doesn't fully register because its words are unfamiliar. The warning is part of the law, but not the culture. In the second regime, the cops often neglect to Mirandize you. Perhaps they never

Mirandize you. But every week of your life you have been taught the *Miranda* warning on your couch, and so, if you are ever arrested, you know your *Miranda* rights down cold. You might still decide to answer the cops' questions, if you are cocky enough to think you can talk your way out of the situation, but your decision to sing would be fully voluntary. (However, most defense lawyers, on TV crime shows and in real life, would say that talking is usually a mistake: The smart move is to keep silent.)

Isn't the second regime obviously more protective than the first? If so, even if the Supreme Court were to overturn *Miranda* tomorrow, how much would it matter?

To say that *Miranda* is here to stay, in our heads if not our law books, is not to say that *Miranda* has been a great thing for America. Under *Miranda* and later cases, a suspect is, in effect, told that if he remains silent, this silence can never be used against him. What incentive does he have to cooperate with the police? When cops are barred from getting information from suspects in a timely fashion, some criminals will likely escape conviction. Even worse, some innocent suspects will wrongly become targets, defendants, and even convicts. When the police are restricted in their ability to get information from guilty suspect A, sometimes they end up going after innocent suspect B. This is a danger that should worry even civil libertarians, yet few of *Miranda*'s partisans have even seen the problem.

Most of these partisans have also urged that the police should be barred from using not only confessions obtained without proper warnings, but also any reliable physical evidence and other "fruits" of *Miranda* violations. These arguments threaten to turn our Constitution upside down: the best argument against coerced confessions is rooted in the protection of innocence. We do not want police forcing "confessions" from those who are not guilty. But where a confession leads to reliable physical evidence or other valuable fruit—a bloody knife, a fingerprint, a witness—the matter is far different.

Though the current Court could not wholly undo *Miranda*, even if it tried, the justices in *Dickerson* could perhaps modify *Miranda* around the edges. Here is one possible compromise, with something for both liberals and conservatives. First, the Court could emphasize that although *Miranda* did not require it, videotaping of police interrogations should be encouraged. Police failure to videotape should be a strong factor suggesting that a confession may have been coerced. This new emphasis on videotaping might reassure civil libertarians, who worry that if *Miranda* goes, it will be open season on suspects.

Second, the Court might modify the precise mix of the suspect's incentives to cooperate. Currently, a suspect is free to clam up and pays virtually no legal price for doing so. Friends of law enforcement have long criticized this feature of *Miranda*.

A different warning might go something like this: "You have the right to remain silent. But if you now choose to stay silent, any alibi or other defense that you later try to offer to a court may be viewed with greater suspicion. Anything you say can be used against you in court, but your silence in the face of police interrogation can also be used against you. If you are innocent, you might be better off cooperating now."

This new warning, closer to modern British practice, may be a little tricky for suspects to understand, at least at first. But after a while, its meaning should become clear. It wouldn't take more than a few new episodes of our favorite TV crime show for us all to learn *Miranda*'s latest stanza.

GETTING TSARNAEV TO TALK[6]

SLATE, MONDAY, APRIL 22, 2013, 4:09 P.M. (ET)

The key legal question in the wake of the Boston Marathon bombing is this: Why should courts exclude highly reliable evidence gathered in a civilized interrogation of a suspect, merely because he has been required by law to answer pressing and probing questions?

This isn't about when or whether Dzhokhar Tsarnaev should be read his *Miranda* rights. He already knows them. So does almost every American—we have all in effect been read the standard warnings countless times, by cop shows that have taught us our basic Fifth and Sixth Amendment entitlements. So what's the big deal if Tsarnaev, or any other suspect in any single case, doesn't get the benefit of this fetishized ritual?

Also, in cases such as *New York v. Quarles* in 1984, the Supreme Court has allowed cops to delay the formal catechism in situations involving an imminent risk to public safety. Any suspect in custody can be asked, "Where's the gun?" or "Where's the bomb?" before being Mirandized.

Even if this public safety exception somehow doesn't apply following the Boston tragedy, the only thing the cops would lose if they fail to give Tsarnaev his *Miranda* warning is the confession itself, so long as the police are acting in good faith. In Boston there is plenty of evidence to convict independent of any confession, and surely the government has acted in good faith. Although some have argued that Boston officials have unduly broadened the public safety exception, this criticism slights the fact that at every point, investigators have been reacting to a fast-breaking, unpredictable, and extraordinarily lethal series of events. Investigators haven't merely been trying to find evidence of the crimes that occurred but have also been seeking to find out, for example, who else might be involved and still at large and what other bombs might be set to blow.

With or without *Miranda*, Dzhokhar Tsarnaev can insist on consulting a lawyer before answering interrogators' questions about his culpability. And this is as it should be. The rule of law and the American system of justice, both civil and military, requires lawyers. Even alleged enemy combatants are entitled to legal counsel. The celebrated 1963 case *Gideon v. Wainwright* guarantees government-appointed counsel to people accused of crimes who cannot afford to pay for lawyers—and this, too, is as it should be. It's essential for sorting the guilty from the innocent.

Here's the real dilemma: With or without a lawyer, Tsarnaev has the right to refuse to answer any questions that might incriminate him. But why is that? Why shouldn't Tsarnaev have to answer questions—with his lawyer present, if he chooses—just like any other witness who may possess vital information?

The short answer is that the Fifth Amendment—the Constitution itself—says that no person "shall be compelled in any criminal case to be a witness against himself." But what, exactly, do these words mean, and why? And how should the Constitution, in letter and spirit, apply to ticking-bomb scenarios?

The best answer is as follows. Our law rightly safeguards against convicting the innocent and tries to structure criminal trials to minimize this risk. A criminal defendant is under special emotional pressure and may end up hurting his own case, even if he is testifying truthfully. He may stutter or sweat or misremember or misspeak or get confused when verbally sliced and diced on the stand by a clever prosecutor. So at trial we don't allow the prosecutor to force the defendant to take the stand. Likewise, we don't allow the government to force a suspect in the police station to answer questions, and then allow those answers to be introduced at trial. Otherwise, our carefully designed trial safeguards could be undone pretrial, in the police station.

But as long as the precise words and testimony elicited in a police interrogation are never introduced in a criminal trial, *the Fifth Amendment will never have been violated.* The defendant will never have been made an involuntary *witness* in his own *criminal case*. And anything else that the interrogation leads to—bombs, guns, other physical evidence, the names of other possible witnesses or accomplices—should be fair game, because this kind of evidence is far more reliable, in general. Imagine, for example, introducing into evidence the fact that a bomb was found in a hideaway controlled by the defendant and filled with the defendant's fingerprints.

In the 1860s, Congress passed a bill based on this understanding of the Fifth Amendment. President Lincoln promptly signed it into law—in sharp contrast to his treatment of other congressional proposals that he believed unconstitutional. Alas, the Supreme Court in the late nineteenth century—a malodorous era that gave us separate but equal in *Plessy v. Ferguson* and many other doubtful rulings—struck down the 1860s law. The Supreme Court currently demands that in general, if a person has been legally required to answer incriminating questions during a civilized interrogation, neither his answers *nor any leads from these answers* can be used in prosecuting him.

Not only does this misinterpretation go far beyond the letter and spirit of the Fifth Amendment, but it also puts police in a special bind in a public emergency. Imagine a case—*not* like Boston—in which there is not much evidence of a suspect's guilt before the police interrogation. If the police can tell a suspect that he must legally answer questions about ticking bombs and the like, they may save lives—but only at the expense of possibly handing the bad guy a get-out-of-jail-free card for his past crimes. In any future prosecution, the government will have to prove that no shred of evidence introduced was a product (or "fruit," in legalese) of the compelled interrogation. And this can be a very hard thing for prosecutors to prove in cases in which a suspect is brought for questioning before the government has compiled an airtight case. Again, this isn't Boston, but it's a scenario that could easily arise.

The best solution would be for the Supreme Court to simply change course and allow the admission of all evidence gathered as a result of a civilized compulsory interrogation. Under current law, a suspect can be forced to hand over a blood sample or a fingerprint, because these items are reliable physical evidence, and they don't violate the Fifth Amendment, because blood and prints are not "witnesses," strictly speaking, and because they are reliable in a way that pure words are not. The same logic holds for admitting all fruit and leads generated by compelled interrogation.

Even if the Court won't go that far, it should hold that in compelled interrogations involving serious and ongoing threats to public safety, evidence and leads obtained by interrogation of the suspect should always be admissible. Let's bring coffee, donuts, and yes, lawyers, into the interrogation room. But the law should also require the suspect to answer all questions under pain of contempt—meaning he can be jailed if he refuses—and under penalty of perjury. His lawyer should understand that her job is not to aid the suspect in lying or stonewalling. Suspects will of course be tempted to lie in some situations. But even lies can often provide cues and clues to trained investigators, and interrogators should also be able to give lie-detector tests with the oversight of a judge. This is the right balance for public safety and a defendant's rights—and the Fifth Amendment, properly understood, allows it.

TAKING THE FIFTH TOO OFTEN

New York Times, Monday, February 18, 2002

By what right do Enron bigwigs stonewall Congress? The Fifth Amendment prohibits a person from being compelled to be a witness against himself in any "'criminal case," but a congressional hearing is hardly a criminal case.

The Fifth Amendment gives criminal defendants the right to refuse to testify at trial. Perhaps the most reasonable justification for this right is the need to protect innocent and truthful defendants from being made to appear guilty if forced to take the stand. They might well sweat, stutter, or misspeak when pressured by prosecutors, and thereby be wrongly convicted.

To protect the core Fifth Amendment right, a person should also be allowed to "take the Fifth" outside his trial. Otherwise, prosecutors might simply be able to adjourn a trial, force the defendant to testify in some other setting, and then offer the transcript and videotape to the criminal jury.

But sometimes a truth-seeking society needs to be able to compel a person to speak outside his trial—in grand jury rooms, civil cases, and legislative hearings, for example. One solution is to require the person to testify in these specific places, but then exclude this compelled testimony from any later prosecution brought against him. This way, he would never become a witness against himself "in a criminal case."

This rule would offer congressional witnesses a narrow type of testimonial immunity. While the testimony itself would be excluded from the criminal trial, evidence that might be drawn indirectly from the testimony would be admissible at a later trial. This would allow prosecutors to use any reliable leads that the testimony might generate. Courts today allow government lawyers to force people to give voice samples and take breath tests for alcohol because these are not considered forms of self-incrimination prohibited by the Fifth Amendment. If prosecutors can compel defendants to provide these kinds of evidence, prosecutors should also be allowed to introduce reliable evidence that is found as a result of earlier immunized testimony.

This is exactly the rule that Congress enacted, and President Abraham Lincoln signed into law, in 1862. Two federal government clerks had embezzled bonds worth $2 million and then confessed in a congressional hearing. They went on to claim that they could never be prosecuted because Congress had required them to talk. Congress cured the problem with a statute obliging future congressional witnesses to speak when so ordered. Anyone refusing to speak could be held in contempt, and anyone lying could be charged with perjury—but all witnesses would be granted only narrow immunity, allowing later prosecutions based on leads generated in Congress. As one senator said at the time, restricted immunity was "all that a rascal ought to have at the hands of justice." If congressional testimony led investigators to find other reliable bits of evidence that could be used to convict, so much the better.

But in 1892, the Supreme Court declared this statute unconstitutional. A person obliged to testify before Congress could never be prosecuted for anything related to his testimony, the Court ruled. In later cases, the Court softened this rule—a person forced to testify before Congress could be prosecuted so long as the testimony and all evidence found as a result of that testimony were excluded.

The Supreme Court has never explained where this ban on other evidence is to be found in the Fifth Amendment's words. Nor has the Court explained how such a ban fits the general innocence-protecting idea that justifies the Fifth Amendment in the first place.

This longstanding reading of the Fifth Amendment has warped the separation of powers. When Congress needs facts to determine whether existing laws are working and how they might be fixed, it often meets a Fifth Amendment stone wall. Congress can find the truth only if it gives witnesses sweeping immunity that then hinders the executive branch's prosecutorial function.

Thus, when Congress sought to investigate the Iran-Contra scandal in 1987, it had to grant immunity to Oliver North in ways that ultimately led judges to overturn North's criminal conviction in 1989 for obstructing justice and other federal crimes. Although the evidence introduced against North was reliable, prosecutors could not prove that witnesses against him were not affected by his nationally televised congressional testimony.

After that fiasco, Congress became cautious in its conduct of important investigations. When Congress sought to investigate campaign-finance abuses and possible Chinese influence in American politics in 1997, it chose not to force John Huang to tell all he knew; such compelled testimony would have shielded Huang from criminal prosecution. Current Fifth Amendment doctrine thus prevents the legislature from doing its job of oversight and law reform.

President Bush has urged strict construction of the Constitution, and the Fifth Amendment is a good place to start. Current case law ignores the Constitution's words, distorts constitutional structure, and overprotects the guilty. But don't expect federal judges to alter this constitutional interpretation anytime soon. Enron executives are not the only ones who dislike confessing error.

WHERE ASHCROFT GOES
TOO FAR IN THE WAR ON TERROR

Time, Friday, April 12, 2002

Zealous advocate, meet zealous advocate.

Criminal defense attorney Lynne Stewart seemed outraged this week when federal prosecutors charged her with conspiring to help her client, Sheik Omar Abdel Rahman, convicted for his part in the 1993 World Trade Center bombing, pass prison messages to outside terrorist groups. While Stewart has declared herself "emphatically" not guilty of the charges, she sees zealous representation of clients as a calling, not a crime. Attorney General John Ashcroft pursues his own job with equal zeal. Terrorists must be vanquished and lawyers who abet them punished.

In principle, the legal line for defense attorneys is clear; in practice things get fuzzy. Lawyers may properly defend clients against prosecution for past criminal conduct, but may not aid and abet new crimes being planned by these clients. Whether Stewart crossed this line will be decided by a jury in the months ahead.

But Ashcroft has already crossed a different line in his determination to fight terror. Tuesday he said that he would begin inserting federal agents into meetings between federal inmates and their lawyers whenever he suspects that these meetings are being used to facilitate acts of violence or terrorism. Never before has any attorney general claimed such power.

Ashcroft bases his authority on a regulation that he himself issued in October, but that lay dormant until this week. This regulation covers not only criminal convicts like Rahman but also jailed defendants awaiting trial and even "material witnesses" who have never been accused of wrongdoing.

The attorney general's announcement restricts one of the most basic of American rights, the right to consult a lawyer in private. This right, rooted in several amendments and their unifying spirit, is not limited to those facing criminal prosecution, but rather applies to all sorts of legal counseling. Much of what clients discuss privately with lawyers is embarrassing or sensitive: family disputes, personal finances, health-care issues, and so on.

If America is to shrink so longstanding a right, this change should come from a congressional law, not a mere executive regulation. In the wake of 9/11, Congress passed a comprehensive anti-terrorism statute. But this law, the USA Patriot Act, said nothing about restricting traditional lawyer-client confidentiality. As finally adopted, the act softened several of the Bush administration's initial proposals that most worried civil libertarians. These adjustments were part of the healthy give-and-take of the democratic legislative process. Ashcroft's regulation simply sidesteps the Constitution's careful system of legislative checks and balances, and indeed drew angry responses in November from Senate leaders who were not even informed of the published regulation, much less consulted beforehand.

The regulation also circumvents the judiciary. Ashcroft says that he alone, and not a judge, should decide whether a given inmate is too dangerous to speak privately with a lawyer. The charges against Stewart, however, were based on evidence acquired in the traditional way, with judicial approval of surveillance directed at the sheik and the lawyer. This indictment would seem to suggest that the traditional system works pretty well.

If the attorney general worries that some overzealous lawyers will cross the ethical line, a more limited intrusion would be to create a roster of approved lawyers who meet the highest ethical standards—say, former Justice Department officials—and allow inmates to consult confidentially with any lawyer on that list. This approach would allow honest inmates to consult honest lawyers without government agents listening in on every word.

Perhaps Ashcroft fears that even honest attorneys may unwittingly transmit some innocent-sounding code word—"ROSEBUD"—to terrorists on the loose. Providing lawyers with security briefings about what to watch out for would reduce this risk. And instead of putting federal agents in the room where inmates meet lawyers, the government could videotape the conversations in exceptional cases. These tapes could be reviewed in private by a judge with top-security clearance and briefing. Unless the judge found lawyer-client misconduct, executive officials would be denied access to the tapes.

There are ways to deal with improper lawyering that are less intrusive to traditional lawyer-client confidentiality than Ashcroft's approach. If new rules are needed to prevent new threats, America should frame such measures democratically, in a process that involves the legislature, the courts, and the people. In that process those zealous for liberty can be heard alongside those zealous for security.

THE FBI'S NEW SURVEILLANCE POLICY

FindLaw, Friday, June 14, 2002 (with Vikram David Amar)

Attorney General John Ashcroft's latest regulation—which expands the FBI's authority to surveil Americans in public venues such as open Internet chat rooms, political rallies, and houses of worship—deserves close analysis under the Constitution's Fourth Amendment, which governs government snooping. The amendment helps identify what is sensible and what is problematic about Ashcroft's new policy. In turn, Ashcroft's regulation helps identify what is sensible and what is problematic about the Supreme Court's Fourth Amendment case law.

The Fourth Amendment provides that "the right of the people to be secure in their persons, houses, papers, and effects, against unreasonable searches and seizures, shall not be violated, and no warrants shall issue, but upon probable cause, supported by oath or affirmation, and particularly describing the place to be searched, and the persons or things to be seized."

The new regulation, issued on May 30, provides (in relevant part) that: "For the purpose of detecting or preventing terrorist activities, the FBI is authorized to visit any place and attend any event that is open to the public, on the same terms and conditions as members of the public generally. . . . For the purpose of detecting or preventing terrorism or other criminal activities, the FBI is authorized to conduct online search activity and to access online sites and forums on the same terms and conditions as members of the public generally."

Does visiting a website or attending a public rally or an open worship service even constitute a "search" that triggers the Fourth Amendment? We think so. In ordinary language, one commonly speaks of performing an "online *search*." Indeed, this is the exact wording of Ashcroft's regulation itself. And when FBI agents engage in extensive naked-eye surveillance at a rally or in a mosque, they are *searching*, according to a standard definition of the verb "search" in the *Oxford English Dictionary*: "To look scrutinizingly at." (Interestingly, the *OED* illustrates this usage with a passage from Justice Oliver Wendell Holmes's father, Oliver Wendell Holmes Sr.: "He searched her features through and through.")

The Supreme Court, however, has sometimes denied that "search" means "search," holding instead that certain sightings of things in plain view lie outside the Fourth Amendment's scope. In *Florida v. Riley*, the Court ruled that hovering four hundred feet over a backyard greenhouse with a surveillance helicopter was not a search; and in *U.S. v. Dunn*, the justices likewise ruled that trespassing onto a person's private homestead, climbing over his fences, and peering into his barn was a nonsearch.

What accounts for such stingy readings at the Fourth Amendment threshold? In part, the modern judicial exclusionary rule, which often suppresses evidence acquired in unconstitutional searches, even if the evidence is highly reliable proof of violent crime. Because many judges dislike suppressing such evidence, they may be tempted to deny the Fourth Amendment was violated in the first place by ruling that no real "search" took place. Thus, expanding Fourth Amendment remedies ends up contracting Fourth Amendment rights. For this reason and others (including the fact that no one at the Founding ever endorsed the exclusionary rule), we are critics of this modern judge-created and truth-suppressing doctrine.

The Court's nonsearch gambit is also a product of its intermittent insistence that searches ordinarily require probable cause or at least individualized suspicion—that is, some particular reason to single out the searchee. But the Fourth Amendment's text does not say this. Rather, the amendment simply requires that a search be "reasonable." (The amendment's rules about "probable cause" apply only to warrants, not to all searches.) The Constitution's wording makes good sense; sometimes a reasonable search may take place without any individualized suspicion, as with airport metal detectors.

The Court has sometimes upheld searches without individualized suspicion, but at other times has insisted that such searches are presumptively unconstitutional. This insistence, in turn, has pressured the Court into denying that a naked-eye surveillance is a search at all. Otherwise most ordinary surveillance would be unconstitutional because police and FBI agents typically engage in naked-eye surveillance *before* they have probable cause or anything like it. Indeed, it is often such surveillance that generates the probable cause supporting a later application for a search warrant.

Once again, an overly broad reading of the Fourth Amendment in one place (presumptively requiring all searches to be supported by probable cause or something like it) creates hydraulic pressure to weaken the amendment in another place (by denying that naked-eye surveillance is even covered by the amendment at all).

A better approach—more commonsensical and textually faithful—would call a search a search, but would recognize that many forms of naked-eye surveillance are often *reasonable* searches, which is all the Constitution requires. If a particular surveillance is unduly prolonged or unjustified, or discriminatory, or expression-chilling, or especially intrusive, it might thereby become unreasonable. For this very reason, judges should treat surveillance as a search, and monitor its overall reasonableness.

There are shards in judicial doctrine that would support this revised approach. The current judicial test for deciding when a Fourth Amendment "search" has occurred speaks of whether the government has intruded upon a citizen's "reasonable expectation of privacy"—thus smuggling the reasonableness inquiry into the threshold determination.

But current doctrine unduly compresses the reasonableness inquiry and limits it to a privacy issue, when in fact constitutional reasonableness encompasses a much broader array of factors, such as the public or private nature of the citizen activity intruded upon; the precise identity of the intruding party; the degree of democratic authorization of the government intrusion; the overall coerciveness and intrusiveness of the government conduct; the impact of the intrusion upon constitutional values of expression and equality; and the precise nature of the government's justifications. The new Ashcroft regulation helps illustrate the importance of these factors to proper Fourth Amendment analysis.

Ashcroft stresses that his new regulation gives FBI field agents only the same surveillance power as ordinary members of the public enjoy: to attend public events or monitor public websites. These restrictions weigh in favor of overall reasonableness, and distinguish Ashcroft's May 30 regulation from his October 30, 2001, regulation intruding into traditionally private conversations between lawyers and clients. Nevertheless, the issue of public surveillance is more complicated than Ashcroft suggests.

For starters, the ability of ordinary citizens to monitor others in public is not unlimited. If a private person stalks and surveils his target for months upon end, following her whenever she leaves the house, this can indeed constitute a tort of invasion of privacy. If the FBI did this without justification, there might likewise be an overall invasion of privacy even if all the surveillance occurred in public.

More generally, the FBI commands vast resources that ordinary members of the public lack. If an individual wants to infiltrate a church or political organization, he can attend a meeting or two. But no single person or group of persons could ever have the chilling effect on religious or political association that the FBI, with its army of full-time employees, could have merely by being present at events open to the public. Being stalked by the FBI—even in public places—is hugely different from being stalked by an individual. Just because a person expects that some individuals may see some things he does in public does not mean that he expects government to see everything he does that might be publicly visible all the time. (Similarly, the formal right of a private jet to fly high above a person's backyard is very different from a government surveillance chopper hovering for hours a hundred yards above his hammock and snapping pictures—a point lost on the Court in *Florida v. Riley*.)

Finally, the Constitution often bars government from doing what private citizens may do. Ordinary Americans are free to spew racial epithets or blacklist liberals. The FBI is not, even though in the past it has done both. Similarly, a private investigator might be free to monitor the speeches only of candidates criticizing the Republican Party; but such selective partisan targeting should be off limits to the FBI.

Thus, it matters not just who is being searched (and why, and how) but also who is doing the searching. Judicial doctrine has been slow to openly recognize this point. But surely a pat-down search of a woman at an airport would generally be more reasonable if done by a female officer rather than a male. So, too, in his famous opinion in *Terry v. Ohio*, Chief Justice Earl Warren noted the special problems of reasonableness raised when largely white police departments performed searches that landed disproportionately on blacks.

Also, the Court has said that certain searches of criminal suspects require more judicial monitoring than noncriminal searches, but the Fourth Amendment's words contain no such distinction. A better rationale for this rule is that searches done by *police departments* raise special concerns because such departments can develop institutional tunnel vision that distances them from the general society and thus requires special judicial oversight.

A similar point applies to the FBI. Prior to the new Ashcroft regulation, rules dating back to the mid-1970s had placed special limits on FBI investigations of political and religious organizations. Before an agent could attend certain public events or meetings, or gather information about certain organizations open to the public, he had to have a particularized reason, as opposed to a simple hunch, for believing that a crime had already been committed there, and he had to obtain special intra-departmental approval.

These rules arose because of an earlier pattern of systematic abuse by the FBI under the leadership of J. Edgar Hoover. Under "COINTELPRO" (Counter Intelligence Programs) initiatives conducted between 1956 and 1971, the FBI surveilled and kept files on hundreds of civil rights and religious activists including Martin Luther King and other leading opponents of the Vietnam War.

The 1970s guidelines were the product not merely of the FBI's own soul searching, but of a series of congressional hearings conducted during 1971–1975, documenting and spotlighting the abuses of Hoover's FBI. Thus, the prophylactic internal rules in place until last week were themselves the result of a dialogue between the executive branch and Congress. Even if Ashcroft's new rules are sound policy, it is troubling that the executive branch issued them without formally consulting Congress or (better still) winning Congress's explicit approval in a statute.

The Fourth Amendment speaks of a right of *the people*—and the people's view about the reasonableness of a government action deserves to be part of a sensible Fourth Amendment analysis. The people are represented not just by the executive branch but by the legislature, too. Any policy that intrudes upon Fourth Amendment interests should receive less deference from judges if it comes with the backing of only one of the elected branches rather than both.

The Rehnquist Court, however, has failed to pay much heed to anyone's view of the Constitution other than its own, and has in general paid less deference to Congress as a coordinate branch than has any previous Court in history. Ashcroft thus had less incentive to win Congress's approval because such approval would not be given much weight by today's Court.

Here is another factor that should inform proper Fourth Amendment analysis: the more coercive or intrusive a given search or seizure, the greater the burden of justification. Simply attending a public meeting is far less coercive than, say, forcing high school students to provide urine samples under teacher supervision.

Also, by singling out "papers" above and beyond all other "effects," the Fourth Amendment reminds us of the importance of protecting free expression, which would be threatened if government could rummage through citizens' books and writings at will. More generally, Fourth Amendment reasonableness should factor in the threat a given government search policy poses to political and religious expression. Likewise, equality values and dignity values should be part of the overall reasonableness analysis. Government surveillance of churches, mosques, and political assemblies raises special concerns if government is allowed simply to pick and choose whom it will surveil and whom it will spare.

Even if such surveillance does not independently violate the First Amendment (because no one is being coercively prevented from speaking) or the equal protection clause (because there is no explicit intent to discriminate, but only a disparate impact on certain minority races or minority faiths), it does call for heightened Fourth Amendment scrutiny.

Finally, reasonableness should obviously turn on the government's reasons. The Ashcroft regulation does not simply allow FBI agents to surveil religious and political meetings for any reason at all. Rather, agents may surveil only "for the purpose of detecting or preventing terrorist activities"—about as compelling a reason as can be imagined after the horror of September 11. Authority to surf public websites is broader—going beyond crimes of terror—but this makes sense, given that reading a public website is less intrusive than surveilling physical meetings.

These restrictions are further reminders of the value of treating FBI surveillance as a search. For if it were not a search, the Fourth Amendment simply would not apply, and government would need not have any reason at all. But if, as we argue, surveillance is a search, it needs to have reasons, and the more intrusive it is, the stronger the reasons must be.

In the end, the biggest problem with the Ashcroft regulation is not that it lacks reasons or restrictions, but that it also poses dangers, when previous FBI abuses are kept in mind, and that these dangers were not openly weighed by the people's representatives in Congress as they should have been.

GO DIRECTLY TO JAIL

NEW REPUBLIC, WEDNESDAY, JUNE 19, 2002

"Thinking like a lawyer" means many things (not all of them flattering), including sizing up a fact situation quickly to identify important legal issues, analogies, and distinctions worthy of further research and analysis. In law lingo, it's called "issue-spotting"—offering a tentative first cut based on limited research and a simplified understanding of the facts. In this spirit, I've spent the last few hours mulling the case of José Padilla, aka Abdullah al-Muhajir. Padilla is an American citizen who, according to the Bush administration, met with a top Al Qaeda leader in Pakistan to plot a "dirty bomb" attack on America. The administration now seeks to detain Padilla without trial as an "enemy combatant." What are the key legal questions, concepts, analogies, and distinctions raised by this case?

Question 1: Can a person—an American!—be detained without being charged with a crime?

Untutored intuition balks at this prospect, but in fact our legal system does detain people outside the criminal justice system in a variety of settings. An eyewitness to a crime can be subpoenaed to show up at a grand jury and/or trial even if these limited detentions significantly disrupt his life plan. If it's doubtful the witness will voluntarily show up for these events, he can be forcibly held as "a material witness" until the government no longer needs his testimony. (In fact, until recently, Padilla was apparently held as a "material witness.") Citizens can be "detained" for jury duty and obliged to serve. At the Founding, Americans were conscripted for militia duty, and ever since the Civil War, the federal government has drafted soldiers into the army as need arose. The draft is a form of indefinite detention; why should the government have less power to detain (and immobilize) disloyal Americans than to detain (and mobilize) loyal ones? Also, those who (perhaps through no fault of their own) pose a threat to others because of mental illness are subject to civil commitment without all the safeguards of the criminal justice system. Persons with dangerous and infectious diseases can in some situations be quarantined. Bringing the matter even closer to Padilla, America has historically detained prisoners of war during wartime even though these prisoners have not been criminally convicted or even charged.

Question 2: What are the substantive limits on this power to detain?

Various global constitutional principles limit all government power, including the detention power. As a rule, the president must have some implicit or explicit constitutional or statutory basis for his actions. The precise boundaries of the president's commander-in-chief power are blurry, but in a military emergency it makes sense to allow the president to act on his own to maintain the status quo from some grave irreversible harm, so long as Congress quickly blesses his action when it convenes. (This is the difference between what Lincoln did at the outset of the Civil War, which the Supreme Court largely upheld, and what Truman did in the Korean War, which the Court struck down in the famous Steel Seizure case.) Beyond this emergency situation, one obvious question is whether any congressional statute or long-standing tradition authorizes Padilla's detention. Presumably, the general power to detain prisoners of war in a duly authorized war is implicit in Congress's general military statutes—which may incorporate or need to be read alongside traditional international law rules—but the issue warrants more research, especially because the precise nature of the "war" America is now facing is murky. Also, the Authorization for Use of Military Force resolution that Congress passed on September 14, 2011, and that President Bush signed into law on September 18 authorizes the president to use "all necessary and appropriate force," but only against those linked to the September 11 attack. It is not clear whether the administration claims that Padilla is so linked; arguably anyone who joins Al Qaeda, even after 9/11, falls within the resolution.[7]

Constitutional principles also generally prevent the government from targeting minority races or religions or political groups. This body of law was less robust during World War II when the government forced around 100,000 Japanese and Japanese Americans into detention centers. The Supreme Court at the time upheld parts of this policy in the *Korematsu v. United States* case, which has never been formally overruled but has been widely criticized. It's useful to remember that *Korematsu*—involving a massive effort to segregate certain nonwhites, allegedly for their own benefit as well as the security of white America—was decided when Jim Crow still reigned in the South and *Brown v. Board* still lay a decade in the future.

Finally, the Fourth Amendment prohibits "unreasonable . . . seizures" of "persons" and requires (among other things) that all bodily detentions must be supported with strong reasons.

Question 3: What procedural rights should Padilla enjoy?

Because detention involves a serious loss of bodily liberty, government must provide "due process." The greater the loss of liberty, the more process is due. Indefinite detention for the duration of a war of highly uncertain length (indeed, with no clear end in sight) is about as severe a form of detention as is imaginable—far more extreme than temporary jury duty. As compared to conventional military service, Padilla's detention might end up being longer than most military stints. On the other hand, he is not being placed at risk of losing life or limb, as were many Vietnam draftees, for example.

Due process need not replicate all the rules of criminal trials—e.g., proof beyond reasonable doubt or the right to a wholly public jury trial, or the right to exclude reliable hearsay accusations—but there must be enough of a hearing to ensure that the person being detained does indeed qualify for detention under the relevant substantive law. Concretely: The government should be required to prove via credible evidence that detention of Padilla is lawful because he is indeed an enemy combatant who can properly be held until he ceases to pose a threat to his country. Many specific due process issues will arise, but the big point is that it should not be enough that President Bush simply claims Padilla is a threat. A hearing is necessary.

Must the hearing be entirely public? Probably not, given that some of the evidence may involve highly classified intelligence and confidential sources. May government introduce affidavits, interrogation transcripts, and other hearsay instead of live witnesses? Probably yes, given that many of the intelligence sources come from abroad, and others may involve electronic intercepts and other statements from persons who would not willingly testify and practically speaking cannot be forced to. Must Padilla be allowed a lawyer, with whom he should be allowed to consult in private? Absolutely. Because his bodily liberty is obviously at stake, Padilla needs a lawyer every bit as much as did Clarence Earl Gideon. If Padilla cannot afford a lawyer, the government should provide one. If the government fears that Padilla might try to use his lawyer to sneak messages out to terrorists at large or to plot ongoing acts of terror, the government could make Padilla pick from an honors list of pre-approved lawyers of unquestioned patriotism and competence—say, former Justice Department officials. If the hearing occurs in a military context, Padilla could be given an attorney who is also a trusted American officer.

Must the hearing be held in a civil court, or can it be held in a military commission or military court? This is the $64,000 question. Eventually, Padilla could bring a habeas petition before a regular Article III court; but will those judges insist on reviewing the evidence themselves on a clean slate, or will it be enough for them that a military tribunal or commission heard the evidence fairly and had a reasonable basis for finding Padilla to be an unlawful combatant? Padilla's lawyers will argue that a military hearing lacks sufficient safeguards because its presiding officers are within the chain of command and are thus ultimately subservient to the president, unlike life-tenured Article III judges. But this argument proves too much, given that military judges are trusted to decide the life and liberty of members of the American military; and military commissions have also been trusted in other settings with power over life and limb.

One big problem for the Bush administration is that it does not appear to have clear rules in place spelling out exactly how, why, and by whom, the evidence that Padilla is indeed an enemy combatant should be heard. (Note that the administration's earlier rules about terrorist trials in military commissions do not apply—more on that below.) Here, too, these rules should ideally be blessed by Congress in a formal statute rather than simply improvised by the executive branch on the fly. Also, these rules should specify what the substantive standards are for being an "enemy combatant"—as opposed to, say, just being a thug or an Al Qaeda sympathizer. The First Amendment requires that we draw a clear line between those who merely admire Al Qaeda or speak out against the U.S. and those who actually attempt or plot to wage war against America.

Padilla, of course, is hardly the only person being held as, in effect, a prisoner of war. But he may well be entitled to more elaborate procedures than the hundreds of detainees in Guantánamo for two reasons. First, Padilla is on U.S. soil, and so Article III judges in America will ultimately have habeas corpus jurisdiction over him in ways they may not over detainees held abroad.[8] Second, the Guantánamo detainees were captured directly by the American military (or their allies) in military operations in a theater of actual war in Afghanistan. Thus, they were captured in the very act of waging war against the U.S. on ground not under the control of U.S. courts. Padilla, by contrast, does not appear to be someone who was a direct combatant in Afghanistan.

Moreover, Padilla is a U.S. citizen, and the Bush administration regulation authorizing military commission trials of certain accused terrorists is limited to aliens. On this last point, however, note that the Bush administration is not now seeking to *try* or *convict* Padilla for anything. It simply seeks to *detain* him.

Question 4: How is detention any different than criminal conviction?

Some have argued that indefinite detention is simply an impermissible circumvention of all the rights of a criminal suspect: It is just like a criminal punishment, but without all the constitutional safeguards.

But is it? A criminal conviction—whether in ordinary civilian court or in a military court or commission—justifies punishment. At the extreme, it can result in death. It can be based on retribution; even if you are wholly nonthreatening and repentant today, if you are found to have committed a crime in the past (perhaps long ago), you can be punished today (and perhaps put to death). A criminal conviction is traditionally based on a definitive finding that the defendant did an evil thing in the past. When a criminal trial ends and a defendant has been found guilty, the government need not (though it may choose to) hold a series of future hearings to decide whether continued incarceration is warranted.

In all these ways, detention is different. It does not justify punishment or death. It is forward-looking and wholly preventive rather than retributive. It may require a series of periodic hearings to determine whether a threat is sufficiently ongoing so as to justify continuing detention. This is the model of civil commitment, or a quarantine. In Padilla's case, it suggests that the government should periodically be obliged to show that Padilla poses an unabated and ongoing threat, that nothing short of detention can prevent this threat, and that the conditions of detention are no more onerous than necessary to prevent the threat.

To see the criminal punishment/noncriminal detention distinction most clearly, imagine a war that is not obviously Good Against Evil. The soldiers on each side fight nobly for their country. If captured by the other side, they can be detained (to prevent them from wreaking future harm), but when the war is over and peace restored, they are free to go. They are prisoner-soldiers and detainees, not criminals.

Of course, one can be both a soldier and a criminal—a war criminal. And perhaps the general sense is that anyone fighting *this* particular terrorist war against America is indeed a criminal, too. But the government is not (yet) charging Padilla with a crime. For now, they are simply treating him as a soldier. Why should he get *more* rights than a typical prisoner of war simply because he may also be a criminal? Why should he get more rights than all the detainees in Guantánamo simply because, unlike the rest, if he is indeed a soldier then he has also betrayed his country (whereas the others owed America no loyalty in the first place)? An analogy: If a rape victim sues the alleged rapist in tort, she need not prove her case beyond reasonable doubt: Even though she is in effect claiming that he is both a tortfeasor and a rapist, he is not in a tort suit entitled to any more rights than any other tort defendant.

One final way of detaining Padilla outside the context of criminal trial and punishment is also worth mentioning. Padilla can be asked to tell all he knows about Al Qaeda. If he refuses, and pleads the Fifth, he can be given a certain kind of immunity (known as use-fruits immunity) and he then must answer truthfully. If he nonetheless refuses to answer he can be held in "civil contempt" and incarcerated until he answers the questions. If he persists in refusing to answer, at some (ill-defined) point the "civil contempt" power may lapse, but until then this mode of incarceration is not deemed criminal because it is forward-looking rather than retributive: At any moment he can stop the incarceration by complying with the order to speak. In effect, he holds the keys to his own cell.

Question 5: What difference does it make that Padilla is an American?

Because he is an American, Padilla could perhaps insist that he be allowed to be detained in America itself. So long as this could be safely arranged without undue danger, the government may have felt it would be wrong to deny this demand. Keeping him out of the country might look too much like banishment or exile—like impermissible punishment rather than permissible detention. This is of course not true for non-American prisoners of war, who have no right to be on American soil in the first place; keeping them from our shores can hardly be deemed punishment.

But because Padilla is now in the U.S., he is subject to ultimate habeas corpus jurisdiction of civilian courts in a way that various other detainees are not—and this complicates the question of how and by whom the evidence against him should be heard and reviewed.

Also, if the administration ever sought to try and convict Padilla as a criminal terrorist, its own current regulation would not allow him to be tried by a military commission (although the administration might decide to amend the regulation). Currently, only alien terrorists fall within the regulation. The administration may have thought this limitation would ease public concern— "Don't worry, Americans: You are safe from being branded a terrorist and tried without all the usual civilian safeguards." But in fact the administration's regulation introduces a discrimination against aliens that is constitutionally troubling. When the infamous Alien and Sedition Acts of 1798 targeted certain aliens for disfavored treatment, the party of James Madison and Thomas Jefferson famously defended alien rights, and after the Civil War, our Constitution was specifically amended to shield the rights of noncitizen aliens to "due process" and "equal protection."

Question 6: How do international law rules and the laws of war affect the picture?

I'm not sure. Part of issue-spotting is identifying what you don't know and need to learn.

A SAFE INTRUSION

AMERICAN LAWYER, JUNE 2001

As scientists unlock the intricacies of the genetic code, lawyers must revise the intricacies of the legal code. DNA technology can work miracles— exonerating the innocent, identifying the guilty, reassuring the public, and vindicating the victim. The technology can also imperil legitimate privacy interests by exposing intimate details of a person's existence to Big Brother and Big Business. Current legal doctrines were not crafted with the promise and threat of this technology in mind. Optimal revisions will require lawyers of all sorts to step back from their narrow job descriptions and see the broader social interest.

A recent ruling from Virginia provides a convenient starting point for analysis. In 1990, the state convicted James Harvey of rape and sentenced him to twenty-five years. Aided by the New York–based Innocence Project, Harvey now seeks access to the rape kit containing biological evidence from the victim and the crime scene in order to test whatever semen DNA may be found. The state prosecutor has resisted, and in mid-April a federal district judge ruled in Harvey's favor, reasoning that withholding the kit and its potentially exculpatory evidence violates Harvey's due process rights. Judges in other jurisdictions have declined to order post-conviction testing on similar facts, and the issue is likely to come before the Supreme Court in the not-too-distant future.

But why are so many of these cases in court at all? Why aren't more prosecutors voluntarily allowing convicts access? Because of the expense of the DNA test? If so, the state can't complain if the defense team is itself willing to shoulder this cost. Because of the state's interest in repose and finality—that is, the interest in not having to reopen earlier adjudications that seemed fair at the time? This ignores our system's compelling counterinterest in substantive justice. If the DNA casts strong doubt on or indeed conclusively disproves the convict's guilt, the state's true interests are ill served by suppressing this information. A just state cares not about upholding convictions, per se, but about finding the bad guys.

If the wrong man is in prison, perhaps the true culprit is on the loose. Sometimes the interest in finality is linked to "closure" for the victim's family and friends. But surely this interest would not allow the state to ban post-verdict private detectives, censor skeptical journalists, or muzzle new eyewitnesses; nor should it allow the state to suppress the DNA evidence. A government with confidence in the general fairness of its criminal justice system should welcome the double-check of independent DNA tests, which can lay to rest all lingering doubts. Indeed, refusal to allow new testing can undermine the confidence of the public and the victim: What is the state trying to hide? And in those cases where the DNA disproves the trial verdict, these tests serve an invaluable auditing function, helping the state determine if there is any systematic pattern to its past mistakes. For example, new DNA tests in Oklahoma have recently led investigators to confront the possibility of serious malfeasance in one particular police lab.

A cynic might say that prosecutors are simply fighting to maintain their winning percentage, resisting anything that might prove their office fallible (or worse). *Res judicata* means never having to say you're sorry.[9] But there are a couple of legitimate prosecutorial concerns that are indeed weighty. First, if the government must hand over whatever biological evidence it retains, courts may eventually require the police to retain the evidence indefinitely at state expense. Second, in many cases the DNA may not be enough to conclusively clear the defendant. For example, in a rape case such as Harvey's, even if testers discover semen that fails to match his, Harvey still could have been involved, since the crime involved two rapists, and the semen could have come from the accomplice. (The victim was unable to provide a conclusive identification and expressed some doubt about whether both rapists ejaculated.) In a case of this sort, the defendant will seek a new trial, arguing that a new jury should hear the new (doubt-raising, though inconclusive) evidence. The prosecutor will often counter, with some justness, that Humpty Dumpty cannot be reassembled. Years might have elapsed since the first trial, perhaps much of the original evidence has faded away, and the witnesses may now be dead or unavailable. A trial truly fair to the state as well as the defendant may no longer be possible.

This is a genuine concern when a defendant seeks the extraordinary remedy of a new trial. But it is hardly an argument for rejecting a new DNA test. So long as it is reasonably possible that the test might completely clear the convict, the test should be done. In Harvey's case, for example, the DNA test might not only fail to match Harvey but might also directly match other culprits in ways that would completely clear the convict. To insist that a convict must prove that the test will conclusively prove his innocence before he can do the test is to make catch-22 a rule of law. What's more, even an inconclusive DNA test can be a valuable aid to a governor or pardon board staffers, who can review old trial transcripts and police files in light of the new evidence in ways that a second trial jury cannot.

But the fundamental problem remains: Often the DNA test will be inconclusive, failing to match the convict while also failing to rule out the possibility that the DNA came from the convict's unknown accomplice. Thus, a purely negative DNA match is often not good enough; we need a positive DNA match as well, telling us not just that the DNA did not come from James Harvey, but also that it did in fact come from Engelbert Smith. Once we make the positive match, we can usually decide whether the prosecution's accomplice theory holds up. Is there any evidence linking Harvey to Smith? Does Smith himself have a record of committing similar crimes on his own or with some other accomplice? With a positive as well as a negative match, everyone wins, except the guilty: Innocent defendants can be freed, past victims vindicated, and future victims protected. Indeed, if we could regularly make a positive match, most stranger rapes could be solved and thus, one hopes, many rapists could be deterred—a truly amazing prospect.

Regularly making positive matches would require creating a far more comprehensive DNA database than currently exists. New technology makes this possible. Every child at birth now has a blood test for medical purposes. A few drops could be diverted to generate a DNA fingerprint. In addition, all adults could be required to submit to a quick cheek swab, perhaps when they get their driver's licenses. This swab is all that would be needed to generate the genetic fingerprint. These DNA fingerprints could also help prevent a now-prevalent form of identity fraud whereby a criminal uses another person's birth certificate, which lacks unique identification markers such as fingerprints or footprints.

Such a database would be in the interest of innocent criminal defendants, yet almost no criminal defense attorney has called for its creation. Instinctively, defense attorneys recoil from broad searches and seizures, and are more comfortable fighting blood tests than demanding them. A defense attorney's job is simply to get his client off the proverbial hook: reasonable doubt at a reasonable price. Actually finding the real culprit is not in the defense attorney's standard job description. (Let the police and the prosecutors worry about that!) But this view is just as misguided as that of the prosecutor who cares only about maintaining conviction rates. Without a comprehensive database, many innocent defendants will never be able to decisively prove their innocence; with such a database in place, prosecutors will be far less hostile to new testing. Many of the convictions a prosecutor's office might lose would be offset by new convictions enabled by positive matches.

Of course there is real danger in allowing the government unlimited access to each person's entire DNA code, which contains oodles of private bits of information that could be used in sinister ways. For example, the complete code may reveal a person's genetic predispositions to various diseases— information that could compromise employability and insurability, and that the person herself might prefer not to know.

But there is a clean way of protecting private information of this sort, by using only part of the DNA code (so-called junk DNA) that identifies a person but tells us nothing truly private—the DNA equivalent of a fingerprint.* The same comprehensive DNA statute that required mandatory blood tests and cheek swabs could also provide that only the DNA fingerprint be done, with the rest of the biological sample destroyed. The law could further provide for elaborate safeguards against the misuse of samples, including an

---

* [One important difference between DNA and fingerprints is that DNA can be used to determine paternity and to track other biological connections—a point I did not make clearly in 2001 but that I did squarely discuss in a follow-up op-ed, "A Search for Justice in Our Genes," which appeared on May 7, 2002, in the New York Times.]

explicit statutory requirement or implicit understanding that the whole program be headed by a distinguished civil libertarian.

If analyzed by the global test of Fourth Amendment reasonableness, this
hardly seems an "unreasonable" search and seizure regime. Our hypothetical
scheme is nondiscriminatory, relatively nonintrusive, well justified, sensitive
to legitimate privacy interests, and no broader than necessary. But it is not
entirely clear that current Supreme Court doctrine would allow such a comprehensive DNA statute, because it contemplates intrusions for criminal law
enforcement purposes in the absence of probable cause, and, indeed, in the
absence of individualized suspicion. This is a category of search that the current Court generally disfavors. And so the new technology may require the
justices, too, to rethink some of their dicta and dogma. Even if law enforcement purposes alone might not justify a comprehensive database, isn't the
case more compelling if such databases can also ride to the rescue of the erroneously accused and the wrongly convicted?

Whether or not comprehensive DNA databases are put in place, the law
needs to provide more protection for the biological samples already in the
government's possession. Current doctrine, for example, does not limit the
government to fingerprinting the "junk" DNA and has failed to make clear
what rules govern the testing of previously acquired biological samples.

More protection against government abuse and more security from private thuggery; more innocent prisoners freed and more violent criminals
caught; more reliable evidence at our disposal and more safeguards for our
medical privacy. This is the world the scientists have made possible. But will
the lawyers make it happen?

WHY THE COURT WAS
RIGHT TO ALLOW CHEEK SWABS

New York Times, Monday, June 3, 2013 (with Neal Katyal)

Something intriguing happened Monday: Antonin Scalia, the Supreme
Court's longest-serving member and one of its most conservative justices,
joined three liberal justices in a sharply worded dissent arguing for the rights
of criminal suspects.

The court decided, 5 to 4, that the Constitution permits the police to
swab the cheeks of those arrested of serious crimes, and then do DNA tests

on the saliva samples to see if the suspects are associated with other crimes. Justice Scalia joined three liberal justices—Ruth Bader Ginsburg, Sonia Sotomayor, and Elena Kagan—in dissenting.

DNA is already revolutionizing law enforcement. The ability of police to use cheek swabs of arrestees rests on a razor-thin majority. The closeness of the vote, and the unusual coalitions on either side, suggest that the matter is far from settled. Justice Samuel A. Alito Jr., who was part of the majority, rightly called the case, *Maryland v. King*, "perhaps the most important criminal procedure case that this Court has heard in decades."

As prosecutors, police agencies, and civil libertarians consider the ruling's implications, analysts should also confront Justice Scalia's stark dissent. Even though he was on the losing side, he seemed quite sure of himself, and President Obama's two appointees to the Court agreed with him. But in fact, his argument is deeply flawed, because he did not get his history quite right.

Justice Scalia summarized his scathing dissent from the bench—a rare act that signals sharp disagreement. His opinion opened with these lines: "The Fourth Amendment forbids searching a person for evidence of a crime when there is no basis for believing the person is guilty of the crime or is in possession of incriminating evidence. That prohibition is categorical and without exception; it lies at the very heart of the Fourth Amendment."

But the Fourth Amendment's text is not as categorical as he makes it out to be. It merely requires that all searches and seizures be not "unreasonable." Its words do not distinguish between intrusions seeking "evidence of crime" and other sorts of intrusions—say, to collect revenue, or preserve public safety.

Justice Scalia failed to identify even one source from the Founders articulating the ultraprecise rule that he claims is the central meaning of the Fourth Amendment. And his version of the Fourth Amendment would lead to absurd results.

The government, for example, permits searches at the border to prevent contaminated livestock and plants from entering the country. Is such authority permitted only because these searches are not seeking "evidence of crime?" Then what happens if the government at some point criminalizes the intentional introduction of diseased animals and vegetables? Why should these searches magically now become unconstitutional?

To take another example: The government requires people to pass through airport metal detectors, both to find evidence of crimes or the tools to commit them, like guns and bombs, and to save lives. These searches occur even when there is no basis for suspicion. (Consider the controversies about searches of small children and wheelchair-using elderly people.)

Justice Scalia properly notes that the Constitution's framers loathed "general warrants," but these colonial-era warrants had odious features that cheek swabs lack. These general warrants lacked statutory authorization, were issued by judges ex parte—that is, in secret, without the affected citizen present—and purported to block the citizen from later taking his complaint to a civil jury and seeking damages against the oppressive official. The Fourth Amendment's words do indeed prohibit general warrants—warrants lacking "probable cause"—but this language regulating warrants simply does not apply where no warrants are involved. For example, the police may stop and frisk without warrants, even where they lack probable cause. Certain kinds of warrantless searches—at the border, in airports, in stop-and-frisk searches, and elsewhere—may exist even though a warrant to authorize these very same actions would indeed be unconstitutional.

In other words, general warrants, which were essentially "get-out-of-jail-free cards" for the police, to insulate them from civil liability, raised special problems at the time of the nation's Founding, problems quite distinct from the issues raised in this week's *King* case.

Maryland's DNA policy is very different from the searches the framers loathed. The DNA in the Maryland case was collected pursuant to a law enacted by the legislature. In approving the law, Maryland's lawmakers knew they themselves would run the risk of being swept up in the DNA database—and balanced that risk against the potential benefits. That is nothing like a secret, immunity-conferring warrant that could be aimed at a single unpopular individual or a group of unpopular individuals without proper individualized probable cause. To be sure, the Framers disliked certain kinds of warrants, but when no warrant has been issued—as in the cheek swab situation—the framers simply required that the search or seizure must be reasonable.

This is precisely the question that Justice Anthony M. Kennedy, writing for the five-justice majority, squarely confronted in this landmark case: Is a policy of swabbing and DNA testing only certain arrestees—who have not been convicted and may never be convicted—truly reasonable?

On one hand, the swabbing itself is not particularly intrusive—no more so than a fingerprint or a lineup. Proper DNA testing can simultaneously exonerate innocent people who have been wrongly accused and find the bad guys—a true win-win situation—and in the process, this amazing new technology can powerfully deter crime. On the other hand, DNA testing without strict safeguards can reveal lots more personal information than a mere fingerprint. (For example, who is the suspect's actual biological father or child?) If members of racial minorities are more likely to be wrongly arrested, they and their relatives will loom disproportionately large in the government's DNA database.

Reasonable minds can differ on this.

And therein lies the real genius of the Fourth Amendment. Contrary to Justice Scalia's view, the framers did not answer the DNA question in 1791. Rather, the framers posed the question for us, their posterity. The distinction between criminal evidence-gathering and all sorts of other government programs and purposes is not an all-purpose touchstone or talisman. Rather, we must ponder how intrusive a given search policy is, how discriminatory it might be in application, how well justified and well administered it is, how democratically accountable it is, how it might bear upon human dignity, and so on.

The words of the Fourth Amendment mean exactly what they say. Warrantless searches are unconstitutional only if they are "unreasonable." That rule, and no other, is the true "heart of the Fourth Amendment."

6

CITIZENS DIS-UNITED
Race, Guns, Gays, and More

OURS IS A SHARPLY DIVIDED COUNTRY on several emotional and high-profile constitutional issues. Many citizens, many lawmakers, many scholars, and, frankly, many Supreme Court justices seem to lean consistently left or consistently right on these matters. Not I. As I see it, neither pole of the current political spectrum has a monopoly on constitutional wisdom; nor is the constitutional truth always "in the middle," as some would have it. Each constitutional issue must be examined on its own merits; partisan and ideological shortcuts cut short proper constitutional analysis.

Consider four major areas of constitutional controversy: affirmative action, gun control, campaign finance, and gay marriage. In four landmark modern cases—cases whose names quickly became household words for many Americans—the Court upheld diversity-based, non-quotified affirmative action in higher education (in a 2003 case called *Grutter v. Bollinger*); struck down a law that in effect prevented an ordinary citizen from keeping an ordinary handgun in his home for self-protection (in a 2008 case called *District of Columbia v. Heller*); invalidated the McCain-Feingold law's spending caps on political advertising by independent groups (in a 2010 case called *Citizens United v. Federal Election Commission*); and affirmed a right of same-sex couples to marry despite state laws to the contrary (in a 2015 case called *Obergefell v. Hodges*). As these cases are conventionally scored, the liberals won two (*Grutter* on affirmative action and *Obergefell* on gay marriage) and the conservatives won two (*Heller* on gun control and *Citizens United* on campaign finance). No justice was in all four majorities—in this sense, none of the justices truly swung. I support all four results, and I made known my stance on each topic well before each landmark case was decided.

ON AFFIRMATIVE ACTION, my then student Neal Katyal and I first registered our views two decades ago, in a piece that we published in the *New Republic* in the summer of 1995 and that now appears as the first essay in this chapter.* The piece was prompted by a June 1995 case captioned *Adarand Constructors v. Pena*, in which Justice Sandra Day O'Connor, speaking for the Court, cast doubt on an affirmative action program involving federal spending for private contractors. Many journalistic commentators were hailing or hooting O'Connor as having, in effect, overruled the landmark 1978 *Bakke* decision, which had dealt with affirmative action in education.

Not so fast, Neal and I said. There were at least two big distinctions between the *Adarand* facts and the sort of affirmative action that had been blessed by the swing opinion in *Bakke*, authored by Justice Lewis Powell. First, the basic affirmative action scheme in *Adarand* was rigid and quota-like. Second and more important, *Adarand* did not involve issues of educational integration, as had *Bakke*. The constitutional calculus was different in the unique domain of public education, we argued.

The question, of course, was whether Justice O'Connor herself agreed. As she would go, so would go the Court. So Neal and I followed up our *New Republic* essay with a much more elaborate scholarly article in the 1996 *UCLA Law Review*.[1] That article was ostensibly crafted for a broad audience of lawyers and law professors, but in truth Neal and I wrote this with two persons chiefly in mind. First, we aimed to persuade Justice O'Connor that she herself believed that education was different from government contracting, and that in *Adarand* she had thus carefully reserved the question of whether Justice Powell's embrace of nonquotified affirmative action in *Bakke* should be rejected or reaffirmed. Second, we aimed to give my former and Neal's future boss, Justice Stephen Breyer, himself a strong believer in educational integration, ammunition in the conversations that he would doubtless

---

* Since his student days, Neal has gone on to a brilliant legal career as a scholar, public servant, and private lawyer. He was acting solicitor general of the United States early in the Obama administration and currently heads the appellate practice group at one of DC's top law firms—a position previously held by another former acting solicitor general named John Roberts. Still in his midforties, Neal has already argued more cases before the Supreme Court than any other minority lawyer in history, with the exception of Thurgood Marshall (who also once served as solicitor general).

have with Justice O'Connor. (I had served as a law clerk to then circuit judge Breyer in 1984–1985, and Neal would end up clerking for Justice Breyer on the Supreme Court in 1996–1997.) Justices Breyer and O'Connor were not just friends but jurisprudential kindred spirits in certain respects. Both had worked in legislatures and both understood the virtues of compromise and consensus. Both were also pragmatists, and one particularly important pragmatic fact loomed large in the years immediately following *Adarand*: Were *Bakke* to be overruled, a massive resegregation of America's top public colleges and universities might occur. And were the Court to construe federal statutes to apply similar principles to any private institution of higher learning that accepted federal funding, this resegregation would affect a wide slice of higher education beyond America's elite public academies.

The world may never know exactly why Justice O'Connor voted as she did to extend *Bakke*'s judicial life span in the landmark 2003 case of *Grutter v. Bollinger*. Perhaps Neal and I were right all along about where she had always stood. Or perhaps she changed her mind sometime between *Adarand* and *Grutter*. (Justice Breyer can be a very persuasive person.) But today, Justice O'Connor no longer sits as the swing justice on affirmative action. That spot has in recent years belonged to Justice Kennedy, and he has always been more skeptical of color-conscious government policies. Indeed, he dissented in *Grutter*, voting with the conservatives in that case to strike down the *Bakke*-style program at issue. But Justice Kennedy takes precedent seriously, and *Grutter* is now an important precedent—as was *Bakke* before it. As this book goes to press in mid-2016, another big educational affirmative action case, *Fisher v. University of Texas*, has just been decided, with Kennedy voting to reaffirm *Grutter* and its diversity rationale, in keeping with the approach Neal and I advocated back in 1996.[2]

ON GUN CONTROL, when the Supreme Court agreed to hear the *Heller* case in the spring of 2008, I wrote a short piece for *Slate* summarizing views that I had articulated long before in scholarly books and articles. Although I myself don't much like firearms (they scare me), guns in homes are part of the American way of life. Even if the Second Amendment didn't exist, the Constitution affirms the importance of unenumerated rights, and one obvious source of unenumerated rights is embodied American tradition: We must look to the actual lived experiences and customs of the American people.[3] If liberals may properly insist on an unenumerated right to have sex in the home, conservatives may likewise insist on a right to have guns in the home. Also, regardless of what the Second Amendment may have meant at the Founding, by the time of the Civil War and the Reconstruction amendments, Americans had clearly come to believe in a fundamental right to have a firearm in one's home for self-protection. So in my *Slate* essay I argued that liberals and conservatives should find common ground. Liberals believe in Reconstruction; conservatives believe in gun rights. Why not write an opinion that appealed to both camps in the culture wars, upholding gun rights with a special judicial nod to the values of Lincoln's generation? Can't we all just get along?

Apparently not, at least not at the Supreme Court. When *Heller* came down several months after my *Slate* piece, the right side—that is, both the correct side and the conservative side—won, but it did so in a 5–4 ruling over a sharply worded liberal dissent. Justice Antonin Scalia's majority opinion over-read the Founding history and paid too little attention to Reconstruction history, which provided better evidence for his bottom-line view.

Two years after *Heller*, the Court revisited the issue of guns in homes in another landmark case, *City of Chicago v. McDonald*. Once again, the Court upheld a right to have a handgun in one's home for self-protection, with conservatives (flanked, as in *Heller*, by the swing justice, Anthony Kennedy) outvoting liberals by a vote of 5–4. Once again, the Court seemed as deeply divided as America at large. But this time, the conservative majority, led by Justice Samuel Alito, did spend a great deal of time and energy powerfully exploring the history of the Fourteenth Amendment—a part of the Constitution near and dear to the heart of every liberal. Although the members of the Court did not explicitly cite to my *Slate* essay, justices across the spectrum did openly rely on my earlier and more scholarly work on gun rights—six citations in Justice Alito's majority opinion, two in Justice Clarence Thomas's concurring opinion, and one in Justice Breyer's dissenting opinion.

Although some liberals may mourn the results in both *Heller* and *McDonald*, they shouldn't. Taking ordinary handguns away from ordinary people in their homes was never going to be a realistic political option in most places, and *Heller* and *McDonald* can in fact make it easier for America to adopt sensible gun regulations short of draconian confiscation. Precisely because *Heller* and *McDonald* make clear that government cannot go all the way to complete confiscation, modest and reasonable restrictions on guns can no longer be demonized by gun fanatics as the first step on a slippery slope that will inevitably end with bans on private possession of all firearms. Liberals should embrace these conservative judicial decisions, and use them to achieve sensible gun control. Or so I argued in "Gun Control After Newtown," which I originally published in the *New York Daily News* only days after a horrific mass shooting took place in a Connecticut community just a few miles down the road from my own hometown.[4]

IN 2002, LONG BEFORE the relevant issues reached the Supreme Court in *Citizens United*, I published a harsh constitutional critique of the McCain-Feingold campaign finance law. This essay attacked McCain-Feingold from the left—as an incumbent-protecting sham reform, and not the kind of real reform that America deserves. And real reform, I believe, is still possible despite the "conservative" (note the scare quotes here) 2010 ruling in *Citizens United*. Indeed, several of the specific reform ideas that I floated in 2002 would easily pass judicial muster today, as would other imaginative and powerful reform ideas that have been put forth by leading scholars more recently.[5]

Some of the reforms that I have advocated involve public financing of campaigns, both directly and via egalitarian vouchers, and changes in law and culture encouraging free and focal candidate debates and enhanced citizen deliberation. Elsewhere,[6] I have endorsed legal limits on campaign contributions, which create quasi-slush funds that can be used directly by candidates for all sorts of quasi-personal purposes. True, these direct contributions are not bribery pure and simple. Campaign contributions go into a regulated campaign fund, not directly into the candidate's pocket. But these contributions are also not entirely unlike bribes because campaign funds can be used for salaries and perks for the candidates' kin and cronies and for other expenses that are utterly distinct from pure political expression.

By contrast, political advertising—advertising that the McCain-Feingold law sought to cap—is itself pure political expression. Even if paid for by big corporations or wealthy individuals, political ads put no money directly into candidates' pockets; nor do they go directly into the pockets of kin and cronies. In fact, political ads work as intended only if they persuade actual voters, who vote on Election Day by secret ballot. And on Election Day, each person counts for one vote and only one vote. Corporations do not vote, and a wealthy individual has no more of a vote than anyone else.

This basic point about First Amendment theory—the theory at the heart of the two leading Supreme Court cases in this field, *Buckley v. Valeo* in 1976 and *Citizens United* in 2010, and a theory I embrace—has been vividly illustrated and vindicated by recent elections. Plutocrat Mitt Romney and his wealthy backers spent tons on ads in 2012, yet Romney lost, big, because the ads did not persuade voters. Billionaire Meg Whitman expended far more money than did Jerry Brown in the California governor's race in 2010, but lost to Brown by more than a dozen points. In my own home state of Connecticut, the near billionaire Linda McMahon spent vast sums on ads in two separate bids for the U.S. Senate and was trounced, twice, by candidates of more modest means who spent less. In the earliest months of the 2015–2016 presidential campaign, backers of Jeb Bush poured out close to $100 million for ads, yet these ads failed to sway actual primary and caucus voters, who forced Bush to drop out in February. Donald Trump ran no ads whatsoever early on, yet soared into the early lead among Republican voters. All these recent developments confirm my view, first expressed in 2002, that real campaign finance reform should not aim at limiting political ads, which both I and the Court consider core political speech.

It's also worth mentioning here, in light of this book's special focus on the role of the media in modern American constitutional discourse, that my 2002 McCain-Feingold article called out and took on the *New York Times* by name. That paper was a ridiculously staunch ally of the reform law that I labeled a sham, but the paper's editors almost never explained to its readers that the so-called reforms that it advocated benefited media corporations over all other corporations. Under McCain-Feingold, a non-media company (say, Exxon-Mobil) was limited in the amount of money it could expend to take out ads favoring a given candidate, but the *Times* itself—like any other media corporation—was not limited in how much money it could spend to give a candidate favorable news coverage or editorial endorsement in its own newspaper or website. Why should sensible reform laws distinguish among corporations in this way? Wouldn't such laws help media companies themselves become kingmakers? If other companies could no longer rent conventional media space via ads, why wouldn't these companies simply start buying media companies or turning themselves into media companies, in part?

ANOTHER ELEPHANT in the culture war room is the issue of same-sex marriage. Here, too, my longstanding views have prevailed in the Supreme Court, albeit quite recently. In countless public lectures, classroom presentations, scholarly footnotes, and oral interviews over the last quarter century, I have argued that bans on same-sex marriage were improper discriminations on the basis of sex and sexual orientation.[7] Until the summer of 2015, however, I never had occasion to fully unfold these arguments in the popular press. In the wake of the Supreme Court's landmark ruling in *Obergefell v. Hodges*, the editors of *Slate* invited me to locate the case against the backdrop of constitutional first principles. The result was a pair of essays that now appear in this chapter.

As so little time has elapsed since the initial publication of these pieces, I cannot confidently report that they have aged well. But I can and do confidently predict that these pieces will age well because they quickly, clearly, and cleanly connect the right of same-sex marriage to the central meaning of the Fourteenth Amendment and to a vast and sturdy corpus of case law vindicating that amendment. Textually and historically, the Fourteenth Amendment promised, at its very core, *birth equality*. Across a wide range of Fourteenth Amendment case law, judges have vindicated that birth-equality principle by frowning on laws that demean a person because that person was born a certain way—for example, born black, or born female, or born out of wedlock, or born to noncitizen parents. So, too, judges should frown on laws that demean a person because that person was born gay. Laws banning same-sex marriage do just that—demean persons born gay—and these laws thus cannot stand, constitutionally.

IN LIGHT OF THE VARIEGATED ideological hues of the essays in this chapter, and in this book more generally, some readers may find this chapter's final two pieces of special interest. The first essay is a remembrance that I composed for *Slate* in late 2012 on the death of Robert Bork, who was my teacher at Yale long ago. Although Bork was a leading conservative, and I reckon myself a liberal on most issues, the man profoundly influenced me in ways that I only later came to appreciate, as I explain in this confessional essay. In mid-April 2015, I composed a companion essay of sorts remembering another bearded Republican who in life was, believe it or not, even more polarizing than Bork. As it turns out, that bewhiskered polarizer, Abraham Lincoln, gives us a great angle on another tall, skinny, constitutional lawyer from Illinois, who now sits where Lincoln once did.

SCHOOL COLORS:
AFFIRMATIVE ACTION IN EDUCATION

NEW REPUBLIC, MONDAY, JULY 17, 1995 (WITH NEAL KATYAL)

Many observers hailed the Supreme Court's decision last month in *Adarand Constructors v. Pena*, which toughened the legal standard by which federal set-aside programs for minorities are judged, as the death of all affirmative action. In fact, though, the Court had surprisingly little to say in that decision about one of the most contentious arenas of affirmative action, admissions to state universities. And for good reason. Opposing affirmative action in the awarding of government contracts while defending it in university admissions is a highly plausible position.

The last time the Court addressed affirmative action in the university context was, famously, in the 1978 *Bakke* case. After Allan Bakke, a white man, was twice rejected from the University of California Davis Medical School, he filed suit contending that the university's special admissions program for minorities was a quota that had excluded him on the basis of race. The Court, in a fractured opinion, struck down the quota program on a combination of constitutional and statutory grounds.

But the upholding of Bakke's claim was only the first part of the Court's ruling. The Court also noted, in now-familiar language, that diversity may be a constitutionally proper goal in the university context and that, while U.C. Davis could not use a racial quota system, it could take race into consideration in its admissions decisions. Justice Lewis Powell, the swing vote and author of the most influential of the six opinions offered in *Bakke*, even attached an appendix detailing the practices of the Harvard College Admissions Program, which did not use quotas but did allow race to "tip the balance" in some cases because "diversity adds an essential ingredient to the educational process." Powell, along with four other justices, held that such non-quota schemes could pass constitutional muster.

Today state university administrators around the country are wondering whether *Bakke* is still good law. In *Adarand*, in an opinion written by Justice Sandra Day O'Connor, the Court overruled its 1990 decision in *Metro Broadcasting Inc. v. Federal Communications Commission*, which judged federal affirmative action by a relatively relaxed standard. But O'Connor's opinion was vague about *Bakke*. On the one hand, she said "all racial classifications, imposed by whatever federal, state or local governmental actor, must be analyzed by a reviewing court under strict scrutiny." Yet, in propounding this nominally harsher test, she watered it down to say "strict scrutiny does take relevant differences into account"—an open invitation to think about education in different terms than construction contracts. As the dissent by Justice John Paul Stevens pointed out, the *Adarand* majority said nothing about "fostering diversity" because the issue was not even "remotely presented."

More generally, O'Connor carefully crafted the *Adarand* opinion in light of her 1992 *Planned Parenthood v. Casey* decision, which argued against over-

ruling longstanding cases around which major social expectations have crys-
tallized. Thus *Casey* affirmed *Roe v. Wade*, while overruling less important
cases that came in its wake. By this test, *Bakke* is arguably more like *Roe* and
should stand even after the less important *Metro Broadcasting* is tossed out.
(Only O'Connor and Anthony Kennedy used this test in *Adarand*, but they
hold the two most crucial votes, as the *Casey* and *Adarand* rulings prove.)

There is, therefore, some reason to think that the Court's recent decision
may not really be the end of affirmative action, at least in education—
especially since, in a number of essential ways, universities are different from
government contracting.

First, set-aside contracts are often given to minority-controlled corporations, not individuals. As such, they are highly susceptible to fraud, for in
some cases, minorities may be present only as figureheads to gain government contracts. Affirmative action in admissions, on the other hand, operates directly on an individual level. (Both schemes pose similarly thorny
issues when it comes to proving minority status: How do you prove that
you're really one-eighth black? Should Aleuts count?)* In addition, those
who award set-aside contracts are often politicians or political appointees, an

*[Neal and I returned to these and closely related questions the following year in a
law review article, "*Bakke*'s Fate," *UCLA Law Review* 43 (1996): 1745. We were of
course aware that the distinction that Justice Powell drew in *Bakke* between strict
racial quotas and softer "plus" factors in school admissions programs has drawn deri-
sion over the years. Aren't plus factors really quotas hiding behind fig leaves? But as
Neal and I explained in 1996, quotas require strict definitions of the group or groups
eligible for affirmative action. How many affirmative action boxes are there on the
admissions form? Just one box, for blacks? Or six separate boxes—for blacks, Hispan-
ics, Asian Americans, American Indians, Eskimos, and Aleuts? Somewhere between
one and six? More than six? And who gets to check a box? A quota system would as a
practical matter require a Nuremberg-like code specifying the quantum of blood that
qualifies. A softer plus system sidesteps some of these problems. Formally, there are
no boxes to check—only a "personal statement" by an applicant describing his or her
lived identity in whatever way the applicant chooses. Also, as Neal and I explained
in 1996, plus-factor systems probably generate less backlash and stigma toward the
minority applicants. Minority status is not singled out as qualitatively different from
everything else in the admissions process. Instead, racial identity is treated holisti-
cally; being black might be a plus, just as being bilingual might, or being a chess whiz,
or a piano player, or a wide receiver, or a farm boy. In a plus system, unlike a formal
quota system, all students are eligible for all seats, and the very fact that fig leaves are
likely involved may dampen racial polarization that a blunt quota system may
exacerbate—polarization that runs counter to the integrationist vision underlying
affirmative action at its best.]

arrangement that doesn't exactly inspire confidence that the programs will reach their targeted groups. Professional educators, with no comparable need to cater to voting blocs, should in theory be less inclined to play racial pork-barrel politics.

Second, contracts are essentially jobs that the government wants done. The goal is simply to carry out a task, not to create a new government entitlement. When the government contracts with a company to provide goods and services, it is not handing out goodies; it is, or should be, getting a job done at the lowest cost. Here, the government's sole concern should be awarding the contract to the lowest bidder. Education, on the other hand, is principally about investing citizens with skills. Its real value accrues only to those who work and learn, which means that those who benefit from it do not reap unfair rewards. In the *Adarand* case, a contractor was paid, in effect, a cash bonus just for being a minority. A cash bonus is a blatant race-based handout, while a seat in a chemistry class is a hand-up. What's more, a wider range of people are helped by preferences in education than by set-asides, which are notorious for benefiting primarily middle- or even upper-class blacks. How many minorities own construction companies?

Third, contracts are awarded to people throughout their adult years and have no logical stopping point. University education typically occurs early in life and then *ends*. Higher education, by making up for educational inequities at early stages in life, can be the ramp to a level playing field—with no further affirmative action—for the rest of your future. It also partially compensates for educational grandfather clauses, the admissions preferences granted to the offspring of the college's alumni. (This is one of the non-merit-based criteria the merit proponents don't seem to talk much about.)

In the end these differences may not be entirely convincing. Allan Bakke and other whites may still feel slighted by virtue of their race. But, before agreeing with this, we should stop to ponder the biggest difference of all. Set-asides compartmentalize people by their race; "black firms" win contracts and "white firms" do not. Set-asides can actually encourage segregation and reward wholly unintegrated minority firms. Education, by contrast, unites people from different walks of life. Instead of atomized corporations fulfilling various contracts, the educational context brings individuals together in an environment where they can mingle with and learn from each other.

There is a way to make affirmative action a gentler, more benevolent force in society than the rigid set-aside. Set-asides don't help in the great American goal of integration, a goal at the heart of the Court's historic 1954 decision in *Brown v. Board of Education*. Instead, set-asides are a recipe for "black" and "white" firms, with no mixture between the two. Integrated education, on the other hand, doesn't just benefit minorities; it benefits all students.

As Powell wrote in *Bakke*, "The Nation's future depends upon leaders trained through wide exposure" to "the ideas and mores of students as diverse as this Nation of many peoples." *Adarand*-like set asides set us apart. *Bakke*-like affirmative action on the Harvard model brings us together.

Until and unless the Court says otherwise, *Bakke* stands as the law of the land.

PUTTING THE SECOND AMENDMENT SECOND

SLATE, MONDAY, MARCH 17, 2008, 3:25 P.M. (ET)

The language of the Second Amendment has been the obsessive focus of just about everyone interested in *District of Columbia v. Heller*, the DC gun-ownership case to be argued before the Supreme Court on Tuesday. That amendment is indeed important and much misunderstood. But *Heller*'s facts, which involve the possession of a handgun inside the home for self-defense, lie rather far from the Second Amendment's core concerns, as originally understood by the Founding Fathers. To think straight about gun control and the Constitution, we need to move past the Second Amendment and pay more heed to the Ninth and Fourteenth Amendments.

Let's begin here: Suppose, for argument's sake, that we concede that everything gun-control advocates say about the Second Amendment is right. Suppose that the amendment focused solely on arms-bearing in military contexts, and that it said absolutely nothing about an individual's right to have a gun while sleeping in his own home or hunting in his own private Idaho. Would this concession mean that no individual constitutional right exists today?

Hardly. According to the Ninth Amendment: "The enumeration in the Constitution of certain rights shall not be construed to deny or disparage other rights retained by the people." In other words, there may well be constitutional rights that are not explicitly set forth in the Second Amendment (or in any other amendment or constitutional clause, for that matter). In identifying these unenumerated "rights retained by the people," the key is that a judge should not decide what he or she personally thinks would be a proper set of rights. Instead, the judge should ask which rights have been recognized by the American people themselves—for example, in state constitutions and state bills of rights and civil rights laws. Americans have also established, merely by living our lives freely across the country and over the centuries, certain customary rights that governments have generally respected. Many of our most basic rights are simply facts of life, the residue of a virtually unchallenged pattern and practice on the ground in domains where citizens act freely and governments lie low.

Consider, for example, the famous 1965 privacy case *Griswold v. Connecticut*. The state of Connecticut purported to criminalize the use of contraception, even by married couples, prompting the Supreme Court to strike down this extraordinarily intrusive state law as unconstitutional. Writing for the majority, Justice William Douglas claimed that a general right of privacy could be found in between the lines of the Bill of Rights. But Douglas did a poor job of proving his case. Writing separately in *Griswold*, the second Justice John Harlan, widely admired for his judicial care and craftsmanship, offered a more modest and less strained rationale: "Conclusive, in my view, is the utter novelty of [Connecticut's] enactment. Although the Federal Government and many States have at one time or another had on their books statutes forbidding the distribution of contraceptives, none, so far as I can find, has made the use of contraceptives a crime." Thus, the basic practices of the American people rendered Connecticut's oddball law presumptively unconstitutional. It is also highly noteworthy that today around a dozen state constitutions and countless statutes speak explicitly of a right to privacy—a right nowhere explicitly mentioned in the federal Constitution.

Now take Harlan's sensible approach to the unenumerated right of privacy and apply it to Dick Anthony Heller's claim that he has a right to have a handgun in his DC home for self-defense. When we look at the actual pattern of lived rights in America—what the people have, in fact, done—we find lots of regulations of guns, but few outright prohibitions of guns in homes as sweeping as the DC ordinance. We also find a right to keep guns affirmed in most modern state constitutions, many of which use the phrase "bear arms" in ways that clearly go beyond the military context. Unlike Founding-era documents, modern state constitutions routinely affirm a constitutional right to "bear arms" for hunting, recreation, and/or self-defense.

In addition to the Ninth Amendment, we should also view the right to bear arms through the lens of the Fourteenth Amendment's command that "No state shall make or enforce any law which shall abridge the privileges or immunities of citizens of the United States." Though this particular sentence applies only to the states, other language in the Fourteenth Amendment affirms that the federal government, too, has a parallel obligation to respect the fundamental rights of citizens.

But the Fourteenth Amendment did not specifically enumerate these sacred privileges and immunities. Instead, like the Ninth, the Fourteenth invited interpreters to pay close attention to fundamental rights that Americans had affirmed through their lived experience—in state bills of rights and in other canonical texts such as the Declaration of Independence and landmark civil rights legislation. And when it came to guns, a companion statute to the Fourteenth Amendment, enacted by Congress in 1866, declared that "laws . . . concerning personal liberty [and] personal security . . . including the constitutional right to bear arms, shall be secured to and enjoyed by all the citizens."

Here, in sharp contrast to Founding-era legal texts, the "bear arms" phrase was decisively severed from the military context. Women as well as men could claim a "personal" right to protect their "personal liberty" and "personal security" in their homes. The Reconstruction-era Congress clearly understood that southern blacks might need guns in their homes to protect themselves from private violence in places where they could not rely on local constables to keep their neighborhoods safe. To paraphrase a modern National Rifle Association slogan: When guns were outlawed, only outlaw Klansmen would have guns. In this critical chapter in the history of American liberty, we find additional evidence of an individual right to have a gun in one's home, regardless of the original meaning of the Second Amendment.

There are at least three advantages of shifting twenty-first-century gun-control discourse in this direction. First, a Ninth and Fourteenth Amendment framework is more modest. Unusually draconian gun laws can be struck down simply because they lie outside the lived pattern of the American experience, while more mainstream gun laws can be upheld precisely because they have proved acceptable to the people in many places. If our nation's capital wants to argue that especially strict gun rules should apply there because the city faces unique risks, no rigid textual language prevents judges from considering such pragmatic claims in the course of interpreting the boundaries of actual American practice. By contrast, if the Second Amendment's language really did guarantee a right to guns in homes, by what authority could judges allow for a different approach in DC? And then, if one has a Second Amendment right to a pistol or shotgun at home, why not a machine gun? Given that the Second Amendment's core right is military, it would seem odd that military arms would be easier to ban than other weapons.

Second, the Ninth and Fourteenth Amendments are more modern and democratically responsive. The Ninth invites us to consider not only rights that have long been part of the American tradition but also rights that have emerged in actual modern practice and in state constitutional clauses of relatively recent vintage that are relatively easy to amend. The Fourteenth directs our attention to the still-relevant problems of race and police protection, or the absence thereof. By contrast, the Second Amendment harkens back to a lost eighteenth-century America, where citizens regularly mustered for militia service on the town square and where the federal army was rightly suspect. This is not our world.

Finally, a focus on the Ninth and Fourteenth Amendments is simply more honest. The open-ended language of the Ninth and Fourteenth Amendments really did aim to invite Americans to ponder state constitutional provisions that declare rights, and these provisions really do focus on individual self-defense. The framers of the Fourteenth Amendment really did focus intently on self-defense in the home. The framers of the Second Amendment did not.

GUN CONTROL AFTER NEWTOWN[8]

New York Daily News, Wednesday, December 26, 2012

As gun controllers and gun enthusiasts continue their conversation in the wake of the Newtown tragedy, several recent Supreme Court rulings may loom large. Ironically, gun controllers can strengthen their case for sensible reform by invoking a pair of pro-gun decisions handed down by the Court's conservatives. In turn, gun lovers should invoke a landmark gay-rights case where the Court's liberals won out.

When Congress last seriously debated gun control in the mid-1990s, the Second Amendment was a virtual dead letter in court. The justices had never used the amendment to invalidate anti-gun legislation, and most scholars read both the Constitution and the case law as providing virtually no protection for ordinary individuals to keep and carry guns. According to then conventional wisdom, only organized state militias were protected by the Second Amendment.

But in the 2008 case *District of Columbia v. Heller*, a challenge to the national capital's restrictive gun laws, the Supreme Court read the Second Amendment to affirm an individual's right to have a gun, especially in his home, for self-defense. Two years later, in a case called *McDonald*, the Court ruled that this basic right applies not just against federal officials—the original target of the Second Amendment—but also against state and local governments.

In both *Heller* and *McDonald*, the Court's five most conservative members—Antonin Scalia, Samuel Alito, Clarence Thomas, John Roberts, and Anthony Kennedy—narrowly prevailed over four vigorous liberal dissenters.

Here's why political liberals tempted to emulate their judicial heroes should resist this temptation and instead embrace *Heller* and *McDonald*: Both cases focused on the right of a law-abiding person to have a handgun in his or her home for self-protection. Neither case foreclosed reasonable gun regulations short of total prohibition—bans on military weapons wholly unnecessary for ordinary self-defense; caps on the amount of firepower a person may stockpile; limits on the size of gun clips; registration and permit requirements; insurance requirements, regular mental health checkups, and so on.

In fact, these two landmark cases not only allow sensible gun regulation, they actually make such regulation *easier* to accomplish. Before *Heller*, many gun enthusiasts sincerely worried that any regulation, however modest, would be the first step on a dangerous, slippery slope that could end in total confiscation. Because the pre-*Heller* Court didn't take gun rights seriously, the only place to defend such rights was in the legislature, and here a hard line had to be maintained. The outer walls of the fortress had to be manned, because once these walls were breached, the inner citadel of gun possession in homes might be at risk. After the rulings, this slippery slope argument no longer works. Precisely because the Court has declared total confiscation off limits, there's no legitimate fear that reasonable regulation will slide into tyrannical confiscation. If sensible liberals embrace *Heller* and *McDonald* instead of trashing them, they can earn the political trust of those who might otherwise resist even the tamest of reforms.

In turn, conservative gun-lovers would do well to embrace an iconic liberal Supreme Court case affirming gay rights, *Lawrence v. Texas*. In that 2003 decision, the Court protected the right of consenting adults to engage in sexual relations in the privacy of their own homes. In this case, the Court's most conservative members—Scalia, Thomas, and then chief justice William Rehnquist—dissented.

Gun enthusiasts who like Scalia's and Thomas's ideas in *Heller* and *McDonald* should side with the liberals in *Lawrence*. For in this case, the liberals recognized that not all rights—in that case, the right of sexual privacy—are explicitly listed in the Constitution itself. Some unenumerated rights deserve protection as well. And to find these unenumerated rights, the Court properly canvassed state laws, state constitutions, and the lived experiences of ordinary citizens. Many state constitutions affirm a right to "privacy"—a word not found in the federal Constitution. Sexual privacy is an important part of American culture and practice, the *Lawrence* Court recognized. Ditto with guns. *Heller* and *McDonald* focused tightly on guns for self-protection, but many state laws and constitutions recognize other aspects of gun use—hunting and sport, for example. Even if the Second Amendment's text did not exist, guns would remain an important part of American culture.

Thus, thanks to three sharply divided cases in the modern culture wars involving guns and gays, conservative justices could end up helping today's political liberals, and liberal justices may have given today's conservatives additional ammunition. Legal arguments, like bullets, can sometimes ricochet.

THE SHAM CALLED CAMPAIGN FINANCE REFORM

AMERICAN LAWYER, OCTOBER 2002

If the ballyhooed McCain-Feingold campaign finance bill signed into law this spring is real reform, exactly what would business as usual or retrogression look like?

One large chunk of the law—the Snow-Jeffords "electioneering" amendment—censors political exhortation during the two months before an election. This amendment openly discriminates against political discourse: A TV spot detailing why challenger Smith is better than incumbent Jones on the key issues of our day is treated worse than an advertisement pushing Pepsi over Coke. The political ad might be an extended infomercial, with enlightening graphs and charts, but no matter. It is legally disfavored compared to spots featuring Britney Spears singing mindless consumerist jingles.

This turns the First Amendment on its head. Political discourse is at the heart of constitutional self-government, especially speech about the elections that our Constitution mandates every two years. It is the speech America cannot do without. Commercial speech hawking products that the government could, if it chose, entirely prohibit is less central to our Constitution's text, history, and structure. The very phrase "freedom of speech" derives from English and colonial principles affirming "freedom of speech and debate" in Parliament and other legislative assemblies. Parliament (from the French verb *parler*—to speak) is a speaking spot—a parley place. But it is a place that privileges a certain kind of speech: political discourse. It is a place where political figures debate the key issues of the day, not where they sing about soft drinks.

The electioneering amendment is not only a content-based discrimination against political discourse but also, in reality, a viewpoint-based discrimination that favors incumbents over challengers. As a rule, congressional incumbents have all the advantages—inertia, seniority, name recognition, franking, pork, perks, and patronage. If no one can talk politics before elections, incumbents generally win. Voters need to be given reasons why they should dump the incumbent in favor of a challenger. In order to give voters these reasons, a challenger's supporters must talk about the candidates—precisely the discourse the amendment constricts!—and must do so when marginal voters are finally paying attention, namely, in the weeks before the vote, precisely the time period blacked out by the amendment. The amendment prohibits various political organizations from running ads explaining just how bad Congressman Jones really is on certain issues, or how much better challenger Smith would be. This is an incumbent-protection provision, pure and simple, muzzling critics of Congress precisely when it counts most.

Many lawmakers who initially resisted the electioneering amendment and indeed thought it unconstitutional nevertheless voted for the McCain-Feingold bill as a whole when forced to vote yea or nay on the entire package. How are these actions to be squared with their oaths of office to support the Constitution?

Presidents are oath-bound, too. Indeed, candidate George W. Bush ran on the oath issue in 2000. His implicit theme was that even though Bill Clinton had betrayed various oaths—of marriage, of office, in depositions—things would be different in a new Bush administration. Candidate Bush also claimed to take the Constitution seriously. When asked whether he thought "a President has a duty to make an independent judgment of what is and is not constitutional, and veto bills that, in his judgment he thinks are unconstitutional." Bush said, "I do." When pressed if he would therefore veto the version of McCain-Feingold then on the table, Bush answered: "Yes, I would. . . . I think it does restrict free speech for individuals."

Perhaps Bush has changed his mind about the Constitution since then. But he didn't say that when signing McCain-Feingold into law. Perhaps he thought the final bill had fewer constitutional flaws than the version he initially opposed. But he didn't say that either, and the earlier version lacked the electioneering amendment, which Bush himself went out of his way to flag as constitutionally dubious—in his statement signing this dubious edict into law.

The constitutional abdications of the House, the Senate, and the president are all the more disheartening because they seem so self-serving. Congressmen protect themselves while President Bush sharpens his own electoral edge as well. Key parts of the "reform" law actually increase the amounts of cash that fat cats can give to candidates, and in fact make it easier for President Bush to opt out of the public financing system for presidential elections in 2004, just as candidate Bush did in 2000.

Nor has America's third branch of government clothed itself in glory here. In recent years, the Supreme Court has increasingly described itself as the center of all constitutional wisdom, and downplayed the constitutional competence of co-ordinate branches of government. Across a wide range of cases, the Court has told Congress and the president that they should not worry their pretty little heads about the Constitution. Leave all that to us justices! This is both self-aggrandizing and self-fulfilling, prompting precisely the constitutional abdications we are seeing in Congress and the Oval Office.

It is also bad history: The framers envisioned a system in which all three branches would take the Constitution seriously. For example, when Congress in its 1798 Sedition Act outlawed criticism of incumbents (sound familiar?), Thomas Jefferson campaigned against this law and later, as president, refused to renew the law when it expired. Jefferson also pardoned all those who had been convicted under the old act, even though courts had upheld these convictions over First Amendment objections. To Jefferson, the question was not simply what judges had done or might do, but what his own independent constitutional conscience dictated. Likewise, President James Madison vetoed a bill he knew courts would uphold and that he favored as a matter of policy but that in his own independent judgment violated the Constitution. As President Andrew Jackson later put the point:

"Each public officer who takes an oath to support the Constitution swears that he will support it as he understands it, and not as it is understood by others. It is as much the duty of the House of Representatives, of the Senate, and of the President to decide upon the constitutionality of any bill or resolution which may be presented to them for passage or approval as it is of the supreme judges when it may be brought before them for judicial decision."

Nor have the Court's pronouncements about free speech and campaign finance been wholly inspiring. The justices have often blurred the lines between money and speech, and between political and commercial discourse. They have failed to elaborate on the central image of "freedom of speech and debate" and the implications of that image for a real system of campaign finance reform.

The media has been as self-serving as the government officials. Television stations have not offered free airtime for candidate debates, and have charged steep rates for political advertising. Other media outlets piously support McCain-Feingold without describing to their audience how the law would end up increasing their own campaign clout. If Amar, Inc. wants to argue for a candidate by buying airtime, that counts as impermissible electioneering; but if the New York Times, Inc. wants to argue for a candidate, that counts as favorable news coverage or editorials exempt from the law's censorship.

For a glimpse of what real campaign finance might look like, we must look past what government officials and media conglomerates are calling "reform" to the Constitution itself. Its text and history provide some suggestive metaphors and models. Consider, for example, the central image of "freedom of speech and debate." Public funds are used to create a space—Parliament, or a legislative assembly, or a town meeting—where proponents of different political visions square off in fair and open debate. Political discourse is thereby subsidized, not disfavored. Debate time is allocated by principles of democracy, not plutocracy. The rich man does not automatically get more time in parliamentary debate than his less wealthy opponent, just because he has more money.

Major aspects of the McCain-Feingold law, of judicial opinions, and of media actions, run counter to this image. They penalize political discourse, spurn debate, make speech anything but free, and privilege wealth over equality, capitalism over democracy.

Imagine instead a genuine model of reform that built on the metaphor of "freedom of speech and debate." The law might require TV stations to offer one hour of free prime time a week, in the two months before elections, for candidate debates for each congressional race. If incumbents refuse to show up, the time goes to their challengers. A stricter rule might prohibit any candidate who spurns these debates from holding a leadership position in Congress. Stricter still, each House could deem such refusal to be a kind of corruption and contempt of democracy akin to bribe taking, and severely discipline such misbehavior with penalties up to and including expulsion. A reform law might further make federal Election Day a national holiday (thus making it easier for working people to vote) and provide that each voter receive $20 if he or she either certifies to having watched at least one debate or spends an hour at the polling place itself reviewing various campaign materials submitted by the various candidates, media organizations, and political groups.

All the details here are of course mere placeholders—starting points and first approximations of what real reforms could and should look like, reforms that would actually try to embody an inspiring constitutional ideal, rather than simply serving the current self-interest of the three branches and the fourth estate.

ANTHONY KENNEDY AND
THE GHOST OF EARL WARREN

SLATE, JULY 6, 2015, 4:17 P.M. (ET)

Every schoolchild knows that in 1954 *Brown v. Board of Education* overruled *Plessy v. Ferguson*, the infamous 1896 separate-but-equal case, but every expert knows that *Brown* did no such thing. Earl Warren's landmark opinion contained no sentence saying, "*Plessy* is hereby overruled." *Brown* did not even say that *Plessy* was wrongly decided. Warren's watershed *Brown* opinion merely said that *Plessy* was a case about segregation in *transportation*—railroads—and that *Plessy*'s separate-but-equal doctrine did not apply to the field of *public education*. The lesson here is that at least for certain world-historical, once-in-a-generation rulings, the basic rightness of the Court's result within the broad sweep of human affairs—the Supreme Court's success in seizing the moment and doing the right thing—sometimes overwhelms the precise language of the Court's exposition. To bend a phrase from Lincoln, in some of the biggest battles, the world may little note nor long remember what the Court said, but it will never forget what the Court did.

The June 26, 2015, ruling on same-sex marriage is the closest the Court has ever come to a repeat of *Brown*. Of course, no two cases decided decades apart on different issues could ever be identical in every respect—Heraclitus taught us long ago that one never steps in the same river twice. But there are obvious parallels between *Obergefell v. Hodges* and *Brown v. Board*. *Brown*'s deepest thrust was to proclaim the dignity and equality of black Americans, and *Obergefell* is likewise a powerful and profound affirmation of the dignity and equality of gay Americans. Beyond equality, the two cases celebrated the substantive and symbolic significance of bedrock societal institutions. *Brown* was an ode to education, and *Obergefell* is an ode to marriage. *Brown*'s majority opinion crossed party lines. A Republican appointee spoke authoritatively for the Court with not a crack of daylight between him and any of the Court's Democrat appointees—no divisive dissent or distracting concurrence from any of the justices from the other side of America's partisan divide. Ditto for *Obergefell*.

Surely these and many other similarities were savored by the author of *Obergefell*, Anthony Kennedy, who grew up in the shadow of Earl Warren. As a youngster in Sacramento, California, Kennedy worked after school in the statehouse, when Warren was governor. "I knew Earl Warren very well," Kennedy said in a 2005 interview. "[I] knew his children and played in the governor's mansion." Warren was famously bipartisan, a fact not lost on Kennedy, who in that same interview highlighted the fact that, as an incumbent governor in 1946, Warren "ran on both the Democratic and Republican tickets." Warren is the only person in California history to accomplish this feat; analogously, Kennedy is the only current justice who routinely sides with Democrat appointees in many key cases and with Republican appointees in many other key cases. (Recall that, although appointed to the Supreme Court in 1987 by a Republican president—another famous California ex-governor named Ronald Reagan—Kennedy had to win confirmation in a Democrat-controlled Senate that had just nixed Reagan's earlier nominee, Robert Bork.)

Because this swing justice truly swings, and at times openly broods on which way he should swing, some consider Kennedy a judicial version of Hamlet. If so, Earl Warren is Hamlet's ghost, a judicial father figure whom Kennedy sees in his mind's eye. In a landmark 1992 decision, *Planned Parenthood v. Casey*, Kennedy coauthored a section of the Court's opinion that detoured to ponder the relationship between *Brown* and *Plessy*, even though the case at hand involved abortion, not race. Four years later, in *Romer v. Evans*, the first major Supreme Court victory for gay rights, Kennedy spoke for the Court to condemn a Colorado referendum that openly bashed persons of "Homosexual, Lesbian or Bisexual Orientation." *Romer* was decided exactly one hundred years, to the week, after *Plessy v. Ferguson*, and this disgraceful case—the case Warren would powerfully undermine (though not quite overrule) in *Brown*—was once again on Kennedy's mind. He opened as follows: "One century ago, the first Justice Harlan [in his now canonical *Plessy* dissent] admonished this Court that the Constitution neither knows nor tolerates classes among citizens."

In the opening minutes of the oral argument in *Obergefell* this past April, it was Kennedy who, unprompted, explicitly invoked Warren's two most famous decisions on race: *Brown v. Board* and *Loving v. Virginia*. *Loving*, of course, was the 1967 landmark case in which Warren struck down a state law banning racial intermarriage. Warren grounded his ruling on two principles, equality and a fundamental (albeit unenumerated) right to marry—the same two principles that Kennedy himself would intertwine in his majority opinion in June.

In *Obergefell*, Kennedy wrapped himself in *Loving*, citing it approvingly almost a dozen times. The only opinion that Kennedy favorably mentioned more often (barely) was his own majority opinion in *Lawrence v. Texas*, the 2003 case striking down state sodomy laws—an opinion that, according to Justice Antonin Scalia's angry and self-fulfilling dissent that day more than a decade ago, portended a right to same-sex marriage. And as Kennedy himself noted in this April's oral argument, in another line full of portent, the time span between *Lawrence* and *Obergefell* roughly matches the thirteen-year gap between *Brown* and *Loving*.

Noting the rhetorical contrast between Warren's spare style in *Brown* and Kennedy's fondness for sweeping and soaring prose, some legal commentators have faulted Kennedy's grandiosity and self-importance. But perhaps Kennedy is simply more honest about the Court and the world beyond. Whereas Warren pulled his punches in *Brown*, Kennedy speaks openly and passionately, yet politely, of the demeaning aspect of the laws he strikes down. And Kennedy's supercharged vision of judicial power is just what one might expect from a youngster who grew up watching Earl Warren lead America and the Court into the history books.

The biggest difference between Warren and Kennedy is that Warren spoke for a unanimous Court. But Warren had all the formal advantages and trappings of the chief justiceship; Kennedy does not. Warren did not have to contend with the operatic diva known as Antonin Scalia. And most important, Warren's world was not deeply and pervasively split along partisan lines. In 1954, there were many liberal Republicans and many reactionary Democrats in America.

No more—and no more in large part because of *Brown* and *Loving*. Once race leaped onto the midcentury American agenda, Congress eventually had to choose sides. When, led by President Lyndon Johnson, Congress sided with *Brown*'s vision of racial justice in a series of civil-rights and voting-rights laws, grateful southern blacks surged into the Democratic Party. Conservative southern whites, encouraged by Republicans Barry Goldwater and Richard Nixon, abandoned the Democratic Party to become Republicans. The party of Lincoln became the party of the Confederacy, pushing liberal northern and eastern Republicans out of the party. Today, the realignment begun by LBJ, Goldwater, Nixon, and the Warren Court has resulted in near perfect polarization. On almost every issue in Congress, the most conservative Democrat is still to the left of the most liberal Republican. Almost no one in high elective office truly swings, mediating between America's two entrenched political parties and their sharply differing worldviews.

This is all the more reason to celebrate rather than to mock Anthony Kennedy, one of America's last remaining Lincoln Republicans, who hails from gay-friendly Northern California and hearkens back to an earlier Lincoln Republican named Earl Warren.

WHAT THE SAME-SEX MARRIAGE CASE SHOULD HAVE SAID (AND ALMOST DID)

SLATE, JULY 10, 2015, 1:28 P.M. (ET)

The fireworks came early this year. When Justice Anthony Kennedy declared a constitutional right to same-sex marriage in *Obergefell v. Hodges* on June 26, each of the Court's other four Republican appointees wrote a separate dissent taking a swipe at him. (The Court's four Democrats stayed mum, content to let Kennedy make the case and take the heat.) Aiming all their firepower at Kennedy, the dissenters missed their real target: the Constitution itself. While persuasively explaining why they could not join Kennedy's majority opinion, they failed to persuasively explain why they voted against the constitutional claims at issue—why they were dissenting ("Kennedy has reached the wrong result") rather than concurring in the judgment ("Kennedy has reached the right result but for the wrong reasons"). Indeed, the four dissenters failed even to identify, much less engage, the best constitutional arguments for same-sex marriage—arguments that have been repeatedly made over many years by many leading lawyers, scholars, and lower-court judges.

Justice Kennedy's majority opinion is not perfect, but it reached the right result, and for many of the right reasons. To be clear: Kennedy is not just right morally and not just right politically. He is not only on the right side of history but also on the right side of the law, based on the Constitution's letter and spirit and original meaning, as properly construed and implemented by the Court in many previous cases.

Had I been whispering in Kennedy's ear, here is the opinion I would have urged him to write:

We begin with the Constitution itself. The Fourteenth Amendment opens with a promise of birth equality: "All persons born . . . in the United States . . . are citizens" and thus *equal* citizens. As full and equal citizens, all persons born in America are entitled to full and equal protection of all fundamental civil liberties, as expressly guaranteed by the very next sentence of the Fourteenth Amendment: "No State shall make or enforce any law which shall abridge the privileges or immunities of citizens of the United States."

The Fourteenth Amendment's opening words about birthright citizenship codified Lincoln's vision at Gettysburg: America is dedicated to the proposition that all are created equal—"born" equal, in the language of the amendment, which echoed leading state constitutions that expressly proclaimed that Americans were *born free and equal*. Persons born black are equal in civil rights to those born white. Persons born female are equal in civil rights to those born male. Persons born out of wedlock are equal in civil rights to those born in wedlock. Those born into Irish American families are equal to Anglo Americans and Italian Americans. Those born into Jewish households are legally the same as those born into Catholic or Protestant households. Children born second or tenth in a family are in law no less than those born first—the amendment prohibits once-common primogeniture and entail laws favoring first-born children as such. A child born in America to a family of noncitizen parents is a full birthright citizen with all the same entitlements and privileges as any other American child. And today we make clear that those born gay or lesbian are no less in civil rights than those born straight.

The Fourteenth Amendment was surely about racial equality—the core case of birth equality—but it just as surely ranged beyond race. The text speaks more generally than race—in pointed and purposeful contrast to the race-specific language of the Fifteenth Amendment that followed shortly thereafter. (That amendment, of course, was necessary, as was the later Nineteenth Amendment, because the Fourteenth Amendment's opening words applied only to "civil rights" and not to "political rights" such as voting, as this Court correctly made clear early on in our 1875 ruling in *Minor v. Happersett*. For more documentation and analysis, see Akhil Amar, *The Law of the Land*, pp. 115–119; Akhil Amar, *America's Unwritten Constitution*, pp. 156–161, 186–187, and sources cited therein.)

The birth-equality principle was expressly and emphatically articulated in a landmark statute adopted alongside the Fourteenth Amendment—by the very same Congress in the very same season and by virtually the same vote. This companion statute, the Civil Rights Act of 1866, opened with language virtually identical to the first sentence of the Fourteenth Amendment and then immediately glossed that language by proclaiming that all birthright citizens were entitled to "the full and equal" benefit of all fundamental civil rights. This birth-equality idea was also expressly articulated by the first Justice Harlan—the great dissenter in *Plessy*—in our 1896 decision in *Gibson v. Mississippi* where, happily, he spoke for the Court as a whole: "All citizens are equal before the law."

This simple yet profound birth-equality principle powerfully organizes and unifies a vast amount of this Court's case law in the modern era, which treats certain legal distinctions as particularly problematic—laws discriminating on the basis of race, sex, ethnicity, or illegitimacy. By contrast, laws that distinguish along most other dimensions—treating wage income differently than rental income; treating opticians differently than ophthalmologists; treating small employers differently than large employers, and so on—are not viewed with the same kind of skepticism.

Some think that the Fourteenth Amendment's framers were not clearly focused on sex discrimination or the related issue of women's civil rights. Wrong. In fact, much of the key language of the amendment's first section tracked a proposal put forth earlier by none other than Elizabeth Cady Stanton. (For details see Akhil Amar, *The Bill of Rights: Creation and Reconstruction*, pp. 260–261 and sources cited therein.) The Fourteenth Amendment's framers thus knew exactly what they were doing in pitching its text at the proper level of generality, condemning not just racially discriminatory laws but all laws creating unequal civil rights on the basis of birth status. This birth-equality principle resonated with Enlightenment ideology and the original Constitution's paired clauses banning both state and federal governments from creating titles of nobility (laws that privileged certain persons by dint of their birth).

Not all laws that distinguish on the basis of birth status are unconstitutional. Some distinctions may be justifiable if genuinely and unavoidably necessary to prevent harm to others. For example, although some persons are born blind, the law may generally prohibit blind persons from flying airplanes; persons born with the HIV virus may be legally prohibited from donating blood; and so on. But judges must carefully scrutinize all such laws to ensure that they do not create an improper caste-like system in which some are legally demeaned and degraded while others are legally honored and exalted merely on the basis of birth status.

Laws that allow straights to marry while denying this basic marriage privilege to gays and lesbians violate this deep and pure Fourteenth Amendment principle. These laws improperly demean our fellow citizens who happen to have been born gay or lesbian and improperly exalt our fellow citizens who happen to have been born straight. True, these laws technically and formally do not hinge on a person's orientation. Even a man born gay is allowed to marry. So long, that is, as he marries a woman! Cf. Joseph Heller, *Catch 22*. But "law reaches past formalism," *Lee v. Weisman* (1992) (Kennedy, J.). Sexual intimacy is part of the core of marriage as a legal and social institution, and denial of same-sex marriage does indeed deprive gays and lesbians of the full and equal enjoyment of this intimacy—a full and equal opportunity for "the pursuit of happiness" that underlies the American project.

We concede that some persons may experience some or all aspects of their sexual orientation as a matter of pure choice. Nevertheless, a vast number of our fellow citizens do in fact understand themselves to be, quite simply, "born this way" in regard to their sexual orientation, and we are in no position to hold that these very widespread self-understandings are inauthentic or delusional. Even if it were conclusively proved at some future point that orientation is typically fixed not at birth but rather very early in childhood, the deep spirit of the birth-equality principle would still apply. Citizens should not be demeaned on the basis of harmless and morally irrelevant traits that they never chose and are not free to change with ease. That is the animating spirit—the underlying logic—of the birth-equality rule.

Religious equality principles are also indirectly relevant here. Even though religion is often chosen rather than fixed at birth, our Constitution allows persons to choose their religion freely and equally. Religion for many is central to identity and so is sexual orientation.

Why, then, did the framers of the Fourteenth Amendment allow discriminatory marriage laws to continue on the books? In large part because they did not know all the facts, scientific and social, that we now know. They did not know that many persons experience sexual orientation as fixed, not chosen. They did not live in a world in which vast numbers of gays and lesbians openly challenged marriage exclusion as a fundamental badge of inequality and degradation.

Similarly, many of the Fourteenth Amendment's framers thought racial segregation was acceptable because racial separation might genuinely be equal. If most blacks and most whites genuinely preferred segregation, then where was the improper demeaning of one race or the improper exaltation of another? Separate could truly be equal under certain factual assumptions in the 1860s (just as today, separate bathrooms and sports teams for males and females are generally seen as equal by both males and females). But once it became clear, in the decades after the enactment of the Fourteenth Amendment, that vast numbers of blacks did object to racial separation, this changed social fact itself was a proper basis for declaring racial segregation unconstitutional. See *Plessy v. Ferguson* (Harlan, J. dissenting); *Brown v. Board* (Warren, C. J.).

A similar story may be told about sex discrimination—discrimination between men and women—within marriage laws. The framers of the Fourteenth Amendment quite clearly did believe in sex equality in civil rights: Within this domain, these framers believed that women should not be demeaned nor men exalted because of their differential birth status. In the 1860s, marriage laws—and many other laws—created differentiated legal roles for men and women, but these differentiated legal roles were in that era not widely understood as ennobling only men or degrading women. Both genders were highly esteemed, but they played different legal roles. Separate roles, distinct roles, but not unequal roles. Women themselves were not en masse demanding an end to coverture laws in the 1860s. And so these laws were widely seen as permissible in the 1860s by the framers of the Fourteenth Amendment. But when later generations of women did en masse come to demand a change—and to highlight that these laws now did indeed appear demeaning to them and improperly tilted toward men—judges in the mid-twentieth century rightly struck down these gendered marriage laws.

We do the same today and for the same reason. Indeed, the laws at issue today do, formally, discriminate on the basis of sex. Under these laws, Pat can marry Jane only if Pat is male (Patrick) and not female (Patricia). This is sex-discrimination pure and simple, and under our longstanding sex-discrimination case law—case law deeply rooted in the text and spirit of the Fourteenth Amendment, as we have just explained—this sex discrimination regime must survive the most exacting judicial scrutiny. We hold today that this regime fails this scrutiny. These sex-discriminatory laws are an improper attempt to enforce a rigid and unequal gender code, telling men that they must not act in effeminate ("sissy") ways and women that they must not behave in a masculine ("butch") manner. Such laws are a violation of genuine sex equality and also of liberty—the liberty of each person, male or female (or neither or both), to be free to be true to himself/herself/oneself.

To put this point about the deep connection between equality and freedom a different way—and to explain from yet another angle why we now must vindicate the enacted letter and spirit of the Fourteenth Amendment without being hamstrung by every specific nontextual and unratified factual or normative assumption that its framers may have held—we today take judicial notice of the following basic and widespread facts of our modern world. Sexual intimacy and human procreation have been profoundly decoupled in the last half-century. Persons can have babies without having sex (in vitro fertilization) and

can have sex without having babies (contraception). Marriage law itself has become gender-neutral, undercutting several of the basic
premises of earlier regimes that structured marriage in deeply gendered
ways. Gender itself has been scientifically transformed. Legally and
factually, men can now become women and women can now become
men. If Patrick, who is married to Jane, undergoes medical and/or legal
gender reassignment and becomes Patricia, Pat is the same human being on both sides of this medical and/or legal procedure. And after the
gender transition occurs, Pat and Jane remain married. This is already
a same-sex marriage, in virtually every state! No jurisdiction has been
brought to our attention that treats Pat's medical transformation as
ipso facto dissolving the marriage—as does, for example, death. Pat is
Pat regardless of what is between Pat's legs or what was once between
them on the day that Pat was born, and regardless of what gender designation appears on Pat's birth certificate or driver's license or pass-
port. Our fundamental nature is not male or female, black or white,
but human, pure and simple. Our most basic law must recognize these
basic facts of modern life, modern law, and modern science.

There are obvious similarities between Justice Kennedy's actual majority
opinion and my alternative. My opinion and his both rely squarely on the
Fourteenth Amendment's vision. We both invoke liberty and equality and
try to highlight ways in which these principles at times intertwine. We both
treat sexual orientation as analogous to race in certain ways. (Kennedy does
this by appealing at every turn to the 1967 case of *Loving v. Virginia*, involving interracial marriage, and by twice explicitly suggesting that sexual orientation is "immutable." I do so by stressing the Fourteenth Amendment idea
of birth equality.) We both candidly confront the fact that the Fourteenth
Amendment's framers did not understand that its words would doom bans of
same-sex marriage. In doing so, we both point to the significance of changed
gender rules within marriage—for example, the demise of coverture laws
that once gave husbands more power than wives in certain key respects.

But I like my version better. I root my opinion in the solid text of the
Fourteenth Amendment's promises of birthright citizenship and the privileges and immunities of citizenship, which include both substantive rights
and equality rights. Also, I make a number of knockdown historical points
about the framers of the amendment and the companion Civil Rights Act of
1866. Kennedy does not play these or any other persuasive originalist notes

and puts most of his weight on the textually inapt due process clause. That clause speaks plainly of procedural rights (fair trials, unbiased judges, and the like) as distinct from substantive rights (such as the right to marry). Kennedy, a libertarian, stresses the word *liberty* in the due process clause, but this liberty has historically been closely linked to negative rights (freedom from government) rather than affirmative rights (freedom to insist on government-recognized benefits such as marriage laws). Kennedy does not make crystal clear the distinction between applying the Fourteenth Amendment's framers' actual and enacted principles to new scientific and social and legal facts, on the one hand, and simply substituting newfangled principles of his own creation, on the other. Kennedy does not treat same-sex marriage bans as simple sex-discrimination laws, nor does he discuss the reality of gender-reassignment in modern America. He offers no overarching way of bringing unity to the Court's treatment of certain kinds of discriminations as particularly invidious. My parsimonious account not only makes sense of the cases as a whole, but powerfully connects them to core principles of constitutional text, history, and structure.

At several points in his opinion, Kennedy takes pains to limit the right to marry to two-person marriages, but he offers no real reason why. My argument cleanly distinguishes same-sex marriage from polygamy. Anti-polygamy laws do not discriminate on the basis of birth status. They do not treat Patrick differently than Patricia, nor do they treat those born gay differently than those born straight. No strong evidence has yet been presented to suggest that a vast number of persons are in fact born polygamous or become polygamous in early childhood and without conscious choice. No broad social movement has arisen in America to insist, authentically, that polygamists were "born this way" and have no real choice in the matter. The distinction between a legally sanctioned two-person institution and a legally unsanctioned three-person arrangement is just like many other generally unproblematic distinctions throughout our law. Tax laws allow different sorts of commuting-cost deductions, depending on whether a person has one employer or two or more employers; discrimination laws treat firms with fourteen employees differently from those with fifteen; and so on.

Still, Kennedy got the right answer. The dissenters did not, and they did not even ask the right questions.

Chief Justice John Roberts himself asked a version of the Patrick/Patricia question at oral argument but then proceeded to utterly ignore this issue in his opinion—as did all the other dissenters in their separate opinions. But the dissenters cannot properly do this if they wish to rule against same-sex marriage. Even if Kennedy didn't squarely rely on this approach, the litigants and amici did make this argument, and so have many other thoughtful scholars and judges. America is entitled to know why this argument is not a proper alternative basis for Kennedy's judgment. And although Kennedy himself did not use magic words such as "strict scrutiny," his repeated emphasis on the immutability of sexual orientation and the long history of anti-gay discrimination surely required that a persuasive dissent confront the claim that laws discriminating on the basis of sexual orientation demand heightened judicial scrutiny. Once again, this was an issue at the very heart of the case at hand, and any justice ruling against the gay and lesbian litigants at hand owed America a careful explanation why heightened scrutiny was inappropriate under the unifying logic of a very long line of landmark precedents involving race and sex discrimination and discrimination against illegitimate children. But Chief Justice Roberts's dissent never explained why heightened scrutiny was unwarranted.

So, too, America is entitled to know how a proper federal system will work if a marriage that is fully valid in the state where it was held fades in and out, legally, as persons cross state lines—perhaps as part of their federal responsibilities, if, for example, they are in the military and sent to a different base or are traveling to the national capital to petition Congress. Kennedy did not need to address these arguments because he was giving the plaintiffs everything they asked for without having to reach the interstate issues. But these issues were squarely before the Court, and the dissenters simply ignored them, proceeding to vote against the actual citizens before the Court in the case at hand without answering all their plausible legal claims. This is judicial minimalism with a vengeance.

The chief justice repeatedly invoked principles of judicial deference but failed to explain clearly why these principles did not apply with equal or greater force in previous landmark cases in which he voted to invalidate an iconic provision of the Voting Rights Act and voted to undo congressional limits on campaign contributions (which are decisively different from purely expressive independent activities such as running political ads on one's own).

Justice Antonin Scalia's dissent insisted that the fact that the framers of the Fourteenth Amendment accepted bans on same-sex marriage was utterly dispositive. He claimed that this fact alone "resolves these cases." But why then are coverture laws, which these same amenders also found proper, unconstitutional? What about the fact that many amenders found segregation and anti-miscegenation laws acceptable? Should this fact alone have resolved *Brown v. Board* and *Loving v. Virginia* in favor of segregationists and anti-miscegnationists? No answer from the good justice.

Justice Clarence Thomas persuasively argued that it was a stretch to say that the due process clause was violated. There was not a clear violation of negative liberty, nor was there any obvious procedural lapse in the laws at issue. But what about the Fourteenth Amendment's birthright citizenship clause and its companion guarantee of full and equal privileges and immunities of citizenship—clauses that Thomas himself has powerfully highlighted and championed in other cases? Once again, silence.

Finally, Justice Samuel Alito was highly persuasive in reminding us that the anti-same-sex-marriage laws at issue were hardly irrational. Following tradition is often quite rational, and every reform is likely to have unintended consequences. Not all of these consequences may be apparent immediately. Same-sex marriage is an experiment, and the jury is still out. Fair enough. But once again, the same could have been said about coverture abolition in 1970, and Alito's arguments merely explain why the laws at hand are rational. What he failed to explain is why mere rationality was enough— why these discriminatory laws should not be treated with special judicial skepticism as are many other traditional gender laws. Laws that discriminated against illegitimate children were not irrational; they arguably incentivized the biological parents to marry, and some of these laws had deep historical roots. Yet the Court rightly invalidated these laws as violative of the birth-equality principle. Jim Crow was a pretty strong tradition in 1954. But *Brown* was nevertheless clearly right—and so is *Obergefell*.

REMEMBERING BORK

SLATE, THURSDAY, DECEMBER 20, 2012, 12:16 P.M. (ET)

The last time I spoke to Robert Bork, who died Wednesday, was thirty years ago this week. In mid-December 1982, I was a second-year law student at Yale finishing up a seminar that Bork taught, a seminar organized around ambitious works by leading constitutional scholars—Alex Bickel, John Hart Ely, Charles Black, and others. I did not entirely love the seminar, or Bork, but today I find myself, weirdly, standing in Bork's shoes. At fifty-four, I am now almost exactly the same age as Bork was then; and I regularly teach a seminar at Yale inspired by the one I took from him, with a reading list that includes several of the books I first read under his supervision. In fact, my seminar usually meets in Bork's old classroom. (And did I mention that I, too, have a beard that some would call scruffy?)

So why didn't I ever converse with Bork after the class ended? And how did a seminar and a professor that I didn't entirely love end up having such a profound effect on me?

I never spoke to Bork after 1982 because, frankly, he could be insensitive and off-putting. In the classroom, he was quick to dismiss imaginative ideas floated by students. In his defense, it must be said that many of these student bubbles deserved to be popped. A law professor's job is to train students to think rigorously. Bullshit does not win cases. So even as I disliked Bork's demeanor at the time, I have since come to admire his honesty. Here was a man who cared enough about ideas to defend his own, and to hit yours head-on if he thought they deserved it. Most important of all, he did not downgrade students who came back at him with tight counterarguments. My term paper for this class was an all-out thirty-page attack on several of Bork's pet ideas, yet he gave me a top grade—without which I might never have been hired by Yale to teach constitutional law.

Bork's truculence in the classroom made me want to fight back—but to do so, I had to work hard and drill down. In the process, I came to love constitutional law, a subject that had not electrified me as a first-year student in an introductory course taught by a gentler and less edgy professor.

The combativeness that Bork brought to the classroom later came into public view during his 1987 confirmation hearings. His arrogance did not serve him well in these hearings—but truth be told, arrogance runs rampant in the higher reaches of the legal academy. (And here I most emphatically do not exempt myself.)

My biggest criticism of Bork thus concerns not his attitude but his altitude: His work in constitutional law never came close to the heights reached by his most gifted contemporaries. John Hart Ely wrote a soaring book on constitutional law—a book that I read while in Bork's class and that I continue to reread and to teach and to learn from every time I re-engage it. Ditto for some of the great works of other modern constitutional law giants, including Charles Black, Philip Bobbitt, Bruce Ackerman, and Laurence Tribe. But as of 1982, Bork's most significant writing in constitutional law was a single middling article on free expression, an article whose best ideas had already been elaborated by other, better constitutional scholars. In his later years, Bork did write several popular books on various issues related to constitutional law, but none of these breezy volumes makes a substantial and enduring contribution to serious scholarship.

By contrast, Bork powerfully contributed to antitrust scholarship with influential articles that culminated in an enormously important 1978 book, *The Antitrust Paradox*. Thus, a fair assessment of Bork's career would properly describe him as a constitutional writer and a towering scholar; but he should not be thought of as a towering *constitutional* scholar.

He did have one big constitutional idea, namely, that original intent should play an important role in constitutional decision-making. Though Bork was hardly the first or the best to put forth this theory, he used his notoriety to popularize it. Many scholars and judges in the late 1960s and throughout the 1970s had begun to talk and act as if the original purposes of the Constitution's founders and amenders were almost irrelevant to serious constitutional analysis in the modern world. Bork thought otherwise, and loudly proclaimed that scholars and judges must pay heed to original understandings.

But Bork was an awkward mouthpiece for this view because he himself knew very little about the Constitution's history. And his extreme political conservativism compounded the problem because much of the history of the document's enactment and amendment is a history of those who were the liberal reformers of their day—nationalist anti-aristocrats at the Founding, egalitarian crusaders for racial justice in the 1860s, suffragists and civil-rights activists in the twentieth century.

Bork failed to see the basic contradiction because he was, to repeat, not an accomplished historian or even a sophisticated consumer of serious historical work. But his clarion calls for renewed attention to constitutional text, history, and structure—alongside similar calls from friends in the political and academic worlds, such as Reagan attorney general Ed Meese and law professor Steve Calabresi—were not without effect. Today, all serious constitutional scholars and most justices are far, far more attentive to originalist arguments than before Bork took the stage. Thanks in part to Bork, we are all textualists of sorts; we are originalists in part.

And by "we," I of course include myself. When I entered Bork's class in 1982, I was inclined to undervalue originalist arguments; I left with much greater respect for the fidelity Bork preached to text, history, and structure.

Over the ensuing thirty years, I have devoted my career to proving, clause by clause, historical fact by historical fact, that faithful adherence to Bork's approved methods does not invariably lead to Bork's politically conservative conclusions. In fact, I've tried to show how many of the methods Bork claimed to embrace often support results precisely contrary to the ones Bork reached.

In short, Professor Robert Bork got under my skin and into my head so much that I have spent the last thirty years taking seriously the issues he first introduced me to. Though I did not entirely love him, I did learn from him. Indeed, I can now see that he profoundly changed my life.

REMEMBERING LINCOLN[9]

TIME.COM, WEDNESDAY, APRIL 15, 2015

Americans yearn for an end to political polarization and partisanship, and many today fault President Obama for failing to achieve consensus on his major initiatives: health care, immigration reform, foreign policy, and so on. But consider Abraham Lincoln. Despite his various efforts at outreach, our sixteenth president was, in life, an intensely polarizing and partisan figure, every bit as polarizing and partisan as our current president.

Lincoln's presidency, which ended exactly 150 years ago today, sharply differed from the experience of his predecessors. Before Lincoln, five presidents had won a second term: George Washington, Thomas Jefferson, James Madison, James Monroe, and Andrew Jackson. Each had carried both North and South in at least one of his presidential bids. By contrast, Lincoln was purely a regional candidate, despised by intense majorities in a large chunk of the country. In 1860, he received zero popular votes south of Virginia, and in 1864, none of the eleven states in Dixie held a valid presidential election, thanks to sectional war precipitated by Lincoln's prior election. Even Lincoln's assassination was sectional: John Wilkes Booth was an intense southern partisan.

In the ensuing century and a half, many of America's most successful presidents have managed to achieve considerable popularity in both North and South. Franklin Roosevelt, Harry Truman, Dwight Eisenhower, John Kennedy, Lyndon Johnson, Ronald Reagan, and Bill Clinton all outdid Lincoln in this regard. But our current president won, twice, by following a more emphatically Lincolnian path to power—that is, a distinctly northern route: Of the eleven states in the former confederacy, Obama lost eight twice, and lost a ninth (North Carolina) once, prevailing twice only in Virginia and Florida.

In our era, as in Lincoln's, regional polarization is on the upswing. Prior to 1850, the winning presidential candidate typically carried both North and South. But that pattern broke down in the 1850s, even before Lincoln rose to national prominence; and a similar fate has befallen Obama. At the presidential level, the North and the South have backed different candidates in every one of the six most recent elections; and many states are becoming increasingly red or blue, presidentially. In 2012, only four states—Florida, Ohio, North Carolina, and Virginia—were decided by less than five points.

If we shift gears from regional polarization to political polarization, Lincoln and Obama once again appear as political doubles. Both made efforts to reach across the aisle. For example, Lincoln, a Republican, chose a former Democrat, Edwin Stanton, to serve as secretary of war; and Democrat Obama has symmetrically chosen Republicans Robert Gates and Chuck Hagel to fill the same slot, now renamed the secretary of defense. Still, Lincoln's signature executive accomplishments were at risk in a judiciary dominated by appointees of the opposite political party; the same remains true for Obama. Shortly after Lincoln's death, every single congressional Democrat voted against the Fourteenth Amendment, which codified Lincoln's dream of birthright equality of all citizens. In our era, every single congressional Republican likewise opposed Obama's signature health care plan aiming to protect those born with unlucky genes from insurance discrimination.

Lincoln's example should remind us that, on some issues, he was on the right side of history despite the fierce attacks of his contemporaries. Even on certain topics where he proposed radical change, his opponents' arguments have not aged well. Shortly before his death, he signed a proposed constitutional amendment providing for an end to American slavery—immediately and with no financial compensation to slaveholders. Nothing like this had ever happened in any American jurisdiction where slavery was widespread. In 1860, less than 1 percent of America's blacks voted on equal terms. In 1870, all racial disfranchisement was constitutionally forbidden, building on another suggestion made by Lincoln himself in his last public speech, just days before he died.

This was a new public stance for Lincoln, much as Obama has only recently evolved to a position of open embrace of same-sex marriage. If the

Supreme Court later this year constitutionalizes this egalitarian vision, following the lead of the latest lanky lawyer from Illinois to occupy the Oval Office, the decision will likely trigger howls of protest. These howls are likely to be loudest in those regions that hated Lincoln and all that he stood for when he was still standing. But Lincoln's example should remind us that contemporary controversy does not necessarily mean that the judgment of history will be equivocal. Lincoln's vision of racial equality has been vindicated by posterity; and the same seems highly likely for Obama' vision of sexual-orientation equality. History never repeats itself, but it sometimes rhymes.

7

CONSTITUTIONAL ANNIVERSARIES

Remembering to Remember

AS A CONTRAPUNTAL CODA stressing commemoration over contestation, this chapter ends Part II of this book by drawing together five essays that I have published in various venues over the years in mid-September. The mid-September timing of these essays is not coincidental. Just as July 4 is Independence Day, and June 14 is Flag Day, so September 17 is Constitution Day, commemorating the date on which the Philadelphia Convention made public its proposed Constitution in 1787. These five pieces—now assembled for the first time as a series—have aimed to say something general and timeless about the American constitutional project.

But when is a timeless truth ever timely? Timely, that is, in a way that the editors of America's leading news outlets will recognize? Special days of remembrance, such as birthdays and anniversaries, offer fitting and proper occasions to bring together the timely and the timeless—to manage the tension between constitutionalism's concern with enduring verities and journalism's obsession with the issues of the hour. The Declaration of Independence has its day, and so, happily, does the Constitution itself. Over the years I have tried to make the most of this fortunate fact.

A closely related fortunate fact is that a constitutional journalist can see a constitutional anniversary coming from a mile away, and can prepare and pitch a proper remembrance essay with more lead time than usual. If fast-breaking news in mid-September requires an editor to bump a remembrance essay off the page, the constitutional journalist can sometimes hold the essay for the next year: Certain kinds of remembrance essays are perennials.

MANY OF THE ESSAYS in other chapters of this book aim to say something quite specific about one particular slice of the Constitution. Some focus on a narrow patch of text—for example, the Twenty-fifth Amendment's rules regarding presidential succession; the Article I, section 5, power of each congressional house to judge its own elections and returns; or the Fourth Amendment's language concerning searches and seizures. Other essays elsewhere in this book range beyond a particular clause, but still concentrate on one distinct and discrete subpart of our constitutional system—for instance, how presidential second terms do and should unfold, how Supreme Court oral arguments should be structured, or how Congress should oversee and hold accountable federal officials. Most of these pieces originally sprang to life in response to specific events in the headlines, although they also aimed to say something more enduring.

The essays in this chapter are rather different. Precisely because they were written to commemorate the Constitution itself—all of it—they seek to say something about our entire constitutional system. How should we interpret the document known as "the Constitution" and the larger constitutional project that revolves around that document? How tightly does that project in fact revolve around the text of the canonical document itself, and how tightly should it revolve? How much have the American constitutional text and the American constitutional project changed in the years between the Founding and the present? What does and what should the future hold for this text and this project, at home and around the world?

I shall let these essays speak for themselves without much more ado beyond a few words on the first and the last essay in this chapter. Recall that modern America is a land of intense political polarization. In response to this basic fact, I have tried to aim my message across the ideological spectrum. It is not entirely coincidental that the first piece in this series is targeted particularly at the left, the last at the right.

The essay that opens this chapter, "Rethinking Originalism," was published in 2005 in *Slate*, whose audience tends to lean left. Liberal academics back then tended to pooh-pooh fidelity to the Constitution's text and history. As many leading liberals saw the matter, only misguided conservatives took originalism seriously. I argued that this anti-originalist liberal mantra was the wrong approach. In my view, the Constitution's text and history provide guidance and inspiration for every American. And liberals especially should wrap themselves in the Constitution, given that the document as enacted and amended is largely the product of triumphant liberal reformers over the centuries.

This essay expressly confronted two towering liberal scholars and good friends, Cass Sunstein and Jack Balkin, who in my view had strayed from the true path. A decade later, I'm not sure I have had any notable effect on Professor Sunstein, but I am delighted to report that Professor Balkin has in recent years moved toward originalism in rich and sophisticated ways. In 2005, Balkin described his own approach as "living constitutionalism." Since then, he has come to champion an approach, much closer to my own, that he openly labels "living originalism." In his important 2011 book, entitled *Living Originalism*, Balkin emphasizes (as he did not in 2005) that the concrete understandings of those who ratified the original Constitution and its amendments—in technical jargon, the ratifiers' original "expected applications and non-applications" of various constitutional provisions—often deserve great weight in later interpretations and implementations, even if those original understandings and expectations should not always be decisive. In 2005, Balkin described constitutional interpretation as a process of openly *evolving away* from founding origins. By contrast, in 2011, he moved to a notably more originalist vision in which faithful interpreters should aim to *redeem* the Founders' original plan by *building on* and *building out* the Founders' original blueprint. That's real progress on the left.

As for the right, the last and most recent essay in this chapter was written at the express request of the Federalist Society, and in fact a sneak preview appeared in that most un-liberal of publications, the *Washington Times*. I used the occasion of the 800th anniversary of Magna Carta in mid-2015 to chastise American conservatives for failing to be sufficiently faithful to one of their own core commitments, namely, American exceptionalism. Enough with Magna Carta! It did not change the world. We, the American people did, and we did so with the Constitution—and its amendments, of course.

In a sustained effort to unify modern America as we remember to remember that we are all children of the Constitution, the essays in this chapter thus address and admonish both sides of the aisle. Liberals must remember that an old text begun in the eighteenth century still sits at the center of our national project. And conservatives must remember that this old text, and all its amendments, young and old, instantiate profoundly liberal principles of freedom, equality, and national power.

RETHINKING ORIGINALISM

SLATE, SEPTEMBER 21, 2005, 12:36 P.M. (ET)

Should constitutional interpreters embrace the document's original intent or evade it? Several leading liberal scholars are urging Americans to choose Door No. 2, because the original-intent game is doomed to reach intolerably conservative—indeed, reactionary—results.

But is it? And once we reject that game, what are the proper legal rules to play by?

The present moment is a perfect time to ponder such foundational questions. The Rehnquist Court is now officially history, two new justices will soon be in place, and the confirmation hearings of Supreme Court nominee John Roberts have introduced a new generation of channel-surfers to detailed debates about constitutional philosophy. Closer to home (i.e., the home page of this website), several recent *Slate* postings by Jack Balkin, Dahlia Lithwick, and Emily Bazelon have made interesting contributions to the original-intent debate.

In late August, Balkin—my Yale colleague and sometime coauthor—correctly pointed out that Justices Antonin Scalia and Clarence Thomas, while proclaiming themselves faithful followers of original intent, do not always practice what they preach. For example, these two justices have consistently voted against affirmative action but have never explained how their votes can be squared with historical evidence that the Reconstruction Congress itself engaged in affirmative action.

But without more, this is merely an argument that Scalia and Thomas should be more consistent and less hypocritical: They should respect original intent across the board—at least in the absence of some compelling legal counterargument, such as justifiable reliance on past practice or precedent.

Balkin himself has reached a wholly different conclusion. Modern constitutional interpreters, says he, should simply stop trying to heed the original intent of the men and women who ratified and amended the document. In his opinion, interpreters should focus on the text, not the original intent.

But constitutional interpretation heedless of enactment history can become a pun-game: The right to "bear arms" could mean no more than an entitlement to possess the stuffed forelimbs of grizzlies and Kodiaks. (And if history no longer constrains, why should spelling? Maybe the Second

Amendment is about the right to "bare arms" and other body parts—e.g., nude dancing.)

How about Balkin's argument that originalism generally leads to outrageously conservative results? Another leading liberal light, Cass Sunstein, has said much the same thing of late. I disagree. The framers themselves were, after all, revolutionaries who risked their lives, their fortunes, and their sacred honor to replace an Old World monarchy with a New World Order unprecedented in its commitment to popular self-government. Later generations of reformers repeatedly amended the Constitution so as to extend its liberal foundations, dramatically expanding freedom and equality. The history of these liberal reform movements—nineteenth-century abolitionists, Progressive-era crusaders for woman suffrage, 1960s activists who democratized the document still further—is a history that liberals should celebrate, not sidestep.

Consider, for example, the landmark 1954 case of *Brown v. Board of Education*. Both Sunstein and Balkin say that *Brown* broke with the history underlying the Civil War amendments, which, they claim, plainly permitted racial segregation. But the Fourteenth Amendment, ratified in 1868, undeniably demanded that government treat blacks and whites with equal respect, equal dignity, and equal protection in their basic civil rights. All Americans— black and white alike—were proclaimed equal citizens by that amendment. True, some framers of this amendment did say that some segregation laws might be permissible. But in saying this, many of them were envisioning a postwar world in which both races in general might prefer separate spaces (as most men and women today probably prefer sex-segregated bathrooms in public places). In such a world, they believed, segregation would not always be unequal.

But the Reconstructionists never said that segregation would always and automatically be constitutional. The Constitution's text does not say that all citizens are equal "except for segregation laws." Rather, it uncompromisingly demands equality of civil rights—no ifs, ands, or buts. In fact, most Reconstructionists understood that a law whose statutory preamble explicitly proclaimed whites superior to blacks would be plainly unconstitutional. The question in both *Plessy v. Ferguson* (in 1896) and *Brown v. Board* (in 1954) was thus a simple one, and simpler than these constitutional scholars might suggest: Was Jim Crow in fact equal? Or was it instead a law whose obvious purpose, effect, and social meaning proclaimed white supremacy in deed rather than in word? For any honest observer in either 1896 or 1954, the question answered itself: Jim Crow was plainly designed to demean the equal citizenship of blacks—to keep them down and out—and thus violated the core meaning of the Fourteenth Amendment. Thus, *Brown* is in fact an easy case for those who take text and history seriously. (Note, by the way, that this basic view of *Brown* has been embraced by a wide range of scholars from Robert Bork on the right to Charles Black on the left.)

Another key originalist point that is often overlooked derives from the Fifteenth Amendment, which was ratified two years after the Fourteenth and reflected a far more robust vision of black rights, including equal-suffrage rules. This amendment was intrinsically integrationist, envisioning a world in which blacks and whites would work side by side at the ballot box, in the jury box, and in legislatures across the country. As the first Justice Harlan understood in *Plessy* (though many modern scholars seemed to have missed the point altogether), the letter, spirit, and original intent of the Fifteenth Amendment thus powerfully reinforce various Fourteenth Amendment arguments against Jim Crow.

Yes, it's true that on today's Court the two leading originalists are both conservative, but perhaps the Court's most influential originalist in history was the great Hugo Black—a liberal lion and indeed the driving force behind the Warren Court. It's also worth remembering that the most towering originalist scholar of the 1970s was also a professed liberal, John Hart Ely.

In short, there are many reasons to question the idea that modern liberals should abandon constitutional history rather than claim it as their own. This short essay is not the place to present all the historical evidence that some modern anti-originalists are overlooking—I've tried to do that more comprehensively in my book, *America's Constitution: A Biography*. But I hope I've said enough here to convince thoughtful anti-originalists to take a second look at the Constitution's first principles.

WE THE WOMEN[1]

PHILADELPHIA INQUIRER, SUNDAY, SEPTEMBER 16, 2012

Two hundred and twenty-five years ago this week—right here in Philadelphia, "where it all began"—America's Founding Fathers went public with a proposed Constitution promising more democracy than the world had ever seen.

Even so, in September 1787, "We the People" basically meant "We the Men." This year, the fate of this manly constitutional project rests more than ever in the hands of women. More women than men will cast votes in November. Just for fun, imagine that women were to vote as a unified bloc. Virtually every election in America at every level of government—both candidate elections and issue elections—would be decided by the female vote. More plausibly, note that in any election in which men are closely divided, the candidate or issue position decisively favored by women will prevail.

For this remarkable turn of events, we must credit not just the Founding Fathers but also their amending daughters, granddaughters, and so on, who have rewritten the Constitution in both word and deed.

The gender-bending of the Philadelphia Constitution began in earnest after the Civil War with the Fourteenth Amendment, which promises "equal protection" to all—not merely racial equal protection but more generally. The amendment also proudly affirms that all homegrown Americans are "born" with equal civil rights. Just as a child born black or brown enjoys the same civil rights as a child born white, so, too, those born female are equal in civil rights to those born male.

A half-century after the Fourteenth Amendment came the Nineteenth, guaranteeing woman suffrage and thereby revolutionizing American politics. Earlier this year, it was obvious to all that Michele Bachmann was eligible to run for president, as Sarah Palin and Geraldine Ferraro were eligible to seek the vice presidency in past electoral cycles—even though the original Philadelphia Constitution repeatedly used the gendered words *he, him,* and *his* to refer to the president. At the Founding and for more than a century thereafter, states were perfectly free to keep women off the ballot; today, such a maneuver would be politically unthinkable and indeed unconstitutional.

Granted, the Nineteenth Amendment's words speak only of women's right to "vote" and not their equal right to be "voted for." But the obvious spirit of the amendment is that women are legally equal to men in all things political—both at the ballot box and on the ballot itself.

Consider also how this amendment has transfigured modern presidential campaign etiquette and the dynamics of presidential succession. President Obama in effect has two running "mates" this season—the vice president and the first lady—and in fact either one could plausibly succeed him in 2017, as could of course another former presidential running "mate" named Hillary Clinton. Nothing of the sort was true at the Founding: Back then, the idea that a Martha Washington or an Abigail Adams might one day become president in her own right would have been preposterous.

Though modern Tea Partiers claim fidelity to the Constitution, their understanding of the document reflects a curious pattern of arrested development, with lots of passionate references to the Founding Fathers and the Sons of Liberty (yes, fathers and sons), but no real embrace of the transformative constitutional amendments of the early twentieth century. To the extent that Tea Partiers focus on the constitutional change wrought during the Progressive era, they are hostile to the Sixteenth Amendment, which ushered in a national and redistributivist income tax, and skeptical of the Seventeenth Amendment, which freed senators from dependence on state legislatures and thus emboldened Congress to aggressively pursue nationalist projects. Together, these two progressive amendments helped set the table for the New Deal, the Great Society, and Obamacare.

But the third Progressive-era amendment—the Nineteenth—has probably proved even more crucial, and the Tea Party is ultimately, if unwittingly, at odds with this amendment, too. Thanks to woman suffrage, America has embraced a far more progressive agenda than she (yes, she) would have accepted had only men been voting. The progressive tilt of female voters over the years helped give America the tag-teams of Franklin and Eleanor Roosevelt, Bill and Hillary Clinton, and now, Barack and Michelle Obama. Earlier this year, the six men on the Supreme Court voted four to two *against* Obamacare. This law—which might also be termed Pelosi-care in honor of the female former speaker of the House who helped birth it—prevailed in Court thanks largely to the three female justices, who stood united in support of the statute's core provisions.

It is unclear what John Adams would have thought of these modern developments. But somewhere, Abigail is smiling.

TWO AND A QUARTER[2]

SLATE, MONDAY, SEPTEMBER 17, 2012, 5:00 A.M. (ET)

Today marks the 225th anniversary of the Constitution of the United States, publicly unveiled in Philadelphia amid considerable fanfare. As Americans think back on the last two and a quarter centuries, we should also think ahead by the same amount. What will and what should the Constitution

look like two hundred years hence? Or if that seems too mind-bendingly fu-
turistic, what will and should it look like in 2020 or 2121?

The most powerful portents of the future are to be found in America's
existing state constitutions, the proverbial laboratories of American democracy. These fifty documents have converged to form a distinctly American
model of governance—call it "American exceptionalism," if you like. For
example, unlike the regimes in various democratic countries around the
world—England, Germany, France, Israel, India, Australia—almost all fifty
states follow the same basic formula, featuring ratified written constitutions,
bicameral legislatures, chief executives who look remarkably like mini-
presidents, and robust bills of rights enforceable in ordinary courtrooms.

This is our basic American model, and it's not going anywhere. Proposals
to amend the federal Constitution are taken seriously when they fit within
this framework—and especially when they have already been adopted and
road-tested by the states. A brief history lesson: The federal Bill of Rights,
ratified in 1791, tracked various preexisting state bills of rights; the federal
Reconstruction amendments of the 1860s, ending slavery and protecting free
blacks, borrowed from the best constitutional practices of antebellum free
states; and the federal woman suffrage amendment prevailed at the continental level in 1920 only after women had won the vote under many state
constitutions.

Indeed, the Philadelphia Constitution of 1787 to which we wish happy
birthday was itself built upon state constitutional templates. In their decision
to put the federal Constitution to a special ratification vote of the people,
the framers copied the models of the Massachusetts Constitution of 1780
and the New Hampshire Constitution of 1784. The idea of a federal census
borrowed from the Pennsylvania Constitution of 1776 and the New York
Constitution of 1777. The elimination of property qualifications for federal
public servants likewise borrowed from Pennsylvania, as did provisions for all
federal lawmakers to be compensated from the public fisc. The broad outlines of executive power combined the best of the Massachusetts and New
York constitutions. Various elements of judicial independence drew upon
state antecedents, as did the U.S. Constitution's basic commitment to trial
by jury.

So much for the past 225 years. Let's now think about the next two centuries. How could we spruce up our founding document based on changes the
states have made to their constitutions?

Many states have term limits for state legislators and also allow voters to recall corrupt or incompetent state lawmakers in certain situations. This invites us to think hard about whether the federal Constitution should provide similar checks against Congress.

Or consider the fact that no state has an upper house in which each county has two seats, regardless of population. Perhaps the Senate could be changed to be more proportionate—a popular idea in *Slate*'s "*How to Fix the Constitution*" series.[3] Imagine, for instance, a federal amendment giving each state at least one senator and capping even the largest state at eight senators. This would keep the Senate at roughly its present size and would respect the existence of the states, while dramatically reducing malapportionment. (There is, of course, a special rule in the U.S. Constitution making it particularly difficult to modify the apportionment of the Senate via a constitutional amendment. But nothing prevents future amenders from preserving the existing apportionment of the official "Senate" while transferring much of the Senate's real power to a newly created, more proportionate, entity—call it Senate 2.0.)

Consider also the way that the states elect governors—directly by the voters, one person, one vote. If the federal electoral college is so good, why does no state closely follow it? Let's scrap it. And if naturalized Americans like California's Arnold Schwarzenegger and Michigan's Jennifer Granholm can be trusted to serve as governors, why not amend the federal Constitution to allow them to run for president? In fact, in 2004, the Senate held hearings on just such a proposed amendment, sponsored by Republican Senator Orrin Hatch and strongly endorsed by several congressional Democrats.

But is it realistic to think that current entrenched interests would ever allow sweeping amendments to prevail? For example, why would Wyoming ever agree to change the way the states are represented in the Senate, given how the current regime favors states with small populations? Or why would our representatives in Congress ever support an amendment to limit their own terms?

The key answer is a long time-delay between the vote on a visionary amendment and its start date—let's call this a "sunrise" rule. A close look at the original Constitution reveals a few clever uses of this device. Although the Deep South refused to give up the power to import trans-Atlantic slaves for the first twenty years, the region was willing to allow Congress to ban importations beginning in 1808, and forevermore. Had the framers been equally clever in the use of sunrise rules on other slavery-related issues—for example, had the original Constitution prohibited slavery in all western territory after 1808, or prohibited three-fifths apportionment credit for all slaves after 1808—perhaps Americans might have ultimately ended slavery without the unspeakable carnage of the Civil War. States in the Founding era, including Pennsylvania, Connecticut, and New Jersey, did use sunrise rules to achieve gradual abolition. Slaves at the time were not liberated, but their children later walked free.

In the same spirit, amendment-minded Americans should imagine ourselves today as representatives of twenty-second-century posterity, tasked with the awesome challenge of framing just rules for that society even though we won't be here to see it. As modern American constitutionalists focus obsessively on the deeds and words of 225 years ago, shouldn't we spend at least some time thinking about what we want two centuries into the future? Much of American constitutional law remains to be written.

THE YEAR THAT CHANGED EVERYTHING[4]

CNN, WEDNESDAY, SEPTEMBER 18, 2013

This season we mark Constitution Day, commemorating the electrifying moment on September 17, 1787, when the Philadelphia framers went public with their proposed Constitution.

Over the ensuing year, Americans debated and ratified this audacious plan, and thereby gave birth to a far better world. Let's recall the central features of that year that changed everything so that we can measure how far we have come, and how far we still need to go, to redeem the Constitution's promise.

After its public unveiling in mid-September, the Philadelphia plan was put to a vote across the continent, in a process that let vastly more ordinary folk than ever before in human history decide how they would be governed.

In most states, standard property qualifications were lowered or eliminated for this special ratification election. New York, for the first time in its history, let all adult free male citizens vote—no property qualifications, no race tests, no religious qualifications, no literacy tests—for ratifying-convention delegates who in turn voted yes on the Constitution several months later.

Later generations have nobly built upon this foundation, repeatedly adding the words "the right to vote" in a grand colonnade of amendments promising a permanent end to all sorts of electoral discrimination and exclusions. That's undeniable progress.

But America no longer leads the world in the integrity and inclusiveness of our elections; several states are now shamelessly trying to roll back voting rights; the Supreme Court has renounced a key piece of the landmark Voting Rights Act; and Congress has yet to mend the tattered statute.

Modern American free speech is a happier story, with robust free expression in almost every corner of the land. Here, too, we have 1787–1788 to thank, a year when Americans dramatically embodied free speech in the very process of establishing the Constitution. No one was censored that year, and the document's opponents were not forever demonized or voted off the island.

In fact, several of the Constitution's early critics came to rank among the new nation's highest leaders—for example, President James Monroe, Vice Presidents George Clinton and Elbridge Gerry, and Supreme Court Justice Samuel Chase. The two camps that had sharply divided over the Constitution's ratification, the Federalists and the Anti-Federalists, soon thereafter found common ground in supporting a Bill of Rights. Is it too much to hope that today's polarized parties might learn something from this inspiring example, and try to find something—anything!—that they can agree upon?

Perhaps because the Constitution's supporters did not try to muzzle skeptics, these skeptics, when outvoted, acquiesced. In several states, the document squeaked through only by the narrowest of margins—for example, 30–27 in New York.

Yet everyone accepted the basic principle of majority rule, even though the document itself did not explicitly specify this voting rule. Here, too, there are lessons for today.

The entrenched filibuster has made the current Senate a deeply dysfunctional body, yet some senators seem to think that a supermajority-rule system has deep roots in founding principles and practices. These senators are mistaken. The early Senate followed the principles of 1787–1788, and the key principle that year in every single state ratifying convention was simple majority rule. Everyone got to speak, and then votes ensued, and simple majorities prevailed. Period.

Finally, let's note the extraordinary religious inclusion championed by the document first unveiled in mid-September 1787. Unlike most revolutionary state constitutions and the contemporaneous rules generally in place elsewhere on the planet, the Constitution opened its doors to office seekers of all faiths and philosophies.

Last year, three of the four men atop the major party tickets—Mitt Romney, Paul Ryan, and Joe Biden—were not members of the mainstream Protestant churches that dominated American society at the Founding. Today's speaker of the House is a Catholic, the Senate majority leader is a Mormon, and no Protestant sits on the current U.S. Supreme Court.

One is tempted to say, "only in America!" but in fact there are other modern countries that are democratic and religiously pluralist. However, many of these democracies have been powerfully influenced by the American constitutional experience.

Before the Constitution went public in 1787, pluralistic democracy existed almost nowhere on the planet, outside America. Today, constitutional self-government reigns across half the globe, and it does so thanks largely to the legal, political, cultural, moral, and military success of the American constitutional project.

In short, the world is becoming more American (and America itself, thanks to trade and immigration, is becoming more global). So we should not say "only in America," but rather "only because of America"—and in particular, because of America's Constitution and because of the year that changed everything.

THE REAL GREAT CHARTER

FEDERALIST SOCIETY BLOG, SEPTEMBER 2015[5]

As the world celebrates the 800th anniversary of Magna Carta this year, we should remember that the true origins of our modern democratic political world lie not in Runnymede, but right here in the United States.

In some modern circles, the significance of Magna Carta has been greatly exaggerated—dare I say Magna-fied? Older is not always better, however, and to the extent this document remains inspiring today, it is largely because its meaning happily evolved over the centuries.

In 1215, one band of unelected strongmen (barons) wrested concessions from another unelected strongman (King John). Ordinary Englishmen were no part of the process, and very little in this charter aimed at anything like modern democracy. The original charter was written in a legal Latin that few ordinary folk could understand. Later generations of Englishmen and

Americans ultimately reinterpreted—and often misinterpreted—Magna Carta's text to range far more broadly than intended. Many of these glosses were normatively admirable, but the credit for them belongs to later generations, not to the men of 1215. For example, in 1215, the charter's affirmation of a right to the "judgment of peers" referred not to jury trials of, by, and for commoners, but rather to a baron's right to be judged by fellow barons—the peerage, the noblemen of the realm. Rather than condemning monarchy and aristocracy, the document entrenched these feudalistic institutions, both in the manner of the charter's adoption (a pact between king and lords) and in the substance of its guarantees.

In short, this old text did not give birth to the modern world—a world in which democracy reigns over half the planet, a world rooted in the consent of the governed, a world committed to free speech for all, and dedicated to the proposition that all persons are created equal.

That modern, enlightened democratic world—the world that is still struggling to prevail against modern forces of unfreedom (Russian and Chinese autocracy, Islamo-fascism, and the like)—was born and reborn in the United States.

In 1787–1788, ordinary American citizens did in actual fact ordain a Constitution for themselves and their posterity. In most states the usual property qualifications for voting were relaxed or eliminated for the special constitutional elections that took place. By a wide margin, more persons got to vote on how they and their posterity would be governed than had ever been allowed to vote on anything in the history of our planet. The proposed new rules for a new world that emerged from the Philadelphia convention were written in plain language precisely so that ordinary folk could read and debate the proposal.

Across an entire continent, for an entire year, citizens discussed and debated first principles, in a world-changing conversation that was truly robust, uninhibited, and wide open. The world would never be the same. That year, not 1215, is the hinge of modern history.

In that entire year, virtually no censorship occurred and no one died in political violence. The men who fiercely opposed the document were not vilified or ostracized. Instead, their reform suggestions were considered respectfully, and many of these Anti-Federalist ideas were in fact incorporated into a series of amendments that emerged from this bottom-up process. Thus, the Philadelphia proposal was crowd sourced—a kind of democratic Wikipedia *avant la lettre*.

The Bill of Rights that emerged after and because of the Constitution's democratic ratification process not only celebrated free speech, but did so in a milieu itself awash in free speech. Five separate amendments (the First, Second, Fourth, Ninth, and Tenth) explicitly spoke of rights of "the people," in an obvious reflection of the fact that they had originated from the people—from the Preamble's "We the People" who had insisted on these amendments in the very process of ordaining and establishing the Constitution.

Although several of these amendments built on foundation stones that can be found in Magna Carta, the 1787–1791 versions of these ideas went far beyond anything that the 1215 barons had contemplated. For example, jury trials by and for ordinary folk were repeatedly guaranteed, and all the rights in the federal Bill of Rights operated to limit not just a king, but the entire government, including the legislative branch.

Alas, America's Founders did little to eliminate the worst feature of the ancien régime that stained our soil: human slavery, which entitled some to lord over others by dint of birth. But in the wake of the Civil War, a low-born commoner named Abe Lincoln proclaimed the need for a new birth of freedom—a second Founding of sorts.

My recent book on the American constitutional project, *The Law of the Land: A Grand Tour of Our Constitutional Republic*, begins with Lincoln, who took old words and repurposed them. The book takes its title from a key phrase of America's Constitution, which describes itself in Article VI as the "law of the land." This phrase traces back to Magna Carta, but Lincoln breathed new life into it, rightly insisting that in America, this key phrase reinforced the impermissibility of unilateral secession. Many other features of the Constitution supported Lincoln's claim that no state could leave the union on its own mere say-so, but the language of Article VI was strong and clear. The Constitution is the law of *our land*; disgruntled Americans have a right to leave, but they have no right to take the land with them. That land, Lincoln correctly insisted, was the inheritance of all Americans.

Here we have yet another illustration of how Magna Carta's words have come to mean many things that they may not have initially meant. So if you are inclined to celebrate a notable anniversary this year, raise your glass to the barons of old, if you must; but also give thanks to Lincoln, a commoner who died exactly 150 years ago and who ensured that the American democratic project—a government of the people, by the people, and for the people—would endure as the last, best hope of earth.

PART III

PRESIDENTIAL DRAMAS

8

BILL CLINTON'S DRAMA
His Partisan Impeachment

WHAT WOULD THE WORLD look like today had Bill Clinton never been impeached?

Here is one imaginable alternate universe: President Clinton leaves office as a relatively popular two-term president, thanks to general peace and prosperity on his watch. Monica Lewinsky gradually fades from view and Ken Starr rides off into the sunset. Starr's replacement, Robert Ray, declines to pursue felony charges against ex-president Clinton, in part because Clinton has already suffered extreme political and personal embarrassment and in part because Clinton remains popular, especially among Democrats; it is hard to envision a criminal jury convicting the former president on any serious criminal charge. As Clinton is heading out the door in 2000–2001, his first and most important running mate—Hillary—wins a seat in her own right as New York senator. Over the next several years, the former president works on burnishing his image and building a family fortune. He is a remarkably young senior statesman with extraordinary energy and imagination, and an incomparable network of contacts, foreign and domestic, political and commercial. He does good and he does well, and he even befriends former president George H. W. Bush, whom he had bested in 1992. Meanwhile, Hillary shines, both in the Senate and around the world, and emerges as a strong candidate for the presidency in her own right.

Oh, wait. All that happened even *with* Clinton's impeachment. (Recall that as events actually unfolded, Clinton was formally impeached—in effect, indicted—by the Republican-controlled House but was acquitted by the Republican-controlled Senate in his impeachment trial, presided over by

Chief Justice William Rehnquist.) Our imagined alternate universe is not so alternative. Perhaps Clinton's impeachment-plus-acquittal was not particularly consequential—an engrossing soap opera, but nothing more.

But consider this: Without the impeachment scandal tarnishing the Democrats' presidential trademark in key swing states in 2000, Al Gore would likely have bested George W. Bush. And here is where two plausible counterfactual scenarios diverge sharply.

In one scenario, alternate-universe President Gore, with the strong encouragement of alternate-universe Vice President Joe Lieberman, reacts to 9/11 much as President George W. Bush actually did react with the strong real-world encouragement of Vice President Dick Cheney. Patriotically rallying behind alternate-universe President Gore in 2004 but eventually disheartened by Gore's expensive and inconclusive interventions in Iraq and Afghanistan, Americans in 2008 elect the Republicans' comeback nominee, George W. Bush. Echoing Warren Harding in 1920, Dwight Eisenhower in 1952, and Richard Nixon in 1968, candidate Bush promises a return to normalcy and an end to yet another dubious war initiated by yet another overly ambitious Democratic president. (The not-so-subtle theme of the 2008 campaign of Bush fils is that his father knew when to stop in the Middle East, and so does he.) Because this alternate-universe President Bush is a "compassionate conservative," he does not try to undo the sweeping medical-insurance-reform law enacted under his predecessor's watch. (Although many hard-core conservatives are outraged by the plan, nicknamed Gore-care, savvy politicos understand that broad entitlement plans, once having taken root, are hard to undo.) As 2016 dawns and a new presidential election looms on the horizon, there is talk about a possible rematch of 1992, with another Clinton (Hillary) poised to go up against another Bush (Jeb), who would if elected be the third member of his immediate family to sit in the Oval Office. New faces in both parties also emerge, urging an end to the Bush-Clinton era.

Once again, this alternate universe is not so different from our own. But imagine, instead, that alternate-universe President Gore holds his fire in the Middle East. Lieberman, after all, was never a clone of Cheney, and as a young man Gore saw the blunder of Vietnam up close in a way that the young George W. Bush did not. Also, the alternate-universe Gore-Lieberman administration cannot lightly ignore the Democratic Party's base, which has generally been far more dovish than the Republican Party's base in the years since Vietnam. In this version of the counterfactual, the Iraq War never happens, and the entire world would today be a vastly different place, for both better and worse.

Perhaps, then, the otherwise ineffectual impeachment of President Clinton did change everything—immeasurably.

I CONFESS THAT I AM NOT a sufficiently subtle historian or a clever enough novelist to choose among these mind-bending counterfactuals. But I do feel more confident regarding two more narrow counterfactuals growing directly out of the essays collected in this chapter.

First, had the views that I put forth in these essays as events were unfolding prevailed, Clinton would never have been vulnerable to impeachment in the first place because the Paula Jones case—*Jones v. Clinton*, the civil lawsuit that spawned the first deeply intrusive judicial thrust into the president's sexual behavior—would have been put on hold during the pendency of his presidency.*

Second, had my understanding of the Constitution been honored as events played out, Clinton would have been safe even had the *Jones* lawsuit gone forward. No perjurious, deceptive, or improper statements from the president in this civil case would ever have occurred because Clinton's Fourth Amendment right to quash certain intrusive and unreasonable questions about his non-Jonesian romantic adventures would have been upheld by the trial judge in the *Jones* case, Susan Webber Wright. Had Judge Wright read the Fourth Amendment and the relevant rules of procedure the right way (meaning, of course, the way I read them back then and still read them now), Clinton's "crime" of perjury would never even have *happened*. Unlike most real-world crimes, which take place far from courtrooms and long before judges are in the picture, Clinton's offense was actually created by the

---

* By way of reminder: Paula Corbin Jones was an Arkansas state employee who sued President Clinton in 1994. Jones's civil sexual harassment suit alleged that in 1991, then governor Clinton propositioned her and exposed his private parts to her in a Little Rock hotel room. The case was eventually settled, but not before President Clinton was deposed about other possible extramarital sexual activities. In the course of that deposition under oath, President Clinton made various statements about his lack of sexual involvement with a White House intern, Monica Lewinsky—with whom, it turned out, he had indeed engaged in certain erotic, albeit non-coital, behavior. Clinton's Lewinsky-related statements ultimately formed the basis of statutory perjury accusations investigated by Independent Counsel Ken Starr and Starr's successor, Robert Ray, and perjury allegations at the center of Clinton's 1998 impeachment by the House of Representatives and 1999 acquittal by the Senate.

judicial system itself; and in my view, wrongly so. (For details, see this chapter's "Unimperial Presidency" essay, which was first published in the *New
Republic* in March 1999.)

OF COURSE, MY CONSTITUTIONAL VIEWS did not win out when the
chips were down. But many years later, I remain comfortable with what I
wrote as history was happening.

This chapter's opening essay, "Advice for the President's Legal Team,"
was first published in 1994 in the *New Republic*. In this short piece, my then
student coauthor Neal Katyal and I suggested that a private (and potentially
politically motivated) civil lawsuit brought by a single person against the
president might in fact interfere with his performance in office, and thereby
improperly obstruct the job the American people elected him to do. At one
key point, Neal and I noted that "Article I explicitly limits certain congressional immunities to times when Congress is 'in session.' But the executive
never sleeps; the president is always in session." Here was the nub of a powerful constitutional argument with strong roots in the founding document's
text, history, and structure.

But it is not easy to persuade newspaper and newsmagazine editors to allow constitutional scholars all the space they (think they) need to unpack
their argument and evidence. Thus, soon after we published this essay, Neal
and I turned to a specialized academic journal, the *Harvard Law Review*, to
make our case more fully. There, we demonstrated in elaborate detail that
the Article I, section 6, arrest clause of the Constitution was designed to
shield members of Congress from certain *civil*—not criminal—arrests whenever Congress was in "session." According to this clause, "Senators and Representatives . . . shall [except in criminal cases] be privileged from Arrest
during their attendance at the Session of their respective Houses." The key
aim of the clause, we showed, was to protect federal lawmakers from certain
private (and perhaps politically motivated) civil suits that might improperly
interfere with—that might "arrest"—the lawmakers' efforts to faithfully represent their constituents while Congress was doing the people's business. For
similar reasons, and because presidents are always in session, Neal and I argued that Article II, which vests the president with executive power, likewise immunized a sitting president from certain civil suits that might impair
the president's ability to do what the American people elected him to do.[1]

When the question finally reached the Supreme Court in the 1997 case of
Clinton v. Jones, the Court gave Neal's and my constitutional argument the

back of its hand. Led by Justice John Paul Stevens, eight justices signed on to an opinion that confidently asserted that there was no substantial risk that the presidency would be improperly intruded upon: "If properly managed by the District Court," Stevens breezily opined, the Jones lawsuit "appears to us highly unlikely to occupy any substantial amount of [the president's] time."

Neal and I had suggested otherwise, and with the benefit of hindsight readers of this book can now decide for themselves who was right when it mattered.

IN 1997 IT WAS SOME CONSOLATION that Justice Stephen Breyer did write a separate opinion that tracked Neal's and my approach in several ways. (At the time, Neal was serving as one of several law clerks to the justice, for whom I had clerked many years earlier.) But even Breyer ended up voting to allow the Jones litigation to proceed, and the 9–0 vote by the Court reinforced a sense among top journalists that Clinton's constitutional claims had little to commend them.

But these journalists were wrong in the 1990s, and they were wrong in a quite predictable way. In general, journalists suffer from at least two major handicaps when it comes to such matters. First, editors, reporters, anchors, and columnists typically know little or nothing about constitutional law, substantively or methodologically. Journalists thus cannot easily and competently evaluate or challenge judicial opinions; journalists can merely report judicial votes and summarize judicial statements. But judicial statements are hardly the only word in constitutional law, and in certain situations they are not even the last word. Sometimes what courts have said runs counter to what the Constitution itself really means, based on its text, history, and structure. (Consider for example, Dred Scott and Plessy v. Ferguson—or Bush v. Gore, for that matter.)[2] At other times—most other times, happily—judicial rulings do fit snugly within the Constitution's basic vision. One needs to know a fair amount about constitutional law to decide which category a given judicial ruling belongs to—to decide, to bend a phrase, whether the umpires nailed it or blew it. And, to repeat, most journalists lack the tools and the training to do this. (To extend the umpire metaphor, journalists do not know how to operate slow-motion, multiple-angled, instant-replay cameras.)

Second, journalists often have little sense of history. They are men and women of the moment—of the day, as their name implies. In the 1990s they remembered Watergate well enough but had no clue that long before Richard Nixon, presidents such as Thomas Jefferson and John Adams and constitutional titans such as Joseph Story had in fact said and written a great deal that argued for Clinton's position and against Jones's claims.

For instance, here is what Jefferson wrote, as president, in 1807: "But would the executive be independent of the judiciary, if he were subject to the commands of the latter, & to imprisonment for disobedience; if the several courts could bandy him from pillar to post, keep him constantly trudging from north to south & east to west, and withdraw him entirely from his constitutional duties." John Adams did not always agree with Thomas Jefferson, but he did on this question: "[T]he President, personally, was not the subject of any [judicial] process whatever. . . . For [that] would put it in the power of a common [judge] to exercise any authority over him and stop the whole machine of Government." And here are the words of Justice Joseph Story, by acclamation the greatest constitutional scholar of the antebellum era, in his magisterial three-volume treatise on American constitutional law: "[W]hile [the president] is in the discharge of the duties of his office, . . . his person must be deemed, in civil cases at least, to possess an official inviolability."[3]

The *Jones* case was decided in a decade of seeming national security—after the collapse of the Soviet Union and before the shock of 9/11. In this narrow sliver of time, perhaps journalists could be forgiven for thinking—quite wrongly, with the benefit of both history and hindsight—that presidents generally have nothing better to do than meet with private lawyers and defend themselves against private lawsuits. But I wonder how the constitutional issue would have looked to both journalists and generalist judges had some private litigant tried to commandeer FDR's time in the middle of World War II. Or Truman's time during the Korean conflict; or Ike's time during the Hungarian uprising or the U-2 spy plane incident; or JFK's time in the season of the Cuban missile crisis; or LBJ's or Richard Nixon's time at the height of the Vietnam War. How would the constitutional question have looked had a lawsuit been brought against President George W. Bush on September 12, 2001, demanding that he turn away from matters of transcendent national import to deal with some wrong he was alleged to have done in his private capacity many years earlier?

IF THE PRECEDING PARAGRAPHS smell like sour grapes, here are some sweeter ones: On two big issues covered in the essays in this chapter, the views that I put forth in the moment have subsequently come to be embraced by the powers that be.

First, in a string of essays collected in the pages that follow—"The Founders' Mousetrap"; "Now Playing . . . a Constitutional Nightmare"; "The Flaw in the Law"; "The Unimperial President"; and "Closing the Book on Clinton"—I argued that the so-called Ethics in Government Act (EIGA), creating a statutory independent prosecutor appointed by judges, was unconstitutional.

My argument both reinforced and refined the analysis put forth by Justice Antonin Scalia, in a powerful solo dissent in the 1988 case, *Morrison v. Olson*. One of my refinements was to highlight the president's pardon power, a power that Scalia had entirely omitted from his analysis, and that made clear the obvious differences between Ken Starr and his successor, Robert Ray, on the one hand, and all prior independent counsels, on the other. All previous EIGA independent counsels, I argued, could have been effectively nullified by forceful presidential pardons, or threatened pardons, of the counsels' investigatory targets. But where a president himself was the target, the pardon pen is unavailable—for surely no man may pardon himself. As a result, Starr's and Ray's post was far more powerful—far less "inferior," as it should have been in order to satisfy the Constitution—than the independent counsel position in the *Morrison v. Olson* case, or, indeed, in any prior EIGA situation.

Today, history has vindicated the Scalia dissent and my refinement of it: The EIGA statute is no more, having expired at the end of the Clinton administration, and never having been revived under Presidents George W. Bush or Barack Obama. Notably, Ken Starr and Bill Clinton, who had disagreed about so much throughout Starr's extended investigations of Clinton, eventually came to agree that the EIGA statute was unconstitutional in just the ways that Justice Scalia and, later, yours truly, had explained. Starr made public his views in comments after his service had ended. Clinton, by contrast, allowed his attorney general, Janet Reno, to speak for him.

In congressional testimony in March 1999, Reno said that she now believed that Scalia (and, by implication, Amar) had been right all along, and thus strongly hinted that any congressional effort to renew the independent counsel statute would meet with a constitutionally based presidential veto. Reno's assistant in preparing her testimony was none other than my own former assistant and coauthor, Neal Katyal, who had first been persuaded of the rightness of Scalia's *Morrison* dissent when he encountered it as my first-year student at Yale in 1992. (Ever since the *Morrison* case was handed down, in 1988, I have featured it in my introductory constitutional law course and encouraged my students to pay special heed to Scalia's dissent. In other words, every year I try to show my students, using the Socratic equivalent of slow-motion cameras, that Scalia made the correct call and that the other umpires goofed.)

Reno's 1999 testimony reflected a change of view on her part. She had come to her position as attorney general in 1993 as a supporter of the independent counsel statute. Many leading constitutional scholars—including Bruce Ackerman, Cass Sunstein, and Laurence Tribe—had also backed the law early on. But by the end of 1999, most academic experts had come around to the view that I had been expressing throughout the preceding decade to any and all who would listen, and that Justice Scalia had powerfully proclaimed in the late 1980s, before my own scholarship on this matter had revved up.

The second major issue on which Beltway bigwigs have belatedly come to their senses involves impeachment standards. As the Clinton impeachment debate was raging, I insisted in essays such as "The Founders' Mousetrap" and "The People's Court" that the key impeachment question was not "what" but "who." Instead of focusing single-mindedly on *what* Clinton did, sober House members should have been asking themselves *who* was calling for his head.

Ours is a two-party system, and if none of the leaders of the president's own party—and no substantial portion of the rank-and-file Democrats who had voted him into office, twice—wanted him out, then at the end of the trial, the requisite two-thirds Senate vote would never be achieved. House Republicans, I argued, should proceed only if joined by leading Democrats. If virtually no Democrats were willing to join the crusade in the House, how could anyone think that any Democrats would vote to convict in the Senate? And without a substantial number of the forty-something Senate Democrats willing to vote against a president of their party, how could an impeachment trial ever end in a conviction? What was the point of the whole process?

The House Republicans did not listen to me in the 1990s, but today the House Republican leadership appears to have gotten the memo. Despite considerable animosity toward President Obama harbored by leading members of the Republican Party today, there is at present no serious impeachment effort afoot precisely because no Democrats are willing to join the crusade. (Likewise, Democrats who controlled the House at the end of the

Bush 43 administration properly resisted extremist calls for W's impeachment.) To repeat, the question is not what, but who: Whether or not some abstract case could be made that this presidential action or that one crosses the threshold of a high crime or misdemeanor, the key fact today is that no leading Democrat thinks President Obama must go. And so he will stay, unmolested—and rightly so.

HAVING OFFERED A stern assessment of contemporary journalists, I must in fairness also critique my own tribe. Constitutional scholars are not trained to write snappy prose on minute-hand deadlines within superstrict word limits. Journalists do this day in and day out; and when constitutional scholars try to play journalist, we—or at least I—do not always shine.

Upon reflection I now think that, in an effort to make my journalistic interventions more reader friendly, I was at times too glib. For example, at one point in my October 1998 essay, "The Flaw in the Law," I depicted Bill Clinton as "the great white whale" being pursued by Captain Ahab—that is, Ken Starr. To be sure, I was merely describing how the titanic struggle between these foes looked to ordinary spectators, but as I re-read these words years later, I wince. And I wince all the more because Ken Starr was at the time I wrote these words my friend, and since then he and his family have become especially dear friends to me and my family. He puts the "gentle" in the word "gentleman"—and yet I had analogized him to a deranged fanatic! And in another passage in that essay, I likened him (again, in the mind of the public) to Godzilla taking on a Kong-like Clinton.

What was I thinking? I was thinking, perhaps, like a journalist seeking to attract eyeballs with colorful writing. Or rather, I was thinking like a *mediocre* journalist, for the true masters of the journalistic craft, honing their skills day after day on tight deadlines, enliven their prose without crossing the line.

My most egregious lapse in this regard fell on the editing floor. But no thanks to me; thanks rather to a professional journalist who firmly restrained me in real time and with good taste. In the first draft of the penultimate essay of this chapter, "Bringing Justice to Clinton," which appeared in the *New York Times* in March 2000, I had ended with a colorful metaphor illustrating the virtues of prosecutorial discretion. Not all crimes should be prosecuted to the hilt, and this general truth about the American criminal justice system applied in particular to whatever crimes may have been committed by Bill Clinton. "Wise prosecutors," I wrote, "know that it is sometimes best to let lying dogs sleep." When I received an edited first draft back from the *Times* staff, I noticed that this line had been eliminated. I asked my editor why; I had been so proud of my pun! "We cut it," she explained, because it was a cliché." "Not at all," I quickly countered. "The cliché is that 'it is best to let sleeping dogs lie.' My line inverts this." She paused and then asked in a cool, almost steely, tone: "Professor, are you calling the president of the United States a lying dog?" "I—I guess so," I stammered, no longer quite so sure of myself. She then said, slowly, and with icy resolve, "Not in the *New York Times*, you're not."

The Gray Lady, evidently, was not amused. And for her good judgment, I am now quite grateful.

ADVICE FOR THE PRESIDENT'S LEGAL TEAM[4]

NEW REPUBLIC, MONDAY, JUNE 20, 1994 (WITH NEAL KATYAL)

No one is above the law, but surely the president is special. This is the legal tightrope Attorney Robert Bennett must walk on behalf of his client, President Clinton. As he drafts an answer to the sexual harassment complaint filed by Paula Jones, Bennett must uphold the role of the office without seeming to betray the rule of law. Bill Clinton must win without looking like Richard Nixon.

Why should Jones be prevented from suing a fellow citizen? Bennett's response must be that the president is, well, the president. Of course, this basic argument can be packaged in several wrappings, each with different consequences for our legal system. Some variants are already on Bennett's radar screen (for instance, a sweeping claim of absolute presidential immunity), but others are not. Here are three Bennett would do well to consider:

The people's president. Our Constitution marks the president as unique, not as a matter of divine right but as an aspect of democratic design. There are over five hundred lawmakers in Congress and roughly a thousand federal judges (headed by nine Supreme Court justices) in the judiciary; these branches can function even if one member is off defending a private lawsuit. But there is only one president. Other branches are only sometimes at work, creating periodic recesses during which a trial could occur—Article I explicitly limits certain congressional immunities to times when Congress is "in session." But the executive never sleeps; the president is always in session.

He must be ready, at a moment's notice, to do whatever it takes to preserve, protect, and defend the Constitution and the people: prosecute wars, command armed forces (and nuclear weapons), protect Americans abroad, negotiate with heads of state, and oversee the economy. Courts should hesitate before arming every citizen with the right to commandeer the president's time, drag him from the White House, and haul him before any judge in America. If suits like Jones's can go forth easily, the American people—not the president—may end up paying the real damages.

Privileges and immunities. In 1982 the Supreme Court held in *Nixon v. Fitzgerald* that a president cannot be sued for his presidential actions. Jones will argue that pre-presidential wrongs are different. Bennett can try to stretch the immunity blanket to cover all presidential sins, past and present, public and private. Yet on that basis, Clinton would win only by out-Nixoning Nixon—hardly something to cheer about.

Presidential counsel Lloyd Cutler and others have floated a narrower solution: "Toll" (that is, stop the clock on) the statute of limitations and let the Jones case proceed only after Clinton steps down from the presidency. Tolling preserves plaintiffs' rights and renders presidents legally accountable, while recognizing the president's special role while "in session" as president. It draws support from the spirit of a 1940 law granting military personnel temporary relief from litigation during their term of service.

Of course, worthy plaintiffs pay a price. They may be forced to wait nearly a decade to get their due, or memories may fade—and not all presidents live to become suable ex-presidents. Imagine a plaintiff run over by a transition team bus driven by Clinton the week before the inauguration. The "tolling" compromise hurts a helpless pedestrian and diligent litigant.

But in the real world, Bennett can argue that Paula Jones is no helpless pedestrian, that she is the reckless one—choosing the constitutionally dubious time of her lawsuit with indifference to its potential impact on the presidency. Why didn't she bring suit before Clinton assumed the high duties of president, when litigation would not have raised grave difficulties? Our hypothetical pedestrian had no choice.

Bennett may also raise the timing issue to challenge Jones's credibility: If it really happened, why did she wait to sue? The problem with this line of questioning, however, is that Jones may have an answer: She could allege, as she does in her complaint, that post-inaugural accusations, denials, and slights induced her to file.

A better idea is for Bennett to fashion an argument around "laches," a little-known but powerful line of defense. This argument would be more technical than a straight-out assault on credibility; it would suggest a quick judicial dismissal rather than an ultimate jury verdict after an ugly trial. Under well-established legal principles, plaintiffs may not always sit on their rights and wait until the last day of the statute of limitations, even if they are telling the truth. Laches prevents a plaintiff from delaying suit in ways that wreak havoc on defendants. It can apply even where a statute of limitations still has time to run.

Although in earlier days laches applied only to "equity" cases (those tried by a judge rather than a jury), the logic of the 1938 merger of "law" and "equity" erases most of those distinctions, and courts have been heading this way for years. Bennett may also sidestep the law/equity question by repackaging the issue as one of constitutional common law: Congress nowhere explicitly enacted a statute of limitations for the claims Jones raises. Where the president is involved, do we want fifty different rules in fifty different states for a lawsuit that is, chiefly, rooted in federal law?

The advantage of laches is that it helps blunt the fairness concern with the Cutler compromise: Jones loses if she cannot explain why she delayed filing for so long. She has been aware of all the facts since May 1991 and says she told many friends within days. Bennett's argument here could nicely bolster his earlier paean to the People's President; laches would encourage people to raise their claims before the public as well as the courts before Election Day. Jones's defamation claim—focusing on the president's statements and actions as president—would require separate attention, but this falls close to the heart of the Nixon case and runs up against a strong free speech defense to boot.[5] Laches has one other possible strategic advantage: Unlike tolling, it might end the lawsuit (and thus litigation discovery) once and for all.

Personal jurisdiction and venue. The specter of a fifty-state patchwork leads to a final and simple but easily overlooked point. If a sitting president can be sued, he should probably be suable only in Washington, DC, to minimize disruption of his constitutionally prescribed duties. Article III guarantees foreign ambassadors the ability to defend suits in DC, so why not the president? In 1787, who would have thought any court on the continent could reach out and grab the president through newfangled long-arm statutes? Adopting this argument would be to Bennett's advantage, for if DC were the only constitutionally apt venue, Jones's lawsuit could be dead on arrival: The statute of limitations in the district arguably lapsed long ago.

Of course, the venue gambit will not always do the trick for a president in all future lawsuits. Then again, Bennett only needs to win the case at hand.

TRYING CASE

WASHINGTON POST, TUESDAY, FEBRUARY 18, 1997

As the justices begin drafting opinions in the case of *Paula Corbin Jones v. William Jefferson Clinton*, grand constitutional principles seem to tug sharply in opposite directions. No man is above the law—and yet a sitting president is special. In a democracy all citizens are equal—yet the president stands first among equals.

As a practical matter, though, lawsuits are delayed for all sorts of good reasons—because soldiers leave the country, because litigants fall sick—yet none of this offends the rule of law. Neither would temporary immunity for sitting presidents. In fact, pro-democracy arguments support Clinton: If a single plaintiff can so enmesh the president in litigation that he cannot do what the people elected him to do, then one voter has effectively undone the votes of millions.

On the other side, sweeping claims that presidents never have a moment to spare seemed too much for even the usually pro-executive Justice Antonin Scalia. Surely, Scalia suggested at oral argument, some small cases might proceed without undue distraction, and so temporary immunity should occur only if the president publicly declares he's too busy—and suffers in public opinion if his declaration is implausible.

But Clinton's lawyers already have conceded that presidents may waive temporary immunity; they argue only that this president has chosen not to waive it in this case. He already has done just what Justice Scalia seemed to call for, by publicly asserting that this lawsuit would be too distracting. How much more public can he get? Surely the court of public opinion is open and in session to judge this president's bona fides.

For their part, Jones's lawyers conceded that if the president had to rush off to an emergency NATO meeting, no judge could demand that he instead sit for a deposition that day. Yet once they (properly) conceded this, they proved the analytical emptiness of their trite trope that a sitting president must be treated exactly like everyone else, lest we slide into monarchy or tyranny.

Various proposed accommodations won't work. The trial court proposed to split the baby by subjecting sitting presidents to pretrial depositions but sparing them from trial. Like actual child partition, this seems a silly or spiteful lose-lose idea: Sitting presidents lose control of their presidential schedule, yet plaintiffs lose their right to win now. The democratic purpose of temporary immunity is to spare the president distraction while he's in office, but pretrial discovery can be endlessly time-consuming.

Another baby-splitting idea came from the Eighth Circuit Court of Appeals, which proposed that trial judges accommodate presidential needs through "sensitive case management." But as Justice Scalia asked in court, do we really want to empower every state and federal judge in America (all of whom are rightly independent of the president and some of whom might be hostile to him) to decide whether a NATO meeting, or a political convention, for that matter, is more important than a deposition? And how can one Supreme Court, sitting miles away, monitor day-by-day scheduling abuses in the middle of pretrial discovery? Would every disputed trial order be faxed to the high court for instant review?

As Justice David Souter pointed out, if judges must be sensitive to presidential schedules, it may be better to be sensitive at the outset rather than in the interior of litigation, postponing everything until the president leaves office. This is a scheme that would enable one-shot review by the high court.

In a recent op-ed piece, law professor Ronald Rotunda floated a variant of the Eighth Circuit approach by demanding that the president certify his pretrial unavailability date-by-date, deposition-by-deposition. But why can't he just certify once at the outset that he's too busy? This would surely be a solemn public act, triggering immense public scrutiny. And as Justices Anthony Kennedy and Stephen Breyer both noted, litigation distractions lie not only in the time actually spent at depositions but in the days and weeks preparing for them with one's lawyers.

For the same reason, another proposal tossed out by Justice Scalia—allow the president to avoid being deposed, but depose everyone else—seems impractical. The president is being sued and claims the suit is baseless; but to avoid unjust liability, he must meet with lawyers to brief them even when others are being deposed. These meetings can be unbelievably time-consuming and profoundly preoccupying.

What, then, is the best solution? Force the president at the outset to openly assert that he's too busy, and let him take the political heat. If the public thinks he's being unfair, public pressure can build up and he can opt to revoke his certification. If members of Congress think he's abusing the system, the Constitution gives them many weapons. In effect, the people—not one plaintiff—can decide how the president must spend his time in office.

THE FOUNDERS' MOUSETRAP[6]

AMERICAN LAWYER, SEPTEMBER 1998

America delights in her inventions. From bifocals at the Founding to light bulbs, flying machines, and computers in the modern era, we constantly quest for the holy grail of the better mousetrap. America's constitutional lawyers over the centuries have also proved remarkably inventive, crafting clever legal contraptions to solve recurring problems. Since Watergate, the problem of wayward presidents has grabbed our imagination, and creative constitutional lawyers have responded with a new invention: an independent counsel, appointed by judges and insulated from executive branch supervision. But the theoretical possibility of a president gone bad did not suddenly arise with the reelection of Richard Nixon. Our inventive Founders foresaw the problem, and forged their own clever machinery to solve it: impeachment. And this machinery, I suggest, is a better mousetrap. Once we understand how it was engineered to work, we will see more clearly some of the design flaws of the modern independent counsel statute.

Presidential impeachment features a brilliant mix of temporary immunity and ultimate accountability. A sitting president is immune from ordinary criminal prosecution, but once impeached by the House and convicted by the Senate, or otherwise out of office, he may be punished just like everyone else. Granted, the Constitution does not say this in so many words, and all other impeachable officers—from vice presidents and cabinet secretaries to judges and justices—may be indicted, tried, convicted, and imprisoned while still in office. But history and structure make clear what the constitutional text leaves open. In two different *Federalist Papers* (Numbers 69 and 77), Publius suggested that criminal prosecution of the president could not occur until after he left office, a point stressed in the First Congress by Senator (and later Chief Justice) Oliver Ellsworth and Vice President (and later President) John Adams.

Structurally, this makes good sense. Unlike other national officers, the president is vested with the power of an entire branch of government. He is not fungible in the way that judges and cabinet officers are, and his duties are far more continuous and weighty than those of the vice president. Suppose a president is actually innocent of wrongdoing, and a given criminal prosecution is simply designed to stop him from doing what he was elected to do. Such a prosecution, even if unsuccessful, could effectively (and perhaps literally, given pretrial detention) incapacitate him and thereby nullify a national election. It is a kind of temporary assassination, a hijacking and kidnapping, of the president. In the spring of 1861, could some clever state prosecutor from North or South Carolina have indicted Abraham Lincoln and demanded that he stand trial down south on some trumped up charge? Surely not. Thus, a sitting president may not be trifled with in this way—but Congress may boot him out if they decide that he has indeed committed offenses that make him unfit to govern. After he leaves office, whether via impeachment or resignation or the natural expiration of his term, he can be tried like any other citizen. If the charges are sound, he will be held to account: No man is above the law. If the charges are instead trumped up, they can be quashed beforehand or overturned afterward by judges, as is true for all other citizens. The ex-president would be inconvenienced by all this, but he could be compensated by Congress, in keeping with the spirit of other congressional statutes defraying legal expenses for various government officials. Most important, the American people would not be denied one millisecond of his tenure in office unless and until Congress made that awesome decision, via impeachment.

Last year's Supreme Court ruling in the Paula Jones case might seem to squint against this reading of the Constitution's structure and history: The *Jones* Court denied that a sitting president should enjoy temporary immunity from a civil lawsuit. But criminal prosecution is hugely different, constitutionally. The *Jones* Court stressed the lack of historical support for civil immunity, but there is clear historical support for temporary immunity from criminal prosecution. In *Jones*, no question arose about who could initiate the lawsuit—in America, any plaintiff can sue any defendant. But not every citizen can indict. Who can indict the president? A county or state prosecutor?

Even in civil cases, *Jones* refused to rule on whether a sitting president could be made to answer in state court, emphasizing that the case at hand would be carefully managed by a federal Article III judge nominated by the nation's president and confirmed by the nation's Senate.

If state prosecution is impermissible—recall Lincoln in 1861—how about federal prosecution? Here the problem is not one of federalism but of separation of powers. How can an "inferior'" executive officer—Independent Counsel Kenneth Starr, who was neither appointed by the president, nor confirmed by the Senate—undermine and overrule his constitutional superior, the chief executive? (This issue did not arise in the 1988 *Morrison v. Olson* case upholding the independent counsel statute, since the investigation in that case targeted a lower-level official, not the president himself.) Doesn't even a federal grand jury pose some of the same risks as a state prosecution, given that any given grand jury will come from a single city or county—the "part" and not the "whole," in the language of *McCulloch v. Maryland*?

Consider next issues of enforcement and remedy. Had President Clinton refused to participate in *Jones*—saying that he was elected to do the people's business, and could not be distracted—a simple default judgment could have been entered. With a push of a button, funds could be transferred from his bank account to the plaintiff's. But if the president were to refuse to acknowledge the legitimacy of a criminal proceeding—claiming that the only criminal court with jurisdiction over him was the high court of impeachment—what are courts to do? Put him in leg irons? Order his imprisonment?

Here, then, are a few of the most impressive features of the framers' mousetrap. First, impeachment is *national*. The president uniquely represents the entire American people, and the decision to arrest his performance in office can only be made by representatives of the country as a whole. A president may need to pursue policies that are nationally sound, but regionally unpopular. Thus the true grand and petit juries eligible to judge a sitting president must come not from one city or county but from all cities and counties. That grand jury is the House of Representatives, and the formal name of its bill of indictment is a bill of impeachment. That petit jury is the Senate, and in impeachment it sits as a great national court, representing the vast geographic diversity of America. A related advantage is that it sits in the capital, thus minimizing any geographic inconvenience to a sitting president. To allow regular federal grand juries into this picture, whether in Charleston or Little Rock, would in the words of President Thomas Jefferson "bandy [the president] from pillar to post, keep him constantly trudging from north to south & east to west, and withdraw him entirely from his constitutional duties."

Next, impeachment is *public* and *accountable*. Ordinary grand juries are subject to strict secrecy rules, but these may tend to break down where something as awesome and interesting as an investigation of the president is afoot. The impeachment process is more flexible—presumptively done in public, as is the rest of congressional business, but allowing secrecy where appropriate. If independent counsels or ordinary grand juries are too hard on presidents—or too soft—there is no recourse for the American people. But if Congress members are too hard or soft, they will pay at election time.

A related point: Impeachment is sensibly *political* as well as *legal*. Politicians judge other politicians and impose political punishments—removal from office and disqualification from future officeholding. The standard of conduct is not narrowly legal but also political: What counts as a "high crime and misdemeanor" cannot be decided simply by parsing criminal law statutes. A statute-book offense is not necessary for impeachment. We should not use state criminal law as the sole test—which state would we pick? And George Washington was surely impeachable for any serious misdeeds he may have committed early on, even though no federal criminal laws had yet been passed. More generally, a president might be unfit to govern even if his misconduct was not an ordinary crime. (Imagine a president who simply runs off on vacation in the middle of a crisis.) Conversely, not every technical offense in statute books—especially offenses that are not ordinarily prosecuted—should count as the kind of high misconduct that unfits a man to be president after his fellow citizens have chosen him. Indeed, what counts as sufficiently high misconduct may be different for judges or cabinet officers—who lack a personal mandate from the electorate—than for a president who enjoys such a mandate. An offense that was made known to electors, or that could have been foreseen by them, may differ from an offense carefully hidden from them. (In this view, lying to the American people—even if not under oath and not technically criminal—might be more serious than technical perjury in a civil deposition.) All these distinctions have little place in our formal criminal law, but they are precisely the sorts of factors statesmen may sensibly consider in the impeachment process. And such statesmen have strong incentives to set the bar of acceptable conduct neither too high—they and their friends will have to live under these rules—nor too low, lest they disgust ordinary voters appalled by back-scratching and self-dealing.

Impeachment is also nicely *nonpartisan*. In the endgame, a president will be ousted only if fair-minded members of his own party condemn him; anything less than a two-thirds vote of conviction is an acquittal. Though the framers did not originally envision the emergence of two permanent parties that would alternate in the presidency, they did expect Congress at any given time to be divided between the president's allies and his enemies; and they devised a beautiful system giving the balance of power to swing senators who could be expected to give the president the benefit of the doubt in close cases. Talk of "vast conspiracies" could be easily laughed off, given the structural safeguards built into the system. And by keeping judges out of the process of investigating, prosecuting, and trying sitting presidents—actions inevitably tinged with politics—the impeachment model keeps judges above the fray of partisan politics.

Impeachment is also beautifully *final*. No appeal lies from the judgment of an impeachment court. By contrast imagine the chaos that might be created by ordinary prosecution and conviction of a sitting president. Could he run the country from a jail cell? This seems outlandish. If, instead, we treated imprisonment as a "disability" triggering vice-presidential succession under the Twenty-fifth Amendment, how will we all feel if a later court invalidates the president's conviction on appeal?

Finally, impeachment is—or should be made—*regularized* and *routine*. An ad hoc independent counsel must build an organization from scratch, and those who volunteer may have an axe to grind, since the target is known in advance. Institutional routines to guard against leaks and other unprofessional conduct may be harder to develop and implement in an ad hoc enterprise. But Congress can and should create a standing committee on impeachment and oversight. The committee could have permanent staff, and be insulated by House tradition from partisanship. Over time, the committee could develop policies and procedures and precedents that can be applied consistently regardless of which party controls the House, and which party occupies the Oval Office. Other high constitutional functions of Congress have been routinized—appropriations, discipline of errant legislators, foreign affairs, and so on. Why not impeachment? If we want the framers' mousetrap to work, we must keep it well oiled.

NOW PLAYING . . . A CONSTITUTIONAL NIGHTMARE

WASHINGTON POST, SUNDAY, SEPTEMBER 20, 1998

Like many adults, I'm dreading the inevitable moment when my kids ask me to explain the Starr report to them. Not because of the sex—the "kids" I'm worried about are my first-year students at Yale Law School, and I assume they know about sex. What they don't (yet) know, and are endlessly curious about, is how the Constitution works, or at least how it was designed to work. If they look to the report for constitutional theory, they may get perverse ideas.

"Professor," I can hear them saying, "you said that the Constitution carefully separates the three branches of government. So how can *judicial* branch officers pick an independent counsel who wields *executive*-branch powers yet reports to the *legislative* branch? If the framers scrupulously excluded ordinary judges from the impeachment process, why were three judges allowed to pick the man who now acts as Congress's designated impeachment adviser? If federal prosecutors are constitutionally confined to punishing violations of federal criminal statutes, then why does this prosecutor's report contain all sorts of material ranging beyond statute-book offenses—charges of lying to the American people and the cabinet, for example?"

I have no good answers. For the truth is that the statute that created the independent counsel—vesting his appointment in judges, arming him with awesome inquisitorial powers and instructing him to hand over all his findings to Congress—cannot be squared with the Constitution designed by the Founders. If this fact wasn't clear to all before the report, it should be clear now.

For the unconstitutional mess we find ourselves in, I blame not Kenneth Starr but the statute itself (first signed into law in 1978 and reauthorized by President Clinton in 1994). Indeed, I have been a critic of this law and its predecessors for a good decade. Starr is just doing what the law allows and indeed tells him to do. He didn't seek out this dirty job—he was chosen, and simply answered when his country called.

But how was he picked, and by whom? Behind closed doors, by three judges. This is bad business. In our constitutional tradition, judges typically act after open argument in open court. By contrast, the independent counsel statute permits ordinarily taboo ex parte (secret) communications under the following logic. Because the statute tells judges not to decide a legal case but to answer an inherently political and policy question—who should investigate the administration?—then judges need to act politically rather than judicially, consulting senators or anyone else they choose, in whatever manner they choose, as they decide who is best for the job.

But this logic only raises the question of why Congress would give judges such a political and potentially partisan task—especially when the investigation is of the president himself. The Constitution says that the House shall prosecute impeachments and the Senate shall try them. This system insulates senators from the prosecution business, so that they may be impartial triers of law and fact. But under the statute, various senators may end up sitting in judgment on a report from a prosecutor they helped pick in secret conversations with lower-court judges (who are supposed to have no role whatsoever in impeachment). Whether any senators in fact helped pick Starr is less important than the fact that the statute allowed them to do so.

The Constitution also says that when a president is impeached, the chief justice shall preside over his trial in the Senate. The idea here was to have a presiding officer utterly free from even the appearance of conflict of interest. (Ordinarily, the presiding officer of the Senate is the vice president, and it would be unseemly for him to preside over a trial that could vault him into the presidency.) But Chief Justice William Rehnquist is the very man who handpicked the three judges who handpicked Starr. The independent counsel statute says that the three judges who pick a special prosecutor should never preside over trials initiated by that prosecutor—lest defendants and the public think that the fix is in, and that the judges will be tempted to make their choice look good. But now, if a trial in the Senate were to materialize, the chief justice can be seen to be linked to one side. If Starr isn't quite the chief's man, he is the man picked by the chief's men.

Consider next a more literal violation of the Constitution made visible by the Starr report. Why in the world are judges ever allowed to pick prosecutors? Judges are members of the judicial branch, and prosecutors wield executive power, which our Constitution vests in the president, not the judiciary. (Remember that, preceding the independent counsel statute, Watergate special prosecutors Archibald Cox and Leon Jaworski were technically appointed by the White House.) Having judges pick prosecutors is as inapt as having them pick generals or diplomats. The Constitution does say that the law may vest judges with unilateral power to pick "inferior" officers, but the obvious idea here is inferior *judicial* officers—magistrates and special masters. However, the Supreme Court rejected this logic a decade ago, in the *Morrison v. Olson* decision upholding an early version of the independent counsel statute. Last year, in the obscure case of *Edmond v. United States*, the Court seemed to repudiate its *Morrison* analysis by insisting that every "inferior" officer must have a clear "superior" with broad power to monitor and countermand his decisions. Under this test, Starr could not be called "inferior" because Janet Reno lacks broad power to control him—but it is unclear whether the Court would now be willing to use *Edmond* to openly overrule *Morrison* and apply its new test to Starr.

Where ordinary special prosecutors are involved, perhaps we could say that they are in some sense "inferior." These prosecutors are targeting officials other than the president, and if the president dislikes what a prosecutor is doing, he may always pardon the targets—even before indictment—and in effect make the prosecutor go away. (This is what President George H. W. Bush did to Iran-Contra independent counsel Lawrence Walsh by pardoning Walsh's target, Caspar Weinberger.) Through the pardon, the president maintains ultimate control over prosecutions, and can, at least arguably, keep special prosecutors in line as his "inferiors."

But when the president is himself the target of the special prosecutor—as was not the case in *Morrison*—he cannot in any conceivable way control the prosecutor because he cannot constitutionally pardon himself. Nor can he exempt himself from the impeachment process.

Thus, when Starr issues a report calling for the president's impeachment, he is clearly acting not as some inferior officer who can be countermanded by the chief executive. Rather, he is acting as one of the largest legal and political actors on our national stage. If we are to create this powerful a figure, the Constitution requires that such a grand officer be appointed by the president and confirmed by the Senate, receiving a personal vote of confidence from both political branches.

It's tempting to respond that Starr's report has no automatic legal significance—it is as if any private citizen "reported" to Congress and called for the president's impeachment. But this is laughable in fact and unsupportable in law. No private citizen is given the government funds and government power that Starr has been given. No private citizen is directed by law to give Congress impeachment reports.

There is a dangerous dance here. Starr does the dirty work and hands his report to Congress, which then publicizes it and even releases evidence gathered under grand jury secrecy. But neither takes full responsibility for its joint product. If Americans think Starr pushed too hard or was unfair, Congress can say, "Blame him, not us—it's his investigation and it's his report." And if Americans think that the report—and the videotape due out soon—should not have been publicized in the way it was, Starr can say, "Blame Congress, not me." The proper lines of constitutional accountability are being blurred.

So are the lines between criminal law and high politics. Presidential impeachment is not a technical issue of statute-book offenses—otherwise, it would have been given to judges, not politicians. Rather, the question of "high crimes and misdemeanors" is whether a president has engaged in such grave misconduct (whether or not technically criminal) that he is no longer fit to lead a great and free nation—whether, in other words, the votes of millions should be undone because of his gross misbehavior. Lying to the American people might well be more serious than lying in a civil deposition, even though the former is not a statute-book crime at all. And so Starr's inclusion of non-criminal matter is fitting in an impeachment report—but unfitting given that Starr is otherwise supposed to be a prosecutor, not an impeachment adviser. Ordinary prosecutors who uncover gross misbehavior that does not constitute a statute-book offense keep this to themselves. The proceedings of ordinary grand juries are secret. Ordinary prosecutors report to the Justice Department, not Congress. The report is a kind of hybrid monster—half indictment, half impeachment—the likes of which America has never seen.

Now that this beast roams among us, what are we to do? There is, alas, no easy way for Congress to cage what it has unleashed. After the havoc, Congress can say "Never again!" by allowing the independent counsel statute to die when it lapses by its own terms next year. But I am afraid we are in for dark and unpredictable days ahead, in which the only advice I could offer Congress would be to approach every issue in the most bipartisan manner possible. But that has not happened thus far, and is unlikely to happen in an election year.

And what shall I tell my students when they ask me to make constitutional sense of this report? It will be painful to tell them that a statute they were told was such a wonderful post-Watergate reform is, in fact, a constitutional abomination.

THE FLAW IN THE LAW

AMERICAN LAWYER, OCTOBER 1998

Awash in lurid detail, confounded by a gaping divide between the public and public opinion leaders, Americans may be tempted to personalize the high politics being played out inside the beltway and beyond. Ken Starr versus

Bill Clinton—Godzilla versus Kong, a fight to the (political) death of one or both. Starr lays out in painful detail Clinton's failings; Clinton, in turn, admits that he has sinned, but attacks Starr's personal ethics and professionalism. At times like this, it's easy to forget that ours is a government of laws and not merely of men. If the independent counsel has gone too far—less is sometimes more—we should blame the statute that made the excess possible rather than the man who carried it out. The fault, dear Bill, is not in Ken Starr but in yourself, and in the law you helped preserve.

In 1994, Clinton himself signed into law a continuation of the independent counsel statute first enacted in 1978, in Watergate's wake. But a prosecutor who answers to no one—who effectively has unlimited budgets and tenure, who is picked by the judiciary while wielding executive powers and performing legislative duties—is a constitutional monstrosity. We can repair the damage wrought by this monster only by fixing blame where it belongs—on the law itself.

Begin with Starr's appointment four years ago. To many, the choice was poetic justice. The great Archibald Cox was solicitor general under John Kennedy—the man who ran against Richard Nixon. Who better to investigate Bill Clinton than Starr, the solicitor general under George Bush—the man who ran against Clinton? But the surface symmetry fails at a deeper level. Nixon's own White House picked Cox and retained the legal right to fire him at will, as dramatized by the Saturday Night Massacre. By contrast, under the Independent Counsel Act of 1994, a special panel of judges named Starr, who cannot be dismissed at will by the attorney general. These key differences have allowed Starr's critics to issue sound bites about vast right-wing conspiracies. From one angle, the whole thing looks (or can be made to look) partisan and conspiratorial: After lunching with Republican senators, Republican judges on a special court crafted by a Republican chief justice pick a Republican independent counsel from a prior Republican administration.

Here we see a huge flaw in the independent counsel statute: It risks sucking the judiciary into partisan and personal politics. Suppose judges did indeed quietly consult senators before appointing Starr. Is it surprising that judges would seek private guidance from politicians when asked to perform a hugely political and nonjudicial task like picking someone to investigate the president? Instead of blaming the judges, or some conspiracy, blame the statute, which, incidentally, is set to expire again in June 1999.

Suppose further that Starr has occasionally blundered and showed poor prosecutorial judgment. The statute tells judges to pick prosecutors. Is it surprising that judges might pick a fellow judge with no prosecutorial experience? Is it surprising that someone with this background might make some rookie mistakes? We should predict that judges may not be good at picking prosecutors, because judges have inadequate information and weak incentives. The attorney general has a wealth of information about the track record of prosecutors. Judges do not—and should not—have access to this treasure trove of intra-executive intelligence, involving as it does various out-of-court behavior that lies beyond the proper province of judicial supervision. And when an appointing body is picking its own assistant, it obviously has strong incentives to pick well. If the subordinate does a bad job, other government officials and ordinary citizens will and should blame the boss. But when an independent counsel messes up, whom can we blame? Who is accountable?

To recast these objections as an argument from constitutional text, judges were allowed to pick independent counsel because such counsel are supposedly "inferior" officers under the Constitution's Article II appointments clause. But to whom is Starr inferior? How can there be an inferior without a superior? How can someone be both truly independent and yet truly inferior? In upholding the original post-Watergate independent counsel act of 1978, the U.S. Supreme Court in 1988 in *Morrison v. Olson* played fast and loose with the word "inferior." But last year in the little-noted *Edmond v. United States*, Justice Antonin Scalia won a strong majority for what was, in effect, his dissenting opinion in *Morrison*, leaving the constitutional status of *Morrison* and statutory independent counsel up in the air. According to *Edmond*, an inferior officer must have a superior, to whom he reports, and who has broad power to monitor and countermand him. If this test were honestly applied to Starr, he would flunk. Surely he is not inferior to the court that appointed him, for these judges do not and cannot monitor all his prosecutorial decisions. Nor is Starr inferior to Attorney General Janet Reno, who did not pick and cannot direct him. But would the Court, in fact, honestly apply its new test to Starr? *Edmond* maintained a coy silence on this $64,000 question.

The 1994 Independent Counsel Act also says that, once appointed by judges, the special prosecutor must be formally independent from ordinary oversight by the Justice Department. Is it surprising that an investigation so carefully shielded from all checks and accountability might become a run-away freight train?

In this context, then, consider the complaint that Starr has spent too long, and has lurched from one supposed scandal to another to another, in his quest to bring down Bill Clinton—Ahab chasing the great white whale to the ends of the earth. Here, too, the fault lies with the statute. It, in effect, designates Starr as Clinton's personal prosecutor: "Here is the man; now go find his crime, no matter how large or small. And spare no expense—the usual budgetary constraints that limit ordinary prosecutors do not apply to you." Combine this with a press and public that measure a prosecutor's success by the number of indictments and convictions rather than exonerations, and you have a dreadful set of incentives.

Why did Starr's investigation keep expanding from one supposed scandal to the next? Because at every juncture the attorney general kept referring new matters to him, and these referrals made a certain sense, given the screwy structure of the statute. Starr's operation was up and running, and the cast of characters in the various events overlapped. (Linda Tripp, it seems, was everywhere—near Vince Foster, in the thick of Travelgate, and as a comforting shoulder for both Kathleen Willey and Monica Lewinsky.) At each point it seemed more efficient to expand Starr's mandate rather than summon into existence a new counsel. A new special prosecutor would need to assemble a new team and get up to speed. What's more, he might be forever bumping into Starr, à la Alphonse and Gaston, as the two (or three or four) counsels decided whom to question when about what, whom to believe, whom to squeeze how hard, whom to immunize, and so forth.

Consider next Clinton's reminder that the Starr investigation is itself under investigation for improper and possibly illegal leaks. Here, too, blame the statute. A permanent organization like the Justice Department has years of experience to develop elaborate safeguards—protocols, routines, audits, and so on—assuring bureaucratic regularity and conformity to department policy. These are much harder to maintain in an ad hoc operation, staffed by volunteers who may sign up precisely because they want to nail the particular target of the investigation, who is known in advance.

To make matters worse, the statute combines the ordinary functions of prosecutors with special duties of impeachment advisers. Ordinarily, prosecutors confine themselves to actual statute-book offenses, and if the dirty laundry they uncover fails to meet that test, it often stays hidden. But when

Congress tells independent counsel to report possible impeachable misbehavior, ranging beyond statute-book crimes, Congress bends the traditional rules and roles beyond recognition. Prosecutors whose ordinary job requires them to screen out borderline material put all this gray stuff in—so that Congress can decide whether it is in fact enough. Traditional rules of grand jury secrecy bend to enable Congress to get all the key evidence. Worst of all, Congress in effect abdicates its own responsibility over the early stages of investigation by creating a cynical scheme of plausible deniability that blurs proper lines of constitutional responsibility. Instead of itself pursuing early impeachment investigations, using permanent House staff and special House appointees—whose abuses may be blamed on the House itself—Congress unloads the job on someone like Starr. If he pushes too hard and comes up empty, congressmen sanctimoniously declare themselves shocked, shocked, at the excess: "This is not what we intended when we passed the statute. Blame Starr, not us." But if a counsel finds something after all, then Congress will use his fruits for its own advantage.

In short, there is plenty of blame to go around in this mess. Blame Congress for having passed such an awful and unconstitutional statute. Blame the Supreme Court for having upheld this monstrosity in 1988, and then for not openly admitting its blunder more candidly in 1997. Blame Starr and the special court that appointed him, if you must, for having faithfully implemented the statute they were charged with faithfully implementing. But most of all, blame Bill Clinton for having resurrected the whole idea of an independent counsel statute in 1994. Of all the untrue and damaging words he has uttered in this sad affair, "This is a good bill that I sign into law today" were as harmful to the Republic as any he's spoken in public. Whoever is president next year, when the 1994 act mercifully expires, should think carefully before repeating this untruth.

HIGH CRIMES AND MISDEMEANORS

PUBLIC LECTURE IN WASHINGTON, DC,
WEDNESDAY, NOVEMBER 11, 1998[7]

The biggest linguistic question confronting America is not what the meaning of "is" is, nor what the words "sexual relations" mean. It is how to construe the phrase "high crimes and misdemeanors." Our legal tradition gives us simple but powerful tools to extract meaning from the Constitution. With these tools in hand, we can test whether Independent Counsel Kenneth Starr's report justifies ousting a duly elected president.

Begin with the hard-boiled realist claim that the Article II, section 4, phrase "high crimes and misdemeanors" means whatever the Congress wants it to mean—it's all politics. But it is not. The Constitution does not say that a president may be ousted whenever half of the House and two-thirds of the Senate want him out. The supreme law of the land prescribes a substantive standard—high misconduct—as well as a procedural voting rule, and conscientious legislators cannot ignore this standard. Even if we view the matter from a purely political perspective, taking hard-boiled realism on its own terms, a senator must say more than "I vote against Bill because I prefer Al (and I vote against Al because I prefer Newt)." Politically as well as constitutionally, lawmakers cannot credibly attack President Clinton for playing fast and loose with words while doing the same thing themselves. They cannot wax sanctimonious about oaths while ignoring their own oaths to uphold the Constitution.

But here is the kernel of truth in the realist claim: the House and Senate will be the last word on impeachment. No Article III court (or state court for that matter) will review their interpretation of the key phrase. Impeachment is, technically, what judges call a "political question" that ordinary courts will not touch. This is not an exception to the basic constitutional principle of judicial review, but a special instance of it. There is indeed "judicial" review of impeachment issues, but this review occurs in the Senate itself, which sits as a high court of impeachment. Its impeachment verdict conclusively binds other courts because this special tribunal has exclusive jurisdiction, and its rulings on fact and law are what lawyers call res judicata—final judgments. Over and over, the Constitution describes the Senate in impeachment as a court—with the power to "try" "cases," render "judgment," and impose "conviction" on the defendant. In presidential impeachments, this judicial character is reinforced by a constitutional rule that the chief justice shall preside over the high court of the Senate. These judicial trappings are further evidence that, contrary to hard-boiled realism, it is not all politics—it is also a judicial trial under the law designed to impose punishment for "high crimes."

If the Senate must act as a court, with a duty to properly construe "high crimes and misdemeanors," how should it go about this task? Ordinary courts often look first to judicial precedent, but this interpretive tool is of little help here. The Supreme Court has never defined "high crimes and misdemeanors"—even if it did, the Senate should feel free to ignore such inappropriate intermeddling—and the precedents in the Senate itself shed little light. In a dozen cases over the last two centuries, the Senate has tried impeachments of judges and cabinet officers, but how much (if any) weight should these precedents carry in a presidential impeachment? The only Senate precedents that could definitively clarify the standards for presidential impeachment would themselves be presidential impeachments. But we have only one of these on the books, and that impeachment—of Andrew Johnson in 1868—resulted in an acquittal, leaving us precisely zero square senatorial precedents telling us what misconduct is enough to oust a president.

Some scholars have suggested that we look to history for answers. But which history? The phrase "high crimes and misdemeanors" took root in fourteenth-century England. Surely this is not the right time and place to search for answers. Practices that may have made sense in a monarchy or in a parliamentary government have no place in a modern constitutional democracy committed to separation of powers. The history of the 1787 Philadelphia Convention helps clarify what was in the minds of the drafters when they inserted the "high crimes" phraseology and rejected the looser idea that presidents could be impeached merely for "maladministration." But these convention conversations occurred behind closed doors. The American people were asked to ratify a public text, not secret intentions. What's more, our constitutional system for selecting presidents differs from the system in place in 1787. Aided by a formal constitutional amendment (the Twelfth) that paved the way for a two-party presidential system to emerge, modern America has committed itself to a kind of populist and partisan presidency that differs from what the Philadelphia draftsmen had in mind.

What, then, is the best way to make sense of our Constitution on the key question of the day? I suggest that we carefully examine the Constitution's text, and attend to its overarching structure. Begin with the obvious tool of textual analysis. The key phrase, in its entirety, says that the president may be impeached for "Treason, Bribery, or other high Crimes and Misdemeanors." Presumably, the word "high" here means something, suggesting that not all crimes (or other forms of misconduct) justify impeachment. If we seek to discover how "high" a crime must be, the text itself gives us two specific examples to anchor the inquiry: treason and bribery. Both are "high" crimes indeed. Treason involves waging war against America, betraying one's country to an enemy power. Bribery—secretly bending laws to favor the rich and powerful—involves official corruption of a highly malignant sort, threatening the very soul of a democracy committed to equality under the law. And in the case of a president who does not take bribes but gives them—paying people to vote for him—the bribery undermines the very legitimacy of the election that brought him to office. Few crimes are as deadly to a democratic republic—as high—as treason and bribery.

Those who argue that any presidential failure to obey the law constitutes a failure to "take care that the laws be faithfully executed," and that all such failures are impeachable, have simply read the word "high" out of the Constitution. On their theory, any crime, high or low, would be impeachable. Consider, in this regard, the words of the Article I, section 6, arrest clause and the Article IV, section 2, extradition clause. Like the impeachment clause, these clauses also speak of treason and other crimes. But they do so in markedly different language—"Treason, Felony, and Breach of the Peace" in the arrest clause, and "Treason, Felony, or other Crime" in the extradition clause. These clauses do encompass virtually all crimes, high and low. And they strongly suggest that the word "high" in the impeachment clause must be taken seriously. When the framers meant all crimes, high and low, they knew the words—and the words are markedly different from those of the impeachment clause.

So much for text. Consider now how the text must be read in light of larger constitutional principles defining the Constitution's overall architecture—its structure. The Constitution's text does not use the words "federalism," or "separation of powers," or "judicial review," but these principles can be discerned from the document's structural blueprint. The first insight generated by structural analysis is that the meaning of a single constitutional phrase sometimes varies, as that phrase interacts with other parts of the document: The words "high crimes" might, in application, mean something somewhat different when applied to presidents than when applied to other impeachable officers.

A blinkered textualist might deny this, pointing to Article II, section 4, in its entirety: "The President, Vice President and all civil officers of the United States, shall be removed from Office on Impeachment for, and Conviction of, Treason, Bribery, or other high Crimes and Misdemeanors." This clause lumps together presidential impeachments with all others (of vice presidents, judges, justices, cabinet officers, inferior officers) and uses the same linguistic standard (high crimes) across the board.

At first this seems a strong argument. But it crumbles on closer inspection—and every senator should intuitively understand why. Consider another patch of constitutional text familiar to every senator and implicating Senate oversight of the president. According to Article II, section 2, "by and with the Advice and Consent of the Senate [the president] shall appoint Ambassadors, other public Ministers and Consuls, Judges of the supreme Court, and all other Officers of the United States." If we applied the same blinkered textualism to this clause, we would say that the Senate must give the exact same deference to a president's choice for Supreme Court justice that it would give to a president's choice for his cabinet, and that the Senate should never apply a stricter standard when considering a nomination to the Supreme Court than to a district court. After all, this clause lumps together all officers, high and low, executive and judicial, and uses the same linguistic standard (advice and consent) across the board.

But this has never been the Senate's view of the matter—and rightly so. The Senate has rejected blinkered textualism in favor of a more structural and holistic approach that ponders all the texts of the Constitution and considers their interrelation. Other parts of the Constitution establish important differences between, say, cabinet officers and judges. Cabinet officers are part of the president's executive branch team under Article II. They answer to him (quite literally, in the Article II, section 2, opinions clause) and will leave when he leaves. Federal judges are not part of the president's team in the same sense. They will not leave when he leaves. Indeed, their independence is secured by life tenure under Article III—a separate article for a separate branch. In light of these important constitutional differences, the Senate has always given the president far more leeway in naming his own executive team than in proposing judicial nominees. And, even within a single branch, the Senate scrutinizes a nominee to the Supreme Court more intensely than a nominee to some lower court. Just ask Robert Bork.

Now apply these structural insights to the "high crimes" clause, and count the ways in which presidential impeachments are qualitatively different from all others. When senators remove one of a thousand federal judges (or even one of nine justices), they are not transforming an entire branch of government. But that is exactly what happens when they oust America's one and only president, in whom all executive power is vested by the first sentence of Article II. In the case of a judge, a long and grueling impeachment trial itself inflicts no great trauma on the nation—but, again, the case of a president is very different. (And don't forget the disruption of the chief justice's schedule, and the commandeering of the entire Senate; only in presidential impeachments must the chief justice preside, and this special rule makes it virtually impossible for the Senate to shunt off important presidential impeachment decisions to smaller committees, as is the current practice for nonpresidential impeachments.) Presidential impeachments involve high statecraft and international affairs—the entire world is watching—in a manner wholly unlike other impeachments.

Most important, when senators oust a judge, they undo their own prior vote (via advice and consent to judicial nominees). When they remove a duly elected president, they undo the votes of millions of ordinary Americans on Election Day. This is not something that senators should do lightly, lest we slide toward a kind of parliamentary government that our entire structure of government was designed to repudiate. Although the Philadelphia framers may not have anticipated the rise of a populist presidency, later generations of Americans restructured the Philadelphians' electoral college, via the Twelfth Amendment and other election reforms, precisely to facilitate such a presidency. Narrow arguments from the high crimes clause in isolation fail to see how holistic constitutional analysis must take account of post-Founding constitutional developments.

To recast these points about constitutional structure into the language of policy, even if the Senate decides that all perjury—of any sort, by any officer—is an impeachable high crime, senators must further decide whether a given perjury warrants removal as a matter of sound judgment and statesmanship. In making this decision, they must be sensitive to the ways in which the presidency is a very different office from a federal district judgeship. Where extremely "high crimes" are implicated—treason or tyranny—senators should probably be quicker to pull the trigger on a bad president, whose office enables him unilaterally to do many dangerous things. (A single bad judge, by contrast, is hemmed in by colleagues and higher courts.) But where borderline or low "high crimes" are involved, the Senate would be wise to spare the people's president—especially if his crimes reflect character flaws that the people duly considered before voting for him, or if the people continue to support him even after the facts come to light. If we absolutely insist on textual (as opposed to structural) evidence supporting our distinction between presidential and judicial impeachments, we can find it in Article I, section 3, which tells us that only in presidential impeachments does the chief justice preside. There are several good reasons for this rule, and one of them is to hammer home the constitutional uniqueness of presidential impeachments.

With the lessons of text and structure in mind, we can now profitably revisit precedent and history. Those who point to three judicial impeachments in the late 1980s as support for a low impeachment threshold have precisely missed the point: We must look to presidential history and precedent for guidance. To counterbalance the 1980s trio of judicial impeachments (of Harry Claiborne, Alcee Hastings, and Walter Nixon), let's look at a trio of presidents over the centuries who had their own troubles with Congress.

Begin with Andrew Jackson, who killed a man in a duel before he was elected president. Technically, this was a crime—although rarely prosecuted. Should Congress have impeached and removed Jackson—even if the people who elected him knew about his crime, and elected him anyway? The duel Jackson fought concerned his wife's honor and chastity. Suppose Jackson had lied under oath to protect his wife's honor. Again, suppose the people knew all this when they voted for him. Should Congress have undone the people's votes, on a theory that all crime is high crime, and that all perjury is the same?

Now consider Andrew Johnson. Given our structural analysis, it seems relevant that Johnson was never elected president in his own right, and that he was in fact trying to undo the policies of the man the people had elected, Abraham Lincoln. If ever our structural argument cautioning restraint in ousting an elected president was weak, it was here, since Johnson lacked a genuine electoral mandate. And his policies toward the defeated rebels could indeed have been viewed as akin to treason, giving considerable aid and comfort to various rebels who were—not to mince words—traitors. And yet even here—an unelected president cozying up to actual traitors—the Senate acquitted.

Finally, consider Richard Nixon, whose extremely high crimes and gross abuses of official power did indeed pose a threat to our basic constitutional system, a threat as high as treason and bribery. Although Nixon was elected by the people, his own unprecedented use of political espionage and sabotage tainted his mandate, in the same way that bribing electors would have. When all the facts were brought to light and the tapes came out, the people did indeed turn against him, prompting leaders of both parties to conclude that the time had come for him to go.

Bill Clinton is not above the law. But the law that the Congress must apply is the law applicable to presidents, not the law applicable to district judges. In trying a man whose name has eerily intertwined with that of Nixon again and again, Congress must remember that Bill Clinton is best judged in light of the case of President Richard Nixon, not the case of Judge Walter Nixon.

Using standard tools of constitutional analysis, then, here are the questions conscientious congressmen should ask themselves as they ponder the Starr report: Are the alleged misdeeds truly as malignant and threatening to democratic government as are treason and bribery? Do they justify putting the nation and the world through the obvious trauma that an impeachment trial itself—whatever its outcome—would involve? Do the misdeeds justify nullifying the votes of millions of Americans, on the assumption that they would never have voted for Bill Clinton had they suspected he was capable of doing what the report alleges? Would virtually all past presidents—none of whom has been removed, and only one of whom was even impeached— have easily passed the standard being proposed by those who argue for Clinton's impeachment?

How high is high enough? The Constitution cannot answer that question for us, but it can give us the right questions to ask.

THE PEOPLE'S COURT

AMERICAN LAWYER ONLINE, JANUARY 1999[8]

Who rules America—the people or the law? Representative Henry Hyde and his fellow House impeachment managers have wrapped themselves in "the rule of law"—the polls favoring President Clinton be damned! But under our Constitution, We the People ordained and established the law, and the law itself often encourages senators to defer to the people's verdict.

Sometimes, the rule of law does require a senator to damn the polls. If in her heart a senator thinks the president is innocent in fact (he actually did not do it) or in law (even if he did it, it is not a "high crime or misdemeanor"), then she must vote not guilty—even if she thereby offends her constituents, who want the man's head. She has taken a solemn oath to do justice, and she would violate that oath if she voted to convict a man she believed innocent. Impeachment is a quasi-criminal affair, in which the Senate, sitting as a court, is asked to convict the defendant of high criminality or gross misbehavior in a trial designed not merely to remove but also to stigmatize the offending officeholder. No senator may properly vote to convict Bill Clinton, merely because, say, her constituents prefer Al Gore.

But none of this helps Henry Hyde and company, who are of course the ones seeking Clinton's head. Impeachment rules are not symmetric between conviction and acquittal. It takes sixty-seven votes to convict, but only thirty-four to acquit; the House must prove the president guilty, but the president need not prove anything. Similarly, although no senator may vote to convict a man she deems innocent, any senator may vote to acquit a man he deems guilty. Like any ordinary criminal juror, each senator is free to be merciful for a wide variety of reasons—because she thinks the defendant has suffered enough, or because the punishment does not fit the crime, or because punishing the defendant would impose unacceptable costs on innocent third parties.

In pondering mercy, ordinary jurors search their souls as the conscience of the community, and senators are free to do the same. But unlike ordinary jurors, senators are elected, and thus they are also free to consult their constituents. Sometimes, deferring to "the masses" might be irresponsible—for example, if the citizenry were ignorant of the facts or incapable of thinking through the complicated legal question at hand. Under these circumstances, Hyde might be right to urge senators to look only to their souls and not to the polls. But is the Clinton case one where the people are ignorant, or simply one where Hyde refuses to heed their judgment?

Again and again, the House managers have invoked "the Founders." But fidelity to the Founders and fidelity to the Constitution are very different things. Since the Founding, We the People have amended our supreme law in many ways designed to make it more democratic than the musty eighteenth-century parchment that the managers wrongly equate with "the Constitution." Consider for example the impeachment court itself. In the Founders' Constitution, the Senate was elected by state legislators, rather than by the people themselves. But the Seventeenth Amendment, adopted in 1913, brought the Senate closer to the people by mandating direct election—and thereby importantly, if implicitly, modified the basic structure of impeachment. Likewise, the presidency created at Philadelphia was vastly different from the one We the People claim for ourselves today. In the late 1780s, a national two-party system did not exist and presidents were not picked by the direct votes of millions of citizens. (Much of the change toward a more populist and party-based presidency occurred as a result of the

Twelfth Amendment, which radically revised the electoral college system forged in Philadelphia.) In 1789, many state legislatures opted to pick presidential electors themselves, and thereby excluded ordinary voters from directly participating in the process of presidential selection; in 1999, it would be unthinkable for any state to revert to this practice. In the Founders' world, presidents were picked without regard to the preferences of blacks and women.

In fact, the Philadelphia framers designed their original electoral college precisely to make it easy for states to disenfranchise blacks and women. A given state—say, Virginia—would receive a fixed number of electoral votes, regardless of whether the state let blacks or women vote. (Under direct national election, by contrast, Virginia would automatically double its clout if—God forbid!—it extended the franchise to women.) But later generations of Americans amended the document to make clear that black and female votes must be counted: That is the basic meaning of the Fifteenth and Nineteenth Amendments.

None of the House managers is black, and none is a woman. Yet they seek to undo the election of a man who was voted for (and who continues to be supported) by large numbers of blacks and women. None of the managers is a member of the Democratic Party. And yet they seek to unseat a duly elected Democratic president. And they continue to insist, woodenly, that removing a man voted for by millions of ordinary people is, under our Constitution, exactly the same as removing any one of a thousand federal judges that none of us ever voted for.

On the merits of the case, maybe the managers are right, and the people are wrong. Maybe Clinton is unfit to lead a great and free people. But as every first-year law student learns, the basic question in constitutional law is often "Who decides?" To succeed, the House managers must persuade the people, not ignore them.

IMPARTIALITY AND IMPARTISANSHIP

AMERICAN LAWYER ONLINE, JANUARY 1999

The Constitution requires that when senators sit as judges and jurors in a high court of impeachment, they must "be on Oath or Affirmation." Earlier this month, each senator took such a special oath, swearing under God to do "impartial justice." Immediately thereafter, the senators—all of them—engaged in conduct that arguably betrayed the letter and spirit of that oath.

Exactly what are the senators supposed to be impartial between? Truth and falsity? Surely not—they should be partial to the truth and dead-set against falsity. The prosecution and the defense? Perhaps, but in key ways the system is designed to be asymmetric. Sixty-seven senators must vote to convict, whereas a mere thirty-four senators will suffice to acquit; this is a partial rule, tilted toward the defendant. So is the notion that evidence of President Clinton's guilt must be proved beyond a reasonable doubt, or at least by clear and convincing evidence. Some forms of partiality toward the defendant are proper and even mandatory.

Given that justice need not be impartial between the prosecutor and the defendant, the better idea is that it should be impartial across potential defendants. A given senator should treat Clinton no differently than she would treat any other defendant president. It should not matter whether she is a friend or an enemy of Clinton—she should treat him the same way.

But this logic has radical implications, which the senators have failed to heed. To be truly, deeply, really, impartial, each senator must be *im-party-al*. That is, each senator should try to wholly blot out of her legal decision making all issues concerning political party. Impartial justice must be the same for Republican and Democratic presidents alike. One way to implement this ideal is to imagine that the defendant on trial is not Bill Clinton, but is instead a Republican president who did the same thing. Another way to do this is for a senator to imagine that she were actually a member of the other political party. But both of these imaginative exercises are psychologically hard to do—akin to writing sci-fi scripts involving parallel universes.

There is, however, one thing that a truly conscientious senator can easily do: Shun any "party" caucus discussing impeachment issues. Senators must be free to talk informally among themselves and in small groups—but party affiliation should play no role whatsoever. Any Democrat who wants to listen in on a "Republican" caucus should be allowed to do so, and vice versa. Ordinary judges, when they deliberate, never break up into Democratic and Republican caucuses, and neither do ordinary jurors. Thus, when senators last week took their oaths and then immediately proceeded to "party" caucuses, they betrayed the deep aspiration implicit in their oath of impartiality—of *im-partisanship*. Although they eventually came together and agreed on a unanimous proposal, none of the senators has said that party caucuses in impeachment are improper, and none has promised to boycott all such caucuses in the future.

It cannot be said that party caucuses are simply unavoidable. The eventual agreement that emerged last week came from a caucus that included all and excluded none, giving us a genuine model of what workable im-partisanship can look like. Party caucuses are a staple of legislative sausage making, but an impeachment trial is not legislative business as usual. Impeachment is in important ways a judicial act, governed by a special ethos. Indeed, the impeachment oath was designed to remind senators (and the rest of us) of the special rules and roles required.

Oaths are serious business. President Clinton is where he is today—in the dock—because of claims that he did not take his various oaths (of marriage, of office, in the *Jones* case, and before the grand jury) seriously enough. Senators who sit in judgment over him—especially those who may be tempted to condemn him—should take a close look at their own oaths and deeds.

THE UNIMPERIAL PRESIDENCY

NEW REPUBLIC, MONDAY, MARCH 8, 1999

The Senate has acquitted Bill Clinton; he will now join Andrew Johnson in obloquy, but he will not join Richard Nixon in utter political ruin. It is a victory, of sorts, for this president. But is it a victory for the presidency? After the many legal battles over sex, lies, and audiotape, what is left of the office itself, its powers and privileges? The answer, alas, is that the legal precedents sprouting from the Clinton scandals have done considerable damage to the presidency, leaving us with an office weaker in key respects than the one that the Founders envisioned.

But, before we begin blaming Ken Starr and Henry Hyde, we should stop to consider that today's Democratic chief executive is reaping what was sown by Republican Richard Nixon's antagonists during Watergate. To be precise, we are all witnessing the consequences of the bad law made during the Supreme Court's celebrated 1974 decision in the Nixon Tapes case. The enemy then was the imperial presidency. But, in hindsight, the tapes case opinion reflects a troubling imperialism of its own—judicial imperialism. The justices reached the right result, but their reasons were remarkably sloppy and self-aggrandizing. As a result, lawyers and judges dealing with big issues raised by the Clinton presidency—the legal status of independent counsels, the amenability of sitting presidents to lawsuits or indictments, the concept of executive privilege, the proper role of Secret Service agents—have seen the world through a distorted lens.

There may still be time to repair our misshapen law of the presidency. Indeed, the best time for reform is now, before we know whether the next president will be a Republican or Democrat. But, before we can move ahead, we must go back and see exactly how the law first went wrong in 1974.

Consider the caption: *United States v. Nixon*. Criminal prosecution is an executive branch function, and the dramatic opening words of Article II of the Constitution vest all executive power in the president. How, then, could special prosecutor Leon Jaworski—an "inferior" officer within the executive branch—claim to represent "the United States" against the pronouncements of its chief executive? In 1974, this was no pedantic quibble. It implicated whether courts could even hear the case and how they would be obliged to rule if they reached the merits. Separation of powers militated against judicial intervention in an intra-executive dispute, and the Court's more general precedents cast doubt on whether a person could sue himself. Given that Jaworski was nothing more than Nixon's subordinate, wasn't the case really Nixon (inferior) v. Nixon (real)? If Jaworski wanted the tapes disclosed for good executive-branch reasons (the need to prosecute criminals), and Nixon wanted the tapes kept secret for good executive-branch reasons (Oval Office confidentiality), shouldn't the president ordinarily and obviously have the last word?

The Court's solution was strained. Chief Justice Warren Burger's unanimous opinion first analogized the dispute to one "between two congressional committees." But this was spurious. Two committees are presumptively coordinate authorities; Nixon and Jaworski were not. Constitutionally, Nixon was president and Jaworski was an inferior officer. Democratically, Nixon had been elected by the nation and Jaworski had not even been confirmed by the Senate. Their dispute was more like one between the Court and a law clerk.

Next, Burger invoked a Nixon administration regulation in which Nixon promised Jaworski a free hand in his investigation and further promised not to fire Jaworski without the concurrence of congressional leaders (to avoid another Saturday Night Massacre). This regulation, said Burger, had "the force of law," empowering executive inferior Jaworski to contest chief executive Nixon. Because of this "law," Burger declared his Court free to decide who was right and to ignore who was boss.

But this was hard to maintain with a straight face: Any legally binding regulation of this kind would have been flatly unconstitutional. As President George Washington and Congressman James Madison established at the Founding, the president does not need Congress's blessing when deciding whom to fire within the executive branch; Congress members cannot legally inject themselves into this removal process. The Court emphatically endorsed this view in a 1926 case, *Myers v. United States*, which remains good law today. If the regulation had legally given congressional leaders a legislative veto over Jaworski's removal, it was invalid under both *Myers* and more general principles that the Court would later reaffirm. Thus, the Nixon regulation could only be understood as a mere read-my-lips political promise.[9]

Even if the regulation somehow counted as law, the Court conceded that Nixon was free to rescind it unilaterally—and then Nixon could tell Jaworski what to do or where to go. But why, then, were the justices insisting that Nixon first rescind, and only then countermand Jaworski? Why wasn't it enough that, in their very courtroom, the president was clearly saying that he disagreed with his subordinate? The best answer is one the Court never stated forthrightly: Richard Nixon was involved in a criminal conspiracy to obstruct justice, and the Court already had evidence under seal that proved this. If Nixon wanted to fire or countermand Jaworski, he would not get a finger of support from the justices; he would have to do it himself (twice!) at high noon on Main Street, for all to see.

Only the Court's private knowledge of Nixon's plain guilt can account for the screwy things that Burger's opinion went on to say. In *United States v. Burr*, an 1807 lower-court case decided by Chief Justice John Marshall riding circuit, Marshall had subpoenaed documents from President Thomas Jefferson. Burger insisted that Marshall's subpoena was indistinguishable from the one sought by Jaworski. But this was obtuse. In *Burr*, a defendant, Aaron Burr, sought to subpoena evidence to prove his innocence, whereas in *Nixon*, the "government" (i.e., Jaworski) sought to subpoena evidence to prove the guilt of various Watergate defendants. Fundamental issues of due process and fairness were at stake in *Burr*: The government cannot prosecute a man while suppressing evidence of his innocence. Had Jefferson resisted the subpoena—based on perfectly legitimate confidentiality considerations— Marshall would never have tried to coerce the president to comply. Instead, Marshall would simply have dismissed the prosecution and released the defendant. The Constitution and laws nowhere demanded that Burr must be prosecuted; they merely required that, if prosecuted, he be given exculpatory evidence. *Burr* thus respected the president's right to decide the executive-branch policy question at hand. It was left up to Jefferson to choose which was more important to him—convicting Burr or keeping confidential communications secret.

But Burger turned *Burr* upside down, insisting that due process demanded that all possible evidence of the criminal defendants' guilt must be produced, even if both the defendants and the president preferred otherwise. He went on to imply that any rule limiting prosecutors' ability to procure "all relevant and admissible evidence" was constitutionally suspect—an odd view that would seem to undermine every traditional evidentiary privilege, from the attorney-client privilege to the one shielding doctor-patient communications.

The Court did purport to recognize a limited privilege for confidential Oval Office conversations but said it had to be balanced against the judicial need for evidence. In this "balance"—with judges holding the scales—the need for confidentiality was, said Burger, ordinarily outweighed (absent national security concerns) if the evidence sought for a judicial proceeding was specific, admissible, and relevant. This was really no privilege at all—*anyone* can resist a subpoena that is overbroad or irrelevant. Thus, on Burger's logic, essential and wholly proper but politically sensitive conversations in the Oval Office were entitled to less protection than ordinary conversations between attorneys and clients.

Imagine, for example, that the president is considering whether to appoint Jane Doe to a high government post. Aides brief the president, reporting various facts and rumors about Doe, her family, and her friends. For the president to do his job right, he needs to hear this sensitive information. But the Nixon Tapes case, if we take it seriously, suggests that any county prosecutor, or any plaintiff in a civil case, could subpoena this conversation in a lawsuit designed to embarrass Doe or the president. If so, aides would hesitate to tell the president what he needs to know to do his job.

Admittedly, the Constitution does not create executive privilege in so many words. But it does create a system of federalism and separation of powers. As a matter of federalism, state and local prosecutors cannot be allowed to disrupt the proper performance of national executive functions. As a matter of separation of powers, each branch must have some space—a separate house, if you will—in which to ponder its delicate business free from the intermeddling of other branches. Senators must be free to talk candidly and confidentially among themselves and with staff in cloakrooms; judges must enjoy comparable freedom in conversations with law clerks; jurors ordinarily deliberate secretly; and the same basic principle holds true for the presidency. This principle was explicitly affirmed in no less a case than *Marbury v. Madison*. When Attorney General Levi Lincoln hesitated to answer certain questions about what President Jefferson had confided to him, feeling "himself bound to maintain the rights of the executive," the *Marbury* Court reassured him that "if he thought that any thing was communicated to him in confidence he was not bound to disclose it." Burger mentioned none of this.

Here is what Burger should have said: "Inherent in the executive power vested in the president by Article II is the general right to decide who shall be prosecuted, and how, and also the right to keep confidential good-faith conversations with executive-branch aides about proper executive-branch policy. But, like other privileges in our law, executive privilege has limits and exceptions. Under the well-established crime-fraud exception, attorneys cannot invoke lawyer-client privilege when independent evidence confirms that they are trying to cover up ongoing criminal misconduct and obstruction of justice. Similarly, conversations by executive officials planning ongoing crimes are not protected by Article II. The conversations sought by Jaworski are conversations among persons designated by the grand jury as coconspirators—including Nixon, though the president was not indicted. The evidence under seal already in the Court's possession provides strong and independent confirmation of this conspiracy. Under these unusual circumstances, executive privilege yields."

Burger instead wrote a sweeping opinion that had the virtue of not attacking Richard Nixon personally and the vice of making no sense when honestly applied to honest presidents.

The tapes case not only trivialized the presidency; it also imperialized the judiciary and marginalized the legislature. The justices doubtless feared that Nixon might defy their orders—this explains why all eight participating justices signed Burger's ill-reasoned opinion. Fear of defiance also helps explain the opinion's overblown rhetoric proclaiming the Court "the ultimate interpreter of the Constitution" (language not found in *Marbury* and never appearing in *U.S. Reports* before the 1960s). But this lofty rhetoric, combined with the immediate effect of the case, shoved Congress offstage. Nixon surrendered the tapes, the smoking gun came out, and soon Nixon was gone. The Court had spared the country the agony of a possibly long and painful impeachment. But the result was to short-circuit an impressive incipient effort by Congress to take its own constitutional role seriously, depriving future Congresses of a modern model for presidential impeachment.

The framers made Congress the main watchdog, via oversight and impeachment, for a reason. Unlike a lone prosecutor trying to take down a president with the aid of judges—sound like anyone we know?—Congress would be democratically accountable. This would deter witch-hunting; the president might be an innocent man and so accusations against him would need to be carefully screened. By giving the primary screening function to Congress, the framers created a structurally superior system to one relying upon unaccountable prosecutors or plaintiffs and unelected judges. But the structural lesson taught by *Nixon* was different: Trust the Court, distrust the president, and ignore the Congress.

The independent counsel statute, passed in 1978, magnified *Nixon*'s pathologies. For starters, the statute dramatically inflated the role of judges. In Watergate, Nixon's White House itself had picked Archibald Cox and Jaworski, and it retained formal power to remove them. Politics, not law, determined whether an outside prosecutor would be named, who he would be, how he would operate, and when (if ever) he would be removed. In making these decisions, the White House had to listen to congressional critics, or risk a political backlash. And the system worked—just the way the framers would have wanted. Cox and Jaworski had great credibility. Nixon retained the right to fire them anytime, but only at his political peril, as the Saturday Night Massacre proved.

Rushing to "reform," post-Watergate lawmakers created a constitutional Frankenstein. Under the independent counsel statute, judges would pick special prosecutors, nominally supervise them, and ultimately decide whether to remove them. But this system was plainly unconstitutional. Under a proper vision of separation of powers, judges should appoint only inferior officers within the judiciary—magistrates, clerks, and masters—not prosecutors within the executive branch. And surely judges should not be in the business of monitoring investigations; this, too, is an executive function, not a judicial one. But the statute naturally flowed from the warped logic of *Nixon*—turning its regulation-as-law gambit into a literal law limiting presidential removal, contra *Myers*, and thrusting judges into intra-executive policy.

The proper job of judges is to decide cases under law in open court after hearing public arguments. But no law can tell judges whom to choose as a prosecutor in a given case. This is a question of personnel and policy, not law; to decide it well, judges must consult leading politicians. But judges should shun this business as altogether too political, partisan, and secretive. Judges may be tempted to pick a fellow judge with no prosecutorial experience, who may in turn make rookie mistakes. (Again, sound familiar?) And, if judges are really to monitor their creature, they must themselves become superprosecutors, considering all sorts of secret material in closed chambers, in violation of deep judicial norms. If not, independent counsels answer to no one, thereby violating the Article II appointments clause, which requires that an "inferior" officer must have a superior.

The judiciary's gain in power was, in part, Congress's loss. Instead of acting as a watchdog, Congress surrenders the job to an independent counsel picked by judges, blurring the lines of democratic accountability. If the counsel errs, Congress says, blame him (or the court), not us. Whereas the Founders carefully kept judges out of the impeachment process, the statute sucks them in. The judicial branch picks an executive officer who serves as formal impeachment adviser to the legislature. This is an obvious distortion of the Founders' model. In the past year, we have repeatedly seen judges involved in the presidential impeachment process—for example, authorizing the transfer of grand jury material to Congress and even obliging a potential impeachment witness to meet (secretly) with House managers in the middle of an ongoing impeachment trial. Federal judges would never involve themselves in procedural issues arising in an ongoing state prosecution, but have shown less restraint vis-à-vis impeachment, again following *Nixon*'s script, where judges rushed into the middle of an impeachment to save the country.

The statute also trivializes the executive branch—and here, too, it tracks *Nixon*. Its hair trigger evinces pathological distrust of the attorney general, the Justice Department, and the entire executive branch. If Kenneth Starr has visions of grandeur—thinking that he, not an elected president, represents "the United States"—these visions are nurtured by a statute nurtured by *Nixon*. If Starr has pushed too hard to uncover every possible crime of every possible defendant by relentlessly pursuing every possible scrap of evidence—subpoenaing bookstores, pressuring a mother to betray her daughter's secrets, piercing presidential privacy, shredding executive privilege, and shrinking attorney-client privilege—this, too, follows the anti-defendant, anti-privilege, anti-prosecutorial-discretion script of *Nixon*.

When the independent counsel statute first came before the Court in the 1988 *Morrison v. Olson* case, seven justices voted to uphold it. *Morrison* winked at the word "inferior," slighted the fact that Article II vests all executive power in the president, and disregarded the objection that judges were performing plainly executive tasks. In each of these respects, *Morrison* followed *Nixon*. Only Justice Antonin Scalia dissented, in a brilliant and prescient opinion that also gave *Nixon* a more narrow reading than was then fashionable.

Then came the Paula Jones case of 1997, and here the presidency didn't even get Scalia's vote. In the three landmark cases of *Nixon, Morrison,* and *Jones,* the combined vote was 24–1 against the presidency. The imperial presidency was surely dead.

But perhaps presidential imperialism was a phony threat all along. The word "imperial" conjures up images of kings ruling by divine right. Presidents are elected by the people. When they are unable to do the people's business because of unilateral decisions of unelected folk—Paula Jones, or Lawrence Walsh, or Ken Starr, or Susan Webber Wright—which way does "imperialism" cut? Kings rule for life. Presidents are limited to two terms, and so, even if lawsuits were generally barred against sitting presidents, plaintiffs could have their day in court after a president leaves office, when the people's business would not be thereby disrupted.

The *Jones* opinion by Justice John Paul Stevens (the first man appointed to the Court in the wake of Watergate) also followed *Nixon*. If Nixon could be obliged to answer Jaworski's call for tapes, shouldn't Clinton be obliged to answer Jones's civil complaint? The overreading of *Burr* in *Nixon* was also key in *Jones*. Stevens leaned heavily on *Burr* but never paused to consider how Jefferson had remained free to disregard Marshall's subpoena by just dropping the case. By contrast, Clinton could disregard the *Jones* ruling only by suffering a default judgment at considerable personal expense. Thus, *Jones* took a big step beyond *Burr*—and beyond *Nixon*, too, given the *Nixon* Court's concession that Nixon could, in two steps, fire Jaworski and keep the tapes. This does not prove that *Jones* was wrong, merely that it was sloppy, making new law without even realizing it—and rather badly misreading the historical evidence to boot.

And, like *Nixon, Jones* reflected a remarkably self-satisfied view of federal judges. Trust us federal courts, said *Jones*, to sensitively manage lawsuits against the president. Against this institutional smugness, is it impolite to note that the entire national agenda of the past year was derailed because of a legal error of Judge Susan Webber Wright's? Under a proper view of Fourth Amendment privacy and Federal Rules of Civil Procedure 26(c) and 45(c), Clinton should never have been forced to answer questions about his consensual sexual activity, given that his answer could implicate serious privacy interests of a nonparty to this civil suit (Lewinsky) in the absence of a compelling need. But on this key issue Judge Wright was Judge Wrong when it counted (at the deposition), and, had it not been for this error, Clinton's alleged crimes *would never have occurred*. In wrongly requiring disclosure of intimate and confidential relations, however, Judge Wright was in a way merely following the twisted logic of *Nixon* and its insistence on evidence over privacy.

Judge Wright is not alone. Most federal judges have internalized a master narrative in which *Nixon* was the work of heroic judges who saved the rule of law: Judges are presumptively good, presidents presumptively bad. This is the theme of a trio of Clinton-scandal-era circuit court decisions involving Secret Service privilege and government-attorney privilege.

In the Secret Service case, a three-judge panel of the United States Court of Appeals for the District of Columbia Circuit dismissed the suggestion that agents should not be obliged to testify against their boss unless they actually saw the president commit a felony. Although the panel thought this suggested balance was "strange," it nicely tracks the crime-fraud exception to attorney-client privilege and fits with what *Nixon* should have said. Quoting *Nixon*'s admonition that privileges "are not lightly created nor expansively construed," the court downplayed national security concerns that presidents would keep Secret Service agents at bay if they couldn't trust the agents to keep their mouths shut. The court's best argument was that national security concerns were strongest when the president was in public, but the proposed privilege would have its greatest bite in shielding information about private meetings. The best response to this is to admit that the privilege should be rooted in privacy as well as national security concerns, even though the language and legacy of the tapes case forced the president's lawyers to push national security while soft-pedaling privacy. Imagine how intrusive it must be to be shadowed everywhere and yet to know that those who wish to humiliate you may subpoena your guardians to talk about wholly lawful and even proper but nevertheless embarrassing activity.

Imagine, in short, how the vision of *Nixon* is wholly inadequate if you are an honest president. If we think about the interaction of the Fourth Amendment and Article II, surely there is a need to protect a zone of presidential privacy. Judges are sensitive to this concern in their own branch—cameras are not even allowed in the Supreme Court's public courtroom, much less their private chambers, and justices would look askance at efforts to force their clerks to testify under oath about the justices' personal lives. More generally, if the chief executive thinks that the Secret Service should remain secret, and an inferior officer disagrees, why do judges heed the inferior rather than the chief?

This is the thread that, when pulled, unravels two circuit court opinions claiming that the president and other White House personnel may not invoke attorney-client privilege when they speak to government attorneys. The attorneys represent "the government," and somehow Starr embodies "the government," thereby displacing a duly elected president. In their own branch, judges think otherwise. The government pays law clerks, but many judges have told their clerks that they owe an absolute duty of confidentiality to the judge under attorney-client privilege. The circuit courts worry about attorney-client privilege shielding evidence of wrongdoing—but the answer to this is that the crime-fraud exception should apply to government attorneys.

But not any broader exception. Imagine an honest president who gets wind of a problem and instructs his aides to cooperate fully with his White House counsel. He assures them that what they say will be kept confidential so that they will tell the truth and he can, if necessary, remove the bad apples from his administration. But the circuit court opinions prevent the president from making this assurance stick—and the result is that judges are interfering with an honest president's ability to run his branch of government. This, too, is the legacy of *Nixon*, which crafted rules that failed to distinguish between White House conversations confessing past crimes, on the one hand, and conspiracies plotting new crimes, on the other.

Modern presidential law is misshapen, and all three branches of government are to blame. Congress has abdicated its proper oversight responsibilities in favor of an abominable independent counsel statute. Presidents have at times been crooked and have opted to litigate key issues of presidential privilege on weak facts. But, most of all, judges have failed to see the big constitutional picture and have succumbed to their own institutional hubris.

Now could be the perfect time to undo the damage. In 2000, the House, Senate, and presidency are all genuinely up for grabs, a truly rare cosmic alignment. Before we know which party will win which branch, let's draft sensible rules for each branch. Let's start by letting the independent counsel statute die. Any successor statute must exclude judges altogether from the process of picking, monitoring, and firing prosecutors. Provision could be made to enable the White House to pick independent counsels on its own (the Cox/Jaworski model), or the president could nominate independent counsels subject to Senate confirmation (as happened during the Teapot Dome scandal in the 1920s). On either approach, independent counsels could be selected ad hoc, or a more permanent set of watchdog positions could be created, to be filled before scandal erupts.

Congress should also craft an omnibus presidential privilege bill—fashioning rules for when (if ever) a sitting president can be sued in civil cases; providing for tolling of statutes of limitation in the event of temporary presidential immunity; and delineating sensible boundaries for various executive, government-attorney, and Secret Service privileges. The statute should also reaffirm the historically sound and structurally sensible rule that a sitting president cannot be forced to stand trial against his will in an ordinary criminal court. The *Jones* case did not decide otherwise; the president had the legal option simply to default the civil case, whereas in an ordinary criminal prosecution, defendants can be physically obliged—with leg irons, if need be—to stand trial. (Indeed, Stevens in *Jones* pointedly distinguished the case at hand from "the question whether a court may compel the attendance of the President at any specific time or place.") Also, unlike a mere civil suit, a criminal conviction and imprisonment could effect a de facto removal from office. As a matter of both federalism and separation of powers, judges and local juries lack this power over the nation's chief executive. The president is elected by the nation, and only the nation's representatives, via impeachment, can properly undo this election.

These reforms cut against the spirit of the Nixon Tapes case, but by now it should be clear that this spirit has itself been a great source of disruption in the institutional balance of our national government. Instead of writing an honest opinion impeding a crooked president, the *Nixon* Court wrote a crooked opinion impeding honest presidents. Crooked presidents need to be straightened out, of course. So do crooked precedents.

BRINGING JUSTICE TO CLINTON

NEW YORK TIMES, MONDAY, MARCH 20, 2000

Just when you thought it was over, think again. Robert W. Ray, the independent counsel who succeeded Kenneth Starr last October, is considering indicting Bill Clinton after he leaves the White House and said yesterday he is expanding his legal and investigative staff.

Many commentators have come out against any such prosecution because, they say, the charges against President Clinton were fully adjudicated in his impeachment trial. There are indeed good reasons not to prosecute Clinton, but an acquittal in an impeachment trial is not one of them.

Clinton's impeachment focused on whether he was fit to complete his term of office. The question in a criminal case is whether he committed a crime of any sort, however small. These two questions overlap but are plainly distinct. The Constitution makes clear that an official who is tried by the Senate may nevertheless be subject to "indictment, trial, judgment, and punishment" in an ordinary criminal court.

This principle makes consummate sense. If presidents received get-out-of-jail-free cards when impeachments failed, senators might be tempted to convict simply to ensure that the wrongdoer did not escape justice altogether. Inevitably, the standard for impeachment and conviction would be watered down—a "high crime or misdemeanor" would be read without the word "high." If impeachment were to degenerate into a search for ordinary as opposed to high criminality, Congress could undo presidential elections whenever some small crime could be found. Precisely to preserve a strong presidency, we must insist that ex-presidents be subject to prosecution just like everyone else.

The possibility of indictment brings up another question: Could Ray indict Clinton now, without waiting for the end of his term, and force him to stand trial in a criminal case?

Although the Supreme Court has never considered this question, there are compelling reasons to support temporary immunity. While in office, a president should not be distracted by a democratically unaccountable prosecutor. The time for trial is later, when he would not be prevented from doing the people's business.

Another reason to insist on waiting for the end of Clinton's term stems from the pardon power that the Constitution vests in the president. A president may issue a pardon even before any criminal trial begins—remember President Gerald Ford's 1974 pardon of Richard Nixon, and President George Bush's 1992 pardon of Caspar Weinberger? A sitting president, however, may not properly pardon himself, and no one else may properly do so either. Thus, if indicted, the president would be the only defendant in America ineligible for a pretrial pardon. Waiting until after Clinton leaves office solves this problem; then the pardon decision would be up to his successor.

None of this is to say that Clinton should in fact be indicted once he leaves office. The strongest reason not to indict is that a jury is unlikely to convict, believing the man has suffered enough. Clinton may have won acquittal in the Senate, but he lost some of his reputation and legacy in the process—a large and poetically proportionate penalty for whatever crimes he may be accused of.

Ray may decide to go ahead and indict; the Senate's verdict in the impeachment trial does not bar criminal prosecution. But in this case, a good prosecutor would use discretion.

CLOSING THE BOOK ON CLINTON

AMERICAN LAWYER, MARCH 2001

On the last full day of the Clinton era, a not quite presidential president signed a less than fully confessional confession as part of a plea bargain with an "inferior" officer who was inferior to no one. Call it a poetic coda to an age when words seemed to lose their meaning, as Clinton lovers denied that "sex" meant "sex" and "is" meant "is," while Clinton haters insisted that "high" crimes meant "low" crimes. And call Clinton's exit rough justice—a proportionate penalty, when heaped atop all the other formal and informal sanctions he has been made to endure. But don't call Clinton's deal with independent counsel Robert Ray a triumph of the rule of law.

Clinton's words at his January 17, 1998, Paula Jones deposition, denying that he had a "sexual affair" with Monica Lewinsky, were indeed self-serving falsehoods. But so were Robert Ray's words almost exactly three years later, on January 19, 2001, when he claimed that his deal "respects America's institutions and demonstrates sensitivity to our constitutional system of government." As a constitutionally "inferior" officer picked by unelected federal judges and answerable to no one, Ray overstepped, wielding powers that the Constitution properly gives to more democratically accountable decision makers.

The substance of the plea bargain, in broad outline, seems fair enough. Ray agreed to decline prosecution "with prejudice," in effect forever immunizing Clinton from any Lewinsky-related federal criminal liability. In exchange, Clinton agreed to give up his Arkansas law license for five years and to pay yet another fine, and finally admitted that he "knowingly violated" judicial orders with deposition answers that were "evasive" and "misleading" and at times downright "false." Better still would have been a forthright admission in person, and not just on paper, that "I lied." Clinton's lies were brazen, yet his confession was not equally blunt. He lied with his own lips, and it would have been better for him to confess in the same way, righting his earlier wrong in the most symmetrical way. Instead, Clinton's legalistic "confession" was read aloud by a press secretary. I confess: He did it. Mistakes were made.

The real problem, however, is not that the wrong person read the confession but that the wrong person demanded and accepted it. Who is Robert Ray, and why was he the one to make the momentous decisions about whether President Clinton had already suffered enough, about how much additional formal and informal punishment would be proper, about when and how Clinton must confess, and about whether permanent immunity is appropriate?

Constitutionally, Ray is supposed to be an "inferior" officer. He was never nominated to his office by the president, nor confirmed by the Senate. Instead, he was picked by a panel of judges, pursuant to a post-Watergate independent counsel statute. (The statute has now expired but investigations already under way are allowed to be wrapped up.) Article II of the Constitution allows judges only to appoint "inferior" officers. Thus, if Ray is not, in fact, an inferior officer, he is a legal nullity, with no authority either to threaten Clinton or to spare him.

In what sense was Ray an inferior officer on January 19, 2001? If he was an inferior officer, who, exactly, was the superior officer authorized to supervise and countermand him? Can an inferior officer properly exist without such a superior? And the decisions Ray took it upon himself to make were hardly the small decisions appropriately resolved by a petty officer lacking the special seal of approval conferred by the advice and consent process required for major officers.

Surely it cannot be said that the judges who appointed Ray were his superiors, with broad power to supervise and countermand him, for that would turn judges into superprosecutors in ways that would make a hash of separation of powers. (The judges would be regularly obliged to meet ex parte, to make secret policy decisions without giving public legal reasons, and to do many other things inconsistent with their judicial roles.) Nor can it be said that Clinton's attorney general, Janet Reno, was Ray's supervisor, given that she did not hire him, could not fire him at will, and indeed could not consistently countermand his decisions or order him to follow her suggestions.

Precisely to the extent that Ray was independent, he was not inferior, as the Constitution requires.

Ray would doubtless seek to wrap himself in the mantle of the 1988 *Morrison v. Olson* case, which upheld the constitutionality of the independent counsel law. *Morrison* did seem to say that an inferior officer could exist without having a clear superior. But in 1997, the U.S. Supreme Court reversed course in the less-noted case of *Edmond v. United States*, proclaiming that "generally speaking . . . whether one is an inferior officer depends on whether he has a superior. . . . In the context of a clause designed to preserve political accountability relative to important government assignments, we think it evident that inferior officers are officers whose work is directed and supervised at some level by others who were appointed by presidential nomination with the advice and consent of the Senate." Although *Edmond* did not formally overrule *Morrison*, it plainly echoed *Morrison*'s dissenting opinion and undermined *Morrison*'s conceptual foundations.

Even if the Court were to reaffirm *Morrison* on its unique facts, that case still provides inadequate support for Ray. Alexia Morrison was investigating underlings in the executive branch. If she had decided to prosecute anyone the president did not want prosecuted, the president could in effect nullify her decision by pardoning her targets. Indeed, the President George H. W. Bush effectively countermanded yet another independent counsel, Lawrence Walsh, by pardoning Walsh's target, Caspar Weinberger, before trial in December 1992.

Because of this presidential pardon power, perhaps we might say that independent counsels are "inferior" in the sense that the president can typically at any time and for any reason countermand any undesirable prosecution they might initiate. But this argument for inferiority fails when the target of prosecution is the president himself. Surely, a sitting president may not properly pardon himself. (This is why President Clinton was not fully presidential in dealing with Robert Ray, for he could not properly wave or wield his mighty pardon pen, which can make all other independent counsel disappear at a moment's notice.) Viewing the issue from another angle, the decision whether a president should be prosecuted should never be seen as a petty issue properly resolved by an inferior officer acting on his own.

Of course, Ray did not seek to prosecute a sitting president, but rather was pondering whether to pursue Clinton after Clinton's term. Yet even the prosecution of an ex-president can raise issues of high statecraft inappropriate for final resolution by an inferior officer. To what extent was Clinton's

presidential impeachment trial itself, with all its publicity and stigma, punishment enough, or close to it? Generally speaking, are national interests
well served by criminal prosecutions of ex-presidents? Even if discretion
counseled against indicting ex-president Clinton, should Clinton be given
permanent immunity—the functional equivalent of an acquittal or a pardon,
a vested legal right that no later administration can undo? These are large
public issues, properly resolved by those with direct public accountability to
the president himself, and his handpicked cabinet, who have been personally vetted and approved by the Senate.

In other words, these were precisely the issues that the Constitution
properly left to President George W. Bush. Had Ray waited one more day, it
would have gradually begun to dawn on his fellow Americans that his very
raison d'être had been overtaken by events. True, Clinton couldn't be trusted
to investigate Clinton, although even that doesn't somehow mean that Ray
should have the last word (as opposed to the House and Senate in impeachment and oversight, or some special independent counsel appointed by the
president or attorney general, à la Teapot Dome and Watergate). But why
couldn't President Bush and his incoming administration be trusted to make
the Clinton call?

According to prominent sources quoted by the New York Times, Ray
"did not want to leave the new president to deal with a problem relating to
Mr. Clinton, especially the thorny issue of whether to pardon him." But the
Constitution is of course designed to give many thorny issues from treaty
negotiation to federal law enforcement to presidents, who are accountable
to the people and to history. To deter and punish presidential misbehavior
in law enforcement—the improper pardoning of friends or persecution of
foes—the Constitution vests a democratically accountable Congress with
important oversight and impeachment powers.

Lame-duck presidents might be thought immune from these checks, but
highly visible exit pardons can be judged by the court of history, whose anticipated verdicts generally weigh heavily in the minds of outgoing presidents. What's more, even ex-presidents are theoretically subject to the
dishonor of impeachment for their official misdeeds: An impeachment court
could declare an ex-president ineligible to hold any future federal office. The
attorney general is another important and accountable decision maker with
a mandate to make big calls deriving from a personal endorsement of both
president and Senate. In special situations, presidents and attorneys general
can name other citizens of high repute to bring independent perspectives to

bear on an issue—an Owen Roberts in Teapot Dome, an Archibald Cox in Watergate, a John Danforth in the Waco investigation. All these actors had democratic credentials that Ray lacked.

Robert Ray's decision to exit the national stage is welcome. Substantively, the deal that he cut seems fair enough and is plausibly in the national interest. Ray may also have done the incoming president a big political favor by whisking a hot potato off his plate.

But constitutionally, Ray overreached by making decisions that were anything but inferior, distorting the Constitution's carefully wrought mechanisms of democratic accountability. By acting as he did, Ray in effect improperly helped President Clinton pardon himself and denied President Bush a decision that belonged to him and his new administration.

For these reasons, Ray would have shown more fidelity to the Constitution by either declining to serve in his unconstitutional office in the first place, or by offering to resign as soon as Bush took over. (Had Bush asked him to stay on, the new administration could then be held publicly accountable for Ray's subsequent conduct.) In short, there were even better exits available than the one that Ray chose.

But even if he missed his constitutional cue, at least he did get off the stage. And he is the last independent counsel we are likely to see, given that the statute that made his office possible—the 1978 Ethics in Government Act—has now expired and is highly unlikely to be resurrected any time soon. For that we should all be thankful. America can now return to the system devised by the framers, in which politically sensitive crimes are handled by politically accountable actors.

9

GEORGE W. BUSH'S DRAMA
His Un-Popular Election

I'VE ALWAYS HAD MY DOUBTS about the electoral college. Each of us is a product of time and place, and several features of my California boyhood in the 1960s and 1970s fed my early skepticism. At a tender age, I was encouraged to question authority. Amazingly, this encouragement came not from trite bumper stickers but from wise authority figures themselves, including my parents, scout leaders, and teachers. And so as a schoolboy I began to ask earnest questions about basic structures of authority—about America's Constitution in general and about the electoral college in particular.

"Equality" was in the air and on everyone's lips in the late 1960s and early 1970s, especially in California, and the first thing I noticed about the electoral college was that it seemed quite unequal. Although all voters in California were treated equally with each other, none of these California voters was treated equally with, say, a Wyoming voter. The precise weight of an American's presidential vote varied drastically, depending on his or her place of residence.

For an earlier generation of constitutional scholars, this type of inequality did not suffice to make the electoral college particularly problematic. Grossly unequal districting—what we would today refer to as "malapportionment"— prevailed in many states, perhaps most. But in a 1964 landmark opinion handed down by Chief Justice Earl Warren (himself a modern Californian, and indeed a former governor of the Golden State), the Supreme Court proclaimed the grand principle of "one person, one vote." The sweeping egalitarian vision of this opinion, *Reynolds v. Sims*, rankled many constitutional scholars of an earlier generation—most notably, the Yale Law School constitutionalist Alexander Bickel, who championed tradition and judicial modesty.[1]

The last half century has not been kind to Bickel on this issue. Our constitutional culture has enthusiastically embraced *Reynolds*. No leading politician today openly calls for a return to malapportioned state legislatures or U.S. House districts; no prominent scholar today echoes Bickel's cri de coeur; and justices from left to right pledge allegiance to the *Reynolds* principle that "as nearly as is practicable one man's vote . . . is to be worth as much as another's."[2] The case that Bickel and others of his era dismissed as outlandish has become the baseline, the cornerstone, the self-evident truth, for boomers like me.

In turn there now arises a need to ask hard questions about *Reynolds* itself—about *its* authority. For example, how broadly should the equal-worth-in-voting principle extend? In the preceding paragraph's quotation, how should we fill in the ellipses? Should we say that "one man's vote *in every election* is to be worth as much as another's?"

The Warren Court did not in fact apply the equal-voting-worth principle to all elections. Thanks to *Reynolds* and its sibling cases, U.S. House of Representatives elections must be equal—meaning that House districts within each state must be equally populous. State legislative elections must be equal—meaning that both houses of state legislatures must be apportioned based on population (though the Court has not yet ruled whether states must count all persons or may instead use some other population metric such as the number of eligible voters in each district). It is also clearly established that no state may structure gubernatorial elections in a way that gives some voters more weight than others. Likewise, all U.S. Senate races within a state must count each state voter the same as every other state voter. But the overall apportionment of the U.S. Senate itself flagrantly flouts the *Reynolds* principle. Wyoming has the same number of Senate seats as does California, even though there are nearly seventy Californians for every Wyomingite. And of course the electoral college itself also lies beyond the sweep of *Reynolds*.

If malapportioned state upper houses are improper, why is the malapportioned federal upper house (aka the Senate) acceptable?[3] And if the young Akhil Amar opposed the electoral college on the simple ground that that it violates the voting-equality ideal, then doesn't consistency oblige Amar to take on the Senate as well? Conversely, if the Senate is constitutionally acceptable, then why not the electoral college?

Questioning authority turns out to be more complicated than I initially understood.

I NEVER MET ALEX BICKEL. He died in 1974, two years before I began my freshman year at Yale. But as a college student and later a law student and law professor at Yale, where Bickel had friends and admirers who kept his memory alive, I did encounter thoughtful traditionalists who forced me to refine the grounds of my disdain for the electoral college.

First, I began to sharpen my formulation of the voting equality ideal. In one of the essays in this chapter, "Countering the Top Ten Arguments for the Electoral College," I explain why the equal-voting-weight idea that supports direct national election of the president does not necessarily entail opposition to the Senate's current apportionment structure.

Second, and more important, I began to move past purely mathematical notions of formal equality to consider larger issues of substantive equality. As a junior professor at Yale, I started to excavate the history of the electoral college, of the Senate, and of America's Constitution more generally. What I found astonished me: The electoral college was designed at Philadelphia and was revised in the wake of the Jefferson-Adams-Burr election of 1800–1801 to advantage the slaveholding South. It was an integral part of the odious pro-slavery three-fifths compromise.

This was not the story that I had been taught by my boyhood textbooks and teachers, nor was it a story familiar to most constitutional law professors in the late 1980s. Several superb legal historians specializing in issues of race and slavery had drawn the connection between slavery and the electoral college, as had a few outstanding professors of political science.[4] But most mainstream professors of constitutional law had failed to build on—or frankly, even notice—this foundational work.

In 1995, I was invited to write a short piece for an academic symposium in which each participant was asked to identify the most mistaken part of the current Constitution. I picked the electoral college and mentioned its pro-slavery roots.[5]

I also mentioned a second vicious feature of the electoral college that makes it different from, and worse than, the U.S. Senate's apportionment structure: Compared to a system of direct national election, today's electoral college system tends to dampen democratic participation. With direct national elections, states would have strong incentives to dismantle needless barriers to voting. If a democratically virtuous state made more persons eligible to vote and made it easier to vote—for example, with same-day-registration laws—more persons in that state would likely vote, and the state would be rewarded for its democratic virtue with more weight in the overall national vote count. By contrast, the current electoral college gives a state a fixed amount of clout in the final vote whether the state enfranchises many or few, and regardless of how easy or how hard it is in that state for voters to vote on Election Day. (The Senate is different from the electoral college in this respect. Were the Constitution modified to create a Senate that tracked the population-based apportionment structure of the House, this change would not itself create any direct incentive for states to facilitate voting or broaden the franchise; each state's clout in the Senate would remain fixed, regardless of how many citizens could and did vote.)

Of course, in a proper system of direct national election, there would need to be effective national or interstate oversight structures to keep a healthy democratic competition among states within proper bounds. But as I confessed in this scholarly essay, "The specter of the national government administering a national election . . . does not give me the cold sweats."

I titled my 1995 essay "A Constitutional Accident Waiting to Happen" and I concluded it as follows:

> [True,] the dreaded specter of a clear popular loser becoming the electoral-college winner hasn't happened in this century. "Why worry?" But that's what someone might say after three trigger pulls in Russian roulette. One day, we will end up with a clear Loser President—clear beyond any quibbles about uncertain ballots. And the question is, will this Loser/Winner be seen as legitimate at home and abroad? If our modern national democratic ethos, when focused on the thing, would balk at a byzantine system that defies the people's choice on Election Day, true Burkean theory would seem to argue against the electoral college. If We the People would amend the Constitution after the Loser President materializes—and I predict we would—why are we now just waiting for the inevitable accident to happen?

Prediction is very difficult, especially about the future.[6] In 2000, a "Loser President" (as I used the term in 1995), did indeed materialize, and We the People have not (yet) amended the Constitution. But it turns out that we Americans *have* taken notable steps in the direction of direct national election—and it further turns out that these steps have apparently been influenced by things I wrote immediately before, immediately after, and on the one-year anniversary of, the very weird election of 2000.

ON THE EVE OF THE ELECTION, I had a premonition that something troubling was about to happen. On October 21, 2000, I published an essay in *Slate* that ended with the following words, echoing what I had said to scholars years earlier: "Last but not least of the democratic accidents waiting to happen: The man who loses the national popular vote next month might nonetheless win the electoral vote. If it doesn't happen next month, one day, statistically, it will. When it does, will the loser/winner have the requisite democratic legitimacy at home and abroad? If not, why are we waiting for this tire to blow rather than acting, via constitutional amendment, to fix the system before it crashes?"[7]

A week and a half later—in *Slate* on Thursday, November 2, 2000, at 6:45 p.m. (ET), to be precise—I expressed a different but related concern. In "President Thurmond?"—the essay that now opens this chapter—I worried aloud (correctly, in retrospect) that the electoral-college vote might be freakishly close and that several of the specific constitutional and statutory provisions for resolving a close presidential contest might misfire. I ended, once again, with a plea for abolition of the electoral college and modification of the current presidential succession statute: "Our current systems of presidential selection and succession are a mess—various accidents and crises waiting to happen. Why not amend the Constitution and provide for direct popular election for all future presidential contests?"[8]

Of course I did not come close to predicting the precise twists and turns of the ridiculous roller-coaster ride that lay ahead—no one did. But one additional idea that I had put forth in 1995 *was* in fact borne out in 2000: "[A] razor-thin electoral-college margin may require recounts in a number of closely contested states even if there is a clear national popular winner." In 2000, there was indeed a clear national-vote winner—Al Gore prevailed by more than half a million votes nationwide—but the razor-thin electoral-college margin (271–266) did end up requiring ultra-careful tabulation in a number of closely contested states: Florida, to be sure, but also Oregon, New Mexico, and New Hampshire.

On the morning after the 2000 election—Wednesday, November 8—my phone rang early. The *New York Times* op-ed department wanted to know if I had anything to say about the divergence between the national popular vote and the apparent electoral-college result. Indeed, I did have something to say—a lot, in fact. Shortly after writing "President Thurmond?" I had drafted two different versions of a piece I aimed to run somewhere on Thursday, November 9, in the all-too-foreseeable event that America picked a Loser President on Election Day. I wrote a "blue" version in case the electoral-college gods ended up favoring Gore, and a different "red" version in case Bush ended up winning the electoral-college game while losing the popular vote. Going into the election, I thought the electoral-college wild card might trump the popular vote either way, but that it was slightly more likely that the blue joker would surface, favoring Gore.

As we all now know—and as seemed most likely immediately after the election, before Florida became a madhouse—the electoral-college tally ended with Bush on top. So I ended up publishing the "red" version of my essay on Thursday in the *Times,* under the title "The Electoral College, Unfair from Day One."

I tried to make four basic points in this brief piece. First, both Bush and Gore had played by electoral-college rules, not national-direct-election rules. Whoever won by the electoral-college rules was thus the legal winner. Any move to a direct-national-election system would need to operate prospectively. Second, in future elections America should scrap the electoral college in favor of direct election. Third—and this was a new point in the broader public debate—modern Americans should realize that the electoral college was conceived in slavocratic sin and continues to have anti-democratic tendencies as compared to a direct-election system that would encourage states to get out the vote.[9] Fourth, and related—and also new in this old debate—states would continue to play a key role, even after the scrapping of the electoral college. Indeed, a direct-national-election system would harness federalism in a more attractive way than does the current system.

In short, only hours after the 2000 election I was trying to make my 1995 prediction come true—trying to make constitutional lemonade out of an electoral lemon by encouraging my fellow citizens to use the triumph of a Loser President as a teachable moment and a spur to sensible reform.

The immediate response to this op-ed was disappointing. Two days after publishing my piece, the *New York Times* ran an op-ed by my friend Charles Fried, a distinguished professor at Harvard Law School and a former solicitor general of the United States, defending the electoral college in the name of federalism. Fried's essay, "How to Make the President Talk to the Local Pol," opened with a sentence that suggested that he was directly responding to me,

albeit not by name: "With Al Gore leading in the popular vote, but the presidential election still up in the air, many constitutional scholars have called
for abolishing the Electoral College." Alas, my friend Charles proceeded to
ignore all the new points I had raised in my piece—namely, that the college
was originally much more about slavery than about a big-state, small-state
balance; that in today's world, the college operates to dampen democracy;
and that "federalism" is no talismanic answer because direct national election would also involve federalism, and indeed would put into action a vastly
superior model of federalism.

On December 19, 2000, the *New York Times* editorial board itself weighed
in, siding with Fried in a piece entitled "The Case for the Electoral College."
I was saddened by the bottom line, of course, but more disheartened because
what the *Times* said was so plainly wrong: "The Electoral College was first
and foremost a compact among states, large and small, designed to ensure
that one state or one region did not dominate the others. As Charles Fried
noted in a recent op-ed piece, it was and is one of those safeguards of a balanced federalism—much like the allocation of two senators to each state,
regardless of size."

My first reaction was harsh. On the basis of years of research I had come
to see that the college was not "first and foremost" about big states versus
small states. It was much more about slavery. And I had explained this in the
Times itself! Didn't these guys read their own paper? Then I calmed down.
The standard stories about the electoral college have been circulating for a
very long time, and it would take time for the new story to soak in. Well-
educated people like Charles Fried and the *Times* editorial board would need
not just to learn something new, but to unlearn something old, and unlearn-
ing is not easy or quick.

Meanwhile, back in the real world, the Florida recount process spiraled
out of control. Americans became increasingly aware that Florida had been
the scene of massive voter suppression and other gross electoral inequalities
on Election Day. And then, in a stunning finish, the Supreme Court bent
legal rules and roles beyond all recognition in its *Bush v. Gore* opinion. With
all these other problems leaping onstage, it was impossible to keep the public
tightly focused on the pure issue of electoral college versus direct national
election.[10]

Two other factors also dampened electoral-college reform efforts once
the shouting in Florida died down. First, reform began to seem to many

Republicans as a retrospective rebuke of George W. Bush. Reform, in other words, came to be seen in many quarters as a *partisan* cause. Second, reform seemed to require a constitutional amendment. Yet the Constitution is notoriously hard to amend—and nearly impossible to amend in the modern era unless both parties climb aboard the amendment bandwagon. The extreme improbability of a formal constitutional amendment was a truth that the younger Akhil Amar had not fully appreciated, perhaps because the 1960s and 1970s had been an era of extraordinary constitutional dynamism and reform.*

AND SO I WENT BACK TO THE DRAWING BOARD. The results of this rethinking may be found in a trio of essays, coauthored with Vikram David Amar, that first appeared in *FindLaw*'s online magazine, *Writ*, on the one-year anniversary of *Bush v. Gore*, and that are reprinted in this chapter.

In the first essay of this trio, "Electoral College History: Slavery, Sexism, and the South," Vik and I reminded readers of the ugly pro-slavery origins of the electoral college. For years, I had been urging Americans to trade the devil they know for the devil they don't. It was thus appropriate to begin this trio of essays by insisting that the devil that Americans (think they) know is indeed a devil—something vicious, not admirable, something very far from the Founding Fathers' finest hour. If the electoral college with all its quirks seems like a rather peculiar institution, we must always remember that several of its peculiarities are intimately intertwined with another famously "peculiar institution"—slavery itself.

Even the superb historians and political scientists who had stressed the electoral college-slavery connection before I came along had tended to dwell only on the role of slavery at the Philadelphia convention. But as I had hinted in my *New York Times* op-ed and now began to elaborate, the real slavery skew of the college became apparent to many Americans only after the 1800–1801 election. The Founders' electoral-college system dramatically

---

* Between 1960 and 1972, four successful amendments became part of the Constitution, all four of them directed, in whole or in part, at the rules of presidential selection or succession. A fifth proposed amendment—the Equal Rights Amendment—was proposed in 1972. Although never formally ratified, the ERA triumphed informally, as the Supreme Court in the mid-1970s embraced the core principle of genuine sex equality.

failed in the election of 1800–1801, in a crack-up almost as spectacular as Florida in 2000. The electoral-college system that emerged to replace the Founders' failed regime—the revised electoral-college system that remains in place to this day, basically—was drafted by and for Thomas Jefferson's pro-slavery party, in the wake of an election that had made clear to anyone with eyeballs that extra slaves meant extra electoral-college clout. This is a theme that has received considerable popular attention in recent years, thanks largely to Garry Wills's powerful 2003 book, *Negro President: Jefferson and the Slave Power*. It is also a theme that I reiterated, with additional evidence and analysis, in my 2005 book, *America's Constitution: A Biography*.

In the middle essay of the 2001 *FindLaw* trio, "Countering the Top Ten Arguments for the Electoral College," Vik and I made clear—as I had not made clear in my previous writings—that the electoral college is not today systematically biased in favor of Republicans. Thus, reform should not be seen as some sort of partisan Trojan horse. Recall that going into the 2000 election, I was predicting—along with most pundits—that if the electoral college ended up inverting the popular-vote results, the more likely beneficiary of such an inversion would be Gore, not Bush.

This middle essay also took aim at several silly claims often made in defense of today's electoral college. The silliness of many of these just-so stories becomes apparent if we ask a simple question: If the electoral-college system is so good and if direct election would be so bad, then why do all the states pick their governors by direct election, rather than by some variant of the electoral college?

This was a question that came especially naturally to me as a former California kid. On the day that Ronald Reagan left the presidency in early 1989, I mentioned to a friend that I had at that point lived more than half my life under Reagan's leadership, given that he had been my governor for eight years and my president for another eight, and I was at the time only thirty. If direct election—counting all votes equally and re-counting them carefully in close cases—has always been the right way to pick governors of California, why wouldn't it be the right way to pick presidents?

There remained the seemingly insuperable problem of amending the Constitution. In 1995, I had explicitly called for a constitutional amendment, and I had emphatically repeated this call in the essays I published just before and after the 2000 election. Then, inspiration occurred. It suddenly hit me that there are least two ways by which a national popular vote could be achieved without amending the Constitution. Strictly speaking, America could have both an electoral-college system (formally) and a direct national popular vote (functionally).

This was the theme of the third essay in the 2001 *FindLaw* trio: "How to Achieve Direct National Election of the President Without Amending the Constitution." Each of the two new routes to reform mapped in this essay had emerged as I rethought what I had written in late 2000. In my *Times* op-ed, I had ended by suggesting that even in a system of direct election, states might constructively compete to promote voting rights. But as I came to see in 2001, states might be able to constructively cooperate and coordinate to create a direct-election system in the first place. My *Times* piece had opened by saying Bush deserved to win because he had played under certain rules. But what if he and Gore had at the outset of the election season agreed to play by different rules—by national popular vote? Most American elections end, as a practical matter, when one candidate concedes, and, indeed, the concession-speech issue loomed large in the Bush-Gore affair. In effect, both major candidates agree at the end of the game about who won. But what if, in some future election, both candidates agree at the beginning of the game to a different set of rules about how the game should be scored, and what should count as winning?

At the same time that these thoughts were occurring to me, Northwestern University law professor Robert Bennett was floating similar reformist suggestions in a popular periodical, the *Green Bag*.[11] In 2004, the reformist cause received another boost: Democratic presidential candidate John Kerry came close to winning Ohio. Had he actually triumphed in the Buckeye State, he would have bested Bush in the electoral college despite having lost the national popular vote by a wide margin—3 million votes. Here, then, was additional and highly visible confirmation of what Vik and I had explained in 2001: The current state-winner-take-all version of the electoral college is not strongly skewed to favor either party, and therefore neither party would be severely hurt were this system to be scrapped in favor of a more egalitarian regime of direct national popular vote.

IN 2006, THE STORY of the electoral college took a startling new turn. A national popular reform movement emerged to implement a version of the reformist ideas that Professor Bennett, Vik, and I had sketched out five years earlier. As I write these words in early 2016, the National Popular Vote Interstate Compact (NPVIC) plan has been formally adopted by ten states and the District of Columbia—a group together totaling 165 electoral votes, more than 60 percent of the 270 electoral votes necessary for the plan to go into operation.

It is still too soon to predict with confidence that the NPVIC plan will reach the 270 mark anytime in the near future. This particular plan also raises several serious legal and logistical issues, in part because it deviates in certain respects from the specific script that Vik and I had sketched out in *FindLaw*.[12] And Republican-controlled states have thus far declined to embrace this plan—an irony, perhaps, given that some evidence suggests that the electoral college in the last decade may be beginning to tilt, slightly, toward Democrats, who enter presidential elections with a substantial electoral-college lead among the states that are safely red or safely blue. (In recent elections, the Democrats have consistently won states totaling 242 electoral votes, whereas the Republicans have had a lock on states totaling less than half this number: 102.)

But whatever the fate of the specific NPVIC plan in the coming years, the national reform movement that gave birth to this plan has confirmed for me that there is an important role for constitutional scholars to play in periodicals aimed at the general citizenry.

I am particularly pleased to note two post-2001 developments of special personal significance. First, the *New York Times* editorial board eventually reversed course and has in recent years become an articulate advocate of direct national election. Here is what the *Times* said in an editorial entitled "Flunking the Electoral College" that appeared on November 20, 2008:

> There is no reason to feel sentimental about the Electoral College. One of the main reasons the founders created it was slavery. The southern states liked the fact that their slaves, who would be excluded from a direct vote, would be counted—as three-fifths of a white person—when Electoral College votes were apportioned. . . .
>
> One of the biggest problems with the Electoral College, of course, is that three times since the Civil War—most recently, with George W. Bush in 2000—it has awarded the presidency to the loser of the popular vote. The president should be the candidate who wins the votes of the most Americans.

Second, in August, 2011, the NPVIC plan was signed into law in my boyhood state of California. The person doing the signing was Governor Jerry

Brown, a friend and fellow Yale Law School graduate whose father had been California governor in the early 1960s, when I first started asking questions about the electoral college back in elementary school.

PRESIDENT THURMOND?

SLATE, THURSDAY, NOVEMBER 2, 2000, 6:45 P.M. (ET)

President Strom Thurmond? Don't laugh. The odds are against it, but there is an outside chance of constitutional meltdown in the days ahead. The problem is created by the Constitution's archaic and confusing rules concerning the electoral college and its intricate provisions concerning Oval Office vacancies.

Constitutionally, the key next Tuesday is not who wins the nationwide popular vote, but who wins the state-by-state electoral vote. Americans will pick 538 electors, and to win, a candidate needs an absolute majority: 270.

But what if George W. Bush and Al Gore tie at 269 apiece? This is not a fanciful scenario. For example, imagine that Gore wins the following states where he seems clearly or slightly ahead today: California (54 electoral votes), New York (33), Florida (25), Pennsylvania (23), Illinois (22), Michigan (18), New Jersey (15), Massachusetts (12), Washington (11), Wisconsin (11), Maryland (10), Minnesota (10), Connecticut (8), Hawaii (4), Rhode Island (4), District of Columbia (3), Delaware (3), and Vermont (3). If Bush wins everywhere else, each man would have 269 electoral votes. Several other easily imaginable permutations could yield the same 269–269 tie.

In this event, our Constitution and statutes allow the race to be decided in the incoming House of Representatives. But in this vote, each state must vote as a bloc, and the winner must win an absolute majority of states—26 out of 50. Some state delegations, however, are likely to be evenly divided between Republicans and Democrats. If each of these delegations could cast a half vote for each man, then one candidate could likely emerge victorious. But the Constitution says that each state shall have "one vote" and says nothing about half votes. House rules and House precedents from the elections of 1800 and 1824 (the only times the House has picked the president), disallow half votes. Thus, divided delegations probably won't count, and neither Bush nor Gore might be able to reach the magic number of 26.

So, what happens then? The presidency would appear to stand vacant after noon on January 20. The Constitution says that the vice president should then take over. But who will be vice president after January 20?

If Bush and Gore tie at 269, so will Dick Cheney and Joe Lieberman. In this event, the Twelfth Amendment provides that the Senate shall pick between them and that the winner must get an absolute majority—51 votes. Here, all bets are off. Imagine the scenarios:

President Lieberman? If the Democrats manage to win every tight race, the new Senate could be evenly split 50–50. The Senate's presiding officer (until January 20) is none other than Vice President Al Gore, and he could cast the tie-breaking vote for Lieberman. Lieberman might possibly be free to later nominate Gore as his vice president under the Twenty-fifth Amendment and then step down once Gore was confirmed, though there are serious unresolved questions here.[13]

President Cheney? If Republicans hold on to the Senate, then they could pick Cheney (who in turn might be able to eventually switch positions with Bush under the Twenty-fifth Amendment).

President Hastert? If the Senate splits down the middle, it is not completely clear that Vice President Gore may cast a tie-breaking vote under the Twelfth Amendment. Arguably the amendment requires an absolute majority of senators, and technically Gore is not a senator. If neither side has 51 senators, federal succession laws could make the speaker of the House the acting president. Republican Dennis Hastert currently holds the speakership and will likely retain it if the Republicans keep control of the House in Tuesday's congressional elections.

President Gephardt? If the Democrats win back the House on Tuesday, the new speaker might be Richard Gephardt rather than Dennis Hastert.

President Thurmond? If the House elections turn out to be very close, the House could be without a speaker at the beginning of the session. (This happened repeatedly in the nineteenth century.) Next in line under the succession law is the Senate's president pro tem, the nonagenarian South Carolina Republican, Strom Thurmond. If Republicans win back the Senate, 51–49,

Thurmond could conceivably, by declining to vote for Cheney and thus denying Cheney the needed 51 votes, crown himself king.

President Albright? The presidential succession laws currently in place probably violate the Constitution. Only "officers of the United States" may be picked as presidential successors, and senators and representatives are not such officers, properly speaking.[14] The next person on the statutory succession list is the secretary of state, Madeleine Albright. Our first woman president!

But wait. Albright is not a natural-born citizen of the United States,[15] so she is ineligible. Next in line is secretary of the treasury Larry Summers.

There is a lesson in all this head-spinning speculation: Our current systems of presidential selection and succession are a mess—various accidents and crises waiting to happen. Why not amend the Constitution and provide for direct popular election for all future presidential contests?

THE ELECTORAL COLLEGE, UNFAIR FROM DAY ONE

New York Times, Thursday, November 9, 2000

As we await results from the Florida recount, two things should be clear. First, if George W. Bush, having apparently lost the national popular vote, does indeed win at least 270 electoral votes when the electoral college meets, he is the lawful winner, who played by the Constitution's rules and won.

Second, we must realize that the electoral college is a hopelessly outdated system and that we must abolish it. Direct election would resonate far better with the American value of one person, one vote. Indeed, the college was designed at the Founding of the country to help one group—white southern males—and this year, it has apparently done just that.

In 1787, as the Constitution was being drafted in Philadelphia, James Wilson of Pennsylvania proposed direct election of the president. But James Madison of Virginia worried that such a system would hurt the South, which would have been outnumbered by the North in a direct-election system. The creation of the electoral college got around that: It was part of the deal that southern states, in computing their share of electoral votes, could count slaves (albeit with a two-fifths discount), even though slaves of course were given none of the privileges of citizenship. Virginia emerged as the big winner, with more than a quarter of the electors needed to elect a president. A free state like Pennsylvania got fewer electoral votes even though it had approximately the same free population.

The Constitution's pro-southern bias quickly became obvious. For thirty-two of the Constitution's first thirty-six years, a white slaveholding Virginian occupied the presidency. Thomas Jefferson, for example, won the election of 1800 against John Adams from Massachusetts in a race where the slavery skew of the electoral college was the decisive margin of victory.

The system's gender bias was also obvious. In a direct presidential election, any state that chose to enfranchise its women would have automatically doubled its clout. Under the electoral college, however, a state had no special incentive to expand suffrage—each got a fixed number of electoral votes, regardless of how many citizens were allowed to vote.

Now fast-forward to Election Night 2000. Al Gore appears to have received the most popular votes nationwide but may well lose the contest for electoral votes. Once again, the system has tilted toward white southern males. Exit polls indicate that Bush won big among this group and that Gore won decisively among blacks and women.

The electoral college began as an unfair system, and remains so. So why keep it?

Advocates of the system sloganeer about "federalism," meaning that presidential candidates are forced to take into account individual state interests and regional variations in their national campaigns.

But in the current system, candidates don't appeal so much to state interests (what are those, anyway?) as to demographic groups (elderly voters, soccer moms) within states. And direct popular elections would still encourage candidates to take into account regional differences, like those between voters in the Midwest and the East. One cannot win a national majority without getting lots of votes in lots of places.

Direct election could give state governments some incentives to increase voter turnout, because the more voters a state turned out, the bigger its role in national elections and the bigger its overall share in the national tally. Presidential candidates would begin to pay more attention to the needs of individual states that had higher turnouts.

The nation's Founders sought to harness governmental competition and rivalry in healthy ways, using checks and balances within the federal government and preserving roles for state governments. Direct presidential elections would be true to the Founders' best concepts—democracy and healthy competition—rather than to their worst compromises.

ELECTORAL COLLEGE HISTORY:
SLAVERY, SEXISM, AND THE SOUTH[16]

FINDLAW, FRIDAY, NOVEMBER 30, 2001
(WITH VIKRAM DAVID AMAR)

On the first anniversary of the very odd election of 2000, it's hard to look back without fixating on Florida and the courts. But these absorbing soap operas should not obscure the other historical headline: The national popular vote loser nonetheless won the electoral-college vote.

Is this a flaw in our Constitution? Should we scrap the electoral college in favor of direct popular vote? Practically speaking, can we do so?

Proper analysis of these questions will require us to cover a lot of ground. Let's start by probing standard historical accounts of, and justifications for, the electoral college. After that, let's consider prominent modern arguments on behalf of the current system. Finally, let's think about how Americans could adopt popular election without amending the Constitution.

Begin by considering why the Philadelphia framers invented an intricate electoral-college contraption in the first place, and why, after its gears jammed in the Adams-Jefferson-Burr election of 1800–1801, the Twelfth Amendment repaired the thing rather than junking it. Why didn't early Americans simply opt for direct national election of the president? The typical answers taught in grade-school civics classes miss much of the real story, both by misreading the evidence from Philadelphia and ignoring the significance of later events, especially the passage of the Twelfth Amendment.

It's often said that the Founders chose the electoral college over direct election in order to balance the interests of big (high-population) and small (low-population) states. The key Philadelphia concession to small states was the framers' backup selection system: If no candidate emerged with a first-round electoral-vote majority, then the House of Representatives would choose among the top five finalists, with each state casting one vote, regardless of population. According to the standard story, although big states would predictably dominate the first round, small states could expect to loom large in the final selection.

But as James Madison insisted,[17] the deepest political divisions in early America were not between big and small states as such; rather, the real fissures separated North from South, and East from West. Moreover, once the modern system of alternating national presidential parties and winner-take-all state contests emerged—a system already visible, though not yet entrenched, at the time of the Twelfth Amendment—the big states obviously had the advantage.

With two national presidential parties, one candidate almost always had an electoral majority in the first round, rendering the framers' pro-small-state backup system irrelevant. (Three or four strong candidates, in contrast, might have split the vote so that no one garnered a majority.) And winner-take-all rules—under which a candidate who won a state got all of its electoral votes, not a number proportional to the extent of his win—compounded the advantage of big states.

Indeed, before the Civil War amendments, which changed the electoral college yet again, only two of the sixteen presidents hailed from small-population states—Zachary Taylor of Louisiana and Franklin Pierce of New Hampshire.[18] And of the more than two dozen men to hold the office since the Civil War, only Bill Clinton of Arkansas claimed residence in a small state.

In sum, if the framers' true goal was to give small states a leg up, they did a rather bad job of it. (As we shall see soon enough, their chief goal was something quite different.)

Another Founding-era argument for the electoral college stemmed from the following objection to direct election: Ordinary Americans across a vast continent would lack sufficient information to choose intelligently among leading presidential candidates.

This objection is sometimes described today as reflecting a general Founding distrust of democracy. But that is not quite right; after all, the framers required that the House be directly elected every two years, sharply breaking with the indirect election of congressmen under the Articles of Confederation. Many leading Federalists also supported direct election of governors.

The key objection at Philadelphia was thus not to democracy per se, but to democracy based on inadequate voter information. The Founders believed that although voters in a given state would know enough to choose between leading state candidates for House races and for the governorship, these voters would likely lack information about which out-of-state figure would be best for the presidency.

This objection rang true in the 1780s, when life was far more local. But the early emergence of national presidential parties rendered the objection obsolete by linking presidential candidates to slates of local candidates and national platforms that explained to voters who stood for what.

Although the Philadelphia framers did not anticipate the rise of a system of alternating national presidential parties, the Twelfth Amendment (proposed in 1803 and ratified a year later) *was* framed with such a party system in mind in the aftermath of the election of 1800–1801. In that election, two rudimentary presidential parties—Federalists led by John Adams and Republicans led by Thomas Jefferson—took shape and squared off. Jefferson ultimately prevailed, but only after an extended crisis triggered by several glitches in the framers' electoral machinery. In particular, Republican electors had no formal way to designate that they wanted Jefferson for president and Aaron Burr for vice president rather than vice versa. Some politicians then tried to exploit the resulting confusion.

Enter the Twelfth Amendment, which allowed each party to designate one candidate for president and a separate candidate for vice president. The amendment transformed the framers' framework, enabling future presidential elections to be openly populist and partisan affairs featuring two competing tickets. It is the Twelfth Amendment's electoral-college system, not the Philadelphia framers', that remains in place today. Yet the amendment typically goes unmentioned in standard civics accounts of the Constitution.

The election of 1800–1801 also helped allay another early anxiety about a popularly elected president. At the Founding, some saw a populist presidency as uniquely dangerous—inviting demagoguery and possibly dictatorship with one man claiming to embody the Voice of the American People. This concern was greater for a president than a governor, given the president's broader electoral mandate and status as continental commander in chief. But beginning with Jefferson's election, Americans began to embrace a system in which presidential aspirants ran national campaigns, sought direct voter approval, and claimed popular mandates upon election.

The biggest flaw in standard civics accounts of the electoral college is that they never mention the real demon dooming direct national election in 1787 and 1803: slavery.

At the Philadelphia convention, the visionary Pennsylvanian James Wilson proposed direct national election of the president. But in a key speech on July 19, 1787, the savvy Virginian James Madison suggested that such a system would prove unacceptable to the South: "The right of suffrage was much more diffusive in the Northern than the Southern States; and the latter could have no influence in the election on the score of Negroes."[19] In other words, in a direct election system, the North would outnumber the South, whose many slaves (more than half a million in all) of course could not vote. But the electoral college—a prototype of which Madison proposed in this same speech—instead let each southern state count its slaves, albeit with a two-fifths discount, in computing its share of the overall electoral college.

Virginia emerged as the big winner—the California of the Founding era—with twelve out of a total of ninety-one electoral votes allocated by the Philadelphia Constitution, more than a quarter of the forty-six needed to win in the first round. After the 1800 census, Wilson's free state of Pennsylvania had 10 percent more free persons than Virginia, but got 20 percent fewer electoral votes. Perversely, the more slaves Virginia (or any other slave state) bought or bred, the more electoral votes it would receive. Were a slave state to free any blacks who then moved north, the state could actually lose electoral votes.

If the system's pro-slavery tilt was not overwhelmingly obvious when the Constitution was ratified, it quickly became so. Slaveholding Virginians won eight of the nation's first nine presidential elections.

Southerner Thomas Jefferson, for example, won the election of 1800–1801 against northerner John Adams in a race where the slavery-skew of the electoral college was the decisive margin of victory: *Without the extra electoral-college votes generated by slavery, the mostly southern states that supported Jefferson would not have sufficed to give him a majority.* As pointed observers remarked at the time, Thomas Jefferson metaphorically rode into the executive mansion on the backs of slaves.

The 1796 contest between Adams and Jefferson had featured an even sharper division between northern states and southern states. Thus, at the time the Twelfth Amendment tinkered with the electoral-college system rather than tossing it, the system's pro-slavery bias was hardly a secret. Indeed, in the floor debate over the amendment in late 1803, Massachusetts congressman Samuel Thatcher complained that "[t]he representation of slaves adds thirteen members to this House in the present Congress, and eighteen Electors of President and Vice President at the next election."[20] But Thatcher's complaint went unredressed. Once again, the North caved to the South by refusing to insist on direct national election.

The Founding Fathers' electoral college also didn't do much for the Founding mothers. Had a system of direct national election existed, a state that opted to enfranchise its women would have thereby doubled its heft in presidential elections. (New Jersey apparently did allow some women to vote in the Founding era, but later abandoned the practice.) Under the electoral college, however, a state had no comparable spur to expand suffrage—each state got an assigned allotment of electoral votes based on population, regardless of how many or how few citizens were allowed to vote or actually voted. As with slaves, what mattered was simply how many women resided in a state, not how many could vote there.

In light of this more complete (if less flattering) account of the electoral college in the late eighteenth and early nineteenth century, Americans must ask themselves whether we want to maintain this peculiar institution in the twenty-first century.

Most millennial Americans no longer believe in slavery or sexism. We do not believe that voters lack proper information about national candidates. We do not believe that a national figure claiming a national mandate is unacceptably dangerous. What we do believe is that each American is an equal citizen. We celebrate the idea of one person, one vote—an idea undermined by the electoral college.

Of course, it remains possible that a system with dirty roots nevertheless makes sense today for rather different reasons than the ones present at the creation. Stay tuned.

COUNTERING THE TOP TEN ARGUMENTS FOR THE ELECTORAL COLLEGE

FindLaw, Friday, December 14, 2001
(with Vikram David Amar)

A year ago, Americans watched the loser of the national popular vote win the electoral vote (with a little help from his friends on and off the Court). In a continental republic of equal citizens, why shouldn't every voter's ballot count equally in a single nationwide vote for president? If one person, one vote is the best way to pick a state governor, why isn't it also the best way to pick a national president?

Many of the modern arguments on behalf of the electoral college are superficially clever, but ultimately makeweight. Often they sweep too broadly and prove too much, with unattractive logical implications. In general, most pro-electoral-college arguments (both those listed below, and other, more minor arguments) unwittingly but unavoidably condemn direct popular election of governors, a deeply established American practice.

Granted, a few arguments for the electoral college do have the right logical shape—explaining why presidential elections should differ from gubernatorial ones—and thus do not have the flaw of proving too much. But these arguments are not weighty enough to outbalance the strong principle of one person, one vote.

Here, then, are the top ten modern arguments for the electoral college and the reasons they do not persuade:

Number 1: The Argument from Political Interest

Some might prefer the electoral college because it advantages a given political interest—say, rural voters or racial minorities. But does today's electoral college strongly and systematically favor any given faction? Not likely.

True, the electoral college was designed to and did in fact advantage southern white male propertied slaveholders in the antebellum era. And in the 2000 election, it again ended up working against women, blacks, and the poor, who voted overwhelmingly for Gore. But it's easy to imagine an alternative 2000 election scenario in which Gore won the electoral vote while losing the national popular vote. Indeed, most pundits going into Election Day thought this the more likely possibility.

Analytically, the electoral college privileges small states by giving every state three electoral votes at the start. This tends to help Republicans, who win among rural whites. But the college also exaggerates the power of big states, via winner-take-all rules. That tends to help Democrats, who win among urban minorities.

In today's world, the two opposing skews largely cancel out. Republicans often win more states overall, but Democrats often win more big states. The net effect is to add to the political deck a pair of jokers—one red and one blue—who randomly surface to mock the equality idea by giving the prize to the candidate who lost the national popular vote.*

In any event, even assuming it could be shown that the electoral college systemically helps some interest group, this is hardly a principled argument in its favor. Our Constitution should not rig elections to favor any particular faction or party. We should treat all presidential voters equally, just as we do gubernatorial voters within states.

---

* [In the decade and a half since I wrote these words in 2001, I have come to think that the electoral college may be beginning to tip slightly in the Democrats' favor, making it a bit more likely in the immediately foreseeable future that if a joker pops up, his color will be blue. For details, see supra pp. 336–337.]

Number 2: The Tennis Analogy

Electoral college defenders also make the following argument: "A tennis player can win more points overall, and even more games, yet still lose the match. So, too, with many other sports. For example, a baseball team might get more hits or win more innings but still lose. So what's the problem if something similar happens with the electoral college?"

The problem is that elections are not sporting events. It matters who wins, and the idea is not simply to make the thing exciting or random. All tennis points are not created equal; but all American citizens are. To talk of tennis is simply to sidestep rather than engage the moral principle favoring one person, one vote.

The tennis trope is a silly analogy, not a serious argument. It also proves too much, calling into question our standard mode of picking state governors. Ditto for a variant of the tennis analogy, which casually dismisses direct popular election as "simpleminded majoritarianism."

Number 3: The Media Argument

Electoral college defenders argue that without the electoral college, candidates will spend all their time trying to rack up big victories in big cities with big media, ignoring the rest of the voters.

But this objection also proves too much. The very same thing might be said of the California governor's election. And the electoral college itself often focuses candidates narrowly on a few swing locations to the detriment of most other regions.

Number 4: The Geographic Concentration Argument

Defenders also contend that the electoral college prevents purely regional candidates from winning by requiring the winner to put together a continental coalition popular in many different regions.

Really? Then how did Lincoln win the electoral college without winning a single southern state, or even being on the ballot south of Virginia? Didn't the elections of 1796 and 1800 also feature sharp sectional divisions between North and South? And if geographic spread is a good argument for a continental electoral college, why isn't it an equally good argument for an intrastate electoral college for vast and populous states like California and Texas?

Finally, under direct election, presidential candidates would continue to wage broad national campaigns appealing to voters in different states and regions: Anyone aiming for a national majority needs to win many votes in many places.

Number 5: The Argument from Inertia

Other electoral college defenders have argued that a change in presidential selection rules would radically change the election game: Because candidates would no longer care about winning states—only votes—campaign strategies would change dramatically and for the worse.

It's hard to see why. Given that, historically, the electoral-college leader has also tended to be the popular vote leader, the strategy for winning shouldn't change dramatically if we switch from one measure to the other.

Granted, had direct election been in place in 2000, the candidates might have run slightly different campaigns. For example, Bush might have tried to rack up even more votes in his home state, while Gore might have avoided badmouthing the state (aka "messing with Texas"). But these likely changes of strategy are neither big nor bad.

Again, why would a system that works so well for state governors fail for the presidency?

That said, the inertia argument has some weight. Reforms often have unforeseen consequences; and it is always possible that we are better off sticking with the devil we know.[21]

Number 6: The Senate Anxiety

Others have claimed that the principle of one person, one vote would likewise doom the equal representation of states in the United States Senate.

This argument at least raises a fair point. The equality idea that favors the abolition of the electoral college does raise questions about Senate malapportionment: Why should the 30-something million citizens living in California get no more senators than the half million citizens living in Wyoming?

But the electoral-college issue is nevertheless distinguishable. On Election Day, Americans vote in thirty-three (or thirty-four) separate Senate races, each featuring a different candidate matchup. These votes cannot simply be added together. To try to add them up—X percent for "the

Democrat" and Y percent for "the Republican" is artificial, given that thirty-three different Democrats are running against thirty-three different Republicans in thirty-three different races.

In contrast, presidential votes can be aggregated across America—indeed, it is artificial *not* to add them together, and the violation of equality is much more flagrant when a person who plainly got fewer votes is nevertheless named the winner.

Number 7: The Third Party and Plurality Winner Problem

Another argument often raised is this one: "Direct election could either lead to a low plurality winner (say, 35 percent) in a three- or four-way race, or would require a high cutoff (say, 45 percent) that would require a runoff. Allowing runoffs would encourage third-party spoilers."

But the very same thing is true for states, which manage to elect governors just fine. Moreover, a low plurality winner in a three- or four-way race is possible even with the electoral college, which has also attracted its fair share of spoilers—just ask Ross Perot or Ralph Nader.

Finally, the problem could easily be solved in a direct national election by a system called single transferable voting, in which voters list their second and third choices on the ballot—in effect combining the first heat and runoff elections into a single "instant runoff" transaction.

Number 8: The Recount Nightmare

Other electoral-college fans are haunted by the specter of recounts: "If you thought the recount in Florida was a disaster, can you imagine the nightmare of a national recount?"

But if California, Texas, New York, and other large states can handle recounts for governors' races, a national recount should likewise be manageable, especially with new technology that will make counting and recounting easier in the future.

Moreover, the electoral college does not avoid, and at times can worsen, the recount nightmare: As we saw last year, a paper-thin electoral-college margin may require recounts in a number of closely contested states even if there is a clear national popular winner. But the recount issue does remind us that direct national election would ideally involve uniform national standards for counting and recounting votes.

Number 9: The Modern Federalism Argument

Many supporters of the electoral college parade under the banners of "federalism" and "states' rights." But direct national election would give state governments a better role than they now enjoy.

Under direct election, each state government would have some incentive to make it easier for its citizens to vote—say, by making Election Day a holiday or by providing paid time off—because the more state voters that turn out, the bigger the state's overall share in the national tally. Direct national election would thus encourage states to innovate and compete to increase turnout and improve democracy.

Of course, national oversight would be appropriate to keep the innovation and competition within proper bounds: No deceased or infant voters, please! Presidential elections would thus continue to reflect a mix of federal and state laws, and respect proper state innovation within a federal framework—in short, federalism at its best.

Number 10: The Futility Argument

A final argument against reform sounds in realpolitik: Adopting direct popular election would require a constitutional amendment, and no such amendment is likely given the high hurdles set out in Article V—two-thirds of the Congress and three-quarters of the states.

But the premise of this argument is wrong. In fact, as few as eleven large states acting together could operationalize direct national election. So could as few as four—yes, four—key persons acting in concert. More on all that soon.

HOW TO ACHIEVE DIRECT NATIONAL ELECTION OF THE PRESIDENT WITHOUT AMENDING THE CONSTITUTION[22]

FindLaw, Friday, December 28, 2001
(with Vikram David Amar)

Imagine this: Americans could pick the president by direct national election, in 2004 and beyond, without formally amending our Constitution. A small number of key states—eleven, to be precise—would suffice to put a direct election system into effect. Alternatively, an even smaller number of key persons—four, to be exact—could approximate the same result, with a little help from their friends.

Begin with the key-state scenario. Article II of the Constitution says that "each state shall appoint, *in such manner as the Legislature thereof may direct*" its allotted share of presidential electors. Each state's legislature thus has discretion to direct how state electors are appointed.

The legislature is free simply to name these electors itself. It is likewise free to direct by law that electors be chosen by direct popular state vote, winner take all. This is what almost all states do today.

So, too, each state legislature is free to direct that its state electors be chosen by direct popular national vote. Each state could pass the following statute: "This state shall choose a slate of electors loyal to the presidential candidate who wins the national popular vote." (Technically, the legislature does not award electoral votes as such, but rather picks from competing slates of electors who have announced in advance their loyalty to particular candidates.)

The eleven most populous states together now have 271 electoral votes, one more than the 270 votes needed to win (out of a total of 538). Thus, if all eleven passed this statute, the presidency would go to the candidate who won the national popular vote.

For those who are counting, the eleven states are California (with 55 electoral votes after the 2000 census), Texas (34), New York (31), Florida (27), Pennsylvania (21), Illinois (21), Ohio (20), Michigan (17), New Jersey (15), Georgia (15), and North Carolina (15).

There is nothing magical about these eleven states; advocates of direct national election need not draw the poker equivalent of a royal flush. If some of the big eleven were to opt out, their places could be filled by any combination of smaller states with as many total electoral votes. The number eleven is used merely to illustrate how few states would be needed, in theory, to effectuate direct national election.*

It's worth pausing to let this soak in. Under the Constitution's Article V, a constitutional amendment providing for direct national election would as a practical matter require two-thirds support in the House of Representatives,

---

* [The 2010 census reshuffled things. The eleven most populous states currently add up to precisely 270 electoral votes, as follows: California (55), Texas (38), New York (29), Florida (29), Pennsylvania (20), Illinois (20), Ohio (18), Michigan (16), Georgia (16), North Carolina (15), and New Jersey (14).]

a two-thirds vote in the Senate, and the further support of thirty-eight state legislatures.

Thus, under the Constitution, any thirteen states—theoretically, even the thirteen tiniest—could block an Article V amendment. In contrast, our hypothetical plan could succeed even if as many as thirty-nine states and Congress (which directs how the District of Columbia's three electors are to be chosen) opted out.

If the eleven biggest states were to pass our law, an odd theoretical possibility would arise: A candidate could win the presidency, by winning the national popular vote, even if he or she lost in every one of these big states! (Imagine a scenario where the candidate narrowly loses in each of these states, but wins big most other places.) Should this theoretical possibility deter big states from passing our law?

After all, the current electoral-college landscape reflects an effort by virtually every state to maximize its own influence, by awarding all of its electoral votes to the candidate who wins the state, rather than dividing its electoral votes proportionately among candidates. Take New Jersey, with its 15 electoral votes. A proportional-voting New Jersey would have only 3 electoral votes truly at stake—the difference between a 9–6 blowout victory and a 6–9 blowout defeat. This would make New Jersey no more important than a tiny winner-take-all state like Wyoming (offering either a 3–0 win or a 0–3 defeat). A winner-take-all New Jersey means not 3, but 15 electoral votes are at stake, so candidates must pay more attention to the state.

For New Jersey to abandon winner-take-all when Wyoming and almost all other states are retaining it would be the electoral equivalent of unilateral disarmament. A similar concern might discourage New Jersey from unilaterally embracing our proposed national popular vote law—this, too, is a form of unilateral disarmament, telling a candidate not to worry about winning votes in New Jersey. Indeed, a candidate could lose New Jersey's popular vote badly and still get all its electoral votes by winning nationwide. Even worse, New Jersey would be unilaterally disarming with no assurance that the presidency would in fact go to the national popular vote winner; acting alone, New Jersey cannot guarantee that its fifteen would be enough to put the national vote winner over the 270 mark.

But New Jersey need not act unilaterally. Its law could provide that its electors will go to the national vote winner if and only if enough other states follow suit. Until that happens, New Jersey and every other like-minded state could continue to follow current (self-aggrandizing) methods of choosing electors. Thus, our new model state law would look something like this: "This state shall choose a slate of electors loyal to the presidential candidate who wins the national popular vote, if and only if other states, whose electors taken together with this state's electors total at least 270, also enact laws guaranteeing that they will choose electors loyal to the presidential candidate who wins the national popular vote."

Acting in this coordinated way, a group of largish states adding up to 270 would not really be disarming themselves. Although it is theoretically possible for a candidate to win a national vote while losing in all (or almost all) of the big states, this is an unrealistic scenario. In general, candidates would tend to lavish attention on most big states because there are lots of voters in these states. As a practical matter, one can't win nationally without winning, or at least coming very close, in various populous states.

Should expressly coordinated state laws of the sort we are imagining be deemed an implicit interstate agreement requiring congressional blessing under Article I, section 10, of the Constitution? Probably not. Each state would retain complete unilateral freedom to switch back to its older system for any future election, and the coordinated law creates no new interstate governmental apparatus. Indeed, the cooperating states acting together would be exercising no more power than they are entitled to wield individually. (The matter might be different if the coordinating states had sought to freeze other states out—say, by agreeing to back the candidate winning the most total votes within the coordinating states as a collective bloc, as opposed to the most total votes nationwide.)

Of course, any coordinated state-law effort would require specifying key issues: Majority rule or plurality rule? Runoff or no? How should recounts and challenges be handled?

It would be hard to rely completely on the laws and courts of each state, many of which might not be part of the cooperating 270 group. For example, the national vote might be close even though the state vote in some non-cooperating state was not, and that state might refuse to allow a state recount. Indeed, a non-cooperating state might theoretically try to sabotage the system by refusing to allow its citizens to vote for president! What if some state let seventeen-year-olds vote in an effort to count for more than its fair share of the national total? And what about Americans who live abroad or in the federal territories?

These questions suggest an even more mind-boggling prospect: Our national-vote system need not piggyback on the laws and machinery of non-cooperating states at all! Let these non-cooperating states hold their own elections, but so long as they amount to less than 270 electors, these elections would be sideshows. The cooperating states could define their own rules for a uniform "National Presidential Vote" system. In that case, our law would read something like this:

> Section 1. This state shall choose a slate of electors loyal to the presidential candidate who wins the "National Presidential Vote," if and only if other states, whose electors taken together with this state's electors total at least 270, also enact laws guaranteeing that they will choose electors loyal to the presidential candidate who wins the "National Presidential Vote."

> Section 2. The "National Presidential Vote" shall be administered as follows. . . .

Section 2 of this model law would proceed to specify the precise rules of this "National Presidential Vote." For example, Section 2 could provide that Americans everywhere who want to be counted must register in a system to be administered by a nongovernmental election commission—made up, say, of a panel of respected political scientists and journalists (not unlike the newspaper consortium that recently announced its tallies of the Florida vote). Section 2 could also specify uniform rules of voting eligibility, uniform presidential ballots, and an election dispute procedure (with the final appeals decided by, say, the legendary presidential debate moderator Jim Lehrer). Alternatively, Section 2 might contemplate that the "National Presidential Vote" should be administered by a new interstate election council or directly by the federal government, and Congress could then pass a statute blessing this more elaborate interstate agreement.

Some will doubtless dismiss all this as mere academic daydreaming, but the daydreams are useful in illustrating how much constitutional creativity is possible within the existing constitutional framework, short of formal amendment. (In an article in the Spring 2001 issue of the *Green Bag*, Northwestern professor Robert Bennett pursues a similar thought experiment.)

Here is a final daydream. What if the two leading presidential contenders in 2004 were asked about their views of the electoral college? After the 2000 election, this seems a perfectly sensible question: It is not purely theoretical to worry about electoral college misfires of various sorts. A question about the legitimacy of the electoral college is one of many questions the candidates should be asked by Lehrer on the *News Hour* or at a presidential debate.

If candidates believe in the college, they should be prepared to give their reasons. If they seek to duck the question as overly hypothetical, they should be pressed. And if they express disapproval of the system, and pledge allegiance to the principle of one person, one vote, then they should be asked if they are willing to put their principles into action. *For the two major presidential candidates and their two running mates have it within their power to move us to direct national election.*

A candidate could pledge that if he loses the national popular vote, he will ask his electors to vote for the national popular vote winner. Having taken this pledge, the candidate could then challenge his rival to take a similar pledge. Each candidate could likewise insist that his vice-presidential running mate take the pledge.

Presumably, the candidates' handpicked electors would honor their respective candidates' solemn pledges when the electoral college met; but if not, each candidate and running mate could further pledge to resign immediately after inauguration in favor of the national popular vote winner.

The candidates themselves can make their pledges stick via the Twenty-fifth Amendment, which allows a president to fill a vacant vice presidency. Suppose for example that Smith somehow is inaugurated even though Jones won the national vote. On Inauguration Day, Smith's vice-presidential running mate would resign immediately. Smith would then name Jones the new vice president under the Twenty-fifth Amendment, and upon Jones's pro forma confirmation by Congress—he is, after all, the man with the mandate in our hypothetical—Smith would step down in favor of Jones.

If this scenario seems odd, it is useful to recall that it is not that different from the one that made Gerald Ford president in 1974: Vice President Spiro Agnew resigned, and then was replaced by Ford, who in turn became president upon Richard Nixon's resignation.

Another analogy: Beginning with George Washington, who resigned after eight years even though he would easily have won a third term, early presidents gave America a strong tradition of a two-term limit on the presidency.

Likewise, presidential candidates today could, via pre-election pledges and (if necessary) post-inauguration resignations, establish a strong tradition that the presidency should go to the person who actually won the national election. Just as the informal two-term limit ultimately became specified in constitutional text, in the Twenty-second Amendment, so, too, a series of candidate pledges could eventually pave the way for a formal direct election amendment.

And all it would take to get the ball rolling is for four persons to take the pledge in the next presidential election. Imagine that.

10

BARACK OBAMA'S DRAMA

His Signature Statute

THIS BOOK BEGAN with a scene from the Supreme Court's steps on June 28, 2012, as the justices handed down their much awaited, closely divided, intensely controversial, enormously consequential, and widely misunderstood ruling in the Obamacare case, *National Federation of Independent Business v. Sebelius*. The health care of millions of Americans hung in the balance that day, as did the constitutional legacies of both President Barack Obama and the Roberts Court. The justices were in effect judging the president, but history will ultimately judge all concerned.

It is now time to return to this case—the most important encounter between the current president and the modern Court—and to describe my own involvement as a constitutional journalist seeking to both analyze and influence events.

THE FOUR OBAMACARE ESSAYS collected in this chapter, presented in chronological sequence, reflect four different deadlines. The first deadline was journalistically created, thanks to a newsworthy birthday on January 20, 2010. To commemorate the first anniversary of Obama's history-making inauguration, the *Los Angeles Times* wanted to run dueling op-eds on the president's biggest unfinished agenda item, an ambitious health-care bill that had yet to clear Congress. The newspaper asked me if I would write something opposite Senator Orrin Hatch, a conservative Republican from Utah who was arguing that the pending bill was not merely unwise but unconstitutional. To counterbalance the senator, I composed a piece titled "Constitutional

Objections to Obamacare Don't Hold Up," which now appears as this chapter's opening essay.

Hatch's constitutional objections to the individual mandate at the heart of Obamacare were newly minted in at least two respects. First, these constitutional claims were new for him. In the 1990s, he had sponsored an individual-mandate alternative to President Clinton's proposed health-care plan (aka Hillarycare). More generally, the idea that a mandate to buy an item is somehow constitutionally problematic was itself a novel proposition in America's centuries-old constitutional conversation. Such mandates go back for centuries. In 1792, George Washington himself signed an individual mandate law regarding the militia. Yet never in American history was there any sustained claim that such a mandate was constitutionally improper—until, that is, President Obama endorsed the mandate idea. As a matter of logic, the mandate's opponents never clearly explained why government could tax me and use the tax money to buy item X and then give me X; but somehow could not require me to buy or procure X myself. Nor did anti-mandate ideologues clearly explain why a mandate that was perfectly okay for a state to impose—remember Romneycare, the similar health-care plan in Massachusetts?—somehow morphed into the very definition of tyranny when imposed by the federal government while regulating transactions that were undeniably parts of, and closely related to, the genuinely interstate commercial system that is modern American health care.

Twelve and a half months after the publication of this *L.A. Times* piece, a second deadline loomed. The law was now on the books, but a federal district judge named Roger Vinson had just ruled that the statute violated the U.S. Constitution. In his ruling, Vinson embraced some of the plainly erroneous claims that my 2010 op-ed had emphatically refuted. And so the newspaper's editors asked me if I could do a follow-up op-ed commenting on the Vinson opinion.

In this February 2011 essay, titled "Constitutional Showdown," I needed to disclose to readers that the federal official who was then responsible for defending Obamacare in the courts, the acting solicitor general of the United States, Neal Katyal, was my protégé. In previous chapters of the book, readers have already encountered a pair of pieces that Neal coauthored with me back when he was a star student at Yale in the mid-1990s; and another essay that we ended up publishing in the *New York Times* in 2013.[1]

Around the time that "Constitutional Showdown" appeared in print, Neal and I spoke by phone. When he mentioned that various briefs would likely be filed in the months ahead in several lower-federal-court proceedings involving constitutional challenges to Obamacare, I began to think that it might make sense for me to compose a longer and more academic statement of my constitutional views. Federal judges trying to sort through the constitutional issues might feel comfortable relying on and perhaps even citing to something of mine that was more substantial than a mere op-ed.

This created a deadline dilemma of its own. The piece that I was envisioning had to be both quick and long—quick enough to be ready for pending lawsuits, and long enough to elaborate the legal argument in a way that would enlighten and persuade generalist judges. The usual journalistic outlets—the *L.A. Times*, the *Washington Post*, *Slate*, and so on—would surely be quick enough for my purpose. Quick is precisely what they do; quick is where they live; quick is who they are. But these great journalistic outlets aim to quickly produce items that can also be quickly consumed—read in real time, read today because tomorrow the reader will want to read something new about the news that the new day will inevitably bring. In order to be fast in time, the usual outlets publish pieces that must be short in length. There are thus many great media outlets for quick and short. But not so many for quick and long.

Enter SSRN. This academic website, formally known as the Social Science Research Network, enables scholars to self-publish pieces of any length at any time—immediately, with the click of a mouse. Quick and long is what SSRN does, where it lives, what it is. Thus, I posted my most elaborate defense of Obamacare on SSRN on June 1, 2011. The piece, "The Lawfulness of Health-Care Reform," is by far the longest piece in this book, for reasons I have just explained. But I include it, in its entirety, in this book precisely because a book—or at least, this book—is not meant merely for a day but for an era. I believe that this piece was, when first published, and remains today, an especially clearheaded constitutional analysis of one of the most misunderstood constitutional issues of our still-young century. Read it and decide for yourself.*

---

* There is some substantive overlap between this long SSRN essay and the shorter op-eds that preceded and followed it. To preserve the accuracy of the historical record—what I said when, in my efforts to both analyze and influence unfolding events—I have not modified these essays in any substantial way. More generally, the slight overlap within this concluding chapter—and within previous chapters, for that matter—is not a bug but a feature. This overlap is entirely characteristic of journalistic contributions, each of which must stand on its own expositional base, even if it is also designed to interlock with other journalistic stand-alone pieces before and after.

But was anyone reading SSRN in real time? SSRN is quick and long—perfect!—but, alas, obscure. It reaches only a tiny fraction of the eyeballs reached by, say, the *Los Angeles Times*.

No matter. This long piece was written especially for a highly select audience: a few dozen judges, justices, and law clerks. With Neal in charge of the government's case until a new solicitor general was formally installed—and given the slowness of the Senate confirmation process, who knew when that might happen?—the ideas in my piece would likely in one way or another come before all the eyeballs that mattered most.

At least that was my hope. However, Neal ended up leaving his post as acting solicitor general in mid-2011. The incoming solicitor general, Don Verrilli, was (and is) an accomplished lawyer, but, unlike Neal, not a constitutional scholar. When the issue of Obamacare's constitutionality eventually reached the Supreme Court in 2012, Verrilli stumbled badly both in his written briefs and in his oral argument.

In Verrilli's defense, he, too, was on deadline. Prior to oral argument, he had to file his briefs within a tight time line. And he faced rigid Court-imposed word limits because the Court itself was on deadline. The justices would have to rule within a certain tight time line of their own, and thus they had to strictly cap the number of pages any litigant, including the federal government itself, could put before them. Although the Court scheduled an unusually long oral argument, stretching across three days, Verrilli still had only so many minutes to drive his points home in a complex and wide-ranging case.

Both literally (when he took a sip of water that went down the wrong pipe) and figuratively, Verrilli choked at oral argument. And his written briefs were less than stellar; in fact, he and his team undid some of the best stuff in Neal's earlier lower-court briefs. Neal would have done better at the Supreme Court precisely because Neal had spent the previous decades perfecting his craft as a constitutional law scholar. In lightning chess, grandmasters shine because their instincts have been honed by years of practice and sophisticated pattern recognition.

The Obamacare case involved a kind of lightning chess. The constitutional challenge to the law was clever in its own way, but loopy. It made the wrong moves; there were clear defenses and devastating counterattacks to it, as I explain in all the pieces in this chapter. But the challenge to Obamacare, designed by ideological academics,[2] was a highly nonstandard chess opening, an utterly unconventional attack. It was an attack that a true constitutional grandmaster, who has spent decades playing and replaying all sorts of openings and gambits and variations in his head, could easily defeat. But Verrilli was no constitutional maven; nor, apparently, was any member of his inner circle. Because these earnest civil servants were not in the habit of thinking daily about the first premises of constitutional law—its deepest roots, its unifying rhythms—they were flummoxed by the challenge. They failed to explain with crystal clarity and ruthless logic why Obamacare was clearly constitutional on any number of alternative theories; and why the ideologically inspired challenges to the law were constitutional flimflam. Because Verrilli failed to make the right moves on paper and in person, the oral argument in late March 2012 was a disaster for the government.

At which point, my phone rang once again. Several friends, both in the press and in the academy, wondered if I might be willing to write something that might bring my SSRN ideas before at least some of the eighteen eyeballs that now mattered, or at least before the eyeballs of their law clerks, and that would also help set the record straight for ordinary citizens who had been auditing the Court's constitutional seminar that week.[3]

My initial reaction to these phone calls was to keep my trap shut. I had already said my piece; it would be weird for me to say anything more now that the case had already been argued. Besides, the odds that anyone on the Court might be swayed by anything that I might say were infinitesimal. After so many hours of oral argument, hadn't everyone already made up his or her mind?

But on second thought. . . . Although some justices had said some troubling things at oral argument, none of the justices had started to write in a serious way. The decisive writing would not begin until the following week, at the earliest. And as one writes, one thinks—and sometimes, rethinks. One sometimes backtracks to do additional research and reading. The deadline for the Court's final decision was still several months away. So I decided to take one last shot at making my argument in a way that might matter. Given that I was, in truth, writing directly for the Court, I explicitly styled the piece as an open letter to the justices, an informal amicus brief. In retrospect, long before oral argument I should have simply filed a slightly revised version of my SSRN essay as a formal amicus brief. Had Neal still been in charge of the case when it reached the Supreme Court I probably would have done just that.

I published my quickly composed piece, "How to Defend Obamacare: What Verrilli Should Have Said," in *Slate* the day after oral argument ended. I knew that the following day, the Court was scheduled to meet in conference, where the justices would likely take a preliminary vote. After that, the judicial writing process would begin in earnest.

I have no hard evidence that any justice, or even any law clerk, at any point over the next three months paid even the slightest attention to what I had written in Slate or SSRN. Still, two things are worth mentioning for the record.

First, my Slate piece correctly prefigured both the final vote and the final rationale. In perfect conformity with the concluding passages of my Slate essay, Obamacare was upheld by Chief Justice John Roberts and the four Democratic appointees (Justices Ruth Bader Ginsburg, Stephen Breyer, Sonia Sotomayor, and Elena Kagan) as a valid exercise of Congress's taxation power. This was the theory that I had advocated first and foremost in my SSRN essay, even though almost everyone else at the time—including CNN's and Fox's pundits, all the way to the end—seemed to be focusing exclusively on the interstate-commerce clause.

In both SSRN and in Slate, I had tried to craft my tax argument in a way that would particularly appeal to Chief Justice Roberts, in light of his professed philosophy of judicial restraint. A similar philosophy had been famously articulated by one of Roberts's avowed role models, Justice Louis Brandeis, in a canonical concurring opinion in a 1936 case, Ashwander v. TVA—an opinion that I thus prominently mentioned in the Slate essay. (Roberts, I knew, had clerked for the great jurist Henry Friendly, who had in turn clerked for Brandeis.) Although Roberts's eventual Obamacare opinion did not explicitly cite Brandeis or Ashwander, Roberts did, at the single most critical turn of his opinion—the nail that saved the kingdom—cite the precise case and the precise page that Brandeis in Ashwander had himself cited, page 62 of a 1932 case called Crowell v. Benson. Neither Ashwander nor the Crowell passage was cited by Verrilli's brief; but thanks to my interventions the previous year, Ashwander had been cited prominently and properly in Neal's brief for the government in the earlier stages of the case.*

---

* For a journalistic account of my earliest conversations with Neal about Obamacare, in the winter of 2011, when I urged Neal to emphasize the tax theory above all and to aim directly at Chief Justice Roberts via an Ashwander approach, see Marcia Coyle, The Roberts Court (New York: Simon and Schuster, 2013), 319–322. I never spoke to Coyle in connection with this book, but I was tickled to read what Neal told her: "I thought Akhil's suggestion was very smart. . . . I didn't think, honestly, at the time, [that this] idea was going to be the thing that won, but you know, it turns out to be."

The second point worth mentioning about my *Slate* piece is that in it I tried to play the *time* card. Given the drift of the oral argument, I was at that moment focusing on one person: John Roberts. He was the key to the case, and I was trying to remind him that even though he was the umpire today, in the long run—in time—future generations will ultimately judge today's judges. Were the Roberts Court to rule against Obamacare, I claimed that such a ruling would not survive *over time*. This was not a close play at the plate, I insisted, and in time, the verdict of history would not be equivocal, especially if the case were decided via a partisan lineup reminiscent of *Bush v. Gore*.

This was a ridiculously cheeky thing for me to say, but I believed it in my bones then and I still believe it now. Constitutional law is not wholly indeterminate. It is not all politics or partisanship. Some constitutional claims are pretty clearly right or wrong; and the arguments against Obamacare were clearly wrong and could not stand the test *of time*. Though any one—a TV pundit, a solicitor general, a Supreme Court justice, or of course a Yale constitutional law professor—can goof badly in real time when acting on deadline, in the long run bad constitutional arguments lose out to good ones. This was a comforting thought back in 2012 and it remains a comforting thought today.

CONSTITUTIONAL OBJECTIONS TO OBAMACARE DON'T HOLD UP

LOS ANGELES TIMES, WEDNESDAY, JANUARY 20, 2010

Critics of Obamacare are now upping the ante, claiming that its basic outlines are not just unwise but unconstitutional. I'm no health-care expert, but

---

Of course, in my various writings and in my conversations with Neal, I also advocated other arguments for Obamacare's constitutionality, in the belt-and-suspenders tradition. To the extent that various justices overlooked or rejected some of these other arguments in the *Sebelius* case, I continue to believe that these justices erred—by which I mean, among other things, that these justices misread the Constitution's text, history, and structure, and garbled prior case law. To recast this point temporally, I predict that future generations of constitutional jurists and scholars who will have the luxury of reexamining the issues free from intense time pressure or political pressure will side with me even on various points that failed to persuade a majority of justices in *Sebelius*.

I have spent the last three decades studying the Constitution, and the current plan easily passes constitutional muster.

It's true that the Constitution grants Congress authority to legislate only in the areas enumerated in the document itself. Other matters are left to the states under the Tenth Amendment. But if enumerated power does exist, the Tenth Amendment objection disappears.

Under the interstate-commerce clause of Article I, activities whose effects are confined within a given state are to be regulated by that state government, or simply left unregulated. But the federal government is specifically empowered to address matters that have significant spillover effects across state lines or international borders.

Federal regulation makes obvious sense if the interstate or international issue involves trade or navigation. But the Founders authorized Congress to act even in situations that did not involve explicit markets, so long as the activities truly crossed state lines or national borders. Today, that power properly extends to regulating such things as air pollution that wafts across state lines or endangered species that migrate across borders. In line with this broad understanding, George Washington signed a law preventing Americans from committing even non-economic crimes on Indian lands because such activities did indeed involve "commerce . . . with the Indian tribes."

The health-care bill clearly addresses activities that cross state lines. These activities are often economic in nature. Currently, workers with preexisting medical conditions may be unable to accept job offers originating in another state—a reality that clogs the free interstate flow of goods and services. Other Americans relocate to states with better public health benefits, creating interstate races to the bottom as states worry about becoming "welfare magnets." Some grandparents now refrain from visiting their out-of-state grandchildren because of anxieties about out-of-network health-care delivery systems. Obamacare addresses all of these matters of interstate commerce.

The Founders' Constitution also gave Congress sweeping power to impose all sorts of taxes. The slogan of those at the Boston Tea Party in 1773 was "No taxation without representation"—Parliament should not tax Americans because Parliament did not represent Americans. But after independence, the Founders created a representative Congress with explicit authority to tax Americans up, down, and sideways.

The longest section of the Constitution's longest article—Article I, section 8, to be precise—opens with the following words: "The Congress shall have power to lay and collect taxes, duties, imposts and excises." During the Progressive era, Americans amended the Constitution to underscore the broad power of Congress to tax, and indeed to tax for redistributive purposes. This is the plain meaning and original intent of the Sixteenth Amendment.

The reason for this sweeping power to tax was clearly set out in Article I: Taxes would "pay the debts and provide for the common defense and general welfare." One special Founding-era concern was national security. Taxes would be needed to fund national defense. Today, national health does indeed affect America's ultimate national strength and national defense posture.

This broad view of national defense is precisely the one endorsed by President Washington in 1791 when he signed a bill creating a national bank. The word "bank" does not appear in the Constitution. Nevertheless, supporters of the bank understood that it would exist in the service of national defense, helping to pay soldiers on site and on time and to manage wartime finances. In 1819, the Supreme Court unanimously upheld the bank as plausibly connected to national security.

After the Civil War, Americans amended the Constitution to give Congress another explicit authority relevant in the health-care debate: Section 5 of the Fourteenth Amendment charges Congress with protecting basic human rights. Health care is such a right—or at least Congress is constitutionally allowed to decide it is. Those who disagree should simply vote for different congressional members rather than hiding behind bad constitutional arguments that do violence to the text and original intent of the Fourteenth Amendment.

Beyond the broad question of federal power, critics of Obamacare have also raised a series of more focused objections. None holds water.

The plan is not a constitutionally improper "taking" of property without just compensation. It is a broad tax connected to a broad set of compensating benefits.

The plan may well have different costs and effects in different states. So do many federal laws, taxes, and expenditures. Thus, federal gasoline taxes bite harder in states with higher gasoline consumption. More NASA money goes to Florida and Texas than to various other states. Federal income tax laws allowing deductions for state taxes benefit high-tax states. Mortgage deductions provide more benefits to states with more expensive housing stock.

True, the plan requires people to buy something from a private industry. But if Congress can tax, and can then spend the tax money to buy a policy from private industry, and can then offer this policy as a government benefit, why can't it do all three at once and cut out the middleman? (Would critics really prefer a government-run single-payer plan?)

True, the plan imposes mandates on individuals. So do jury service laws, draft registration laws, and automobile insurance laws.

Maybe Obamacare is good policy; maybe not. But it is clearly constitutional. Recent critics of the plan are mangling the very Constitution they claim to cherish.

CONSTITUTIONAL SHOWDOWN

Los Angeles Times, Sunday, February 6, 2011

Earlier this week, after grading student papers from my Yale Law School class on constitutional law, I began reading Federal District Judge Roger Vinson's recent opinion declaring "Obamacare" unconstitutional. One thing was immediately clear: My students understand the Constitution better than the judge.

I strive to be apolitical in evaluating students and judges alike. Over the years, many of my favorite students have been proud conservatives, while others have been flaming liberals. The Constitution belongs to neither party.

As every first-year law student learns, lower-court judges must heed Supreme Court precedents. The central issue in the Obamacare case is how much power the Constitution gives Congress, and the landmark Supreme Court opinion on this topic is the 1819 classic, McCulloch v. Maryland.

In McCulloch, when states' rights attorneys claimed that Congress lacked authority to create a federal bank, Chief Justice John Marshall famously countered that the Constitution gives Congress implied as well as express powers. Marshall said that unelected judges should generally defer to elected members of Congress so long as a law plausibly falls within Congress's basic mission. Though the words "federal bank" nowhere appear in the Constitution's text, Marshall explained that Congress nevertheless had the power to create such a bank to facilitate national security and interstate commerce. Other words not in the Constitution include "air force," "NASA," "Social Security," "Peace Corps," and "paper money," but all these things are constitutional under the logic of McCulloch. Obamacare is no different.

In thirty-four years as chief justice, Marshall never struck down an act of Congress as beyond the scope of federal power.[4] The modern Supreme Court has followed Marshall's lead. Since 1937, only two relevant cases—U.S. v. Lopez in 1995 and U.S. v. Morrison in 2000—have held that federal laws transgressed the limited powers conferred on Congress by the framers.[5]

Neither of the laws at issue in these cases plausibly fell within the Constitution's grant of congressional power to regulate "commerce among the several states"—a phrase that includes all interstate transactions, such as a national market in goods or services or a situation in which people, pollution, water, or wildlife cross state lines.

By contrast, Obamacare regulates a health-care industry that obviously spans state lines, involving billions of dollars and millions of patients flowing from state to state. When uninsured Connecticut residents fall sick on holiday in California and get free emergency room services, California taxpayers, California hospitals, and California insurance policyholders foot the bill. This is an interstate issue, and Congress has power to regulate it.

Even were it conceded that a particular piece of Obamacare regulates a wholly intrastate matter, that piece is OK so long as it is a cog within a truly interstate regulatory regime. In 2005, the Court allowed Congress to criminalize private possession of homegrown marijuana plants because, even if these plants did not themselves cross state lines, a blanket prohibition was part of a legal dragnet regulating a genuinely interstate black market in drugs.

There is nothing improper in the means that Obamacare deploys. Laws may properly regulate both actions and inactions, and in any event, Obamacare does not regulate pure inaction. It regulates free riding. Breathing is an action, and so is going to an emergency room on taxpayers' nickel when you have trouble breathing.

Nor is there anything improper about requiring people to buy or obtain a private product. In 1792, George Washington signed into law a militia act that did just that, obliging Americans to equip themselves with muskets, bayonets, cartridges, the works.

Strictly speaking, Obamacare does not mandate the purchase of insurance. It says that those who remain uninsured must pay a tax. Vinson says this mandate cannot be upheld under Congress's sweeping tax powers. Wrong again. A basic purpose of the Founders was to create sweeping federal tax power, power that was emphatically reinforced by the 1913 income tax amendment.

If Congress can tax me, and can use my tax dollars to buy a health-insurance policy for me, why can't it tell me to get a policy myself (or pay extra taxes)? Vinson offers no cogent answer to this basic logical point.

He also mangles American history and constitutional structure. In a clumsy wave to today's "Tea Party" groups, he rhetorically asks whether Americans who fought a tax on imported tea in the 1770s would have authorized Congress in the 1780s to mandate tea purchases.

Huh?

Surely Congress was authorized to do the very thing that Parliament could not—tax imported tea. Congress could do so precisely because Congress, unlike Parliament (and unlike Vinson) is elected by voters who can vote the bums out if they do not like the taxes. The rallying cry of the American Revolution was not "No Taxation!" but "No Taxation Without Representation!" Congress represents voters, so it can tax voters, or impose mandates on voters, regarding tea or militia service—or insurance policies.

(In the interest of full disclosure, I should note that Acting Solicitor General Neal Katyal, who will defend Obamacare in the appellate courts, is a former student of mine. But my views today have nothing to do with him, and everything to do with constitutional first principles.)

Obamacare's opponents are free to vote for politicians who will repeal it. They should not use seats on lower courts to distort the Constitution, disregard applicable precedents, and disrespect a duly elected Congress, which gave Americans in early 2010 exactly what the winning party platform promised in November 2008.

In 1857, another judge named Roger distorted the Constitution, disregarded precedent, disrespected Congress, and proclaimed that the basic platform of one of America's two major political parties was unconstitutional. The case was *Dred Scott v. Sanford*, involving a slave who sued for his freedom because he had lived with his master in places where Congress had banned slavery. In an opinion by Chief Justice Roger Taney, the Court not only ruled against Scott on the narrow facts of the case, but also sweepingly declared that Congress's famous 1820 Missouri Compromise, which had outlawed slavery in northern territories, was unconstitutional. Under Taney's preposterous and activist illogic, the basic Republican Party platform of the 1850s—advocating a congressional ban on slavery in all federal territory—was likewise unconstitutional.

History has not been kind to that judge. Roger Vinson, meet Roger Taney.

THE LAWFULNESS OF HEALTH-CARE REFORM[6]

POSTED (I.E., SELF-PUBLISHED) ON *SSRN*.COM, JUNE 1, 2011

Call it Obamacare, if you like. Or call it the Affordable Care Act, if you prefer. But don't call it unconstitutional.

In what follows, I shall often call it "Obamacare." Some readers might wonder whether anything turns on labeling choices such as this. Shakespeare reminds us that "a rose by any other name would smell as sweet." After asking his audience how many legs a dog has "if you call its tail a leg," Abraham Lincoln, according to legend, answered "four." Calling a tail a leg, Lincoln explained, doesn't make it so. More recently, Justice Antonin Scalia warned that judges should not be "faked out" by statutory labels.

But names and labels sometimes do matter, even when they shouldn't. The names "Montague" and "Capulet" mattered all too much in Renaissance Verona, with tragic consequences. Lincoln's tail tale got a laugh precisely because of its initial misdirection. Scalia's warning occurred in dissent; the Court majority in that case was in fact faked out by the popular label "line item veto," even though the statute at issue actually created no such unconstitutional contraption.

Critics of Obamacare are likewise hoping to fake out judges with sly word games. For example, critics argue that Obamacare's individual mandate cannot be justified as an exercise of Congress's sweeping tax powers because Congress did not incant the magic word "tax" in this subsection. As we shall see, the critics' name-game claim that all taxes must be explicitly labeled "taxes" to count as taxes mangles the Constitution's text, distorts the document's deep structure, has no historical support, and flouts binding precedent.

If labels can sometimes matter and mislead, why then do I routinely use the label "Obamacare"—the nickname preferred by the law's leading critics, whose main constitutional arguments I emphatically reject and indeed deem preposterous? First, I use the label to signal that the health-care reform law is easily and obviously constitutional even when analysts grant every genuinely reasonable point made against this law. Because it is indeed plausible to call the thing "Obamacare," and because using that plausible label directly engages critics on their own terms, my previous public pronouncements on health-care reform have regularly referred to "Obamacare," and I shall continue to use this nickname today.

Second, the "Obamacare" label usefully locates the health-care debate in a broader political and constitutional context. Many critics of the 2010 law are so contemptuous of Barack Obama, a man whose very legitimacy as president has been denied by a notable minority of Americans, that these critics believe that linking the law to the man is actually a prima facie constitutional argument against the law. As some see it, Obama himself is constitutionally illegitimate, and any law tightly linked to him must also be unconstitutional.

Whether or not this spin works on Election Day 2012, it should operate precisely the other way for any sober-minded federal judge. Indeed, the very label "Obamacare" is ultimately evidence of the constitutional cluelessness of many critics insofar as they actually aim to enlist the federal judiciary in their political crusade. Unwittingly, the critics' label of choice highlights why federal judges should exercise special restraint when this law is challenged in court. President "Obama" did indeed push for and sign the 2010 health-care reform. This program is indeed the signature achievement of President "Obama"—the main thing he ran for in 2008 and the main thing he must run on in 2012. The reform measure is indeed all about "care." The 2010 health-reform law does in fact echo an earlier landmark law with the word "care" in its popular title: the Social Security Act of 1965 that established the iconic "Medicare" program. "Obama" plus "care" does indeed equal "Obamacare."

All of which means that judges should approach health-care reform with far *more* deference than what is due ordinary, everyday, less-than-iconic, inside-the-beltway acts of Congress. Not all laws aim to extend care to especially vulnerable Americans, and a handful of the federal laws that do extend such care in certain special ways properly qualify as civil-rights or human-rights statutes, meriting special judicial respect as congressional enforcements of Amendments Thirteen and Fourteen above and beyond whatever enumerated powers Congress can claim under Article I. Rarely in history can a congressional statute as plausibly claim to rest on an emphatic presidential mandate to which judges should defer in the absence of patent unconstitutionality—unconstitutionality so clear that jurists of *all* stripes, appointed by presidents of *both* parties, broadly concur in the verdict that the law cannot stand. Seldom is America's system of national elections so structurally superior to ordinary Article III adjudication as a forum for judging a clearly defined and easily understood constitutional question.

"Six Impossible Things Before Breakfast"

Obamacare critics' central constitutional claim is that the 2010 law's individual-mandate provision exceeds Congress's proper regulatory authority. In essence, this provision requires a broad swath of Americans to procure health insurance that conforms to certain federal standards. Those who do not procure this insurance must generally pay a penalty to the Internal Revenue Service.

The critics' central constitutional claim sounds in federalism. In essence, critics argue that Congress lacks enumerated power to impose this mandate. This claim does not sound in separation of powers. Critics do not, for example, argue that while the federal government has power to impose an individual mandate, the mandate fails to provide proper federal legislative standards for the IRS or proper federal judicial oversight of the IRS. Nor do critics generally contend that Obamacare's individual mandate violates the Bill of Rights. If it did, so, too, would the individual mandate underlying Massachusetts health-care laws (popularly known as "Romneycare"), given that states are generally held to the same Bill of Rights rules that apply against the federal government. Rather, the critics' central contention is that Obamacare's individual mandate usurps the power of states. While states may properly impose an individual mandate, the federal government may not, claim the critics.

As it turns out, however, Obamacare is not only a proper exercise of federal constitutional authority, it is proper under at least six different theories, each one of which has deep roots in constitutional text and common sense, and five of which also have compelling support in binding Supreme Court case law. Any one of the six theories outlined below suffices to uphold the act in court. Critics must thus persuade the judiciary to reject each of these six sensible theories. To borrow from Lewis Carroll, any judge who claims that Obamacare exceeds federal power must in effect believe "six impossible things before breakfast."

I. The Mandate as a Tax

First, a judge must believe that Obamacare's individual mandate cannot be upheld as a simple, straightforward tax. Under Obamacare, those persons who choose not to obtain insurance pursuant to the individual mandate are generally required to pay a tax instead. The moneys raised from this tax in turn enable the government to finance emergency health care for the uninsured and to subsidize health-care insurance for those who would like to purchase such insurance but cannot easily do so without financial assistance.

It is outlandish to think that these provisions exceed the sweeping power that the Constitution confers upon Congress to "lay and collect Taxes, Duties, Imposts, and Excises." This sweeping tax power is the opening sentence of the longest section of the Constitution's first and longest article. A primary goal (indeed, perhaps the single most important and frequently expressed goal) of the Federalist Founders was to empower the federal government to impose taxes upon individuals to finance basic federal functions—to "pay the Debts and provide for the common Defence and General Welfare of the United States," in the language of the Article I tax clause. This language, in turn, notably echoed the Preamble, thus providing yet more evidence— visible to Americans of the ratifying generation and of every subsequent generation—of the central importance of sweeping federal taxation power to the entire constitutional project.

In short, a dozen years after staging an anti-tax revolution against the British, Americans, led once again by George Washington, effectuated a pro-tax revolution. This pro-tax revolution (also known as the "Constitution of the United States") underscored what should have been plain to careful observers all along: Patriots in 1776 had not challenged all taxation as such, but had rebelled against the oppressive British practice and theory of taxation *without representation*. In the words of the Declaration of Independence, Americans revolted because George III and Parliament had conspired to "impos[e] Taxes on us *without our Consent*."

Article I, section 8, opened with a resounding commitment to sweeping federal taxing power precisely because earlier provisions of Article I, and of the Preamble, made clear that this taxation would occur *with actual consent and actual representation*. Thus, the Preamble proclaimed that the entire constitutional system, taxes and all, would go into effect only thanks to a special electoral ordainment of the document by a special vote of the American people themselves. Article I, section 2, made clear that the new Congress would include a House of *Representatives* worthy of its name, composed of men who would be directly elected to *represent* the ordinary Americans who would be subject to taxes and other congressionally imposed burdens. Section 7 of this article provided that all bills raising revenues—essentially, all tax bills—would need to originate in this special house of representation.

Section 3 of Article I mandated that the upper house of Congress would also be chosen by the American people, albeit indirectly, as would the president, who under the explicit provisions of section 7 would play a role in enacting all proposed federal legislation, including all federal tax legislation.

The upshot of all this for Obamacare is that Congress was purposefully given sweeping power to tax ordinary Americans, subject to the key textual and structural principles that Congress must vote for these taxes; that Congress and the presidency must be truly representative institutions; that all taxes must originate in the House of Representatives; and that these representatives must regularly come before the electorate, as must senators and presidents. *The check on abusive taxation was emphatically not activist judicial review, but popular elections.*

This was precisely the theme sounded by Chief Justice John Marshall, himself a former congressman, in his most elaborate judicial discussion of congressional power, which of course occurred in the iconic 1819 case of *McCulloch v. Maryland*. In this case, forbears of the modern Tea Party trumped up various ad hoc states'-rights objections to a landmark congressional statute, and tried to dress up these political objections as constitutional arguments. Marshall would have none of it, emphatically rejecting these objections in a unanimous opinion for the Court that every federal judge considering a challenge to Obamacare should read slowly from start to finish at least three times. (I am not joking here. Over the course of the last quarter-century, I have re-read *McCulloch* in its entirety at least fifty times, and have profited from each re-reading. This opinion is the centerpiece of the first chapter of the constitutional law casebook I have the honor to coedit, and *McCulloch's* sweeping vision of federal power is a prominent theme of my 2005 book, *America's Constitution: A Biography*, and its recently completed sequel, *America's Unwritten Constitution*.)

In passing, here is what Marshall said about the nature of the taxing power, and about the key check on this power: "[T]he power of taxing the people and their property is essential to the very existence of government, and may be legitimately exercised on the objects to which it is applicable, to the utmost extent to which the government may chuse to carry it. *The only security against the abuse of this power is found in the structure of the government itself. In imposing a tax the legislature acts upon its constituents. This is in general a sufficient security against erroneous and oppressive taxation.*"

Although Marshall in this passage was speaking directly about state taxation, his point rings equally true for federal taxation. Those who do not like

Obamacare's tax scheme are free to vote for new representatives, senators, and presidents, who in turn are free to repeal and/or replace Obamacare. Political critics should not be allowed to use federal courts to undo Obamacare in the name of the Constitution when the Constitution contains no relevant textual provision or structural principle that casts doubt on Obamacare.

This general point can be recast as a specific response to Federal District Judge Roger Vinson's preposterous opinion proclaiming the individual mandate unconstitutional. In a clumsy and consummately injudicious wave to the modern Tea Party movement, Vinson rhetorically asked whether Americans who fought a tax on imported tea in the 1770s would have authorized Congress in the 1780s to mandate tea purchases.

To which the only legally and historically sound response is that *of course* Congress was authorized to do all sorts of things that Parliament could not properly do. That was the whole point of the American Revolution and the American Constitution. As made clear by the logic of Marshall's above-quoted passage in *McCulloch*, Congress in the 1790s could, for example, tax imported tea whereas Parliament in the 1770s could not properly do so, precisely because Congress, unlike Parliament, would be elected by American voters who could vote the bums out if they did not like the taxes. Congress represents voters, so it can tax voters, or impose mandates on voters, whether these mandates oblige constituents to serve on militias or juries, or to buy muskets or tea or health-care insurance. As we shall see in more detail below, if Congress may tax its constituents and may use this money to buy tea, which Congress in turn may distribute to its constituents, it follows that Congress may also mandate that constituents buy the tea directly.

THE T-WORD

Obamacare's critics try to sidestep the taxing power with a word game. Because the individual-mandate clause of the statute does not explicitly use the word "taxes" but instead speaks of a "penalty" that must generally be paid to the IRS for those who refuse to procure proper health insurance, critics claim that the mandate cannot be upheld as a constitutionally proper tax.

Let us now count the ways in which this word game legally fails. First, it does violence to the Constitution's text. The text contains no such requirement that every proper federal tax must explicitly be called a "tax" in the federal statute itself. Taxation is, as we have seen, a central concern of the document. The document takes pains to specify various special rules for taxes—for example, the rule that revenue laws must originate in the House of Representatives. But the text has no rule that every tax must be labeled a "tax."

Indeed, the Constitution itself does not always use the T-word when referring to taxes, broadly defined. It also uses the words "excises," "duties," and "imposts" in the opening sentence of Article I, section 8, and elsewhere refers generally to all generic "Bills for raising Revenue." If the critics' Simon Says word game were accepted—if every tax must explicitly say "tax"—then the Constitution itself would be unconstitutional, because the Constitution itself does not always and invariably use the T-word.

If Congress passed a tax law but did not use the word "tax," surely it could not thereby avoid the House-origination clause of Article I, section 7. The tax would still be a tax, and thus subject to section 7, whether or not it used the word "tax." Perhaps for that very reason, section 7 featured a broader, more generic word, "revenue." In perfect synch with this broader constitutional word, the key penalty section of Obamacare, 26 USC section 5000A, is in fact codified in title 26—the Internal *Revenue* Code. The "penalty" is paid to the Internal *Revenue* Service via forms administered by that very same Internal *Revenue* Service. Constitutionally, Obamacare does use le mot juste.

Second, the insistence that all federal "taxes" be labeled "taxes" has no historical support. There is, for example, no clause in the Declaration of Independence scathing Parliament for imposing taxes under the label "penalties."

Third, the basic structural precept underlying the Constitution, as explained by Chief Justice Marshall in *McCulloch*, is that those who impose taxes must be politically chosen and removable by those on whom the taxes are imposed. But surely members of the American electorate understand, when they are obliged to pay extra taxes to the IRS if they refuse to procure proper health insurance, that they are being taxed; and that they are being taxed by Congress and the president; and that if they do not like these taxes (howsoever labeled), that they are free to vote the bums out and vote for a new set of bums—er, lawmakers. No structural purpose would be served by a judicially fabricated Simon Says rule that taxes must always say "taxes."

Section 5000A undeniably aims at raising revenue. It is part of a larger Obamacare statute whose central purposes included amelioration of the federal government's fiscal situation. The individual mandate is a key part of a statute whose overall effects were scored by the nonpartisan Congressional Budget Office (CBO) as bending down the federal deficit by more than $100 billion. The CBO also estimated that individual mandate and related penalty provisions would themselves generate roughly $4 billion annually.

Partisan skeptics of these nonpartisan numbers are free to criticize these numbers and to vote against Congress members and the president who relied on these numbers, but judges are not equally free to dismiss these numbers, which conclusively establish for judicial purposes that Obamacare should be simply and straightforwardly upheld as a good-faith effort to improve the federal government's financial picture—a proper federal goal hearkening back to the central purposes for which the federal Constitution was drafted and ratified in the 1780s. Congress itself enacted Obamacare under special internal House rules applicable to revenue measures, and the Obamacare statute itself explicitly recites the following Senate findings: "Based on Congressional Budget Office (CBO) estimates, this Act will reduce the Federal deficit between 2010 and 2019. . . . CBO projects this Act will continue to reduce budget deficits after 2019."

Fourth, the critics' proposed Simon Says rule squarely contradicts binding Supreme Court precedent. Marshall's *McCulloch* opinion upheld the bank law by relying on the following powers listed by the chief justice: "the great powers to lay and collect taxes; to borrow money; to regulate commerce; to declare and conduct a war; and to raise and support an army." These powers, Marshall wrote, sufficed to uphold the bank *even though several of these powers were not explicitly cited in the bank bill itself*. In particular, the word "tax" nowhere appeared in the bank bill, yet Marshall nevertheless upheld the bill by relying (among other things) on Congress's sweeping tax power. The Supreme Court made this implicit aspect of *McCulloch* explicit in 1948, when the Court declared that the "constitutionality of action taken by Congress does not depend on recitals of the power which it undertakes to exercise."[7] No lower court is free to change these rules of statutory interpretation, and if the Supreme Court itself seeks to revisit the matter, it may not properly change these rules retroactively in a way that would defeat proper legislative reliance upon preexisting canons of statutory construction. Nor do the rules of construction that may bear on whether a congressional law is a proper "tax" within the meaning of the federal Tax Injunction Act have any relevance to the very different question of *constitutional* taxing power at issue in the Obamacare litigation.

Fifth (as if the preceding points were not enough!), it turns out that the key penalty section of Obamacare—the section that generally requires those who do not obtain proper health-care insurance to pay the IRS an extra amount—in fact does explicitly provide that "[a]ny penalty imposed by this section with respect to any month shall be included with a *taxpayer's* return under the chapter 1 for the *taxable* year which includes such month." In fact, this section—26 USC section 5000A, to be specific—refers to cognates and variants of the word "tax"— "tax," "taxpayer," "taxable," "taxation," etc.—a whopping thirty-four times.

Finally, even if a willful judge were to disregard all of the above, what would be the proper remedy for the fact that in certain passages the Obamacare law uses the word "penalty" instead of the magic word "tax"? Under long-standing and elemental principles of severability and construction, the remedy would simply be for judges to issue an opinion making it crystal clear to all Americans that the public should understand that the "penalty" of section 5000A is in fact a "tax" and that judges will treat the "penalty" indistinguishably from a tax. True, this remedy arguably "rewrites" the statute, but in a manner little different from the way in which Chief Justice Marshall "rewrote" the Judiciary Act of 1789 by ignoring the plain meaning (as Marshall saw it) of one clause of the statute in the 1803 case of *Marbury v. Madison* and by construing certain other provisions of this law to mean something different than their plain meaning suggested in the 1809 case of *Hodgson v. Bowerbank.* (The Court did these things even though the 1789 Judiciary Act had no explicit severability clause. Neither does the Obamacare statute.) More recently, the Rehnquist Court "rewrote" the federal criminal sentencing guidelines in the 2005 case of *United States v. Booker,* and the Roberts Court "rewrote" certain provisions of the Voting Rights Act in the 2009 case of *NAMUNDO v. Holder.*

OTHER TAX-POWER QUIBBLES
Apart from their Simon Says word game, Obamacare critics have also argued that the insurance mandate cannot be upheld as a tax because the mandate operates as an independent regulation from the tax penalty. But the Obamacare law does not, for example, seek to criminally punish or otherwise condemn those who refuse to get insurance; the law simply seeks to tax them and it does nothing else to them. A person who pays the tax is not violating the Obamacare law; he is complying with it—much as modern contract doctrine understands that promises in many a contract should be construed as promises to perform *or to pay damages.* Obamacare essentially tells covered individuals to obtain health insurance or to pay taxes in lieu of obtaining insurance. If a person is otherwise not required to file a return with the IRS, the "mandate" is simply inoperative as to that person. (Again, if judges find these points debatable as a matter of statutory meaning but critical as a

matter of constitutional principle, judges are free simply to construe the statute in a manner that would render it constitutional, in keeping with a
centuries-old line of cases from *Hodgson* to *NAMUNDO*. Perhaps the most
famous judicial opinion in this long line is Justice Louis Brandeis's concurrence in the 1936 case, *Ashwander v. TVA*.)[8]

What about the argument that Obamacare's sponsors truly want Americans not to pay taxes/penalties but to procure insurance, and that the taxes/
penalties are simply a small-revenue tail wagging a big regulatory dog? First,
the Obamacare's tax provision is in fact projected to raise lots of money. Under long-standing Court case law, if a statute is "productive of some revenue," Congress may exercise its taxing powers free from any "collateral
[judicial] inquiry as to the measure of the regulatory effect of a tax."[9]

Second, Congress may properly impose taxes to discourage certain antisocial behaviors that impose costs on others and therefore violate "the
general welfare." This principle is visible on the surface of the relevant constitutional text, which speaks of taxes that aim to both "pay the debts" (and
as we have seen, Obamacare aims to reduce federal deficits), and also to
"provide for the common defence and general welfare of the United States."
(We shall return to the common defense idea shortly.) Here, too, long-
standing case law and practice reinforce the textual principle. Congress is
free to tax cigarettes or foreign oil so as to discourage their use—free, that is,
to tax well in excess of the revenue-maximizing point on the economic
curve. As the Court made clear more than sixty years ago, a tax "does not
cease to be valid merely because it regulates, discourages, or even definitely
deters the activities taxed."[10]

Next, what about the argument that Obamacare in effect taxes inaction,
and that such taxes are categorically improper? The short answer is that
there is no such blanket constraint on the taxing power, which is plenary,
subject of course to various cross-cutting principles clearly set out elsewhere
in the Constitution.* Indeed, the framers themselves expressly demonstrated
their awareness that future congressional taxes might in effect be imposed

---

*For example, a tax imposed only on Catholics as Catholics would violate the First
Amendment's religion clauses; a tax aimed at critics of the government would offend
structural principles of free expression, principles also embodied in the First Amendment's free speech clause; a tax on blacks only would transgress Fourteenth Amendment rules of equal protection and equal citizenship; a new tax targeting only sitting
federal judges would run afoul of the salary non-diminution rules of Article III; and
so on. [Footnote in original SSRN essay.]

upon persons just for inaction. A tax on each person regardless of his or her actions was understood at the Founding as a classic head tax/capitation, and such taxes are explicitly countenanced by Article I, section 2, and Article I, section 9.

True, the Constitution sets out special rules for pure capitations and other direct taxes, rules that Obamacare does not even attempt to meet because Obamacare, strictly speaking, is not technically a direct tax or capitation. (Nor have critics emphasized these special direct-tax rules, for the more they talk about these rules, the more obvious it becomes that there is nothing whatsoever unconstitutional about a tax that taxes inaction.) The Obamacare tax does not apply to various individuals who make less than a certain amount of income, and the tax thus easily falls on the income-tax side of the line for those who attempt to sharply distinguish between "income" taxes and various "direct" taxes. Unlike a classic direct tax, the Obamacare tax is avoidable, either by refraining from earning a certain amount of taxable income, or, of course, by obtaining health insurance. (These are not the only ways of avoiding the tax, but they are among the most obvious ways.) Strictly speaking, one need not even *buy* health insurance to avoid the tax. One might receive health insurance as a gift (for example if one is a dependent on another person's family health-care policy) or as a tax-free fringe benefit from one's employer.[11]

No sober judge should seek to widen the domain of the Constitution's special rules regarding direct taxes beyond the very limited category to which these rules originally applied: pure head taxes, and possibly also taxes imposed directly upon possession of real property. These special rules about direct taxes have ugly roots. They were consciously designed to protect slavery and slaveholders, and thus lost much of their point after the Civil War. Supreme Court justices in 1796 sharply and sensibly constricted the domain governed by these direct-tax rules, as did the Court for nearly a century thereafter. When the Court in 1895 infamously reversed course in a 5–4 decision in *Pollock v. United States*, Justice Harlan in dissent proclaimed this decision "a disaster to the country." Ultimately, the American people rose up to overturn the *Pollock* case via the Sixteenth Amendment, much as they had previously risen up to overturn the malodorous *Dred Scott* case. For any judge who seeks to avoid the worst mistakes of his predecessors, *Pollock* stands as a sharp reminder of the consummate unwisdom of aggressive anti-tax rulings lacking proper foundations in constitutional text, history, structure, or precedent.[12]

Finally, Obamacare's critics believe that, legal technicalities and pettifog-ging aside, it is simply unfair to tax or regulate inaction. At some extreme point, a law might indeed be so unfair as to plausibly be unconstitutional under various open-ended clauses of the Constitution, such as the equal pro-tection, due process, and privileges-or-immunities clauses. But Obamacare is laughably far from this extreme point. (And if Obamacare's mandate is un-constitutional on basic fairness grounds, so is Romneycare.)

The basic moral intuition supporting Obamacare (and Romneycare, for that matter) is that it is utterly fair to tax or regulate certain things that in fact create costs for others and that impose risks on others. Even if a person intends to drive very safely and in fact does drive very safely, the very fact that this person gets behind the wheel and enters the stream of traffic creates a risk that the driver will injure someone else. Hence most states require au-tomobile insurance because uninsured driving itself creates risk to others.

So does uninsured breathing. If a person falls sick, he may well infect others—and he may be more likely to fall sick if he does not get good pre-ventive health care because he is not insured. Even if an uninsured person poses no incremental threat to others' health (in the way an uninsured driver poses an incremental risk to other drivers and to pedestrians), a person with-out health insurance poses an enormous risk to himself, a risk that he may later need expensive emergency care that he cannot pay for when the need for such care urgently presents itself. If and when the emergency arises, other members of society may well feel morally obliged to provide emergency care at their own expense. This urge to help is not immoral. Rather, this urge is deeply human, and wholly admirable. And it is not fundamentally unfair to insist that a person who may well later benefit from the kindness of strangers pay (via insurance) for that kindness if he or she is able to do so.

II. The Mandate as a Tax Equivalent

Any judge not persuaded by the mandate-as-tax argument still has miles to go before he can sleepily vote to invalidate Obamacare. Indeed, there are five more arguments he must confront and dismiss. Here, then, is the second argument for Obamacare: Even if the mandate cannot be upheld as a proper tax, it should be upheld as a constitutionally proper tax-equivalent.

If Congress may tax me (and surely it can); and if Congress can then use this tax money to buy an insurance policy for me (and again, it can surely do so); and if it can then give me that policy (and once again, this seems clear beyond doubt), then why can't it do all three at once by mandating that I procure my own health-insurance policy?

Any judge voting to invalidate Obamacare must tee up and persuasively answer this simple question. It is possible to imagine the abstract shape an argument might take. The seemingly "greater" power does not always encompass the seemingly "lesser" power; certain means are qualitatively off limits; the law of the excluded middle does not always apply; there is such a thing as the "unconstitutional conditions" doctrine; the whole is sometimes different than the sum of the parts; and so on. But thus far, no legal or judicial critic of Obamacare has carefully teed this question up and persuasively answered it. Surely Judge Roger Vinson's shoddy opinion holding Obamacare unconstitutional did not come within miles of asking or answering this question, even though this question had long been a prominent feature of the public discourse supporting the constitutionality of Obamacare.

Also in the public discourse long before Vinson's ruling was a venerable legislative precedent for the Obamacare mandate, namely, the Militia Act of 1792, an act signed into law by none other than George Washington— a mind, as Marshall reminded readers in *McCulloch* "as pure and as intelligent as this country can boast." This 1792 statute imposed an individual mandate—that is, an effective mandate to buy or otherwise procure an item in the private marketplace—as follows: "Every citizen, enrolled [in the militia] shall, within six months thereafter, provide himself with a good musket or firelock, a sufficient bayonet and belt, two spare flints, and a knapsack, a pouch, with a box therein, to contain not less than twenty four cartridges, suited to the bore of his musket or firelock, each cartridge to contain a proper quantity of powder and ball; or with a good rifle, knapsack, shot-pouch, and powder-horn, twenty balls suited to the bore of his rifle, and a quarter of a pound of powder; and shall appear so armed, accoutred and provided, when called out to exercise or into service, except, that when called out on company days to exercise only, he may appear without a knapsack."

Similarly, jury-service laws effectively mandate individuals to buy or procure transportation to the courthouse when summoned for service. There is nothing especially problematic about such laws, so long as the lawmakers are truly representative. As Marshall emphasized in *McCulloch*, the power to tax involves the power to destroy, financially, and therefore also the lesser-included power to impose various individual mandates to spend money. To repeat Marshall's key insight, "the only security against the abuse of this power is found in the structure of the government itself. In imposing a tax"—or, we might today add, in imposing a mandate to buy some item from the marketplace—"the legislature acts upon its constituents." And this, said Marshall, "is in general a sufficient security against erroneous and oppressive taxation"—or against erroneous or oppressive mandates, for that matter.

To put the point differently, critics of Obamacare must ultimately show that there is something distinctly unconstitutional—something sinister or something un-American, something ultimately "improper" and violative of the "spirit" of the Constitution—about a mandate to purchase a private item in the marketplace. But critics can point to no deep structural or textual or historical or traditional support for their ad hoc objections. Marshall in *McCulloch* confronted a similar sort of ad hoc objection, by those who insisted that Congress could not create a corporation. Marshall responded by acknowledging that Congress may not pass laws that are "improper" and that violate the "spirit" of the Constitution, and he then proceeded to explain why the bank law was perfectly fine even though it created a corporation. Marshall's reasons remain relevant today, and indeed have uncannily close analogues in the Obamacare debate.

First, Marshall insisted that there was nothing particularly problematic about a corporation-creating law—just as there is today nothing inherently wrong with a purchase-mandating law. Both are simply means fairly available to the Congress: In Marshall's words: "The power of creating a corporation . . . is not, like the power of making war or levying taxes, or of regulating commerce, a great substantive and independent power, which cannot be implied as incidental to other powers, or used as means of executing them. . . . A corporation must be considered as a means not less usual, not of higher dignity, not more requiring a particular specification than other means." Ditto for a purchase mandate.

Second, Marshall reminded his audience that states had a long history of creating corporations—a fact that strongly suggested that there was nothing un-American about such laws. Similarly, states have long mandated that residents procure various sorts of items from the private marketplace and even various forms of private insurance. Indeed, state lawmakers have even mandated purchase or procurement of private health insurance. (See, once again, Romneycare.)*

---

* A brief aside regarding the now-viral hypothetical of a congressional law mandating that Americans buy and/or eat broccoli. The hypothetical is outlandish because it abstractly posits a law with no obvious purpose. If and when Congress actually passes such a law, it would be well to consider why Congress in fact did this, and

Finally, Marshall showed that Congress had previously created corporations as means to enforce various other enumerated powers. This proved that there was nothing intrinsically improper about a corporation-creating law. Marshall placed special emphasis on the fact that Congress had previously created particular corporations as a means of enforcing its powers to "*make all needful* rules and regulations" for the federal territories. How, Marshall asked, was it any different if Congress chose to create a corporation pursuant to its textually similar power to "*make all* laws *necessary* and proper" to its other enumerated powers? Similarly, the Militia Act of 1792 proves that there is nothing intrinsically improper about a purchase mandate or a procurement mandate. The militia law aimed to govern "a well-regulated" militia. How is this any different from Congress's power to tax and spend or to "regulate" interstate and international commerce? If the militia clauses can support a proper procurement mandate, why can't other congressional empowerment clauses—and especially the clause empowering Congress to regulate interstate and international commerce—do the same? Note, interestingly enough, that "well-regulated" and "regulate" are textually cognate words, much as "needful" and "necessary" were textually cognate in *McCulloch*. If good regulation of a well-regulated militia may properly entail a purchase/procurement mandate, why may not good regulation of interstate and international commerce?

With this last point, we at last come face to face with the interstate-and-international-commerce clause as a proper constitutional foundation for Obamacare in general and the individual mandate in particular. As it turns out, there are no less than three distinct interstate-and-international commerce clause arguments supporting Obamacare. Any judge seeking to overturn Obamacare must reject all three. To this trio we now turn.

---

whether the law in fact was connected to a constitutionally valid federal goal. Today, for example, virtually all Americans are obliged to buy ethanol when they buy gasoline. Ethanol is nowadays made mainly from corn but might in the future be derivable from broccoli. (Who knows what future technology will permit?) Insofar as broccoli hypotheticals posit a law mandating that Americans not only *buy* but also *ingest/eat* broccoli, these hypotheticals slyly trade upon all sorts of different constitutional anxieties that properly arise regarding laws invading personal bodily autonomy. An Obamacare-style law that simply mandates purchase of items on private markets does not implicate these privacy/autonomy/bodily integrity concerns. It should also always be kept in mind that not all dumb laws are unconstitutional laws, and that the best remedies for certain bad laws are political and not judicial. [Footnote in original SSRN essay.]

III. The Mandate as a Regulation of Interstate Commerce

INTERSTATE COMMERCE AND NATIONAL SECURITY

For those who have not recently and carefully re-read *McCulloch*, it may come as a surprise to learn that the Marshall Court upheld the federal bank law in large part as a national security measure. In order to win wars, the federal government might need to ensure that money would flow easily from state to state, and thereby guarantee that American soldiers would be paid on site and on time, lest they desert or mutiny, and further guarantee that war suppliers would likewise be paid in a timely fashion so that goods and services would reach the troops when needed. As anyone can attest who has ever tried to cash an interstate check or get emergency funds away from home—or who recalls what interstate travel was like before ATMs—a bank with interstate branches in every locality can make life immeasurably more convenient. Marshall's *McCulloch* opinion explicitly rested on this national-security-meets-interstate-commerce argument:

> Although, among the enumerated powers of government, we do not find the word "bank" or "incorporation" [or the words "individual mandate," for that matter] we find the great powers, to lay and collect taxes; to borrow money; to regulate commerce; to declare and conduct a war; and to raise and support armies and navies. The sword and the purse, all the external relations, and no inconsiderable portion of the industry of the nation, are intrusted to its government. . . . [A] government, intrusted with such ample powers, on the due execution of which the happiness and prosperity of the nation so vitally depends, must also be intrusted with ample means for their execution. The power being given, it is the interest of the nation to facilitate its execution. It can never be their interest, and cannot be presumed to have been their intention, to clog and embarrass its execution, by withholding the most appropriate means. Throughout this vast republic, from the St. Croix to the Gulf of Mexico, from the Atlantic to the Pacific, revenue is to be collected and expended, armies are to be marched and supported. The exigencies of the nation may require, that the treasure raised in the north should be transported to the south, that raised in the east, conveyed to the west, or that this order should be reversed. Is that construction of the constitution to be preferred, which would render these

operations difficult, hazardous and expensive? Can we adopt that construction (unless the words imperiously require it), which would impute to the framers of that instrument, when granting these powers for the public good, the intention of impeding their exercise, by withholding a choice of means?

In short, interstate commerce and national security intertwined at the Founding, as Marshall (who had served alongside Washington at Valley Forge) understood in his very bones. Nor was this intertwining limited to the Founding era. President Abraham Lincoln's transcontinental railroad and President Dwight Eisenhower's interstate highway system both famously promoted national defense and interstate commerce.

And so does Obamacare. In the twenty-first century, the next war may well be biological—that is, conducted via germ warfare. As the towering constitutional scholar Philip Bobbitt has explained in his magisterial book on *Terror and Consent: The Wars for the Twenty-first Century*: "More than 140 million persons enter the U.S. by air every year; the flight time between points of departure and arrival is seldom more than twenty-four hours. Yet diseases such as plague and smallpox have incubation times ranging from three days to two weeks, respectively. . . . If we are to redress this vulnerability [to biological warfare] from the supply side, we must strengthen public health systems." Like Marshall, Bobbitt—a former senior director for strategic planning at the National Security Council—knows whereof he speaks when he discusses national defense matters and their connection to issues of federal constitutional power.

How does Obamacare help address the issues raised by Bobbitt? Preventive health care enhances herd immunity and therefore makes America more secure from threats posed by viruses unleashed by enemies, foreign and domestic—viruses that do not stop at state borders. Obamacare encourages preventive health care by subsidizing care, by ensuring access to those with preexisting medical conditions, and by requiring individual Americans to "arm" themselves with health insurance, which will incentivize individuals to get regular checkups, vaccines, and other preventive care. In 1792, national defense required individuals to have muskets and powder. Today, national defense requires individuals to have health insurance and vaccines. Or so Congress might properly find, and it is not the proper role of judges to deny Congress the right to make this call in the name of national security and interstate/international commerce.

The issues raised by biological warfare highlight the central idea—and the obvious limits—of congressional power over interstate and international commerce. The central idea is that Congress may properly regulate transactions that spill across state and national borders—transactions that create "externalities" that individual states are ill equipped to handle. Issues of war and peace and foreign affairs affect all Americans, and so our Constitution gives these matters to the central government. Congress decides whether and how foreign travelers may cross our borders and enter the heartland. But precisely because germs and people so easily cross state lines, individual states acting on their own cannot adequately provide for the nation's common defense and promote the nation's general welfare. Developing national herd immunity requires collective action among many states, collective action that Congress is uniquely charged with organizing under America's Constitution.

All this also highlights the central limit of Congress's power under the interstate-and-international-commerce clause. Where a given issue does not truly generate interstate or international externalities—when there are no true cross-border spillovers, where neither money nor people nor germs nor pollution nor costs nor benefits, etc., are truly crossing state or national lines—the matter should be left to the states. The 1995 case of *Lopez v. United States* beautifully exemplified a situation in which no truly interstate problem existed and where the Court therefore properly held that Congress had overstepped.*

But Obamacare involves matters where massive interstate flows—of money, germs, patients, doctors, medical records, and so on—occur on a daily basis, in ways that warrant a federal role along the lines of Obamacare, if Congress so chooses. Consider, then, two other basic interstate commerce theories that undergird the Affordable Care Act.

UNCLOGGING BARRIERS TO INTERSTATE
TRAVEL AND PROMOTING INTERSTATE FAIRNESS
A central purpose of the Constitution at the Founding was to eliminate interstate trade barriers and to enable Congress to create a continental free

---

* *Lopez* was of course critically distinguished in the 2005 case of *Gonzales v. Raich*, in which the Court made clear that even an individual clause of a statute that did not itself regulate interstate commerce should be upheld if the statute as a whole did plainly regulate interstate commerce and the clause in question was an integral feature of this overall statutory scheme. [Footnote in original SSRN essay.]

market. Major commerce-clause cases in the past—both dormant commerce-clause case law and case law upholding congressional enactments—have stressed the idea of eliminating clogs and impediments to the free flow of goods, services, and people across state lines. In 1964, Congress found that blacks hesitated to travel interstate for fear that they could not find motels or restaurants that would serve them, and in turn the Supreme Court pointedly relied on these findings in upholding the constitutionality of the Civil Rights Act of 1964.

In years past, some persons likewise hesitated to travel out of state for fear that they might not receive emergency services in out-of-state emergency rooms. Before Obamacare, people also hesitated to seek out-of-state jobs for fear that their preexisting condition would preclude a new (out-of-state) employer from hiring them, even if they would be able to contribute more to the economy in a new job. Obamacare solves the second problem by banning discrimination against preexisting conditions.

The first issue—the need for travelers to receive emergency care out of state, even if they are uninsured—raises obvious issues of interstate fairness. Some states might end up paying far more than other states per capita to provide emergency services to those temporarily visiting from out of state. Obamacare fixes the interstate unfairness issue when patients fall sick out of state by minimizing the likelihood that the financial burden of this emergency-room care will be borne by the host state.

The individual mandate provisions are tightly linked to the achievement of these basic purposes. Without Obamacare's ban on discrimination based on preexisting medical conditions, people will be trapped in their current state and their current job even if they are more valuable in another state—the very thing the Constitution was designed to prevent. Without Obamacare's individual mandate, either out-of-state patients might be denied emergency services—a shocking situation that may also discourage even persons with ample means and insurance from traveling out of state lest they be *erroneously* denied out-of-state care when in distress—or some host states might be obliged to bear an unfair share of the financial burden of emergency care.

Here, too, the key point is that persons and money are flowing across state lines in ways that warrant congressional regulation. At any given instant in twenty-first-century America, a very substantial number of Americans, in both absolute and percentage terms, are physically present in a state not their own—because, for example, they are away at college, or visiting friends, or on holiday, or simply because they live in one state and work in a neighboring state. If they fall sick when away from home, their host state should provide them emergency services, and generous host states should not suffer for this generosity of care to fellow Americans. Or so Congress might reasonably think, and federal judges have no proper basis to undo this congressional judgment.

THE INTERSTATE ANALOGY TO
UNEMPLOYMENT INSURANCE AND SOCIAL SECURITY

The Sixteenth Amendment to the Constitution squarely authorizes congressional measures that to some degree redistribute from wealthy to indigent. When this proposed amendment was pending before the American people, it was understood by both its supporters and detractors as inviting Congress to enact a progressive—that is, redistributive—income tax. Individual states may hesitate to adopt such redistributive measures lest the wealthy move out and the indigent move in. Even if virtually every state wants these measures, individual states cannot accomplish these goals on their own without triggering races to the bottom and concerns that properly generous states will become welfare magnets. Thus, a long line of Supreme Court cases has recognized the propriety of federal legislation in such situations.[13] Obamacare is no different. It creates certain subsidies for the indigent, and these subsidies must of course be properly paid for. Hence the individual mandate, enforced via a tax penalty administered by the federal taxing authorities in the Internal Revenue Service.

IV. The Mandate as a Civil Rights Statute

The foregoing five stories—a tax story, a tax-equivalent story, and three distinct stories about interstate commerce and national security—have tended to focus on the Founding and the Sixteenth Amendment, with special emphasis on the broad lessons of *McCulloch v. Maryland*. *McCulloch* of course encouraged readers to view the Constitution as whole: "We must never forget, that it is *a constitution* we are expounding." In that spirit, let us finally consider one final part of the document that provides yet another argument for upholding Obamacare: the Reconstruction amendments.

The Civil War and its amendments connect up to every one of the five theories we have already considered. The war itself prompted Congress to adopt a broad view of its powers to tax and to impose individual mandates— hence the first income tax in American history and the first federal draft.

National security and interstate commerce intertwined with Lincoln's vision of intercontinental railroads; and the first sentence of the Fourteenth Amendment reinforced the right of Americans to travel to other states and indeed to choose to reside in any new state to which they traveled. The war also generated pension plans for soldiers and their widows that foreshadowed the later Social Security system in certain respects.

The Civil War amendments also echoed *McCulloch* by authorizing Congress to enact sweeping laws enforcing freedom and equality. The key language of section 2 of the Thirteenth Amendment and section 5 of the Fourteenth Amendment explicitly borrowed from *McCulloch*'s gloss on the necessary-and-proper clause—a point stressed by many Reconstruction congressmen themselves in the 1860s and by many later Supreme Court cases. Recent Supreme Court case law, however, has suggested a more cramped view of congressional power outside the context of race discrimination. Lower federal courts are of course bound by these recent cases.

But if and when Obamacare reaches the Supreme Court itself, which has the right and duty to correct its past mistakes on the subject of Congress's Reconstruction powers, the justices should focus their attention on the central meaning and deep spirit of the Thirteenth Amendment and the first sentence of the Fourteenth Amendment, and on Congress's explicit power to "enforce" the central meaning and deep spirit of these commands.

A person who is unable to get necessary health care to save his life or to make his life livable is, in many ways, a slave. He is utterly dependent on the will or whim of others, as many an antebellum slave was utterly dependent on his master's will or whim. He does not have the minimum autonomy and control over his life needed to be truly free. Or so Congress might properly believe.

A person who cannot get private insurance because he was born with a preexisting condition is not truly born equal in keeping with the deep spirit of the first sentence of the Fourteenth Amendment. The grand idea of this glorious sentence is that all Americans—black and white, male and female, those born with a genetic disposition to disease X and those born without this genetic disposition—are all born equal and should in some sense have equal life prospects.[14] Private insurance discrimination against blacks or women or those with genetic predispositions violate that abiding ideal of birth equality—an ideal that as expressed in the opening sentence of the Fourteenth Amendment has no state action requirement. Or so Congress might properly believe.

The individual mandate provision, of course is logically distinct from the other portions of Obamacare. But practically, the provisions are related. Congress has chosen both to subsidize health care so as to ensure each American's basic civil right/human right to be truly free from servile dependence on others, and also to prohibit discrimination against preexisting conditions in order to ensure each American's entitlement to be truly equal at birth. Congress has further and quite plausibly decided that the best way to achieve these two Reconstruction aims is via a complementary individual mandate to ensure the financial and practical integrity of the reformed health-care delivery system. Congress, in other words, has taken seriously its constitutional mandate to "enforce by appropriate legislation" the letter and spirit of Reconstruction.

If and when the matter reaches the Supreme Court, the justices should defer to Congress's landmark legislation, enacted as it was by the only branch of government explicitly tasked with enforcement in the text of the Reconstruction amendments themselves, and signed into law by a man whose very election as America's first black President was a poetic and profound culmination of the Reconstruction vision.

"Obamacare" indeed.

HOW TO DEFEND OBAMACARE: WHAT VERRILLI SHOULD HAVE SAID

SLATE, THURSDAY, MARCH 29, 2012, 4:07 P.M. (ET)

May It Please the Court,

I have never written an open letter to Your Honors, but I now do so in response to several things that were said—and not said—in this week's historic oral argument on the Affordable Care Act, aka "Obamacare." In the spirit of the season, please permit me to proceed in the same style of Socratic dialogue powerfully on display in the oral argument itself.

Q: *What are the limits of congressional power?*

A: The limits are those found in the Constitution itself, of course—its text, its history, and its structure as glossed by subsequent practice and precedent. The Constitution expressly gives Congress the power to "Regulate commerce . . . among the several states." Here, we have a genuine *regulation*—both the micro-mandate/penalty/tax and the larger regulatory regime of which it is an integral part. We have *commerce* under any reading of the word. Insurance is a purely commercial or economic question about who pays whom. And we have an underlying problem that is truly *"among the several states."* The problem of health care creates spillover costs that cross state lines, problems that result in some states in effect imposing costs on other states or bearing costs that properly belong to other states.

Q: *How so?*

A: At any given instant, literally millions of Americans are out of state. Most of my students come from other states. I myself am out of state three days a week. If any of us falls sick while out of state, we can seek emergency-room care in the host state. And unless we have insurance, we will be imposing costs on other states. Obamacare addresses this obvious interstate problem in a direct way. The two leading cases in which the court has recently invalidated congressional laws as going beyond the scope of the commerce clause—U.S. v. Lopez in 1995 and U.S. v. Morrison in 2000, involving guns in schools and violence against women—did not involve similar interstate spillovers. Those cases were thus rightly decided on commerce-clause grounds, as I myself have argued. And these cases prove that limits do really exist.

Q: *Isn't the obligation to offer emergency-room care itself created by federal law? So isn't your argument pure bootstrap—one intrusive federal law generating another?*

A: With due respect, no. The obligation to care for the urgently sick—including the strangers in our midst—is ultimately rooted in morality and centuries of tradition. Many ERs would and should pitch in even without a federal requirement, and the interstate problem is ultimately created by travel itself—travel that the interstate-commerce clause in fact was designed to promote. Which leads me to a second and independent argument supporting Obamacare, namely, . . .

Q: *Before you get to that, wouldn't your argument allow the feds to mandate burial insurance? Indigents sometimes die out of state, don't they?*

A: Yes, but in what numbers, Your Honor? With due respect, it is easy to hypothesize from an armchair—but is there really, truly, an interstate problem of indigent interstate burials anywhere near the magnitude of the actual emergency-room problem in America? States can individually handle burials, but any state that on its own tries to generously handle the health-care issue risks becoming a massive magnet for out-of-staters. Sick people can flock to states with generous medical benefits. And this really doesn't happen with dying people leaving their home states just so that they can die on some other state's nickel.

Q: What about a federal mandate to buy broccoli?

A: Thank you for that softball, Your Honor. There is no real, substantial, honest-to-goodness interstate spillover/externality problem with broccoli that I see at the moment. [Pause] Even if nothing I have said yet persuades Your Honors, my second commerce-clause claim is that millions of Americans suffer from preexisting medical conditions. If they get a better job offer out of state, they should take it so that they can contribute more to their families and to the general economy. But they will not be able to do so if the out-of-state employer discriminates against preexisting conditions. This discrimination creates a huge lock-in of labor. It prohibits interstate mobility—the free interstate flow of services. The core purpose of the interstate-commerce clause is to allow Congress to remove interstate barriers—legal, physical, economic—such as this.

Q: That explains the ban on preexisting condition discrimination, but how does that explain the mandate?

A: The two are of course intertwined, as Your Honors recognized on Day Three of oral argument, regarding the law's "severability." The ban on discrimination will work only if almost all are obliged to insure before they become expensively sick.

Q: But nothing you've said so far addresses the unprecedented issues raised by a federal mandate that a person buy a private product.

A: Several answers, Your Honor. First, this law is hardly unprecedented. The Militia Act of 1792 had a similar mandate, obliging Founding-era Americans to privately procure muskets, ammo, pouches, and so on. George Washington signed onto that law. And no one at the time said that mandates such as this were somehow intrinsically improper regulatory tools.

Q: Even if so, that law was passed under a different clause of the Constitution?

A: It's hard to see why that matters. If a mandate is a permissible *regulation* of a *well-regulated* militia, it is an equally permissible *regulation* of interstate commerce. In the most important case ever decided on the scope of congressional power, the iconic 1819 case of *McCulloch v. Maryland*, Chief Justice John Marshall said that because a corporation-creating law was valid under one clause of the Constitution (the territories clause), a corporation-creating law should be equally valid under other clauses. What is true of corporation-creating laws is also true of mandate laws.

Q: If two hundred years ago, national security enabled government to mandate muskets, might national security today enable government to mandate vaccines?

A: Yes, Your Honor. The next terrorist attack might very well be biological, and our best national defense is herd immunity, which does mean that
we need a large percentage of Americans to have vaccines. They will be
more likely to have such vaccines if they have insurance. And states cannot
individually handle these issues well because viruses do not stop at state
lines. They spill over. They create interstate externalities. *McCulloch* itself, I
might add, was decided on national security grounds. In the wake of the War
of 1812, Marshall explained how a national bank was useful in fighting wars
and supporting armies.[15]

*Q: You said that no one in 1792 thought mandates were somehow especially
troubling. Why not?*

A: Because they understood simple logic—and we must do the same
today. If government can tax me, and use the money to buy a musket/insur-
ance policy with my name on it, and then give me the musket/insurance
policy, then government can for the very same reason oblige me to procure
the musket/insurance policy myself. I am being taxed/mandated by persons
that I helped elect and that I can vote against. That is the main guarantee
against abuse, as Chief Justice Marshall stressed in *McCulloch* and is obvious
from the Constitution's basic structure. And speaking of taxes, another easy
way to handle this case is simply to uphold the mandate/penalty as a genuine
revenue measure, enforced by the IRS and predicted by the Congressional
Budget Office to improve the federal government's fiscal situation by several
billion—with a "B"—dollars a year.

Q: But isn't liberty especially at risk with these kinds of federal mandates?

A: Respectfully, no. Not at all. I emphatically deny Your Honor's key
proposition. It flunks a logic test, and a history test, and a structure test, and,
well, just about every other legal test I can think of. If government can take
my money and pay it to Detroit, there is no liberty difference than if government tells me directly to buy from Detroit. And if one thinks that money is
speech such that a compelled payment is a First Amendment problem, then
the 1792 act was unconstitutional; and all state mandates of health insurance (Romneycare) and automobile insurance are unconstitutional. And a
vast range of other state and federal laws would also be unconstitutional.
Nothing in the Constitution or history or structure—or precedents, for that
matter—provides suitable support for the "mandates are different" intuition,
which cannot survive analytic scrutiny. Such an opinion will not write—or
if it does, it will not last.

Q: Meaning what?

A: Meaning, with the greatest of respect for an institution and individuals whom I hold dear, I have to teach the stuff that Your Honors write year in and year out to my students. And if a judicial opinion simply fails tests of text, history, structure, and logic—and if it comes down by a 5–4 vote; and if the vote seems to track the party alignment of appointing presidents; and if the four dissenters are emphatic that the majority's arguments simply don't wash; and if the vast majority of us who study constitutional law professionally, including most conservative scholars, agree that these arguments simply don't wash; and if I already have to do a lot of work to explain *Bush v. Gore*, in context—well, what will I tell my students when they say to me, cynically, that "it's all politics"? What will I say, when they ask me (as I have already been asked by one former student), "Just how many presidential elections are five conservative justices allowed to undo?"

Q: Are there any middle positions that might generate a broader consensus on the Court?

A: One possibility, perhaps, might build on various comments by Chief Justice Roberts and Justices Sotomayor, Kagan, Breyer, and others, at oral argument. The "mandate" should not be understood as free-floating requirement but simply as connected to the tax penalty. In turn, the penalty can be upheld as a genuine revenue measure designed to bend down the cost curve. If the relevant statutory section needs in effect to be "reworded" to achieve this result, a judicial re-writing/re-reading of this section would be in keeping with various earlier cases, including the 2005 sentencing guidelines case of *U.S. v. Booker* and the 2009 Voting Rights Act case of *NAMUNDO v. Holder*. Both cases, in turn, can be seen as rooted in principles of judicial restraint and charitable interpretation famously put forth by Justice Brandeis in his concurrence in the 1936 *Ashwander v. TVA* opinion. With all due respect, several other possible approaches are also sketched out *in an SSRN essay I wrote last summer.**

And I'm sure that there are many other possible consensus positions that may emerge as Your Honors begin to deliberate among yourselves. Perhaps it would be too much to expect the kind of unanimity this court achieved in *McCulloch, Marbury v. Madison*, and *Brown v. Board of Education*—to name

---

* http://papers.ssrn.com/sol3/papers.cfm?abstract_id=1856506 [hyperlink in original online column].

some of the most iconic cases. But an opinion that in some way genuinely crossed party lines would, with all due respect, be just what America now needs, and needs desperately, from the highest court in our land.

Respectfully submitted,
Akhil Reed Amar

CONCLUSION

Just, in Time

IMAGINE THAT, IN THE WEE HOURS of April 13, 1861, President Abraham Lincoln sends you a terse telegram summoning you to the White House to advise him on the most momentous and terrible constitutional question ever to arise in America. You are one of Lincoln's closest confidants, and he knows that you have studied the Constitution with care over many years. When you reach his office on the evening of April 14, Lincoln confirms that the newspaper accounts are correct. Confederate troops have captured Fort Sumter. "I am in a fix, old friend," he says to you, softly. "What shall I do?"

The president is asking you a legal question—a constitutional question. For him, it is also an intensely moral and deeply personal question. Several weeks ago at his inauguration, with the eyes of the world upon him, he took a solemn oath "registered in heaven" to "preserve, protect, and defend the Constitution of the United States." That day, he publicly proclaimed his view that "no State, upon its own mere motion, can lawfully get out of the Union" and that various purported ordinances of secession adopted in late 1860 and early 1861 were thus "legally void." These were brave words when spoken, but only words. Now that cannons have begun to roar and blood has begun to flow, Lincoln seeks your thoughts about whether the views he expressed that day were indeed constitutionally correct. If they were not, there is still time for him to change course.

Much may turn on your answer to the president—the fate of America, and perhaps the fate of the earth. Having been defeated fair and square on Election Day last November, can southern slavocrats now be suffered to use bullets to overturn the verdict of ballots? What then will become of the very idea of democracy on the world stage, a world whose great powers in 1861 openly scoff at the revolutionary American conceit that ordinary people can govern themselves without a hereditary monarchy or aristocracy to keep the populace in check? Will the American project in continental self-government reveal itself, in this testing hour, as a failed experiment? If so, will government of the people perish from the earth, at least for the foreseeable future? Will the American Constitution's bold self-description as "the supreme law of the land" be reduced to empty words that do not really mean what they say? And speaking of the land, how will a proudly pro-slavery Confederate regime, positioned as it is all along the Union's soft underbelly and wielding complete control over the mouth of the Mississippi River, affect the global balance of power in the years and decades ahead?

On the other hand. . . . If the words of the Constitution's supremacy clause and many other supporting words and phrases in the Constitution really do mean what they say; and if these strong unionist words are clearly in keeping with the Constitution's overall spirit and structure; and if the history of the Constitution's ratification in 1787–1788 surely supports Lincoln's inaugural argument; and if, as even his craven predecessor James Buchanan has publicly admitted, not a single prominent Federalist, in the entire year in which the Constitution was ratified, ever floated the idea of future unilateral secession as a sop to induce fence-sitters to say yes; and if many of the Constitution's leading advocates in that world-changing year instead explicitly and famously insisted that the Constitution must be ratified "in toto and for ever"—if all of these things are true, and if Lincoln's constitutional oath obliges him to be true to all these things—then what lies ahead is the horrible prospect of a continental civil war. No one can be sure, on April 14, 1861, just how much carnage might ensue, and for how long, in the name of democracy and the Constitution.

What, then, do you say to President Lincoln?

ALTHOUGH FICTIONAL IN CERTAIN SPECIFICS—the telegram and the quiet late-night meeting—the foregoing 1861 vignette is designed to dramatize the real-life historical truths about America's Constitution that are at the heart of this book.

First, our Constitution does in fact squarely address certain epic issues. Some scholars have suggested that the document is clear only on trivial and technical matters. For example, everyone needs to know when one quadrennial presidential term ends and another begins—and our Constitution today does specify this—but the world would be pretty much the same had the text said 3:00 p.m., rather than noon, January 20. According to some scholars, most of the Constitution is a glorified version of the noon rule; the text, they say, is clear only when the stakes are small.

The Lincoln vignette refutes this suggestion that the Constitution's text, history, and structure don't much matter on big issues. In April 1861, the Constitution mattered for the most momentous issue of the century. A Confederate world in which each state may lawfully secede whenever it so desires would be an entirely different world than Lincoln's world—our world. Our Constitution addresses certain big topics—the wrongness of state secession laws, the importance of voting rights, the centrality of majority rule, and so on—with genuine clarity.

In this spirit, I have included in this book essays on many of the most consequential questions of the last two decades. Of course, none looms as large as the question Lincoln faced in mid-April 1861. But surely it matters whether Obamacare, the most significant domestic legislative achievement of our still-young century, is properly upheld or invalidated; whether an effort to undo a presidential election via a partisan impeachment is or is not constitutionally appropriate; whether current filibuster rules can or cannot be abolished at any moment by a mere majority vote of the Senate; whether same-sex couples do or do not rightly retain the same rights to marry as heterosexual couples; and whether excluding reliable evidence of criminal guilt is or is not a generally sound constitutional approach.

Here is a second, and closely related, truth that emerges from the Lincoln vignette: Proper rules for constitutional interpretation do in fact exist, and sometimes these rules generate decisive answers. In 1861, the Constitution's text, history, and structure were not indeterminate on the secession question. Lincoln was legally right.

Of course, many of Lincoln's contemporaries disagreed, to put it mildly. These men in gray risked their lives, their fortunes, and their sacred honor in defense of their constitutional view, and many eventually lost everything. But that fact alone does not make their secessionist view right or even highly plausible, when judged by proper rules of constitutional interpretation— rules of text, history, and structure; interpretive rules that were firmly in place in 1861; rules that had been in place since the Founding; rules that were in fact both articulated and followed by the likes of George Washington, James Madison, Alexander Hamilton, John Marshall, and Joseph Story, to name just a few.

And these rules of proper constitutional interpretation continue to remain in place today. True, the *substance* of constitutional law has changed dramatically over the centuries. Slavery is no longer enshrined or even allowed; women and blacks now vote; the Bill of Rights today rightly limits state governments; and so on. But the basic *methods* of constitutional law and rules of *constitutional interpretation* have largely remained the same across the centuries. Constitutional text, history, and structure still matter, as they did for Washington, Madison, Hamilton, Marshall, Story, and Lincoln. Precedents are still important, though no precedent may as a general matter trump a clear constitutional text. (Complications still arise, as they have always arisen, in situations where mistaken precedents have created reliance interests of a certain special sort.)[1] American practices and traditions since the Founding also matter, especially practices and traditions that have glossed an ambiguous constitutional phrase or that are arguably baked into an open-ended constitutional clause, as when the Constitution prohibits "unreasonable" searches and seizures or "cruel and unusual" punishments.

I admit that I have long been obsessed by the secession question and that I have always been a Lincoln man. Lincoln's rightness on this question is the punch line of the first section of the first article I ever wrote as a law professor, of the first chapter of my first big book for a general audience, and also of the opening chapter of my last book. And now, in the concluding section of this book, I am returning to this issue yet again, and insisting, once more, that the secession debate was not indeterminate or evenly balanced. Secessionists, I have always claimed and continue to claim, were constitutional flat-earthers.

The obvious counterargument is that Lincoln's legal rightness is clear only in retrospect, and only because in the end his side won on the battlefield. I disagree, and my vignette seeks to sharpen this point by asking you— the reader—how you would have advised Lincoln, *before* the die was cast and *before* the grand armies clashed.

In the same spirit, many of this book's essays show readers how to analyze constitutional questions *before* the issue at hand was decided by some salient decision maker—the House in the wake of the lurid Starr Report; the Senate in deciding whether to seat the undeniably corrupt governor Rod Blagojevich's presumptively corrupt appointee, Roland Burris; the president and attorney general in case of the American dirty-bomb suspect, José Padilla; the Supreme Court in the high-profile Obamacare litigation; and so on.

Here is a third truth about American constitutional law: Persons who have spent time carefully thinking about a very wide range of previous constitutional issues are somewhat more likely to think sensibly about the next constitutional issue that may arise. Practice may not make perfect, but it often makes less imperfect. This truth about American constitutional law is tucked into my fictional vignette: Lincoln seeks your views in part because he knows that you have been a careful student of the Constitution.

More generally, this truth animates the basic structure of this book. The preceding chapters aim to expose you to an extremely broad cross-section of constitutional cases and controversies so that when new constitutional issues arise (as they inevitably will), you will already know how to think constitutional law and how to do constitutional law because you have been thinking it and doing it in every chapter of this book. This book's various topics and case studies, I submit, are particularly good laboratories because readers are likely to have brought to this book a general familiarity with many of these specific episodes, having themselves already lived through these events.

A fourth truth about constitutional law highlighted by the Lincoln vignette is that constitutional decisions must be made on deadline. Lincoln did not have all the time in the world to decide how to react to the first wave of secession ordinances or to the fall of Fort Sumter. As his fictional adviser, you are called upon to make your case under the gun, so to speak, with the clock ticking down fast.

The essays that form the meat of each chapter in this book were likewise composed in the heat of the moment. The key claims take shape quickly, but at their best these claims are buttressed by longer, slower, and more scholarly articles that were published elsewhere, both before and after my journalistic interventions, and that provide much more documentation and elaboration than was possible on deadline.

In the 1861 crisis, the relevant constitutional decision maker was not a court. Here lies a fifth major truth about the American constitutional system: Not all constitutional questions end up in court. This truth is reflected in this book's sustained attention to constitutional issues outside the judiciary, alongside other essays that focus more tightly on pending or recently decided court cases. As the Lincoln vignette reminds us, some constitutional issues are simply unfit for judicial resolution. They are, in technical legal jargon, "nonjusticiable"—beyond the ken of courts under a long line of cases, tracing back to *Marbury v. Madison*, known as the "political question doctrine." Certain aspects of the issues faced by Lincoln in 1861 were classically nonjusticiable.

And happily so, for the Supreme Court in mid-April 1861 was, frankly, disgraceful. One of its justices, John Archibald Campbell, would soon resign from the Court to join the Confederacy. The Court's chief justice, Roger Taney, was the author of the 1857 *Dred Scott* opinion—an utterly preposterous decision that Lincoln in 1858 rightly condemned as "an astonisher in legal history."

Implicit in Lincoln's harsh criticism of Taney in 1858, and in the actual historical fact that Lincoln did not solicit Taney's informal advice in mid-April 1861, is a sixth basic truth of American constitutional law: The right constitutional answers do not depend wholly on what judges have said or would say (if asked) about the Constitution. If constitutional law is simply judge-made law, no more and no less, then it is hard to make sense of Lincoln's 1858 criticism of Taney and *Dred Scott*. If the Constitution is simply what judges say it is, then there is no proper basis for nonjudges (such as Abraham Lincoln, or for that matter, Akhil Amar) to claim that the judges are "wrong" or, more forcefully, "clearly wrong." But Lincoln believed and I believe and virtually all sensible constitutional thinkers over the course of American history have believed that constitutional law cannot be entirely reduced to what judges think. Above and beyond judicial pronouncements, the text, history, and structure of the written Constitution itself surely count for something, as do relevant nonjudicial practices and traditions. A well-trained constitutionalist outside the judiciary might indeed prove that the judges are flat-out wrong. That is what Lincoln himself did in 1858 in his "astonisher" speech and in the Lincoln-Douglas debates that quickly followed, and that is what I have tried to do in several of the essays in this book. In many other essays, of course, I have sided with the Court—even though this stance at times has obliged me to explain where and how the Court's dissenters goofed.

But then who decides in the end what the Constitution, rightly read, really means? You do, dear readers. We—the People—do. We are the ultimate supreme court, and in the long run we judge the judges, and all other government officials—and, indeed, we judge each other's claims and counterclaims. This is what it means for the citizenry to be, in a word, *sovereign*. Or to put the point a different way: Presidents, with the Senate's advice and consent, pick the Supreme Court, and we, the people, pick presidents and senators. The rules by which we seat and unseat presidents and senators are central to our entire system, and thus it is no coincidence that these rules and their various wrinkles and nuances loom particularly large in the essays that compose this book.

These essays thus address not only the formal rules of presidential (and senatorial) selection and succession but also the sensibilities that constitutionally sophisticated voters should bring into the polling booth on Election Day. On that day, we are all advisers to the president, in a manner of speaking. We advise and consent to our presidents on Election Day in a manner not entirely unlike the process by which the Senate advises and consents to cabinet officers, ambassadors, generals, admirals, and Supreme Court justices. We, the voters, cannot responsibly shirk this role as constitutional advisers. It is an intrinsic, if implicit, part of every election, when we, the sovereign citizens, choose to empower persons with a particular set of constitutional credentials and sensibilities over other candidates offering up a different set.

My fanciful 1861 vignette seeks to dramatize the critical constitutional role of the ordinary American citizen. The vignette does so by inviting you, whoever you might be, to imagine yourself as a literal adviser to the president at a critical moment in history. And, to repeat, this book's largest aim is to enable you, the reader, to develop and hone your constitutional skills by showing you, by example, how to think constitutional law and how to do constitutional law in a broad range of recent, high-profile, real-life constitutional case studies—the issues of our era.

IT MIGHT BE ASKED WHY the current generation of Americans should ever resolve any genuinely difficult and important modern issue by paying close attention to words penned and deeds done long ago by now-dead men.

This is hardly a new question. It might also have been asked in 1861, and in some small intellectual circles it doubtless was asked in that year. But in general, neither side in the great secession debate claimed that because all the leading framers were long dead, the Constitution's text and enactment history were simply irrelevant. Instead, both blue and gray invoked the Founding text and Founding deeds. Although one side was far more plausible in its appeals to constitutional text, history, and structure, each camp claimed that it, and not the other, carried aloft the true flame of the fallen fathers.

Despite—or perhaps because of—their age, the Constitution's text and traditions provide important sources and resources for modern constitutional conversation and contestation. This old text and the history of its implementation furnish a common vocabulary for our common deliberations—a shared national narrative that can facilitate social cooperation and coordination for a diverse and highly opinionated populace. Also, many of the difficult issues faced by modern constitutional decision makers are in fact surprisingly similar to those faced by their predecessors because today's constitutional institutions lineally descend from the Founders' institutions. Presidents still sign and veto bills, the Senate still remains the judge of its own elections, the House continues to enjoy the power of impeachment, and so on.

Modern interpreters should attend to various elements of the Constitution's original intent not because these old unwritten understandings always and everywhere tightly bind us today, but rather because we can learn from our constitutional predecessors. The evils that they lived through—that they experienced firsthand at epic moments in American history such as the Revolution and the Civil War—can help us understand why they put certain things in the text, to spare us from having to suffer as they suffered. Various rights emerged from real wrongs, wrongs we ignore at our peril.

Simply put, the written Constitution is often wise—typically, wiser than judges acting on their own steam—because the document distills the democratic input of many minds over many generations. More ordinary people voted on the Constitution in 1787–1788 than had ever voted on anything else in world history. In saying yes to the Constitution that year, everyday people up and down the continent wisely insisted that a Bill of Rights be added—a Bill in which the phrase "the people" appears no fewer than five times. Later generations of ordinary Americans mobilized to enshrine in this terse text an end to slavery, a sweeping guarantee of equal birthright citizenship, an emphatic commitment to protecting civil rights against all levels of government, and radical expansions of the rights of political participation—to blacks, to women, to the poor, to the young, and more. These were epic democratic achievements, and they are all worthy of profound respect by today's Americans. We, the people of the twenty-first century, thus do well to ponder the collected and collective wisdom of this old and intergenerational text.

WHICH BRINGS US BACK, one last time, to the special problem of constitutional journalism. Journalists by training are neither historians nor legal scholars. They may well be unaware of the deep wisdom of the past. They are men and women of the day, of the hour, of the minute.

Here, in conclusion, are a few friendly suggestions from one part-time, amateur journalist to my full-time, professional journalistic colleagues.

The beginning of wisdom is self-knowledge and self-criticism. Journalists—both writers and editors—must constantly remind themselves of their limitations and their structural biases. In particular, they must always keep in mind, so that they may properly make allowances for, their inherent bias toward newness and nowness, and their general unfamiliarity with law and history.

Today's journalists often tend to compensate for their lack of legal expertise by deferring unduly to judges. "I may not be a legal expert," the journalist tells herself, "but surely judges are legal experts, so I can simply report their rulings at face value. After all, they are our constitutional system's impartial umpires." But judges are not always—indeed, not usually—genuine constitutional experts. They are generalist lawyers, and all are chosen in a process that is broadly political. Judges are not the unproblematic umpires of the American constitutional system; they are also players in the game with their own agendas, interests, and biases.

Journalists should thus cover judges more in the way journalists cover other branches of government—with less credulity and more critical scrutiny of the public pronouncements of these public officials. Presidential press conferences are skeptically analyzed in the popular press; Supreme Court opinions deserve the same sort of critical analysis. In short, America's leading newspapers, newsmagazines, and news journals must question what judges say and do so that the American people—the system's ultimate umpires—can judge the judges and can judge the presidents and senators who pick the judges.

Many journalistic writers who lack extensive legal expertise may not be up to the task of detailed and critical appraisal of judicial opinions and judicial practices.* But legal experts do exist, and journalistic gatekeepers must find these experts and must open their journalistic gates to these experts. To do this, however, journalistic gatekeepers—print editors and broadcast producers—must do a better job vetting self-described experts to assess both their impartiality and their expertise.

---

* The sort of penetrating journalism that I am advocating here is not so much investigative journalism about how the Supreme Court justices in fact came to compose their various opinions—the locus classicus of this genre is Bob Woodward and Scott Armstrong's 1979 book, *The Brethren: Inside the Supreme Court* (New York: Simon and Schuster)—but rather analytic journalism independently assessing the strengths and weaknesses of the Court's factual assertions and legal arguments.

On impartiality, here are basic questions that gatekeepers could ask self-described experts, but almost never do: "Can you identify important recent topics on which your constitutional views diverge from your political preferences? Have your views been cited with strong approval, or has your work otherwise been endorsed, by judges, lawmakers, and scholars from differing points along the political spectrum?"

In asking these questions, gatekeepers and other journalists should not lazily assume that on every constitutional issue, the truth is always in the middle and thus that the most credible expert is never to be found strongly on one side or another of a currently controverted issue. Gatekeepers should look for experts who are widely respected across the spectrum, but on any particular issue, it might simply be true that one side is rather clearly right and the other side rather clearly wrong—by which I mean, in part, that *history* will so view the matter with the benefit of cool hindsight once the current political spin cycles have run their course. In 1861, sharp divisions about secession existed, but the right answer was not somewhere in the middle. Later that decade, every single congressional Democrat opposed the proposed Fourteenth Amendment and every single congressional Republican save one supported it, but our best constitutionalists today do not view each side of this sharp constitutional debate with equal admiration and respect.

To recast this point with reference to the essays in this book, I claim that all or virtually all Republicans in Washington, DC (including the Republicans on the Court), were constitutionally wrong on *Bush v. Gore*, constitutionally wrong on Obamacare, and constitutionally wrong on same-sex marriage; but constitutionally right on the Second Amendment and constitutionally right on *Citizens United*. Nor is the Court's current swing justice, Anthony Kennedy, much as I admire him, pitch-perfect every time. For example, his position in *Bush v. Gore* was an embarrassment and his initial attack on Obamacare was an astonisher in legal history. (These are falsifiable claims: I predict that history will share my view.) The truth, to repeat, is not always and everywhere in "the middle," as too many inexpert journalists are wont to write in their columns and to reflect in their gatekeeping choices.

A second set of questions that journalist gatekeepers should ask supposed constitutional experts in the vetting process concerns expertise as distinct from impartiality. Here are the obvious questions to ask: "What is your track record as an expert? In particular, can you name various issues on which you have beaten the market either as a predictive or a prescriptive matter or both? As a matter of prediction, how well have you foretold the outcomes of past constitutional controversies? As a matter of prescription, are there important constitutional issues on which you took positions that are now widely accepted as correct but that were far less well accepted when you first weighed in?" These are precisely the sorts of questions that business journalists and sports journalists ask: "Which investors and which hedge funds have beaten the market? Who bought Google early and sold Enron short at the peak? Which sports analysts have done best year after year at forecasting the Sweet Sixteen and the Final Four in March Madness?" These are precisely the sorts of questions that political pundits ask pollsters: "How well have your past polls predicted past elections?" But at least in my experience, broadcast producers and print editors rarely ask the right track-record questions when vetting supposed constitutional experts.

Here is one final suggestion for my professional full-time journalistic colleagues: Journalists must do more than simply publish "the first draft of history." This first draft is what journalists do, daily: They publish the truth as they see it and uncover it day by day. Alas, they only rarely revisit an old story years later and publish their considered revision—their second (or third or fourth) draft of history.

Happily, there are notable exceptions to this journalistic disinclination to revisit, and perhaps the most famous exception is also modern America's preeminent journalist: my friend and mentor Bob Woodward, to whom this book is dedicated. Woodward, in fact, has published many drafts, over time, of the most important political and constitutional saga of the 1970s, the Watergate scandal.

Woodward's first draft of history consisted of a long string of blockbuster investigative articles—one after another after another, each more eye-popping than its predecessor—that appeared in the *Washington Post* as he and his intrepid colleague Carl Bernstein smoked out and sleuthed out a story of massive political sabotage and lawlessness at the highest levels of politics and government, leading all the way up, eventually, to the president of the United States. As events were still furiously unfolding, Woodward and Bernstein published their second draft of history as a book in 1974, *All the President's Men*. In this canonical work, the journalists reworked and revised their earlier *Post* pieces into a gripping overarching narrative that also described in detail, for the first time, the role that they themselves had played in influencing and driving some of the political and governmental events they were covering.

But Woodward did not stop there—and here he offers a profound object lesson for his fellow journalists. In 2014, he and Bernstein released a fortieth anniversary edition of the 1974 book with a new epilogue that placed the events of 1974 in a properly historical and more sweeping intellectual framework. Thanks to the passage of time, Woodward and Bernstein were able, in this fine epilogue, to explain to ordinary Americans certain large truths— historical truths and constitutional truths—about Watergate that had been obscured to some extent amid all the fascinating details of "Woodstein's" earlier and engrossing journalistic whodunit. And in 2015, Woodward returned once more to the scene of the crime, so to speak, by uncovering another trove of archival material, adding still more depth to the story as originally told. This new material, with additional exposition and analysis, appeared in Woodward's most recent draft of history, *The Last of the President's Men*. And perhaps more drafts may follow.

The book you now hold in your hands is inspired by Woodward's model. Exemplifying the advice I am hereby offering my fellow journalists to revise and revisit important stories after some time has passed, this book supplements and contextualizes my original journalistic essays with later thoughts about these early pieces, thoughts informed by the passage of time and the benefit of hindsight.

This book, in other words, has aimed to combine the first and the second drafts of history. I have sought to show readers how the most important constitutional issues of my adult lifetime looked to me as they were still unfolding and also how these issues look to me now that they are slipping into the recent past. Both temporal perspectives—the first *and* the second draft of history—are essential for understanding the ongoing American constitutional project, a project that at every moment of our history has been and must remain both timely and timeless.

Acknowledgments

I've been working on this book for most of my adult life. My debts, intellectual and personal, are thus many and profound.

THANKS, FIRST AND ALWAYS, to my family and friends. I began writing op-eds as a high schooler in the early 1970s, with the sustained encouragement of my parents, who continue to encourage me in every way, lo, these many years later. Ruth Ann White, my high school journalism adviser, helped me take my first baby steps as an aspiring essayist. Every would-be author needs an audience, and back then, my best buddy, Kevin King, was also my most faithful reader. (In Chapter 6 of my 2015 book, *The Law of the Land*, I tell the story of how Ruth Ann, Kevin, and other friends stood by me when my high school principal sought to censor my anti-Nixon op-ed columns.) In 1973, my inspired and inspirational cousin Raj Chabra—himself a student journalist at a nearby high school—gave me one of the best gifts ever: a book of journalistic essays by the *San Francisco Chronicle* political satirist, Art Hoppe. That book, *Mr. Nixon and My Other Problems*, along with another early 1970s journalistic tour de force, *All The President's Men*, first got me thinking about how seemingly discrete and separate journalistic pieces might over time add up to something much more.

In 1976, on my eighteenth birthday, I arrived at Yale, sight unseen, and I have never left. Here I made an additional set of friends, and several of my closest friends eventually became occasional journalistic partners. Ian Ayres, Steve Calabresi, Josh Chafetz, and Neal Katyal all fit that category, and so does my most intimate and frequent journalistic collaborator, Vikram David Amar. True, I met Vik long before Yale—on the day he was born, in fact. But it was only when my kid brother arrived as a student at Yale Law School—on the same day that I started teaching as a professor at Yale, in 1985—that we met intellectually, and began to talk law and think law together.

Memory's fog makes it hard for me now to compile a complete list of all the other friends at Yale who have nurtured me in connection with the various ideas in this book. But special mention must be made of my most stirring teachers—Bruce Ackerman, Guido Calabresi, Owen Fiss, Paul Gewirtz, the late Burke Marshall, and Peter Schuck—and my closest Yale conversation partners over the years (other than those already mentioned): Jack Balkin, Philip Bobbitt, Stephen Carter, James Forman, Heather Gerken, Abbe Gluck, Linda Greenhouse, Oona Hathaway, Harold Koh, Tony Kronman, John Langbein, Jed Rubenfeld, Reva Siegel, Kate Stith, and John Witt. Among my students and assistants, I am especially indebted to Robert Black, Maggie Goodlander, Sundeep Iyer, Iulia Padeanu, Monika Piotrowicz, Anthony Ramirez, and Jacqueline Van de Velde for their incisive editorial and logistical aid as this book took shape.

Beyond Yale's ivied walls, I must also offer special thanks to two more coauthors, Gary Hart and Timothy Noah, and to various other faithful friends and interlocutors: Todd Brewster, Rick Brookhiser, Jennifer Brown, Jon Blue, Stephen Colbert, Walter Dellinger, Alan Dershowitz, Ken Gormley, Dale Gregory, Paul Johnson, Ed Larson, Sandy Levinson, Eric Liu, Gene Meyer, Trevor Morrison, Mike Paulsen, Bob Pushaw, Diane Rehm, Dean Reuter, Charlie Rose, Paul Solman, Ken Starr, Steve Susman, Jeff Toobin, Nina Totenberg, Laurence Tribe, Bruce Wessel, Evan Wolfson, Sam Zurier, and the late Peter Jennings and Doug Kendall. Si Lazarus—himself a gifted legal journalist—was particularly helpful in the final stages of this book, offering detailed suggestions just when I needed them.

On the home front, few of the pieces in this book would likely have been written without the steady support of my wife, Vinita. On the other hand, many more pieces would likely have been written had it not been for our kids—Vik, Kara, and Sara. But most of these pieces would likely have been miserable because I would have been miserable without our kids. To put the point within the intellectual frame of this book: Day to day, the kids can drive me crazy, but over time they make life worth living.

IN THE WORLD OF PROFESSIONAL JOURNALISM and book publishing, I owe thanks to many friends and mentors. I have already mentioned that Art Hoppe's journalistic writing motivated me in the early 1970s. When I graduated from high school in 1976, he moved me yet again by sending me a sweet and witty letter of encouragement and discouragement. One of my teachers had apparently sent him several of my high school columns and he wrote me back directly, telling me that I had talent and should thus stay out of the newspaper business and find honest work instead: He didn't want the competition.

I have generally found inspiration in a series of academic authors who have combined high-quality journalism with penetrating legal, political, historical, and/or constitutional analysis. These academic role models span the political spectrum and I love reading them: Will Baude, Stephen Carter (again), Garrett Epps, Noah Feldman, Linda Greenhouse (again), Jeff Rosen, Cass Sunstein, Garry Wills, and Eugene Volokh.

I owe particular thanks to three journalistic editors who repeatedly helped me place my work before the public in real time: Emily Bazelon, Jeff Rosen, and Chuck Lane—Emily when she was at *Slate*, Jeff and Chuck when they were at the *New Republic*. Far and away, Emily accepted and edited more pieces in this collection than anyone else, and her edits were unfailingly incisive. Plus, she was always a dream to work with—fast, witty, and generous. She is, quite simply, the best. So are Jeff and Chuck, gifted former students who drew me deep into the world of professional journalism by bringing me into the *New Republic* family as a contributing editor in the late 1990s. Other great editors deserving special mention are: Linc Caplan, Sue Horton, Ken Ikenberry, Kate Julian, Dahlia Lithwick, Lily Rothman, Allison Silver, Mark Joseph Stern, June Thomas, Michael Tomasky, Gary Spiecker, Scott Stossel, and Terry Tang.

Another memorable editor, Peter Beinart, ran the *New Republic* from 1999 until 2006. When I shared with Peter my desire to write a series of *New Republic* pieces using timely hooks to say something more timeless, he listened politely and firmly said no. As he put it in an e-mail to me, "The stuff for us has to clearly respond to today's news. It can't be a contemporary peg for a historical point." At the time, these were hard words for me to hear, but today I would like to thank Peter publicly for helping me see clearly the temporal tension at the heart of my effort to do what I am calling here "constitutional journalism."

My deepest professional thanks are reserved for three unindicted co-conspirators who have stood by me to bring this book to market: my literary agents, Glen Hartley and Lynn Chu, and my publisher, Lara Heimert. I have never told her this, but Lara is my muse. When I close my eyes at the keyboard and try to think of something smart to put on the page, I picture myself talking to her. This is the third book that Glen, Lynn, Lara, and I have done together, and I can't wait to get cracking on the next one. I would also like to offer my public thanks to Lara's entire Basic Books team, especially Brian Distelberg, Carrie Majer, Leah Stecher, Michelle Welsh-Horst, and Michele Wynn.

IT REMAINS TO SAY A FEW MORE WORDS about one more muse, whose influence has, I hope, been evident from start to finish. This book is dedicated to Bob Woodward for many reasons. Several are elaborated in the final paragraphs of this book's Conclusion: Woodward offers a powerful model of a journalist who is willing to acknowledge his own role in shaping as well as covering events, who listens to all sides and who commands respect across the spectrum, and who is willing to revisit earlier stories with the benefit of hindsight. But that is not all. As I now have come to see things, my entire career owes a huge debt to this good and great man, whom I am today tickled to call my friend.

Here's the story (with the benefit of hindsight): I was lucky to get into Yale College in 1976, and I have often wondered what got me in. I now think it was my high-school journalistic achievements and adventures, and I now see that I was obviously entranced by Woodward's example. He took on Nixon and so would I. He investigated the power structure and so would I. (In an investigative piece in my junior year, I uncovered and publicized sex discrimination in my high school's sports program.) And then, while I was still in college—the same college that Woodward himself had attended only fifteen years earlier—he published another book, with another coauthor, probing judicial decision making on the highest court in our land.

I received a copy of *The Brethren: Inside the Supreme Court* as a Christmas gift in my senior year. I read and re-read and re-re-read it over Christmas break. A week later, I composed and submitted my application to law school.

Permissions

Special thanks to all the newspapers, newsmagazines, and other outlets that allowed me to retain rights to revise and reconfigure my journalistic essays for comprehensive assembly and analysis in this book. Eighteen of the essays in this volume first appeared in *Slate*, ten in the *New Republic*, eight in the *American Lawyer*, eight in *FindLaw*, seven in the *Los Angeles Times*, six in the *New York Times*, six in the *Washington Post*, three in *Time*, and two in the *Daily Beast*. Other essays first appeared in the *Atlantic*, CNN, the *Daily News*, *Democracy Journal*, the *Los Angeles Review of Books*, the *Philadelphia Inquirer*, *Roll Call*, SSRN, the *Wall Street Journal*, and the *Washington Times*.

Notes

Unless otherwise indicated, all endnotes have been composed solely for this book and did not appear in the essays as originally published. Note also that some essays have been retitled in this volume and that subheadings in the original essays are generally omitted.

INTRODUCTION

1. True, several of modern America's most distinguished legal journalists are law-trained superstars such as the *New York Times*'s Linda Greenhouse, Adam Liptak, Charlie Savage, and Emily Bazelon; CNN's and the *New Yorker*'s Jeff Toobin; *Reuters*'s Joan Biskupic, *Slate*'s Dahlia Lithwick, and the *National Law Journal*'s Marcia Coyle. But even they are not general constitutional scholars in the strictest sense. With perhaps one or two exceptions, no modern professional journalist has managed to do sustained scholarship on the Constitution's origins and implementation across the centuries and across a wide range of topics.

2. My claims about Court insiders and current views among conservative scholars draw upon multiple confidential conversations and off-the-record interviews over the years. For a smattering of recent scholarly opinion, see Andrea Sachs, "The Worst Supreme Court Decisions Since 1960," *Time.com*, October 6, 2015.

3. Long-shot candidate Lincoln Chafee was also a dynastic candidate, but he dropped out early on. His most notable moment in the spotlight was, fittingly, a dynastic moment, when, in the only televised presidential debate in which he participated, he fumblingly answered questions about a Senate vote that he had cast by repeatedly reminding the audience that this vote happened shortly after he had been appointed [*sic*] to the Senate to fill the vacancy created by the death of his father, Senator (and former governor) John Chafee.

4. Readers seeking detailed constitutional analysis of the other main element of today's executive branch—the large bureaucratic officialdom of departments and agencies headed up by presidential appointees—should consult Akhil Reed

Amar, *America's Unwritten Constitution: The Precedents and Principles We Live By* (New York: Basic Books, 2012), 319–332, 369–387, 409–410.

5. See *California v. Acevedo*, 500 U.S. 565, 581–83 (1991) (Scalia, J., concurring in the judgment); *City of West Covina v. Perkins*, 525 U.S. 234, 247 n. 2 (1999) (Thomas, J., concurring in the judgment); *Atwater v. City of Lago Vista*, 532 U.S. 318, 332 n. 6, 336, 339 n. 10 (2001); *Virginia v. Moore*, 553 U.S. 164, 170 (2008); *Riley v. California*, 134 S. Ct. 2473, 2495 (2014) (Alito, J., concurring in part and concurring in the judgment).

6. See Jack Balkin, *Living Originalism* (Cambridge: Harvard University Press, 2011).

7. I am here as elsewhere profoundly influenced by Jed Rubenfeld, *Freedom and Time* (New Haven: Yale University Press, 2001).

CHAPTER 1. THE PRESIDENCY

1. Like anniversaries and holidays, surveys of this sort can often be excuses to divert popular attention, momentarily, to some timeless issue worth discussing every so often. For more thoughts on anniversaries and holidays as windows of special opportunity to counterbalance everyday journalistic myopia and amnesia, see pp. 255–257.

2. My original opening sentence contained a whopping error, in which I strongly implied that King George III was older than George Washington. Oops.

3. Jefferson here was borrowing from Richard Rumbold, an English Leveler. See Akhil Reed Amar, *America's Constitution: A Biography* (New York: Random House, 2005), 384, 610 n. 73.

4. A few sentences from this paragraph and the following two paragraphs later reappeared at p. 161 in ibid.

5. He does of course have a nephew—Jeb's son—named George P. Bush, who was in 2014 elected Texas land commissioner, a traditional stepping-stone for higher statewide office.

6. This essay was originally published online under a different title: "Dynasty Dooms JFK."

7. For more elaboration of this admittedly harsh criticism, see "The Sham Called Campaign Finance Reform," pp. 232–236.

8. "So far" was of course circa 2008. The Clintons have made a lot since then. See, e.g., "A Look at Hillary Clinton's 2007–2014 Federal Tax Returns," nytimes.com, July 31, 2015, Associated Press report: "The Clintons earned $139.1 million over the past eight years . . . The couple paid nearly $44 million in federal taxes and donated nearly $15 million to charity."

9. Some of the material in the ensuing paragraphs borrowed snippets from chapter 2 of Akhil Reed Amar, *America's Unwritten Constitution: The Precedents and Principles We Live By* (New York: Basic Books, 2012).

10. For details and documentation, see ibid., 63–79.

11. The original essay said that "most presidents" uttered the words "so help me God," but subsequent research inclines me to scale back this claim from "most" to "many."

12. This paragraph has been beefed up for this book.

CHAPTER 2. THE VICE PRESIDENCY

1. Letter from John Adams to Abigail Adams, December 19, 1793 (style altered); *Journal of William Maclay*, ed. Edgar S. Maclay (New York: D. Appleton and Co., 1890), 3 (entry of April 25, 1789).

2. *Preserving Our Institutions—The Continuity of the Presidency: The Second Report of the Continuity of Government Commission* (June 2009, Brookings Institution).

3. The original essay incorrectly implied that Cheney had formally "invok[ed]" executive privilege.

4. The original essay used improper lingo, referring to the anti-Stalwart faction in 1880 as "Mugwumps" rather than "Half-breeds."

5. This essay was originally published under a different title: "This Is One Terrorist Threat We Can Thwart Now."

6. For more details and analysis of this claim and the claims in the ensuing paragraphs, see Akhil Reed Amar and Vikram David Amar, "Is the Presidential Succession Law Constitutional?" *Stanford Law Review* 48 (1995): 118.

7. The original version of this point was more emphatic. I have now inserted the word "perhaps." Upon reflection, I see more problems with "snap" off-year presidential elections. Also, it must be noted that the general structure of the Twenty-fifth Amendment allows for a string of successors who lack a strong personal national mandate. For example, Nelson Rockefeller was never directly elected by the American people, nor was he appointed by a president who himself was directly elected by the American people. Moreover, any system that gives the party that wins the presidency less than its standard four years in the Oval Office might unduly increase the perceived payoff of politically motivated assassinations.

8. For example, under certain circumstances, separate ballots might lead to an increased likelihood that the president and veep would be from different parties, which could in turn create various unhelpful frictions and even increase incentives for political assassinations and partisan impeachments. But these scenarios can occur even under the existing system, and it is possible that separate ballots would actually make these worrisome outcomes less likely. For more details and analysis, see Akhil Reed Amar, *The Law of the Land: A Grand Tour of Our Constitutional Republic* (New York: Basic Books, 2015), 173–174, 186 fn. *; Akhil Reed Amar and Vikram David Amar, "President Quayle?" *Virginia Law Review* 78 (1992): 913.

9. For more on conditional resignations, and their astonishing implications for Supreme Court replenishment practices, see pp. 135–137.

CHAPTER 3. THE CONGRESS

1. Apart from FDR, only one other post-Lincoln non-incumbent Democrat had even won a popular vote majority—Jimmy Carter in 1976, who did not even break 51 percent and whose electoral college margin was also razor thin.

2. A few years later, Tim Scott from South Carolina and Mo Cowen of Massachusetts would join the club, as would another one of my amazing former students, New Jersey's Cory Booker.

3. Akhil Reed Amar, *America's Unwritten Constitution: The Precedents and Principles We Live By* (New York: Basic Books, 2012), 361–369.

4. This paragraph has been beefed up to reflect more recent research on the Reconstruction Congress that appears in Akhil Reed Amar, Lindsey Ohlsson Worth, and Joshua Alexander Geltzer, "Reconstructing the Republic: The Great Transition of the 1860s," in *Transitions: Legal Change, Legal Meanings,* ed. Austin Sarat (Tuscaloosa: University of Alabama Press, 2012), 98–129.

5. This essay was later retooled for a section of my 2012 book, *America's Unwritten Constitution* see supra n. 3.

6. This essay was originally published under a slightly different title: "Threatening Eric Holder with a Contempt Citation Is Just Cheap Talk."

7. This essay was originally published under a slightly different title: "Filibuster Changes Made Simple."

CHAPTER 4. THE JUDICIARY

1. For more on this commentary, see pp. 362–365, 392–397.

2. On the interesting electoral-vote question that arose in 1872–1873, see pp. 69–70.

3. See Akhil Reed Amar, *The Law of the Land: A Grand Tour of Our Constitutional Republic* (New York: Basic Books, 2015), 140–162.

4. On direct presidential election without an amendment, see pp. 351–357. On avoiding lame ducks without an amendment, see pp. 77–80.

5. In our *Washington Post* essay, Steve and I referred vaguely to "some commentators" who had floated a precursor of our idea—a reference to an oral exchange we once had with a distinguished federal circuit judge who did not want his/her name mentioned. Although Steve later raised constitutional doubts about this proposal, these doubts are easily sidestepped. Imagine a statute allowing senior justices to remain on the Court, but as back-benchers hearing only special cases.

6. See Steven G. Calabresi and James Lindgren, "Term Limits for the Supreme Court: Life Tenure Reconsidered," *Harvard Journal of Law and Public*

Policy 29 (2006): 769; Robert Barnes, "Legal Experts Propose Limiting Justices' Powers, Terms," *Washington Post*, February 23, 2009.

7. On vice presidents, see pp. 49–83. On statutory successors to veeps—successors who might be thought of as vice-vice-presidents, so to speak—see pp. 70–77.

8. This essay was originally published under a slightly different title: "The Supreme Court's Unfree Speech."

9. This essay was originally published online under a different title: "Too Much Order in the Court."

10. Several paragraphs from this op-ed later appeared in an endowed lecture I gave in Florida in 2009, a lecture that was in turn revised and reprinted as chap. 7 of my 2015 book, *The Law of the Land*.

11. As I explained in greater detail in later work, the electorally accountable Florida legislature deserving deference in the 2000 election was the state legislature that enacted the state election code before Election Day, not the state legislature acting after the election that was tempted to intervene, improperly, ex post facto. See Amar, *The Law of the Land*, 150–154.

12. This essay was originally published online under a different title: "Merrick Garland Is Like Barack Obama and Hillary Clinton." The penultimate paragraph borrows from Amar, *The Law of the Land*, 275–276.

13. This essay was originally published online under a different title: "Democrats Should Demand Hearings but Not a Vote."

14. In 2013, the title given this book review by the editors of *Democracy Journal* was "Originalist Sin." Back then I paid little attention to the title, but I now see it as doubly misleading. First, my review has little to do with originalism and much to do with a technical rule of interpretation known as the absurdity doctrine—hence my revised title in this book. Second, I do not consider originalism an interpretive sin. All serious constitutional interpreters—myself included—are and must be originalists to some extent, see pp. 250–251, 255–260, 405–406.

15. This paragraph and several others in this book review have been revised to make clear that I am criticizing Scalia and Garner for misstating and misunderstanding the absurdity doctrine more generally, above and beyond their treatment of Blackstone's formulation in particular.

CHAPTER 5. CRIMINAL PROCEDURE

1. The various acts of misconduct of the Texas cop described in this 2001 op-ed—his brutish bullying of a woman who had committed a mere traffic offense, and his unreasonable determination to flex his power by arresting her for this traffic offense—eerily anticipate the fact pattern of a more recent incident involving another outrageous Texas cop in July 2015. The woman involved in

this 2015 case, Sandra Bland, was later found hanged in her jail cell—a cell she should have never been placed in, had my commonsense views of the Fourth Amendment prevailed in Court in 2001. Bluntly, the Supreme Court badly blew it in 2001, and this gross error was obvious at the time.

2. This 2002 *New York Times* essay does not appear in this book because, apart from the paternity issue, it largely overlapped the 2001 *American Lawyer* essay, which does appear in this volume. On the general issue of overlap and repetition in constitutional journalism, see p. 361 fn. *.

3. Alas, the key provisions of this proposed legislation, S.3, The Violent Crime Control and Law Enforcement Improvement Act of 1995, were never enacted. In a Senate hearing on March 7, 1995, I had testified in support of this reform at the invitation of Senator Orrin Hatch. For a later issue on which I directly squared off against Senator Hatch—the constitutionality of Obamacare—see pp. 359–360 and pp. 365–368.

4. This essay was originally published under a different title: "The Fourth Amendment Does Not Say What Most Libertarians or Judges Think It Does."

5. See "The Don't-Bother-to-Knock Rule," *New York Times*, June 16, 2006. This citation appeared as a hyperlink in the original column.

6. This essay was originally published online under a different title: "What If Dzhokhar Tsarnaev Decides Not to Talk?"

7. In the original essay, I included the following paragraph at this juncture:

> In claiming the power to designate "enemy combatants," the administration would be on firmer ground had the president secured from Congress a general declaration of war (against Al Qaeda specifically, or against anti-American terrorists more broadly), or something similar. If the basic idea is that Padilla is a kind of prisoner of war, shouldn't Congress formally declare war or otherwise specifically authorize the detention of enemy combatants who cannot be tied to 9/11? (In a famous World War II case involving Nazi enemy combatants found on American soil, Congress had of course already declared war.)

I now believe that Congress's 2001 Authorization for Use of Military Force (AUMF), enacted shortly after 9/11, should indeed be read as "something similar" to a declaration of war, and that this paragraph thus added more confusion that clarity.

8. Years after the publication of this essay, five justices took the position that Guantánamo should be treated as American soil for habeas purposes. See *Boumediene v. Bush*, 553 U.S. 723 (2008).

9. *Res judicata*—Latin for "a thing adjudicated"—is a legal doctrine barring relitigation of certain issues already decided in court. The doctrine is subject to various exceptions, as this essay seeks to make clear.

CHAPTER 6. CITIZENS DIS-UNITED

1. Akhil Reed Amar and Neal Kumar Katyal, "*Bakke*'s Fate," *UCLA Law Review* 43 (1996): 1745.

2. It is worth noting, in this context, that in our 1996 law review article following up on the 1995 essay that appears in this chapter, Neal and I suggested that a sound regime of educational affirmative action might indeed, at some foreseeable point, properly fade away. Ibid., 1754, 1779 n. 148.

3. For extensive elaboration and illustration of this approach to a certain subset of unenumerated rights, see chap. 3 of Akhil Reed Amar, *America's Unwritten Constitution: The Precedents and Principles We Live By* (New York: Basic Books, 2012).

4. Readers seeking more elaboration on what the Second Amendment meant at the Founding and during Reconstruction and how that amendment and its state constitutional counterparts have unfolded in modern times and should be understood today are invited to consult chap. 10 of my 2015 book, *The Law of the Land: A Grand Tour of Our Constitutional Republic* (New York: Basic Books)—a chapter devoted entirely to the Second Amendment as a case study in modern constitutional interpretation.

5. See, e.g., Bruce Ackerman and Ian Ayres, *Voting with Dollars: A New Paradigm for Campaign Finance* (New Haven: Yale University Press, 2002); Bruce Ackerman and James Fishkin, *Deliberation Day* (New Haven: Yale University Press, 2004); Lawrence Lessig, *Republic, Lost: How Money Corrupts Congress—and a Plan to Stop It* (New York: Twelve, 2011).

6. See Amar, *The Law of the Land*, 100–103; Akhil Reed Amar, "The First Amendment's Firstness," *UC Davis Law Review* 47 (2014): 1015.

7. See, for example, Akhil Reed Amar, "Attainder and Amendment 2: *Romer*'s Rightness," *Michigan Law Review* 95 (1996): 203, 204–205 n. 7.

8. This essay was originally published under a different title: "When Legal Bullets Bounce Back."

9. This piece was originally published under another title, which I have altered to highlight its connection to the Bork essay that precedes it in this collection. Both are essays of remembrance.

CHAPTER 7. CONSTITUTIONAL ANNIVERSARIES

1. This essay was originally published under a different title: "Constitution Not Same, Thankfully."

2. This essay was originally published under a different title: "Happy 225th Birthday, U.S. Constitution!"

3. The original online column here provided a hyperlink to this series, which is available at http://www.slate.com/articles/news_and_politics/the_hive/2012/07/u_s_constitution_as_rewritten_by_slate_legal_experts_and_readers_.html.

4. This essay was originally published online under a slightly different title: "The Year That Changed the World."

5. This essay was originally published, with the help of the Federalist Society, in the *Washington Times*.

CHAPTER 8. BILL CLINTON'S DRAMA

1. Akhil Reed Amar and Neal Kumar Katyal, "Executive Privileges and Immunities: The *Nixon* and *Clinton* Cases," *Harvard Law Review* 108 (1995): 701.

2. On the wrongness of *Dred* and *Plessy*, see Akhil Reed Amar, *America's Constitution: A Biography* (New York: Random House, 2005), 252–254, 264–266; *America's Unwritten Constitution: The Precedents and Principles We Live By* (New York: Basic Books, 2012), 143–151, 270–275; and *The Law of the Land: A Grand Tour of Our Constitutional Republic* (New York: Basic Books, 2015), 109–222.

3. Letter of June 20, 1807, from Thomas Jefferson to George Hay, reprinted in *The Works of Thomas Jefferson*, ed. Paul L. Ford (New York: G. P. Putnam's Sons, 1905), 10: 404 (emphasis deleted); *Journal of William Maclay*, ed. Edgar Maclay (New York: D. Appleton and Co., 1890), 167; Joseph Story, *Commentaries on the Constitution of the United States* (Boston: Hilliard, Gray and Co., 1833), 3: 418–419, sec. 1563. For detailed analysis of these and other sources, see Amar and Katyal, "Executive Privileges and Immunities."

4. This essay was originally published under a headline that both Neal Katyal and I—and many readers, I suspect—found highly offensive: "Pounding Paula." This headline was puerile, misogynistic, and completely beside the point. Our analysis focused on the law of the presidency, not Paula Jones as a person. Authors typically have no control over headlines in newspapers and newsmagazines, both print and online. Books, happily, are a different matter.

5. On the free speech of executive-branch officials, see the chap. 2 essay "Stealing First: Dick Cheney and the First Amendment," at pp. 56–60.

6. A few phrases that first appeared in this op-ed later reappeared in my more general discussion of independent counsels in *America's Unwritten Constitution* at pp. 369, 372–378.

7. Portions of this public lecture, delivered to a National Federalist Society conference, were later published in the *New Republic* on Monday, January 18, 1999.

8. Portions of this were also published in ibid.

9. This paragraph has been fine-tuned to reflect the slightly more precise account of the relevant constitutional issues put forth in 2012 in *America's Unwritten Constitution* at pp. 319–324, 369–386, 568–569 n. 18.

CHAPTER 9. GEORGE W. BUSH'S DRAMA

1. See generally Alexander M. Bickel, "The Supreme Court and Reapportionment," in *Reapportionment in the 1970s,* ed. Nelson W. Polsby (Oakland: University of California Press, 1971), 57–74; Alexander M. Bickel, *The Supreme Court and the Idea of Progress* (New York: Harper and Row, 1970).

2. *Reynolds v. Sims*, 377 U.S. 533, 559 (1964) (quoting *Wesberry v. Sanders*, 376 U.S. 1, 14 [1964]). In the 2016 case of *Evenwel v. Abbott*, Justice Thomas wrote separately to pose profound questions about the logic and conceptual foundations of the *Reynolds* principle but stopped short of calling for the overruling of this landmark case, a case he himself has previously relied upon—most famously in the Court's per curiam opinion, which he joined, in *Bush v. Gore*. For my own critique of the Court's deployment of the *Reynolds* principle in that case, see chap. 4 at pp. 124–127. And for my defense of *Reynolds* and explication of the constitutional logic that underpins it, see *America's Unwritten Constitution: The Precedents and Principles We Live By* (New York: Basic Books, 2012), 183–199, 223–230.

3. For one answer, see ibid., 224 fn. * (explaining that the constitutionally entrenched rules of Senate apportionment limit the extent of realistically imaginable federal malapportionment as compared to the nearly infinite imaginable state malapportionment that could occur absent the limiting principles of *Reynolds* or something loosely akin to *Reynolds*). From time to time, individual new states have been added to the union and a few state boundaries have changed, always with congressional consent; but these occasional and localized events, with entrenched and complexly bundled consequences sweeping far beyond the mere allocation of Senate seats, have not resulted in the sort of massive and/or mushrooming malapportionment that had in fact occurred in various states in the decades prior to *Reynolds*. In general, the apportionment structure of the Senate has not skewed federal electoral results to the same extent that various state apportionment rules, prior to *Reynolds*, operated to severely penalize urban and disproportionately nonwhite voters. Indeed, in recent years the political party with the stronger urban and nonwhite voter base (the Democratic Party) has held a higher proportion of U.S. Senate seats than U.S. House seats, and the party balance in the Senate has rather closely reflected the party balance in the overall national electorate—more closely in fact than has the party balance in the House. (Strikingly, in the 2012 election, Republicans won a wide majority of House seats even though more Americans nationwide voted for House Democrats than for House Republicans.) Also, as a matter of constitutional text, history, and structure, cities, counties, and/or mere voting districts within states have never been closely comparable to semi-sovereign states within the federal

union. And of course the Constitution itself explicitly and emphatically requires that the Senate not mimic the population-based apportionment structure of the House, whereas no comparably explicit and emphatic federal constitutional text protects state-senate malapportionment. Not all states even had senates at the Founding, and not all do today.

4. See., e.g., Paul Finkelman, "Slavery and the Constitutional Convention: Making a Covenant with Death," in *Beyond Confederation: Origins of the Constitution and American National Identity*, ed. Richard Beeman, Stephen Botein, and Edward C. Carter II (Chapel Hill: University of North Carolina Press, 1987), 188–225; Donald L. Robinson, *"To the Best of My Ability": The Presidency and the Constitution* (New York: W. W. Norton, 1987), 82–83. See also Shlomo Slonim, "The Electoral College at Philadelphia: The Evolution of an Ad Hoc Congress for the Selection of a President," *Journal of American History* 73 (1986): 35.

5. Akhil Reed Amar, "A Constitutional Accident Waiting to Happen," *Constitutional Commentary* 12 (1995): 143.

6. An insight variously attributed to Mark Twain, Niels Bohr, and Yogi Berra—the last of whom, it must always be remembered, didn't say everything he said.

7. Akhil Reed Amar, "Dead-President Elect," *Slate*, October 21, 2000.

8. For more discussion of the flaws in current presidential-succession laws as distinct from presidential-election laws, see the various essays in chap. 2 at pp. 70–77, 80–83.

9. I have found almost no mention of slavery's linkage to the electoral college in America's most prominent newspapers and newsmagazines between 1980 and 2000; and I have not found any op-ed before mine that mentioned even in passing the key role that slavery played when the Founders' electoral-college system was revised in light of the election of 1800–1801. An important caveat: The various computer databases that I used to conduct my searches doubtless have gaps and glitches. (For example, my own passing reference to slavery's role in the electoral college in "Speak Softly"—an essay originally published in the *New Republic* in 1999 and reprinted in chap. 2—did not consistently pop up in my various searches.)

10. For more on this stunning finish and on the U.S. Supreme Court's embarrassing performance, see Akhil Reed Amar, *The Law of the Land: A Grand Tour of Our Constitutional Republic* (New York: Basic Books, 2015), 140–162.

11. See Robert W. Bennett, "Popular Election of the President Without a Constitutional Amendment," *Green Bag 2d* 4: 241 (2001); Robert W. Bennett, "State Coordination in Popular Election of the President Without a Constitutional Amendment," *Green Bag 2d* 5: 141 (2002).

12. For a powerful analysis and useful correctives, see Vikram David Amar, "Response: The Case for Reforming Presidential Elections by Sub-Constitutional

Means: The Electoral College, the National Popular Vote Compact and Congressional Power," 100 *Georgetown LJ* 237 (2011).

13. Strictly speaking, Lieberman in this scenario would not be "president" but would merely be a vice president acting as president—a wrinkle that prompts a serious question whether he could invoke the nomination provisions of section 2 of the Twenty-fifth Amendment. The amendment seems to distinguish clearly between true presidents and "acting presidents," and explicitly reserves the power to nominate a new vice president to a true president. Put another way, if Lieberman were merely a vice president acting as president, there would be no true vice-presidential vacancy to fill under section 2. For more analysis, see Akhil Reed Amar and Vikram David Amar, "Is the Presidential Succession Law Constitutional?" *Stanford Law Review* 48 (1995): 118, 138 n. 145. See also chap. 2 at pp. 60, 71–72.

14. See pp. 72–75, 81.

15. I originally said that Albright was constitutionally ineligible because she "was not born in the United States." This was an imprecise and misleading formulation of the constitutional test, which focuses not on where a person is born but on whether a person is a citizen on the date of his or her birth, under the laws on the books on that date. John McCain, for example, was constitutionally eligible even though he was born outside the boundaries of the United States, narrowly understood, and Ted Cruz is eligible even though he was born in Canada; see p. 38 and fn. *. For more discussion, see Akhil Reed Amar, *America's Constitution: A Biography* (New York: Random House, 2005), 164, 554 n. 91, which in turn relies upon Jill A. Pryor, Note, "The Natural-Born Citizen Clause and Presidential Eligibility: An Approach for Resolving Two Hundred Years of Uncertainty," *Yale Law Journal* 97 (1988): 881. For more recent scholarship supportive of this basic thesis, see Michael Ramsey, "The Original Meaning of 'Natural Born,'" *SSRN*, January 7, 2016; see also Akhil Reed Amar, "Why Ted Cruz Is Eligible to Be President," *CNN.com*, January 13, 2016.

16. Several snippets from this op-ed were later sprinkled into my 2005 book, *America's Constitution*.

17. *The Records of the Federal Convention of 1787*, ed. Max Farrand (New Haven: Yale University Press, 1911), 1:486 (June 30, 1787). This citation appeared as a hyperlink in the original column.

18. The original column erred in omitting mention of Zachary Taylor.

19. *The Records of the Federal Convention of 1787*, at 2:56–57. This citation appeared as a hyperlink in the original column.

20. *Annals of Congress*, 13:538 (Oct. 28, 1803). This citation appeared as a hyperlink in the original column.

21. This important concession did not appear in the original op-ed, although it did appear in earlier writings of mine on the electoral college.

22. This op-ed was later revised for use in the final chapter of my 2012 book, *America's Unwritten Constitution.*

CHAPTER 10. BARACK OBAMA'S DRAMA

1. See pp. 212–215, 223–227, 282–285.

2. One of the leading academic architects of the constitutional challenge was a Georgetown law professor, Randy Barnett. Georgetown's DC location—featuring proximity to conservative think tanks, to conservative Congress members' offices, to the national media, and to the Court itself—has given Barnett unique opportunities to promote his intellectual agenda. Though I find his efforts to fuse originalism, federalism, and libertarianism deeply unpersuasive (to put it mildly), I have long admired his energy and originality. In fact, he got his job at Georgetown in 2006 in part because I strongly urged the chair of the faculty appointments committee back then to hire him. The name of that appointments chair: Neal Katyal. Small world!

3. Auditing, quite literally: the Court chose to allow the oral argument in this high-profile case to be broadcast live by NPR, something that only rarely is permitted by the Court. For more on cameras and/or microphones in the courtroom, see pp. 119–124.

4. In the famous 1803 case of *Marbury v. Madison*, the Court did strike down a federal statute, but not on grounds of federalism, states' rights, or lack of federal power. The statute in that case plainly involved a matter of federal power, namely, the federal legislature's power to regulate the jurisdiction of federal courts—something far removed from the authority of state governments to regulate.

5. In another, less relevant, modern case, the Supreme Court held that Congress lacked power to set the voting age for state elections. The Court's ruling in this 1970 case, *Oregon v. Mitchell*, did not involve federal power to raise taxes or regulate interstate commerce. In 1971, the Twenty-sixth Amendment was added to the Constitution to overturn *Mitchell* and guarantee eighteen-year-olds the right to vote in both state and federal elections.

6. I borrowed my title from a classic essay by my teacher and mentor Charles Black, who held a Sterling chair at Yale—a chair I am now honored to hold—while I was a student. Black's 1960 *Yale Law Journal* article, "The Lawfulness of the Segregation Decisions," was written to make clear for all time that the 1954 *Brown v. Board of Education* decision was not just right but plainly so. There were some who doubted *Brown*'s legal correctness when the decision came down, and for some time thereafter; but today, almost everyone embraces *Brown*. Via my titular allusion to Black's essay, I was suggesting that the lawfulness of Obamacare will likewise in the future seem clear, despite the ruckus that was being raised in the moment.

7. *Woods v. Cloyd W. Miller Co.*, 333 U.S. 138, 144 (1948).

8. I have revised this paragraph to include an explicit reference to *Ashwander*.

9. *Sonzinsky v. United States*, 300 U.S. 506, 514 (1937).

10. *United States v. Sanchez*, 340 U.S. 42, 44 (1950).

11. For a more detailed analysis of direct versus indirect taxes, see *America's Constitution: A Biography* (New York: Random House, 2005), 405–409, 613–614 n. 6.

12. For more background and details, see ibid., 405–409, 613–615.

13. See, e.g., *Steward Machine Co. v. Davis*, 301 U.S. 548, 588 (1937); *United States v. Darby*, 312 U.S. 100, 115, 122 (1941); *Hodel v. Virginia Surface Mining & Reclamation Ass'n*, 452 U.S. 264, 281–282 (1981).

14. For more on this principle in the context of same-sex marriage, see pp. 240–248.

15. On the individual rights issues implicated by vaccines—as distinct from the federalism issues of national power versus state power at the heart of the *Sebelius* case—see supra p. 385 fn. *, discussing the analogous issue of a hypothetical law mandating the eating of broccoli as distinct from the purchasing of broccoli.

CONCLUSION

1. Where a litigant has relied upon a precedent now deemed erroneous and has thereby placed himself/herself in a worse position than he/she would have been had the judicial error not occurred, judges may sometimes properly consider this fact of reliance in seeking to do law and justice in the case at hand. For more on reliance interests, see chap. 5 of my book, *America's Unwritten Constitution: The Precedents and Principles We Live By* (New York: Basic Books, 2012).

Index

for political participation, 37;
enfranchisement of blacks and
women, 308; increasing power of the
female vote, 261; Tea Partiers'
hostility towards, 262
Ninth Amendment: enumeration of gun
rights in the Second, Ninth, and
Fourteenth Amendments, 227–230
Nixon, Richard: connection to
independent counsel, 296;
Eisenhower presidency, 45;
impeachment, 305–306, 310–312,
314–315; Nixon Tapes case,
310–312; presidential pardon, 321;
presidential succession, 79, 356;
reasonableness of paper searches,
183; second term, 43
Nixon, Walter, 305–306
Nixon Tapes case. See United States v.
Nixon
Nixon v. Fitzgerald, 56, 283
Noah, Timothy, 89–90
North, Oliver, 164–165, 193–194
note taking in the Supreme Court,
121–122
Notes on the State of Virginia (Jefferson), 99
"nuclear option" of filibuster reform, 7,
91–93, 109

oath of office, 233–235
Obama, Barack, 78(fn); awkward political
transitions, 78–79; black suffrage, 39;
Bush as lame duck, 78; filibuster
reform effects, 7; Hillary Clinton's
political career, 26–27; historical
and political importance of the
second term, 45–46; increasing
political power of women, 261–262;
invoking executive privilege for the
House Oversight Committee,
104–106; political link to
Obamacare, 372; political
polarization, 251–252; presidential
eligibility, 38(fn); presidential
succession, 82; recess appointments,
89–91, 93(fn), 103–104; second
term, 43–44; senatorial succession,
13, 85–89; significance of the
decision, 401; Supreme Court

nominee, 135–139; 2012 reelection,
25–26
Obamacare: Breyer's judicial contribution,
147; broadcasting the Court's oral
arguments, 115; constitutional limits
on congressional power, 392–394;
constitutional objections, 365–368;
female justices' support for, 262;
Hatch's challenge to the individual
mandate, 359–361; inadequacy of
the Supreme Court oral arguments,
362–365; McCulloch defending the
constitutionality of, 368–370;
partisanship over, 408; paths of
constitutional validity, 17–18;
semantic manipulation of the
constitutional context, 371–372. See
also interstate-commerce argument
for Obamacare; taxation-clause
argument for Obamacare; individual
mandate (Obamacare)
Obergefell v. Hodges, 217, 222–223,
238–240
O'Connor, Sandra Day: affirmative action,
224; Breyer's bond with, 151;
conditional congressional
resignations for navigating lame-
duck periods, 80; longevity on the
Court, 133; retirement from the
Court, 135; similarities and
differences in Bakke and Adarand,
218–219; state judicial elections, 128
originalism, 15–16; anti-originalist
liberalism, 256–257; Bork's
popularization of, 250–251; Breyer's
decision on Noel Canning, 148–149;
Scalia absurdity doctrine, 141–147

Padilla, José, 202–208
Pakistan, dynastic succession in, 31
Palin, Sarah, 261
partisan politics: aftermath of the Clinton
impeachment, 273–274; alternating
national presidential parties, 344;
alternative-universe scenario of the
Clinton impeachment, 273–275;
Brown and Obergefell decisions
crossing party lines, 237; Bush v.
Gore and the exclusionary rule,

454 INDEX

Watergate, 33, 293, 295–297, 310, 312, 315, 409–410
Weinberger, Caspar, 294, 321, 324
The West Wing (television program), 53, 74–75, 77
White, Byron, 33
Whitman, Meg, 221–222
Why Not?: How to Use Everyday Ingenuity to Solve Problems Big and Small (Ayres), 118
Wilkes, John, 164, 182–183
Wilkes v. Wood, 182–183
Wills, Garry, 335
Wilson, James, 340, 344
Wilson, Joseph, 56–57, 59–60
Wilson, Valerie Plame, 56–57, 59–60
Wilson, Woodrow, 43, 79
wiretap warrants, 173

women and women's rights:
    discrimination through electoral college design, 308; dynastic succession, 31; Equal Rights Amendment, 334(fn); expansion of rights, 260–262; Fourteenth Amendment framers addressing, 241–242. *See also* gender
Wood, Gordon, 23
Woodward, Bob, 407(fn), 409–410
World Trade Center bombing, 68, 194–196, 203
World War II, 203
Wright, Susan Webber, 275, 317–318
Wydra, Elizabeth, 16

Zenger, John Peter, 57
Zurcher v. Stanford Daily, 183–184

Akhil Reed Amar is the Sterling Professor of Law and Political Science at Yale University. The author of several books, including *America's Unwritten Constitution*, and winner of awards from both the American Bar Association and the Federalist Society, Amar lives in Woodbridge, Connecticut.